Lecture Notes in Artificial Intelli

Edited by J. G. Carbonell and J. Siekmann

Subseries of Lecture Notes in Computer Science

Springer

Berlin
Heidelberg
New York
Barcelona
Hong Kong
London
Milan
Paris
Tokyo

Maria A. Wimmer (Ed.)

Knowledge Management in Electronic Government

4th IFIP International Working Conference, KMGov 2003
Rhodes, Greece, May 26-28, 2003
Proceedings

 Springer

Series Editors

Jaime G. Carbonell, Carnegie Mellon University, Pittsburgh, PA, USA
Jörg Siekmann, University of Saarland, Saarbrücken, Germany

Volume Editor

Maria A. Wimmer
University of Linz
Institute of Applied Computer Science
Altenbergerstr. 69, 4040 Linz, Austria
E-mail: mw@ifs.uni-linz.ac.at

Cataloging-in-Publication Data applied for

A catalog record for this book is available from the Library of Congress.

Bibliographic information published by Die Deutsche Bibliothek
Die Deutsche Bibliothek lists this publication in the Deutsche Nationalbibliografie;
detailed bibliographic data is available in the Internet at <http://dnb.ddb.de>.

CR Subject Classification (1998): I.2.4, I.2, H.4, K.4, K.6.5, K.5, K.3, J.1

ISSN 0302-9743
ISBN 3-540-40145-8 Springer-Verlag Berlin Heidelberg New York

Springer-Verlag Berlin Heidelberg New York
a member of BertelsmannSpringer Science+Business Media GmbH

http://www.springer.de

© 2003 IFIP International Federation for Informtaion Processing, Hofstrasse 3, 2361 Laxenburg, Austria
Printed in Germany

Typesetting: Camera-ready by author, data conversion by PTP-Berlin GmbH
Printed on acid-free paper   SPIN: 10931585   06/3142   5 4 3 2 1 0

Preface

The importance of Knowledge Management (KM) is increasingly recognized in business and public sector domains. The latter is particularly suitable for KM implementations since it deals with information and knowledge resources at a large scale: much of the work of public authorities deals with the elaboration of data, information and knowledge on citizens, businesses, society, markets, the environment, law, politics, etc.

Even most products of public administration and government work are delivered in the shape of information and knowledge themselves. This especially applies to policies, management, and the regulation and monitoring of society, markets and the environment. Governments expect advanced support from KM concepts and tools to exploit these huge knowledge and information resources in an efficient way.

Not only does the trend towards a knowledge society call for KM solutions, but current e-government developments also significantly influence the public sector. Ample access to remote information and knowledge resources is needed in order to facilitate:

- Citizen- and businesses-oriented service delivery, including one-stop service provision;
- interorganizational co-operation between governmental agencies;
- cross-border support for complex administrative decision making;
- e-government integration of dislocated information and knowledge sources into a fabric of global virtual knowledge.

Support for the collection, elaboration and accessibility of domain knowledge and project knowledge (on which decisions have been made, why have these been made, and how have problems been solved) needs to be designed properly. E-government implies a fundamental knowledge redistribution and requires a careful rethinking of the management of project know-how, domain expertise, information resources and knowledge bases. At the same time, the specific problems of public administration and governance (e.g., data protection, security, trustworthiness, etc.) need to be taken into account.

The annual international working conferences on "Knowledge Management in e-Government" (KMGov)[1] bring together academics and practitioners to discuss and disseminate ideas, concepts and experiences on the many perspectives and issues that deserve attention when developing e-government systems and KM applications. The contributions to the KMGov 2003 conference proceedings address, among others, the following topics:

---

[1] KMGov has become of big interest, and so it has grown into a working conference.

- concepts of knowledge management and knowledge engineering for inter-organizational cooperation in the public sector;
- requirements for KM systems in government;
- improving government activity through KM;
- representing government knowledge;
- innovative technologies to support KM;
- KM tools for public administration;
- approaching KM solutions for the public sector;
- examples of KM in public administration, and case studies.

At this point I'd like to express my special thanks to the conference chairs, the members of the Program Committee and the additional reviewers (see below) for their great help. The editor is particularly grateful to Ute Holler for her exceedingly engaged assistance in coordinating the preparation of the program and proceedings.

May 2003   Maria A. Wimmer

Program Committee

Program Chairs

Gregoris Mentzas, National Technical University of Athens, Greece
Roland Traunmüller, University of Linz, Austria

Conference Coordination

Maria A. Wimmer, University of Linz, Austria

Members

Heide Brücher, Competence Center e-Government, Switzerland
Jean-Loup Chappelet, University of Lausanne, Switzerland
Marcella Corsi, LUISS University, Italy
Christian S. Friis, Roskilde University, Denmark
Fernando Galindo, University of Zaragoza, Spain
Tom Gordon, Fraunhofer Center for e-Government, Germany
Hermann Hill, German University of Administrative Sciences, Germany
Klaus Lenk, Oldenburg University, Germany
Andrew McCosh, University of Edinburgh, UK
Gregoris Mentzas, National Technical University of Athens, Greece
Pierre-Andre Merlin, MTA - Marketing & Technologies Avancées, France
Michael Milakovich, University of Miami, USA
Erich Neuhold, Fraunhofer IPSI, Germany
Gerald Quirchmayr, University of Vienna, Austria
Ignace Snellen, Erasmus University of Rotterdam, The Netherlands
Thanasis Spyridakos, 01 Pliroforiki S.A., Greece
Roland Traunmüller, University of Linz, Austria
Antonio Rizzo, University of Siena, Italy
Efthimios Tambouris, Archetypon S.A., Greece
Gerrit van der Veer, Free University of Amsterdam, The Netherlands
Tom van Engers, Dutch Tax and Customs Administration, The Netherlands
Maria A. Wimmer, University of Linz, Austria

Additional Reviewers

Kim Viborg Andersen, Copenhagen Business School, Denmark
Nicolae Costake, Consultant, Romania
Alexandra Dörfler, CIO Operation Unit, Austria
Johann Eder, University of Klagenfurt, Austria
Margrit Falck, University of Applied Sciences for Public Administration and Legal
    Affairs, Germany
Andreás Gábor, Budapest University of Economic Sciences and Public
    Administration, Hungary
Michael Gisler, Bundesinstitut für Informatik und Telekommunikation, Switzerland
Dimitris Gouscous, University of Athens, Greece
Ake Grönlund, Örebro University, Sweden
Ralf Klischewski, University of Hamburg, Germany
Andrea Kö, Budapest University of Economic Sciences and Public Administration,
    Hungary
Ronald Leenes, Twente University, The Netherlands
Claire Lobet-Maris, Namur University, Belgium
Peter Mambrey, Fraunhofer Institute for Applied Information Technology, Germany
Oliver Märker, Fraunhofer Institute of Autonomous Intelligent Systems, Germany
Thomas Menzel, University of Vienna, Austria
Jeremy Millard, Danish Technological Institute, Denmark
Andreas Rapp, City of Vöcklabruck, Austria
Reinhard Riedl, University of Zürich, Switzerland
Michael Sonntag, University of Linz, Austria
Witold Staniszkis, Rodan Systems, Poland
Janis Stirna, Stockholm University, Sweden
Jörgen Svensson, Twente University, The Netherlands
Martin van Rossum, The Netherlands
Francesco Virili, University of Cassino, Italy

Table of Contents

Representing Governmental Knowledge

Innovative Technologies to Support KM

KM Tools for Public Administrations

Distributed Knowledge Repositories for Pan-European Public Services

Otmar Adam, Dirk Werth, and Fabrice Zangl

Institute for Information Systems (IWi)
at the German Research Centre for Artificial Intelligence (DFKI)
Stuhlsatzenhausweg 3, Bld. 43.8
66123 Saarbrücken
Germany
{adam,werth,zangl}@iwi.uni-sb.de

Abstract. The free movement of persons is a concept that has been settled on a European strategic level. In reality there are still a lot of steps to be followed in order to achieve this ambitious goal of mobility. Both the complexity of and the problems encountered in pan-European administrative processes interfere this aim. Interferences can be Knowledge Management (KM) specific (decentralization, implicitness, non-reusability, creation of process knowledge) as well as KM non-specific problems (linguistic, legal, document handling, cultural problems).

To solve these problems both administrative processes have to be made transparent to the citizen and the knowledge about these processes has to be managed. Thus, public administrations must interact seamlessly vertically (Europe, nation, region, municipality) as well as horizontally (between countries) with each other. This implies not only the use of standards but also the interoperability of process systems. Coping with the above mentioned problems a solution requires Knowledge Management. As public administrations are in strongly heterogeneous legal environments a centralised and harmonised solution is not feasible.

In this article a possible solution is described that has been developed in the European research project "InfoCitizen". Within InfoCitizen a Distributed Knowledge Repository and an intelligent agent-based Architecture is identified as an appropriated approach. InfoCitizen is a "proof-of-concept" project in which a Distributed Knowledge Repository and an agent platform are core concepts. The experiences and intermediary results of the successfully ongoing project are presented.

1 Citizens' Mobility in Theory and Practice

In 1985 free movement of persons was decided in the Schengen Agreement. Being integrated into the EU Treaty with the Treaty of Maastricht in 1993 it aims at increasing the mobility of work forces inside the European Union (EU). [1] This enhanced mobility should improve the flexibility of the employment market inside the EU. The lack of mobility of work forces causes significant macroeconomic damages on the employment market and the current situation should therefore be improved. [2]

M.A. Wimmer (Ed.): KMGov 2003, LNAI 2645, pp. 1–12, 2003.
© IFIP 2003

Hence, an effort must be done to reduce those barriers hindering the mobility of persons within the European Union. One of these barriers is the high variety of procedures and responsibilities for similar services, e.g. the delivering of a birth certificate. As everyone has already experienced, it can be quite difficult to receive such services within one country. A certain amount of documents has to be submitted to the administration and the result of the service obtained might have to be forwarded to other administrations. As such chains of processes can be difficult to follow in the own country, it often becomes almost impossible to do so across borders. The consequence is an impediment to international mobility of persons and "imprisons" people in there own country in terms of employment. Furthermore, the current proceeding allows errors in the process since the citizen is also bound to transport documents from one administration to another and to know about his/her duties involved in submitting such documents to an administration. [3] In order to overcome this problem public services and processes have to be integrated.

The knowledge about these processes is dispersed over several administrations, if available at all. Budgetary funds of public administrations are getting shortened every year and yet there is still a problem of public finances. Reducing costs of administrative processes therefore becomes a necessity. An efficient Knowledge Management [4] of administrative processes can not only help to make cross-border mobility easier. It also helps to reduce the costs of these processes.

2 Process Knowledge as an Enabler for Pan-European Interoperability

2.1 Basic Considerations

Knowledge Management is the creation of value or respectively reduction of costs by an organization (here public administrations) from their knowledge-based assets. The value adding or costs reduction can be as much on a microeconomic level as on a macroeconomic level. On a microeconomic level travel costs can be reduced because the citizen can obtain the same service without transporting paper documents from one administration to the other. Furthermore prices for public services could be lowered, if the internal operating expenses are cut off. On the same level costs can be reduced for public administrations by more time and resource efficient processes. On a macroeconomic level the costs are reduced by a higher efficiency in the working population's mobility and a more balanced budgetary structure concerning the costs of public administrations.

Concretely Knowledge Management means the creation, dissemination and utilization of that knowledge. [5] How the creation, dissemination and utilization of Knowledge can be achieved in Public administrations will be shown in the third section of this paper. Knowledge Management is often assimilated to the use of Information Technology. That is not necessarily true. Nevertheless, Information Technology can be helpful as a supportive tool for Knowledge Management. It will also be shown in this paper how Knowledge Management can be achieved on a strategic business level. Only after this analysis has been done, the possibilities of the support from Information Technology to Knowledge Management in the creation, dissemination and utilization will be covered in detail.

2.2 Scope of Problem

For a successful use of Knowledge Management in cross-border interaction between public administrations several problems have to be solved. A major problem is the fact that process knowledge is distributed, tacit and only shortly gathered with the citizen. Hence it is not accessible and reusable for the process executing administration. The knowledge required to execute is held decentralized, redundant and unstructured on various types of systems. Even within a country the process knowledge is not necessarily available in a structured manner. Figure 1 shows the As-Is-situation and its resulting problems described above. Currently the citizen goes to the employee of a Public Administration (PA) and asks for a service. The PA employee implicitly knows about the partial service (process segment) he has to execute, the input(s) he needs to execute the service (e.g. a certificate of birth) and the outputs that the service provides (e.g. a marriage notification). It is yet the task of the citizen to know where to get the required input and where to bring the output produced by the service that he requires. Furthermore the input and output providers will again implicitly know about the process segments that they have to execute. Summed up, on one hand it is the citizen who knows for the duration of the service provision what process segments have to be executed and who can execute them. On the other hand it is the Public Administrations as well as the input and output providers who know how to execute the process segments. After the service has been provided the knowledge of process segments sequence and its executor is kept by the citizen and therefore is not reusable. This shows that knowledge is decentralized and implicit.

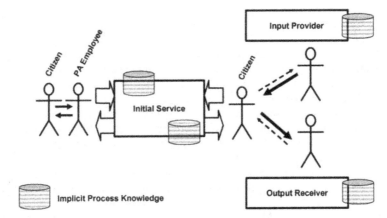

Fig. 1. As-Is-situation in public administration's procedures

Figure 1 shows the present situation where the citizen has to start every single public service himself. The citizen gets information from the public administration employee on the documents required to fulfil the initial service. The citizen then gets these documents from other second level public services that again might need some additional documents to be accomplished. The knowledge on required documents for the initial service is distributed between the concerned public administrations and the citizen is in charge of the transport of the documents as well as the process order, i.e. the public service to start in order to get the documents.

Apart from the Knowledge Management specific problems in public administrations a citizen can encounter further problems when executing an international process. The language in which the required documents (inputs) or out coming documents (outputs) are written is most likely to differ between one country and another. To resolve that difficulty the citizen has to have the documents translated and the translated documents certified. More over following international processes also implies for the citizen to pull information from many different sources to gather knowledge on how to "build" the process. A further problem can occur when the citizen brings paper-based documents to a public administration and the administration has to enter data manually into its system. Some required information might also be missing on a document from a foreign administration requesting the citizen to bring even more documents. Finally, there also might be legal differences between two or more countries which can make international administrative processes more difficult.

2.3 Requirements

In order to remove the above mentioned barriers and problems process knowledge needs to be created, disseminated and utilized [6]. To create process knowledge its knowledge assets have to be selected and documented. However there is too many information to be all taken into account. Therefore methods have to be used or even developed to document (process) knowledge in a formal way and also to enable continuous knowledge growth.

For dissemination purposes (process) knowledge needs to be made available so it is accessible at the right time in the right place. That knowledge also has to be sustainable and accurate over time. Furthermore the knowledge needs to be pushed to concerned entities. This implies that full process knowledge has to be brought to the citizen; if this is necessary at all. A more improved solution would avoid making it necessary for the citizen to acknowledge the process and make the latter completely transparent to him/her. This way the use of public services would be greatly facilitated for the citizen and hence also reduce barriers to (cross-border) mobility.

In order to utilize (process) knowledge efficiently it has to be retrieved methodically from the above mentioned documentation. Thanks to these methods the knowledge would be adapted to the entities using it, hence the knowledge should be citizen or administration aligned oriented.

Finally, knowledge has to be reusable. Therefore it has to be made understandable for any entity accessing it, e.g. a system of a public administration. The reusability of knowledge is a condition for interoperability. If knowledge is stored but cannot be accessed or used by concerned public administrations, interoperability can per se not be achieved. Therefore process knowledge enables interoperability, which is the final condition to cross-administration and cross-boarder process and knowledge management.

Interoperability is the ability of two or more systems to exchange information and to use the information that has been exchanged, as well as the capability of two or more environments to handle the same input (information or service) in the same way. The interoperability can be obtained ether by adhering to public interface standards or by using an agent that converts one system's interface into another. With this understanding of interoperability it becomes evident why first, Process Knowledge enables interoperability and second, why interoperability is needed for a platform that intends to support transparent pan-European and cross-administration processes with the exchange of electronic standardized documents. [7]

3 Process Knowledge for Integrated Public Service Provision

As described above the main focus of current integration projects is to facilitate the use of public services by the citizen. In order to achieve the demanded transparent service provision the public authorities must communicate and interact seamlessly with each other. Current approaches are mostly limited to standardization of data exchange so that documents are well-defined and can be generated and interpreted unambiguously by each participant. These efforts are necessary but not sufficient to enable interoperability between European Public Administrations. Within the local offices the procedures are analyzed and optimized with process management tools from an intra-organizational perspective and are supported by IT. Considering inter-organizational aspects in contrast the local interfaces to procedures in other public administrations are treated manually. To improve this situation for both the citizen and the public administrations an automated execution of cross-level and cross-national procedures must be established.

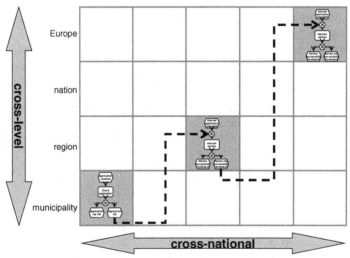

Fig. 2. Interaction of Public Service Offers

To enable this kind of interoperability the local service must retrieve information about services that provide needed inputs and services that process the outcomes at least on a meta-level. The initial service must know the characteristics of these services i.e. the service or process knowledge [8] must be accessible through standardized mechanisms. As the potential impact of managing process and service knowledge is clarified now the needed knowledge management activities are characterized in the following.

A common segmentation of KM activities distinguishes between the identification of existing knowledge assets, lacks of knowledge and external resources to fill these gaps, the augmentation and documentation of available knowledge and the use respectively reuse of knowledge. [9] This basic scheme can be applied to the management of process knowledge in e-Government scenarios.

Identification:

- Business process modelling and redesign within the local offices is the foundation to document existing procedures. Thus the created and maintained process models represent the knowledge assets of the local offices.
- Undetermined interfaces to other authorities with which the local public administration collaborates vertically and horizontally have to be identified. Thus the missing knowledge is determined.
- Resources for external knowledge acquisition (knowledge base) means black box knowledge about inputs and outputs of external services. The local knowledge is extended by the documents that have to be exchanged in a cross-organizational scenario. A distributed service knowledge repository is potentially able to fill this gap.

Augmentation/Documentation:

- By establishing standardized request operations that regulate the search for appropriate preceding and subsequent services the service instances can look for the input providers and output receivers that are needed to successfully execute a local service.
- At the local service interfaces the retrieval mechanisms must be added and integrated.
- The interaction mechanisms and communication acts are modelled so that the connection to other systems possibly through adequate adapters can be established. One subtask in this context is the standardization of data exchange.
- The knowledge gathered in this stage is static knowledge with a medium- to long-term validity.

Use/Reuse:

- The static knowledge described above is used to retrieve potential input providers and output receivers. The routing of documents is generated dynamically at run-time.
- The dynamic knowledge is cached and reused when the same or a similar business process is executed. This can be seen as a learning component of the system.

As illustrated the process knowledge is to be identified, documented, stored and made available on the right time at the right place. The easiest way would be to set up a central database that holds all the information that is needed. At this point the specifics of the e-government domain have to be taken into account. On a pan-European level or in a federally structured country no such central database can be established, amongst others because of legal restrictions on personal data protection. Further more there are major performance and reliability concerns considering central IT-systems in decentralized structures.

4 Designing Distributed Knowledge Repositories

The inappropriateness of a central solution arises from the circumstances described above. An alternative solution is the use of concepts that follow the paradigm of decentralization by keeping distributed data. This approach implies that all data that represent routing decisions (concerning input and output) are not maintained centrally but in logically many repositories. These repositories are virtually aggregated and integrated without establishing one central repository. For this purpose intelligent search and retrieval mechanisms are used. As static information the services that are offered by a Public Administration are stored in the local repository and are made accessible. At run-time the retrieval function determines the input providers and output receivers dynamically by accessing the virtually aggregated repository. Thus the business process fragments that are stored as modules in the decentralized on-site-repositories are connected and the customized and integrated overall-process can be executed. This effect is illustrated in Figure 3.

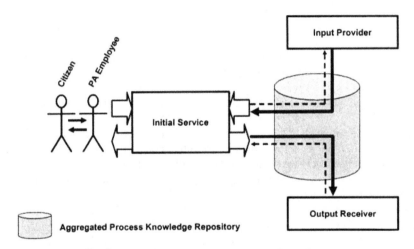

Fig. 3. Process Knowledge Management Repository

This dynamic process customisation can be explained with the following example. A citizen has moved from one country to another. According to the law he has to register the change of residence at the Public Administration of the municipality he has moved to. Additionally he has to deregister with the authorities of his former home country where a national agency is responsible for residential issues. To perform the service "change of residence" the certificate of birth of the citizen is needed. An authority of the region where he was born can issue this document. Without automated service interaction the citizen has to know these interdependencies and get the certificate of birth. At the new registry he hands out the certificate and after checking the documents his change of residence is officially registered. The citizen gets a certification of the new registration with which he or she can go to the former registry and the deregistration is performed. All these activities, especially the exchange of documents, were carried through manually by the citizen. The non-availability of cross-organisational process and service knowledge causes this lack of integration. With the distributed services repository described above the procedure would be customer-friendly. The citizen just moves to the new place and initiates the "change of residence" service. The employee checks the ID of the citizen and triggers the process. The service itself "knows" which inputs are required; in the underlying case this is the certificate of birth. The service retrieves the services that are potentially able to provide this input document as an output by asking the knowledge repository.[10] An intelligent search mechanism or a software agent finds the respective services and returns the list. These services are invoked sequentially by priority order as long as the main service can be successfully executed. This can be called a kind of "pull strategy". After that the output of the main service is delivered to the Citizen. Additionally other outputs have to be distributed to services that need the generated output as initial input. In the described scenario this is the notification about the change which implies the deregistration with the former registry. The so called "push strategy" retrieves a list of services that need this kind of input from the knowledge repository and they are started by delivering the generated output documents. At this point the translation of process knowledge into control knowledge[11] is needed. The static process knowledge has been used to generate the service instance. This instance requires now dynamically composed routing which is specific for the current service. The control knowledge is able to provide that information.

5   The InfoCitizen Approach

5.1   The InfoCitizen Project

The Project InfoCitizen, funded by the European Commission under the 5th Research Framework Programme, aims to create a pan-European Information Architecture for EPA interoperability as well as to develop specific information technology that supports this Architecture and ensures a seamless information exchange between European public administrations on a pan-European level. Moreover, with this solution EPAs are able to provide transparent and integrated public services for their citizens as well as for external clients.

InfoCitizen started in September 2001 with a project volume of 3.3 million euros for a duration of 24 months. Eleven organizations within five different EU-countries are working together to succeed the challenge of pan-European interoperability. The showcase scenario is tested in the municipalities of Colleferro (Italy), Schmelz (Germany), and Tres Cantos (Spain), and the prefecture of Thessaloniki (Greece).

5.2   The InfoCitizen European Architecture

The first major milestone was the development of a generic Interoperability Framework, the InfoCitizen European Architecture. It describes the relations and specifications of knowledge and information exchange between EPAs, i.e. the inter-PA interaction. The major requirements that were addressed with this Architecture are to support and describe the two key goals of the user needs, namely:

- transparent public service provision to the European citizen
- multi-agent / multi-country setting of public service provision

The InfoCitizen European Architecture will conduct electronic transactions in multi-agent settings/multi-country settings in a transparent as possible manner for the European citizen.

In order to create a long-living and stable result, we decomposed the European Architecture into three parts:

1. The Conceptual Architecture provides a business level view on the solution. It addresses the EPAs and their scope of description.
2. The Technical Architecture transforms the conceptual solution into a system-level architecture that describes the technological system without specifying concrete technology; it is technology-independent and therefore disconnected from the rapid-changing technology layer.
3. The System Architecture describes the system to be build. It is the blueprint of the InfoCitizen software solution based on an appropriate selection of state-of-the-art technologies.

The main challenge of the European Architecture, esp. of the Conceptual Architecture was the management of the control knowledge for the interaction. The central object in this context is the public service provided by a specific EPA. As already explained both the inputs needed for processing the service as well as the outputs produced by the service have to be received respectively distributed to the citizen in a transparent manner. Therefore the service itself has to conduct two different strategies for information retrieval and delivery.

1. The "Pull" strategy means that the required input of a service should be automatically accessed when needed from its relevant source (which is another service).
2. The "Push" strategy means that the consequences of the PA service provided should be "propagated" to all relevant PAs (respectively their appropriate services).

Besides the information exchange problem, that will be discussed later, the difficulty is how to identify the appropriate service. The knowledge for answering these kinds of questions is distributed over the different EPAs. Therefore InfoCitizen uses a distributed knowledge management approach. Each EPA publishes both the services it provides and detailed information about the services, such as mandatory or optional information inputs, outputs and preconditions.

Looking at a single instance of a service provision, it is necessary to find a mapping between services looking for specific information and services able to provide these. These mapping is an individual action, specific for each instance of service provision. As an example a service "marriage" with instance "Man A (German) and Woman B (Italian)",both needing certificates of birth, naturally has to communicate with different services than the instance "Man C (Greek) and Woman D (Spaniard)". To enable this mapping search a service uses the knowledge published by the other EPAs and determines potential information sources and targets. For technical reasons within InfoCitizen we decided not to hold the complete knowledge in each EPA but in a central repository, where they can access it. This is not opposed to our distributed knowledge management concept, as the central storage represents only a simplified communication media.

Obviously, to successfully communicate the services must understand each other. To solve the Babylonian problem of data format mapping a "Common Document

Language" has been developed. It is an open and extensible specification describing the data to be exchanged within InfoCitizen. It relies on state-of-the-art XML technology and is based on existing standards. Using the "Common Document Language" we provide a flexible instrument to find a common definition of the syntax and semantics of data within EPAs without forcing them to change internally.

5.3 InfoCitizen Platform

The information-technological realization of the concepts described uses agent-technology. This is most suitable for our purposes because it assists and facilitates the process of service search and discovery. Therefore the main component of the InfoCitizen platform is the interoperability agent. It plans controls and executes the information exchange. Using the emerging agent-technology enables the platform to efficiently search for, retrieve and distribute documents in order to satisfy the information demand of the EPAs that are connected to the InfoCitizen platform.

Figure 5 shows the central role of the Interoperability Agent within the structure of the InfoCitizen system architecture.

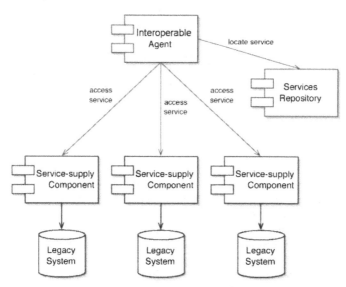

Fig. 4. InfoCitizen System Architecture

We implemented a services repository where all relevant information about services and input respectively output documents are stored. The service information was set up in a distributed manner and updated by the EPA that is responsible for this specific service. When searching for an appropriate service, the Interoperability agent queries and analyses the data of the services repository and finally locates the specific service.

A problem in real scenarios is the heterogeneity of EPAs. Within the context of the electronic support of service transactions triggered from or targeted to external systems, the existing legacy systems of the EPAs have to communicate with the other systems and therefore have to be-at least indirectly-connected to them. This connection will be realized through the Service Supply Component, which acts as an adapter between the existing legacy or standard-software application systems of EPAs and the InfoCitizen platform. The Service Supply Component Architecture is a Source code-Framework that simplifies and fastens the implementation of specific Service Supply Components. Moreover we provide precompiled and customisable Standard Service Supply Components that can be deployed instantaneous for widely common applications such as JCA compliant ones or JDBC compliant databases.

The front-end should satisfy user needs in usability and process support. Based on internet-technologies we are developing a multi-lingual, customizable information portal solution that interfaces between the user and the InfoCitizen platform.

In order to prove our concepts and implementations we are setting up a pilot system, which includes

- Local pilot showcases in the four participating countries that will focus on commonalities of business processes,
- and a generalised, pan-European InfoCitizen trial, which will reflect experiences and results in the international information exchange between the particular pilot sites.

Even as this pilot is showing interoperability only between four different European public administrations, we not only evidence the conceptual and technical feasibility of integrating these four specific offices. In view of the general approach we created with both the conceptual ideas and the technical realization, we can show that at least an interoperability between any public administration within these four countries can be established using the InfoCitizen European Architecture and the InfoCitizen Platform.

6 Conclusion

As a first result relevant processes in the Public Administrations of the four user-partners were documented and analysed. This serves as a basis for the improvement of existing processes and the invention of new services that facilitate the usage for the citizen. Furthermore generic models for almost any governmental service provision have been deducted by abstraction. These models are integrated in the InfoCitizen European Architecture which offers support for administrative business processes considering standards and interoperability. On this foundation a prototype consisting of locally installed Service Supply Components, an agent platform and a front-end is implemented. To prove the validity and practicability of the developed architecture the prototype is used in the showcase enabling the interaction of EPAs in four European countries. The move, marriage and adoption procedures in multi-country settings can be executed using the InfoCitizen System.

In the long run the InfoCitizen results are intended to serve as reference models for the electronic interaction of any Public Administration and thus establishing cost-effective and time-saving interoperability procedures that also improve the service quality considering the citizen. The Services Repository implementing distributed Knowledge Management enables this interoperability between EPAs. But the use of the repository is not limited to this purpose. In order to generate new added value of public products and services EPAs need more knowledge. Therefore the content of the repository will grow in quantity and quality to satisfy this future needs. Enabling the public administrations in Europe to provide transparent and integrated services on local, regional, national or pan-European level is the challenge for the future. The InfoCitizen project is a first step towards that future.

References

1. Fontaine, P.: Europa in zehn Lektionen, in: Europäische Kommission (Hrsg.): Veröffentlichungen für ein breites Publikum, 1997, <URL: http://europa.eu.int/comm/publications/booklets/eu_glance/ 12/txt_de.htm>.
2. Jansen, S. A.; Priddat, B. P.: Electronic Government – Neue Potenziale für einen modernen Staat, (Klett-Cotta) Stuttgart, 2001, S.22–23.
3. Meir, J.: Geschäftsprozesse im eGovernment – Ein Überblick, Arbeitsbericht Nr. 5 des CC eGovernment, Berner Fachhochschule – Institut für Wirtschaft und Verwaltung, Bern, 2002, S. 19–20.
4. Attenda: Government e-enables neighbourhood renewal – Attenda operates online knowledge management system, M2 Presswire; Coventry; Feb 6, 2003.
5. Newman, B.: An open discussion of Knowledge Management, 1991.
6. Kresner, Richard: Building a knowledge portal: A case study in Web-enabled collaborations, Information Strategy; Pennsauken; Winter 2003.
7. Fumio, Hattori; Takeshi, Ohguro; Makoto Yokoo; Socialware: Multiagent systems for supporting network communities, Association for Computing Machinery. Communications of the ACM; New York; Mar 1999.
8. Rolland C.: "Modelling the Requirements Engineering Process", Proc. Fino-Japanese Seminar on "Conceptual Modelling", 1993.
9. Probst, G.; Raub, S.; Romhardt, K; Doughty, H.A.: Managing Knowledge: Building Blocks for Success, John Wiley & Sons, 1999.
10. Seokwoo, Song: An Internet knowledge sharing system, The Journal of Computer Information Systems; Stillwater; Spring 2002.
11. Wilkins, D.; Jardins, M.: A call for knowledge-based planning, AI Magazine; La Canada; Spring 2001.
12. SAP: Next generation of manufacturing solutions to more tightly link shop floor with supply chain networks; Development resources dedicated to design solutions that will reduce working capital requirements and improve asset turns and cycle times, M2 Presswire; Coventry; Oct 29, 2002;
13. DATA PROTECTION REGISTRAR: Data Protection Registrar welcomes proposal for information commissioner, M2 Presswire; Coventry; May 26, 1999.

An *E*-service-Based Framework for Inter-administration Cooperation

Mariangela Contenti[1], Alessandro Termini[2], Massimo Mecella[2], and
Roberto Baldoni[2]

[1] Università di Roma LUISS "Guido Carli"
Centro di Ricerca sui Sistemi Informativi
mcontenti@luiss.it
[2] Università di Roma "La Sapienza"
Dipartimento di Informatica e Sistemistica
{termini,mecella,baldoni}@dis.uniroma1.it

Abstract. In order to provide electronic service delivery, several activities involving different public agencies need to be related and carried out in coordinated manner, thus resulting in a cooperative process. Currently, e-Service technologies seems to offer the enabling infrastructure for supporting cooperative process enactment, even at inter-country level. In this position paper, we outline the architecture we are proposing in the EU-PUBLI.com project, in which *orchestration of* e-*Services* constitutes the basis for provision of *e*-Government services. We discuss how such an architecture could support a form, although simple, of management of the *cooperative process knowledge*.

1 Introduction

In many countries, laws and administrative provisions usually fragment all the aspects of the life of a citizen according to *sectors* (i.e. taxation, health, labor, etc.): different responsibilities are then assigned to different agencies of the Public Administration (PA). This fragmented assignment of responsibilities produces difficulties in delivering services to citizens, as such services often result composed by several activities interleaved within complex business processes and involving different agencies. Therefore, in order to be able to provide services satisfactory from the point of view of a citizen agencies should make huge efforts, in term of knowledge and practice of the business processes.

In past years, some experiences (e.g., [1]) have shown that the introduction of consolidated distributed object technologies within the information systems of the agencies represents a mean to render accessible all the data and information stored in their own legacy systems . The proper design and implementation of wrappers allow to abstract from the data physical representation (access wrapper) and to create new information as new relations among the stored data (integration wrapper) [2].

But the adoption of different solutions by different agencies in terms of distributed object platforms and semantic frameworks have hampered interoperability among the different information systems, thus resulting in poor cooperation among their employees and a scarce knowledge management.

M.A. Wimmer (Ed.): KMGov 2003, LNAI 2645, pp. 13–24, 2003.

Emerging technologies such as *e*-Services and XML can currently represent the mean to overcome PA boundaries and can offer the technological and conceptual solution to design and to implement cooperation among employees belonging to distinct agencies. In the EU-PUBLI.com project, an approach based on *macro-processes* [1] and *orchestration* of *e*-Services [3] is being proposed and experimented, in order to enable cooperation and knowledge management among agencies belonging to different European countries.

A macro-process is a complex business process involving different agencies; *e*-Service technologies can be used to (semi-)automate macro-processes through cooperative applications, thus obtaining *cooperative processes*, which are enacted in order to offer added-value services to employees, citizens and businesses. Enactment of the cooperative processes is obtained by suitably orchestrating *e*-Services offered by different cooperating agencies.

Such an approach does not necessarily require initial radical modifications either in the macro-process structure nor in the organization internal processes: each agency interfaces the others by offering specific *e*-Services, independently on how it realizes them, its autonomy in changing its own processes is therefore guaranteed. Internal changes do not impact on the macro-process, as they are hidden by the service interfaces exported towards other agencies.

In such an approach, knowledge management, specifically focused on cooperative processes, is enabled and enforced in two specific ways:

- all the information collected in the analysis phase, aimed to identify the macro-process, produces a coherent and homogeneous documentation of the business practices that are often scattered and never formally documented; this is especially true in an inter-country *e*-Government scenario, as the one we are experimenting. Then such a documentation can both *(i)* be offered to citizens and employees through informative *e*-Services, and, *(ii)* formalized in an appropriate manner, it is stored as part of the supporting architecture and drives the orchestration of the different *e*-Services. This is especially true in the case of the mappings among different legal frameworks;
- orchestration of *e*-Services (i.e., the enactment of the cooperative processes) produces information on effective run-time executions, exceptions, bottlenecks, etc.; such information can be analyzed and mined in order to infer new process knowledge (business process intelligence, [4]).

In this paper we outline, in Section 2, some of the organizational aspects concerning the emerging need of cooperation and knowledge management; in Section 3 we will present the technologies on which our approach is based. In Section 4, first we briefly describe the EU-PUBLI.com project, then the novel architecture proposed in the project, and in Section 5 we will approach, on the basis of previous and current experiences, some aspect concerning knowledge management and we highlight the architectural subsystems of our architecture specifically supporting it. In Section 6 we compare with related work and finally Section 7 concludes the paper by remarking open issues and future research directions.

2   Organizational Issue

As defined in [5], "a *stakeholder* in an organization is any group or individual who can affect or is affected by the achievement of the organization's objective". A good organization should then identifies and strengthens its strategies for satisfying as a whole the often conflicting needs and claims of its different stakeholders. The dynamically changing actions a firm performs to comply the stakeholder theory have been then recognized as the mean for guaranteeing the survival and the maintenance of a sustainable competitive advantage for the firm itself.

Although, differently from private-sector firms, the PA's primary mission is to operate on behalf of citizens to pursue public interests and they are by their own nature monopolistic organizations, one of the PA's fundamental task is the provision of public services: the environment turbulence, changing the firms' approach towards a wider customer-oriented flexibility, is influencing the PA's approach, too. Also, the several stakeholders of a public agency are substantially incarnate by citizens, as they play both the role of "investors" (through the tax payment) and of "customer" (as service user) of the PA's acting[1].

This implies the the past and consolidated vertical configuration of the PA's, that, focusing on the efficiency rather than on the effectiveness, allowed to reach economy of scale and concentrate all the experiences and knowledge in specific *sectors*, is currently moving towards different aims and different configurations, driven by the citizens-centric view of service delivery. The new context implies renewing a wide range of operative business processes as often: *(i)* fragmentation of responsibilities translates in fragmentation of complex processes in atomic administrative activities, each of which assigned to different specific organizational units; *(ii)* the lack of integration implies frequent interruptions of processes inside each administration resulting in inefficient provision of services, as it often requires that citizens serves as messenger, providing the information needed to establish the communications required.

To design and implement new operative procedures both cost saving and citizen-oriented, is then necessary a new approach which binds together the efficiency and effectiveness of the service delivery: the Information and Communication Technologies (ICT) progress could represents the enabling technological instrument to sustain these efforts, at least for those services characterized by an high *information intensity* [6].

In this context, the Australian National Audit Office (ANAO) recently published a report focused on the opportunities and challenges that PA should evaluate for delivering services via electronic channels [7]. From the information collected via a questionnaire filled by 66 Commonwealth agencies emerged the main beneficiaries of IT initiatives are individuals and government agencies and the more suitable technology is Internet: the introduction of Internet should reduce the cost and improve the quality of the services. Specifically, the report has identified a framework according to which an agency offering services through

---

[1] With this view we are neglecting many other stakeholders, e.g., the employees which instead should be taken into account as they could represents, in some cases, a source of resistance to the change.

the Internet can be in one of four stage, as depicted in Figure 1; each stage represents a different level of service delivery: the higher the stage, the higher the technological and organizational complexity as well as the range of electronically provided services.

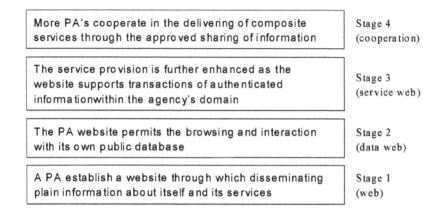

More PA's cooperate in the delivering of composite services through the approved sharing of information	Stage 4 (cooperation)
The service provision is further enhanced as the website supports transactions of authenticated information within the agency's domain	Stage 3 (service web)
The PA website permits the browsing and interaction with its own public database	Stage 2 (data web)
A PA establish a website through which disseminating plain information about itself and its services	Stage 1 (web)

Fig. 1. Our elaboration from the ANAO report [7]

Such a framework has been adopted by the British Central IT Unit of the Cabinet Office in an *e*-Government benchmark [8], focused on the comparison of the progress status in several *sectors* among G7 and other leading nations: many countries are positioning their public sectors at stage 2 and 3, whereas only few countries, i.e., USA, Canada and Singapore, have reached stage 4 and only in few sectors (only in *e*-Procurement). Such studies confirm the difficulties in establishing a stage 4 *e*-Government initiative; such difficulties stem mainly from organizational issues rather than technological ones, as laws and administrative provisions strongly constraint the cooperation processes. Indeed stage 4 requires that agencies identify cooperative processes, that is complex processes involving and "crossing" them in order to furnish added-value services to citizens and businesses [1].

Based on our past experiences, we are convinced that a viable approach to the design of public administration services at stage 4 implies, rather than *deep business process reengineering*, *macro-process technological improvement* and this is the one we have adopted in the EU-PUBLI.com project.

In a deep business process reengineering approach, redundant processes in specific organizational units would be eliminated, and some activities would be re-assigned to new organizational units: this would eliminate many information exchanges, thus addressing the main issue of the excessive fragmentation of responsibilities among agencies. Unfortunately, certain issues hamper large-scale radical changes in the short and medium term, such as the impossibility of assigning new legal responsibilities to given organizational units (due to the difficulty of changing existing laws), the lack of specific skills and resources in some agencies, the time needed to create such skills, and so on.

In the technological improvement approach, each agency is seen as a domain with a proper information asset, made available as data and application services exported on such data; separate agencies are loosely coupled as each agency interfaces the others by offering specific services, independently from their realization; the reengineering of an agency's internal processes does not impact the cooperative processes and the former improvement and enrichment enable the way to more radical macro-process reengineering.

3   Technological Background

As the EU-PUBLI.com architecture is based on *e*-Services, in the current section we briefly describe such a paradigm and related technologies. *e*-Services, also referred to as Web-Services, are Web-enabled applications exported by different organizations consisting of well-defined functionalities that allow users and applications to access and perform tasks offered by back-end business applications.

A Service Oriented Architecture (SOA, [9]) is a framework for *e*-Services consisting of *(i)* some basic operations and *(ii)* roles, as shown in Figure 2:

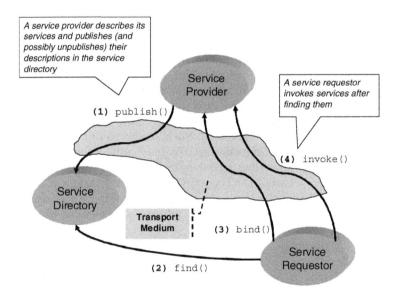

Fig. 2. Basic elements of an *e*-Service framework

– **Service Provider:** it is the subject providing software applications for specific needs as services; *(i)* from a business perspective, this is the owner of the service (e.g., the subject which is possibly paid for its services), and

(ii) from the architectural perspective, this is the platform the service is deployed onto. Available services are described by using a *service description language* and advertised through the `publish()` operation on a public available service directory.

- **Service Requestor:** it is the party that uses the services; *(i)* from a business perspective, this is the business requiring certain services to be fulfilled (e.g., the payer subject), and *(ii)* from an architectural perspective, this is the application invoking the service. A service requestor discover the most suitable service in the directory through the `find()` operation, then it connects to the specific service provider through the `bind()` operation and finally it uses it (`invoke()` operation).
- **Service Directory:** it is the party providing a *repository* and/or a *registry* of service descriptions, where providers publish their services and requestors find services.

As the transport medium is a parameter of a SOA, this framework is easily integrable on different technologies and then well suited for open and dynamically changing environment as the Web is.

Currently, some competing solutions for *e*-Services and Web Services are emerging in commercial contexts, such as the Universal Description, Discovery and Integration (UDDI)[2] initiative, and the ebXML[3] standardization effort. All such proposals, on the basis of a common transport medium, consisting of Web technologies such as HTTP, SOAP and XML Protocol, address some basic technological issues of a SOA, that is the definition *(i)* of the service directory, *(ii)* of the service description language, *(iii)* of how to define possible interactions a service can be involved in (conversations), and *(iv)* of how to compose and coordinate different services, to be assembled together in order to support complex processes (orchestration).

In the UDDI initiative, the architecture of a distributed service directory is proposed [10]; many service description languages are being proposed for specific purposes:

- Web Service Description Language (WSDL, [11]) for describing services, specifically their static interfaces; on top of it, a specific ontology-based language for *e*-Services has been proposed, namely DAML-S [12];
- Web Service Conversation Language (WSCL, [13]) for describing the conversations a service supports;
- Web Service Choreography Interface (WSCI, [14]) for describing the observable behavior of a service in terms of temporal and logical dependencies among the exchanged messages;
- Web Service Flow Language (WSFL, [15]) for the design of composite Web Services starting from simple ones (composition of Web Services);
- XLANG [16] for both the specification of the behavior of services and their orchestration;
- Business Process Execution Language for Web Services (BPEL4WS, [17]) with the aim of merging WSFL and XLANG.

---

[2] UDDI.org: `http://www.uddi.org`.
[3] ebXML.org: `http://www.ebxml.org`.

The architecture of EU-PUBLI.com, outlined in the next section, is based on the previous technologies, that are adopted and homogeneously integrated in an *e*-Government framework.

4   The **EU-PUBLI.com** Architecture

The EU-PUBLI.com project attempts to achieve cooperation amongst European agencies by designing and implementing a cooperative system that can interconnect, at application level, the different information systems, in order to (semi-) automate inter-country macro-processes providing complex *e*-Government services; as an example, in the project demonstrator, the macro-process of establishing in Greece an affiliated company (i.e., an independent "branch office") of an Italian company will be experimented.

Figure 3 shows the overall EU-PUBLI.com architecture; the basic vision consists on defining an overall architecture, respecting the autonomy of the single involved agency; ad hoc development and integration are feasible, but they will produce complex distributed application difficult to maintain and evolve. Instead, the choice of a SOA ensures an high level of flexibility to the system.

The cooperation of different agencies is achieved by making them responsible for exporting some views of its own information system as *e*-Services; the **Cooperative Gateway** sub-system represents "where" and "how" *e*-Services are deployed; it includes the definition on how different cooperating organizations are organized and connected and how pre-existing legacy applications (Local IS in the figure) can be integrated in a common cooperative process. Roughly speaking, it exports the set of data and application services offered by a single agency through well-defined interfaces. In the architecture, each cooperating agency offers its own cooperative gateway. Clearly, cooperative gateways has the role of service provider in the SOA.

e-Services exported on cooperative gateways can be either *informative e*-Services, i.e., providing only static information (stage 1 and 2 of the ANAO model) or *transactional e*-Service, i.e., allowing dynamic retrieve of data and update on back-end databases (stage 3 and 4).

The **Orchestration Engine** sub-system is the responsible of coordinating all the *e*-Services involved in a cooperative process: through "cooperative process definitions" (technically referred to as orchestration schemas) stored into the Information Manager, it dynamically finds and links suitable *e*-Services. In some sense, this sub-system can be viewed as a particular service requestor of the SOA.

The core of the architecture is represented by the **Information Manager**: this sub-system stores both *(i)* *e*-Service definitions and *(ii)* orchestration schemas. Moreover, it stores and manages all information needed to convert and map different legal frameworks.

In general, it is accessed at design-time by the cooperating agencies, in order to publish and register their *e*-Services, and to define and register the cooperative schemas with the needed mappings. The information manager is also accessed at run-time by the orchestration engine, in order to gain access to both *e*-Services specifications and instance data, and to update running process instance data. In next section it will be discussed how this sub-system supports knowledge about

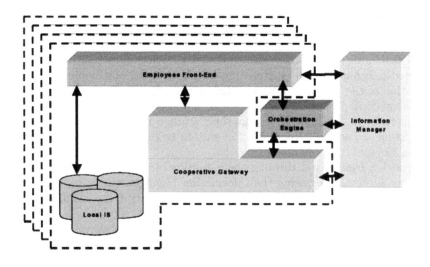

Fig. 3. EU-PUBLI.com Architecture

cooperative processes. With respect to the SOA, the EU-PUBLI.com information manager plays the service directory role.

Finally the **Employees Front-End** sub-system is responsible for the presentation to end users of the results of cooperative process executions.

5   Knowledge Management in **EU-PUBLI.com**

As discussed in the previous sections, building cooperative process applications requires the integration of different heterogeneous systems, which are different not only from the technological point of view but also for the information asset they export. Whatever the progress in ICT could afford a syntactic interoperability among the PA information systems, an effective and durable cooperation, founded on the dynamic sharing of information and services, can be automated via electronic channel only after the achievement of a semantic agreement, among the interacting parties, about the meaning of the information and services exchanged. Thus, a relevant aspects to be dealt with, for a real cooperation among different agencies, is the knowledge management, at least at level of definition and use of explicit knowledge.

In the last years the problem of the semantic agreement on the information and services interleaved in a cooperative process is being approached through the definition of atomic semantic entities, the ontologies, whose meaning is globally defined and shared within a community. Through the ontologies, each participant of the community can make use of this basic building block to describe its own information and knowledge asset. The definition and the adoption of such a semantic reference model can thus automatize the knowledge mapping within the community; moreover it can represent the starting point for further community-wide automatic composition and retrieval of other knowledge.

What the EU-PUBLI.com architecture represents is a technological solution which is able to realize an overall cooperative information system spanning national and cross-country agencies. Its adoption requires a deep analysis phase, aimed to identify macro-processes, followed by a formalization phase of all the collected information. These steps produce a coherent and homogeneous documentation of the business practices that are often scattered and rarely formally documented. A proper formalization and representation of the collected information through XML dialects and their storage in the Information Manager sub-system are actually mandatory operation to the correct run of the Orchestration Engine.

In such a framework, through the definition of additional appropriate informative *e*-Services interfacing the Information Manager, the overall architecture can provide the functionalities of an electronic library from which old, current or specific administrative procedures can be retrieval.

Moreover, the Orchestration Engine produces data on effective run-time executions, bottlenecks, etc., that can be stored, analyzed and mined in order to infer process knowledge [4] and to enhance a deeper comprehension of each public agency role within both the national and the cross-country public service scenario. A deeper knowledge of the causal relation among the several activities will become, in an iterative fashion, the starting and the target point for process reengineering involving not only the information system reengineering but even legal constraints; in this cycle the *e*-Governance and the the Electronic Service Delivery become overlapping disciplines.

At current stage of our project and investigation it is not yet clear whether the description of the signature and the behaviour of the involved *e*-Services is a sufficient description, or also dictionaries of each single involved data are required. Currently both *e*-Service descriptions and orchestration schemas in the EU-PUBLI.com architecture are based on specific XML dialects, and this is coherent with the DAML approach to ontology definitions; therefore extensions to more sophisticated techniques should be simple.

6   Related Work

The problem of inter-agency cooperation at European level has been already emerged in several different research contexts, as, for example, in the IST FASME project [18]. The project focused on the integration of an European citizen with many European PA's through the prototyping of a set of services relying on the technological support of Internet and smartcards.

In the project, one of the considered services was the residence registration service by mobile Europeans at local administrations. What emerged was that the registration procedure generically require information about one' own birth, marriage and children, but these concepts does not have neither a European-wide representation nor a European-wide meaning: *(i)* the certificates attesting these kind of information, have in each country its own different format and data contents; *(ii)* taking as example the marriage, it could be referred to monogamy, polygamy, polyandry or same-sex marriage according to the country in which the concept is instantiate.

A crucial point for the effective realization of ICT-aided cooperation among European PA's is, thus, the cross-countries information exchange. Actually, as a legal concept, generally spans a legal framework ruling several different rights (as in the case of marriage, the tax payment and inheritance, for instance) the project strengthen that to prevent legal confusion it was - and it still is - important to agree on the meanings of the information explicitly or implicitly exchanged, also because a specific aspect caught in a country could not exist or could be even explicitly not recognized in other countries.

To face these problems the FASME project relied on standardized "template solution" derived from a legal and administrative harmonization at European level. By following such an approach the transition to e-Government solutions might be hampered by the need of a deep business process reengineering moving towards an hardly, slowly and unlikely reachable common legal framework. A more feasible approach to integration and cooperation at European level should, instead, *(i)* preserve different culture, ideologies and legal framework and *(ii)* detect, collect or even trigger commonalities and harmonizations at process level among two or more national legal framework.

In this view, the EU-PUBLI.com architecture could represent the information repository where to store cross-nation agreements and partnership; as an example, in the demonstrator we are investigating, the Information Manager will store and manage the mapping rules among those certificates and forms in the two different pilot countries, which are needed for the business establishment. Compared with a static template solution, a framework in which process and data schemas are dynamically loaded and linked together to reflect well-defined administrative provisions, could actually facilitate and accelerate the actuation of cooperative e-Government initiatives. Such a widely configurable solution can be flexibly queried and enriched to reflect social evolution and trigger legal changes.

Along the way towards the definition of common metadata and data schemas definition, an important experience is the one related with the British e-Government Interoperability Framework (*e*-GIF) project [19], in which the issue has being faced with a centralized approach relying on XML technologies. The *e*-GIF currently comprises a wide set of XML documents, publicly available, defining mandatory technical policies and specification *(i)* for achieving interoperability and data integration; *(ii)* for ruling information access and content management and thus *(iii)* for ensuring information system coherence across the British public sector.

The XML schemas definition process is realized through an interactive and iterative procedure: *(i)* proposals and revisions for an XML schema involve a central coordination team but also all the stakeholders so to ensure its wide acceptance; *(ii)* the order in which the XML schemas are defined or refined is driven by the need of citizens.

The *e*-GIF initiative is claiming more and more interests and it could represent an important methodological and technical reference for the next step along the way to a real adoption and and effective use of approaches and architectures similar to the one investigated in the EU-PUBLI.com project.

7   Conclusions

In this paper, we have presented the EU-PUBLI.com architecture, specifically focusing on *e*-Government service provisions based on orchestration of *e*-Services. The basic concept of our approach is the one of cooperative process, as unifying element among different inter-country agencies providing value-added services to European citizens.

Moreover, we have discussed how the proposed architecture support a form, although simple, of knowledge management, specifically focused on cooperative processes:

- all the information collected in the analysis phase, aimed to identify the cooperative process, produces a coherent and homogeneous documentation of the business practices. Such a documentation *(i)* must be formalized in an appropriate manner to be stored as part of the supporting architecture and to drive the orchestration of the different *e*-Services (e.g., in the case of the mappings among different legal frameworks); and *(ii)* can be later offered to citizens and employees through informative *e*-Services;
- orchestration of *e*-Services (i.e., the enactment of the cooperative processes) produces information on effective run-time executions, exceptions, bottlenecks, etc.; such information can be analyzed and mined in order to infer new process knowledge.

Focusing on processes, on the other hand, tends to underestimate the importance of automatizing the knowledge mapping and the automatic composition and retrieval of other knowledge, which conversely are addressed by ontology-based techniques. Therefore an important issues that need to be resolved in order to develop a complete *e*-Government framework, is how an ontology-based approach to knowledge management can be integrated and complemented with the one based on cooperative process execution and *e*-Service orchestration proposed in this paper.

Acknowledgments. This work has been supported by the European Commission under Contract No. IST-2001-35217, Project *EU-PUBLI.com (Facilitating Cooperation amongst European Public Administration Employees)* (http://www.eu-publi.com/). The authors would like to thanks the other project partners: CERTH/ITI (Greece), ICE (Italy), ALTEC (Greece) and IBERMATICA (Spain) for discussing many issues dealt in this paper.

References

1. C. Batini and M. Mecella, "Enabling Italian *e*-Government Through a Cooperative Architecture", *IEEE Computer*, vol. 34, no. 2, 2001.
2. M. Mecella and B. Pernici, "Designing Wrapper Components for *e*-Services in Integrating Heterogeneous Systems", *VLDB Journal*, vol. 10, no. 1, 2001.
3. M. Mecella, F. Parisi Presicce, and B. Pernici, "Modeling *e*-Service Orchestration Through Petri Nets", in *Proceedings of the 3rd VLDB International Workshop on Technologies for e-Services (VLDB-TES 2002)*, Hong Kong, Hong Kong SAR, China, 2002.

4. D. Grigori, F. Casati, U. Dayal, and M.C. Shan, "Improving Process Quality through Exception Understanding, Prediction and Prevention", in *Proceedings of the 27th International Conference on Very Large Data Bases (VLDB 2001)*, Roma, Italy, 2001.
5. R.E. Freeman, *Strategic Management: a Stakeholder Approach*, Pitman, 1984.
6. M.E. Porter and V.E. Millar, "How Information Gives You Competitive Advantage", *Harvard Business Review*, 1985.
7. Australian National Audit Office, "Electronic Service Delivery, including Internet Use, by Commonwealth Government Agencies", The Auditor-General, Audit Report No.18 (1999-2000), 1999.
8. Central IT Unit of the Cabinet Office (CITU), "Information Age Government. Benchmarking Electronic Service Delivery", CITU Report, London, United Kingdom, July 2000.
9. T. Pilioura and A. Tsalgatidou, *"e-Services: Current Technologies and Open Issues"*, in *Proceedings of the 2nd VLDB International Workshop on Technologies for e-Services (VLDB-TES 2001)*, Rome, Italy, 2001.
10. UDDI.org, "UDDI Technical White Paper", http://www.uddi.org/pubs/lru_UDDI_Technical_Paper.pdf, 2001.
11. Ariba, Microsoft, and IBM, "Web Services Description Language (WSDL) 1.1", W3C Note. http://www.w3.org/TR/2001/NOTE-wsdl-20010315, March 2001.
12. A. Ankolekar, M. Burstein, J. Hobbs, O. Lassila, D. Martin, D. McDermott, S. McIlraith, S. Narayanan, M. Paolucci, T. Payne, and K. Sycara, "DAML-S: Web Service Description for the Semantic Web", in *Proceedings of the 1st International Semantic Web Conference (ISWC 2002)*, Chia, Sardegna, Italy, 2002.
13. H. Kuno, M. Lemon, A. Karp, and D. Beringer, "Conversations + Interfaces = Business Logic", in *Proceedings of the 2nd VLDB International Workshop on Technologies for e-Services (VLDB-TES 2001)*, Rome, Italy, 2001.
14. BEA, Intalio, SAP, and Sun, "Web Service Choreography Interface (WSCI) 1.0", Document. http://wwws.sun.com/software/xml/developers/wsci/wsci-spec-10.pdf, 2002.
15. F. Leymann, "Web Service Flow Language (WSFL 1.0)", IBM Document. http://www-4.ibm.com/software/solutions/webservices/pdf/WSFL.pdf, May 2001.
16. T. Satish, "XLANG. Web Services for Business Process Design", Microsoft Document. http://www.gotdotnet.com/team/xml_wsspecs/xlang-c/default.hm, 2001.
17. F. Curbera, Y. Goland, J. Klein, F. Leymann, D. Roller, S. Thatte, and S. Weerawarana, "Business Process Execution Language for Web Services (Version 1.0)", IBM Document. http://www.ibm.com/developerworks/library/ws-bpel/, July 2002.
18. FASME Project: http://www.fasme.org.
19. Office of the *e*-Envoy, *"e*-Government Interoperability Framework", 2002.

Evaluation of Life-Event Portals:
Multi-attribute Model and Case Study

Anamarija Leben[1] and Marko Bohanec[1,2]

[1] University of Ljubljana, School of Public Administration, Gosarjeva 5, 1000 Ljubljana,
Slovenia
anamarija.leben@vus.uni-lj.si
[2] Jozef Stefan Institute, Ljubljana, Slovenia
marko.bohanec@ijs.si

Abstract. The provision of life-event based public services is one of popular
development trends of e-government programmes that have emerged in recent
years. In the article, first a concept of life-event portal is briefly presented. The
main emphasis of the article is on the methodology for the evaluation of life-
event portals, which is based on multi-attribute modelling. The methodology
helps to assess and compare electronic services, life-events and portals as a
whole. The results of an analysis of sixteen life-event portals are presented.

1 Introduction

1.1 The Concepts of an Active Life-Event Portal

Government portals as one of the development trends of e-government programs have
an important role in the provision of public services. They allow us to join or even
integrate services that are in the competence of different public institutions into one
single entry point via the Internet. One of the key questions in developing such portals
is how to structure and design services to gain real benefits for the customer (citizens
and business) and the government as well.

The problem lies in the fact that the existent organization of government is based
on a division of work between several fields or competences. Accordingly,
government processes and services are adapted and distributed over several public
institutions. However, the problems of customers do not usually apply merely to one
single competence or one single public institution. The solution of customer's
problem typically requires starting several different administrative procedures at
several different public institutions. Moreover, businesses are often involved as well.
In such situations a citizen often knows only what *he* wants (e.g. get married, build a
house), but does not know which administrative procedures are relevant in his
particular case, in what order, which public institution is competent for handling that
case and what else is needed to complete the procedure (what application, which
supplements, where and how to find all the necessary information, etc).

One of the possible solutions in this respect is the development of services based
on life-events. This approach considers government operation from the perspective of
everyday life and customer's needs rather than the internal needs of the government.

M.A. Wimmer (Ed.): KMGov 2003, LNAI 2645, pp. 25–36, 2003.
© IFIP 2003

Therefore, one life-event has to comprise all services as well as the corresponding processes (either administrative or business processes) needed to solve the customer's problem from the beginning to the end. The government portal, which includes the system to help the user to identify and solve his life-event, is called a life-event portal. The core system of such a portal is a knowledge-based system (Fig. 1), which is a computer program that employs the relevant knowledge and is based on inference mechanisms to solve a given problem [7, 8]. The knowledge-based system in an active life-event portal (intelligent guide trough life-events) uses a pre-defined structure of a particular life-event to form an active dialog with the user. In this way, the user is an active partner in the overall process of identifying and solving his/her problem. The Singapore 'e-Citizen' portal [4] uses such a system for the life-event 'starting a business'.

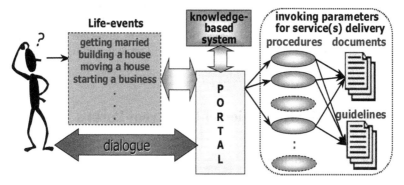

Fig. 1. Concepts of an active life-event portal

An 'intelligent' user interface of an active life-event portal that employs corresponding knowledge-management system should meet three objectives [10]. The first goal is to select an adequate life-event. This could be achieved through a hierarchical structure of topics. This structure helps the user to identify the life-event that corresponds to his problem. Other instruments for selecting an adequate life-event are, for example, a search engine or alphabetical list of life-events with their brief descriptions. The second goal is to identify the processes needed to solve this life-event. This could be achieved through a decision-making process, which is comprised in the structure of the life-event. This process results in a list of generic processes. The third aspect is to identify an adequate variant of each generic process in this list. This is also a decision-making process, where parameters needed to define a variant of process depend on the values of decisions. These parameters are, for example, different documents needed as supplements to the application form for particular process, and their corresponding guidelines. The list of procedures and corresponding documents and guidelines are called invoking parameters for e-service delivery. These e-services can be presented as information, interaction or even transaction.

As described above, a particular life-event comprises a considerable amount of knowledge about the customer's needs as well as a government structure and operation needed to meet these needs. In this way, a life-event portal can be regarded as a knowledge-management system. On the one hand, the knowledge is represented and maintained within this system, and on the other, this knowledge is made operational and accessible to the citizen.

1.2 Background

A preliminary study of existent life-event portals, carried out in the beginning of 2002, indicated that portals differ mainly in the following characteristics:
- the selection of instruments that are used to identify and select an adequate life-event,
- the extent to which a particular life-event corresponds to the real user's problem,
- the way how life-events are designed and represented to the user together with the corresponding electronic services, and
- the level of on-line sophistication at which life-events and electronic services are offered to the user.

These findings suggested that detailed analyses of portals should be conducted. Therefore, a methodology for the evaluation of life-event portals was developed to assess the state of the art of portals in terms of contents and applied technology, to identify portals' strong and week characteristics, and to compare the portals. This methodology and the results of the analysis of 16 life-event portals are presented in this paper.

2 Methodology for Evaluation of Life-Event Portals

2.1 Underlying Methodology

The core of our assessment of life-event portals was based on multi-attribute models. This approach, which originates in the field of decision analysis [3], is aimed at assessing the utility of options (or alternatives) that occur in decision-making problems. In principle, a multi-attribute model represents a decomposition of a decision problem into smaller and less complex subproblems. A model consists of attributes and utility functions. Attributes (sometimes also referred to as performance variables or parameters) are variables that represent decision subproblems. They are organized hierarchically so that the attributes that occur on higher levels of the hierarchy depend on the lower-level ones. According to their position in the hierarchy, we distinguish between basic attributes (leaves or terminal nodes) and aggregate attributes (internal nodes, including the roots of the hierarchy). Basic attributes represent inputs of the model, while the roots represent its output. Utility functions define the relationship between the attributes at different levels, i.e., for each aggregate attribute they define a mapping from its immediate descendants in the hierarchy to that attribute. Thus, utility functions serve for the aggregation of partial subproblems into the overall evaluation or classification.

For the purpose of our research, we have developed qualitative models using the software tool DEXi. Qualitative models contain qualitative (cardinal or ordinal) attributes, and use if-then rules for the aggregation of attributes. DEXi [6] is a decision-support computer program that facilitates the development of qualitative multi-attribute models and the evaluation of alternatives. The developed model is comprehensible; it allows validation, different analyses and simulations (such as what-if analysis), as well as the interpretation, justification and graphical representation of results. DEXi and its predecessor DEX [1, 2] have been used in more than fifty real-life decision problems in various areas [9], such as selection and evaluation of computer hardware and software, performance evaluation of enterprises and business partners, project evaluation, and personnel management.

We have developed three qualitative models for the assessment of life-event portals at three different levels: (1) electronic services, (2) life-events and (3) life-event portals as a whole. The latter is the model at the highest level, as each life-event portal supports one or more life-events. Thus, the model for assessing life-events subsumes one or more evaluations of life-events. Similarly, each life-event offers one or more electronic services, so again each life-event model refers to one or more models for assessing electronic services.

When assessing particular life-event portal, first the electronic services of each selected life-event (see section 3.1) are assessed. The assessments of services influence the assessment of the life-event in which these services are included (see section 2.4). Finally, the assessment of observed life-events at particular life-event portal is included in the assessment of this portal (see section 2.5).

2.2 Model for Assessing Electronic Services

The European Commission, DG Information Society [5] proposes a four-staged framework for the classification of e-services regarding the level of on-line sophistication, as follows:

- Stage 1 - Information: online information about public services;
- Stage 2 - Interaction: downloading of forms;
- Stage 3 - Two-way interaction: processing of forms, including authentication;
- Stage 4 - Transaction: case handling, decision and delivery (payment).

In our methodology, this framework was used as a basis for the development of the model for assessing e-services. In this model, the individual characteristics that define a particular stage are analysed separately and then combined (aggregated) into the overall assessment of e-service. In addition to these characteristics, the clarity of e-services is also considered (Fig. 2).

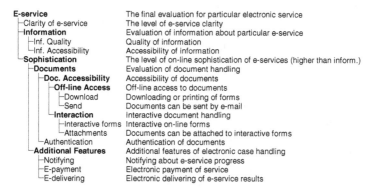

Fig. 2. The hierarchical tree of attributes of the model for assessing electronic services

2.3 Model for Assessing Life-Events

In the proposed model, the final assessment of life-event is aggregated from the assessments of the following attributes (Fig. 3): life-event maturity, life-event usage and clarity of life-event.

Fig. 3. The hierarchical tree of attributes of the model for assessing life-events and corresponding attribute scales

The *maturity of life-event* is further composed of life-event on-line sophistication, the scope of life-event and life-event coordination. These attributes are described in more detail, since they form a very important part of the overall assessment of life-event.

A life event comprises different electronic services. Some of these services are vital for the life-event, meaning that if they are not accomplished, the life event cannot be considered as solved. For example, the company has to be registered before you can start a business; thus, the service 'registering the company' is a vital service for the life-event 'starting a business'. Other services within life-event are considered as additional as they contribute to the quality of life-event or add the value to the final result. For example, information about benefits and weaknesses of different business types can simplify the decision about which business type corresponds to a particular user's situation.

According to this classification, the *scope of life-event* is defined to evaluate how well a particular life-event is covered with electronic services. This characteristic is evaluated for the vital services and additional services separately and then aggregated into the final assessment of the scope of life-event.

A life-event can be considered a complex electronic service. Thus, the *level of on-line sophistication* is one of the characteristics for the assessment of life-events. In the proposed model, this characteristic is calculated from the assessments of electronic services assessed in a particular life-event in the following way:

1. The average assessment is calculated separately for the vital and additional services within life-event.
2. The average assessment for the life-event (LE_{avg}) is a weighted sum of the average assessment for the vital services (VS_{avg}) and average assessment for the additional services (AS_{avg}): $LE_{avg} = 2/3\ VS_{avg} + 1/3\ AS_{avg}$.
3. Finally, the intervals to transform the average assessments into the assessment of life-event on-line sophistication are defined as follows:

Average assessment of services	Life-event on-line sophistication
between 1 and 1.7	1 - unacceptable
between 1.8 and 2.5	2 - acceptable
between 2.6 and 3.3	3 - good
Between 3.4 and 4.1	4 - very good
between 4.2 and 5	5 - excellent

The *level of coordination* within a life-event defines the way in which electronic services are combined into a particular life-event. The manner of the integration of the processes that correspond to these services is not an issue here. This characteristic evaluates only the coordination, as it is perceived by the user. The levels of coordination are defined as (Fig. 3):

− dispersion: services, which are normally comprehended within particular life-event, are provided on different web sites;

− one entry point: this entry point offers links to the web sites of institutions, where the corresponding services are provided;

− step-by-step coordination: the services are provided on one web site; however, the user must apply each process that corresponds to the electronic service separately, and wait until it is finished before applying the next one;

− one-step coordination: the user applies only the first process, and the next one is triggered automatically when the preceding one is finished.

The *use of life-event* combines two elements: the access to services and the standardization of electronic services design and structure. The access to services evaluates different instruments helping to access electronic services within life-event. In addition to standard instruments (e.g. the list and the description of key steps, check-list with the most important services and frequently asked questions with answers helping the user to solve his problem), an 'intelligent' electronic-guide through life-event (see section 1.1) is specially included in the proposed model.

The *clarity of life-event* was added to the model during the assessment of portals. Sometimes so little information about particular life-event was provided that it was difficult to evaluate especially which services are vital and which are additional, or to determine the structure of the life-event.

#	Maturity 35%	Use of LE 31%	Clarity of LE 34%	Life-event
1	unacceptable	*	*	unacceptable
2	<=acceptable	unsuitable	*	unacceptable
3	*	unsuitable	inadequate	unacceptable
4	acceptable	partly-suitable:suitable	*	acceptable
5	acceptable	>=partly-suitable	<=partly-adequate	acceptable
6	acceptable:very-good	>=partly-suitable	inadequate	acceptable
7	>=acceptable	partly-suitable:suitable	inadequate	acceptable
8	>=good	unsuitable	>=partly-adequate	acceptable
9	acceptable	very suitable	adequate	good
10	good	partly-suitable:suitable	>=partly-adequate	good
11	good	>=partly-suitable	partly-adequate	good
12	good:very-good	partly-suitable:suitable	partly-adequate	good
13	>=good	partly-suitable	>=partly-adequate	good
14	excellent	very suitable	inadequate	good
15	good:very-good	very suitable	adequate	very-good
16	very-good	>=suitable	adequate	very-good
17	very-good	very suitable	>=partly-adequate	very-good
18	>=very-good	very suitable	partly-adequate	very-good
19	excellent	>=suitable	partly-adequate	very-good
20	excellent	>=suitable	adequate	excellent

#	Access to Services 63%	Standardisation of Services 37%	Use of LE
1	unsuitable	*	unsuitable
2	<=partly-suitable	inadequate	unsuitable
3	partly-suitable	partly-adequate	partly-suitable
4	suitable	inadequate	partly-suitable
5	partly-suitable:suitable	adequate	suitable
6	suitable	>=partly-adequate	suitable
7	very suitable	inadequate	suitable
8	very suitable	>=partly-adequate	very suitable

#	Access Instruments 55%	E-guide 45%	Access to Services
1	unsuitable	<=partly-adequate	unsuitable
2	unsuitable	adequate	partly-suitable
3	partly-suitable	<=partly-adequate	partly-suitable
4	partly-suitable:suitable	inadequate	partly-suitable
5	partly-suitable	adequate	suitable
6	suitable	partly-adequate	suitable
7	very suitable	inadequate	suitable
8	>=suitable	adequate	very suitable
9	very suitable	>=partly-adequate	very suitable

#	LE Sophistication 34%	Scope of LE 34%	Coordination within LE 32%	Maturity
1	unacceptable	*	*	unacceptable
2	<=acceptable	inadequate	*	unacceptable
3	<=acceptable	*	<=one entry point	unacceptable
4	<=good	inadequate	<=one entry point	unacceptable
5	<=good	*	dispersed	unacceptable
6	*	inadequate	dispersed	unacceptable
7	acceptable	>=partly-adequate	>=step-by-step	acceptable
8	good	inadequate	>=step-by-step	acceptable
9	>=good	inadequate	step-by-step	acceptable
10	good	>=partly-adequate	one entry point	acceptable
11	>=good	>=partly-adequate	one entry point	acceptable
12	>=very-good	inadequate	one entry point:step-by-step	acceptable
13	>=very-good	<=partly-adequate	one entry point	acceptable
14	>=very-good	partly-adequate	<=one entry point	acceptable
15	>=very-good	>=partly-adequate	dispersed	acceptable
16	good:very-good	partly-adequate	>=step-by-step	good
17	>=good	partly-adequate	step-by-step	good
18	very-good	<=partly-adequate	one-step	good
19	>=very-good	inadequate	one-step	good
20	very-good	adequate	one entry point	good
21	good	adequate	>=step-by-step	very-good
22	good:very-good	adequate	step-by-step	very-good
23	excellent	partly-adequate	one-step	very-good
24	excellent	adequate	one entry point	very-good
25	>=very-good	adequate	one-step	excellent
26	excellent	adequate	>=step-by-step	excellent

#	Key Steps 33%	Check List 33%	FAQ 33%	Access Instruments
1	inadequate	inadequate	<=partly-adequate	unsuitable
2	inadequate	<=partly-adequate	inadequate	unsuitable
3	<=partly-adequate	inadequate	inadequate	unsuitable
4	inadequate	<=partly-adequate	adequate	partly-suitable
5	<=partly-adequate	inadequate	adequate	partly-suitable
6	inadequate	partly-adequate	>=partly-adequate	partly-suitable
7	inadequate	>=partly-adequate	partly-adequate	partly-suitable
8	inadequate	adequate	<=partly-adequate	partly-suitable
9	<=partly-adequate	adequate	inadequate	partly-suitable
10	partly-adequate	inadequate	>=partly-adequate	partly-suitable
11	>=partly-adequate	inadequate	partly-adequate	partly-suitable
12	partly-adequate	>=partly-adequate	inadequate	partly-suitable
13	>=partly-adequate	partly-adequate	inadequate	partly-suitable
14	adequate	inadequate	<=partly-adequate	partly-suitable
15	adequate	<=partly-adequate	inadequate	partly-suitable
16	inadequate	adequate	adequate	suitable
17	partly-adequate	partly-adequate	>=partly-adequate	suitable
18	partly-adequate	>=partly-adequate	partly-adequate	suitable
19	>=partly-adequate	partly-adequate	partly-adequate	suitable
20	adequate	inadequate	adequate	suitable
21	adequate	adequate	inadequate	suitable
22	>=partly-adequate	adequate	adequate	very suitable
23	adequate	>=partly-adequate	adequate	very suitable
24	adequate	adequate	>=partly-adequate	very suitable

#	Vital scope of LE 71%	Additional scope of LE 29%	Scope of LE
1	inadequate	*	inadequate
2	partly-adequate	<=partly-adequate	partly-adequate
3	>=partly-adequate	inadequate	partly-adequate
4	>=partly-adequate	adequate	adequate
5	adequate	>=partly-adequate	adequate

Fig. 4. Utility functions for the aggregated attributes of the model for assessing life-events

The attributes that occur in the model for assessing life-events (Fig. 3) are aggregated according to the utility functions shown in Fig. 4. Utility functions are represented in tabular form. For each aggregate attribute, a corresponding table defines how the value of that attribute is determined from the values of lower-level attributes.

For example, the topmost table on the left of Fig. 4 defines the mapping of the attributes *Maturity*, *Use of LE* and *Clarity of LE* into the final assessment of *Life-event*. Each row of the table represents a rule that defines the value of *Life-event* for some combination of values of the former three attributes. Rule 1, for example, defines that *Life-event* is unacceptable, whenever *Maturity* is unacceptable, regardless on the assessment of the *Use* and *Clarity of LE* (notice that the asterisk represents any value of the corresponding attribute). Similarly, rule 2 specifies that *Life-event* is unacceptable, too, whenever *Maturity* is worse than or equal to acceptable, and *Use of LE* is unsuitable, regardless on *Clarity*. All the remaining rules can be interpreted in a similar way.

2.4 Model for Assessing Life-Event Portals

The assessments of life-events influence the final assessment of life-event portal through the characteristic that evaluates the way in which life-events are handled. The intervals to transform the average assessment of life-events into the assessment of life-event handling are as follows:

Average assessment for life-events	Life-event handling
between 1 and 1.4	1 – unacceptable
between 1.5 and 2.3	2 – acceptable
between 2.4 and 3.3	3 – good
between 3.4 and 4.2	4 - very good
between 4.3 and 5	5 – excellent

Other characteristics, included in the proposed model (Fig. 5), evaluate the scope of life-event portal (how well the portal is covered with life-event and topics), different instruments helping to identify an adequate life-event (access to life-events), the standardization of life-events design and structure and personalization.

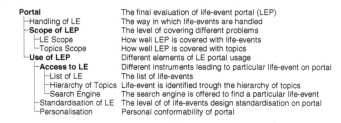

Fig. 5. The hierarchical tree of attributes of the model for assessing life-event portals

3   Analysis of the Life-Event Portals

3.1   Scope of the Analysis

This analysis, which was conducted in August 2002, was aimed at the assessment of a selected sample of sixteen life-event portals (Table 1).. The portals were selected for analysis according to the following criteria:

– The portal provides services based on life-events.
– The portal is considered a good practice with respect to the structure of the portal or to the level of on-line sophistication.
– The services, provided by portals, are comparable with services that are provided by the state government in Slovenia. In some countries, these services are provided by the cities (for example in Germany) or by the federal lands or provinces (for example in Germany and Australia).
– The portal should be available in one of the languages that are adequately mastered by the research team members (English, French, Spanish, Italian, German, Slovene).
– The research focused mostly to European countries, but included also some representative portals from the rest of the world.

The number and selection of life-events provided by the portals varies considerably. Thus, only a few common life-events were selected and analysed at each of the selected portals:
- moving a home,
- driving license (learning to drive and getting a driving license),
- passport (applying for or renewing a passport),
- starting a business.

In this analysis, about 300 services were evaluated within 65 life-events.

3.2 Results of the Analysis

The final assessments of analysed portals (Fig. 6) show that these portals are still at the early stages of development of life-event based electronic services, as half of the portals are assessed as unacceptable. The assessments for life-event handling mostly contribute to these poor results. The remaining characteristics included in the model for assessing life-event portals were generally assessed quite well. The scope of life-event portals mostly (at 10 portals) reached the highest possible value, whereas the elements of portals' usage (personalization of portal, standardization of life-events and instruments helping to identify an adequate life-event) were assessed at least as suitable at 11 of the observed portals.

Table 1. The list of analysed life-event portals

State/Land-Province/City	Internet Address
Europe	
France: Service Publique	http://www.service-public.fr
Italy: Italia.gov.it	http://www.italia.gov.it
Spain: Administración.es	http://www.administracion.es
Great Britain: UKonline	http://www.ukonline.gov.uk
Ireland: Information on the Irish State	http://www.irlgov.gov.ie
Austria: Internet service HELP	http://www.help.gv.at
German Federal Land Rheinland-Pfalz-Lotse: RLP-Lothse	http://rlp.bund.de/rlp-lotse.htm http://www.rlp-buergerservice.de/
The city of Bremen (Germany): Bremer-online-service	http://www.bremer-online-service.de/
Slovenia: e-Uprava	http://e-gov.gov.si/e-uprava/index.html
Rest of the world	
Australia-Commonwealth	http://www.fed.gov.au/KSP/
Australian Province Capital Territory	http://www.act.gov.au/
Australian Province Tasmania: ServiceTasmania	http://www.servicetasmania.tas.gov.au
Australian Province New South Wales	http://www.nsw.gov.au/
Canada: Government of Canada	http://canada.gc.ca/
Singapore: eCitizen	http://www.ecitizen.gov.sg
Hong Kong: Government Services	http://www.info.gov.hk/eindex.htm

In general, the Singapore eCitizen portal is evaluated as the best, as all characteristics (except the handling of life-events and personal conformability of the portal) have reached the highest possible assessment.

The assessments for life-event handling are very poor (Fig. 7). At almost a half of observed portals, this characteristic was evaluated as unacceptable, mostly because of the lowest possible assessment for the life-event on-line sophistication. On the other hand, at the Singapore eCitizen portal and the portal Bremer-online-service, the life-event handling is evaluated as good. However, one must take into account, that at Bremer-online-service only one life-event was analysed.

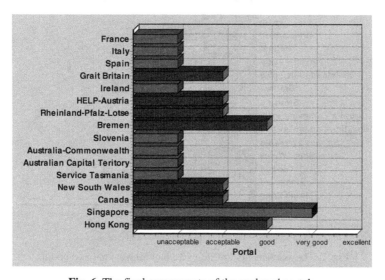

Fig. 6. The final assessments of the analysed portals

At the eCitizen portal, five life-events were analysed. Three of them ('getting married', 'starting a business' and 'issuing a passport') were assessed as very good, mostly because of the highly evaluated life-event maturity, which combines the level of on-line sophistication, the level of coordination and the scope of life-event. The other two life-events at this portal ('moving a house' and 'getting a driving license') were on the contrary assessed as unacceptable (the lowest possible value), mostly because of poor assessments for the on-line sophistication and the level of coordination.

4   Conclusions

The idea of life-event based electronic services seems to be widely recognized as an appropriate way of providing public services. However, the analysis of life-event portals revealed different approaches to developing electronic services, based on life-events. In some cases, the focus of the development is placed on a high on-line sophistication with a limited scope of life-events offered to the public (for example the Bremer-online-service), whereas some other portals provide a wide range of well-structured and defined life-events with good information and a possibility to download corresponding forms (Austrian HELP portal, British UKonline). We believe that both aspects are important. On the other hand, some other important aspects of design and development of life-events are still somehow neglected, such as for example a high level of coordination of services within life-events and the tools, helping to navigate through life-events, which is still inadequately designed.

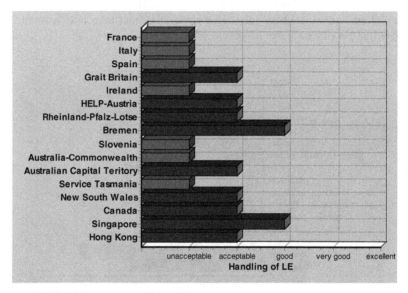

Fig. 7. The assessments for life-event handling at analysed portals

The proposed methodology provides a powerful tool for assessing the life-event portals and life-events themselves, and for comparing them. When implemented in the periodical analyses (for example once or twice a year), it may also show the trends in developing electronic services based on life-events. It offers a vehicle to understand the characteristics of life-event based services provided through government portals. On the other hand, it can serve as a guideline to outgrow the present state and to develop public services of higher quality.

References

1. Bohanec, M., Rajkovič, V.: DEX: An expert system shell for decision support. Sistemica 1(1), 1990, Pg. 145–157.
2. Bohanec, M., Rajkovič, V.: Multi-Attribute Decision Modeling: Industrial Applications of DEX. Informatica 23, 1999, Pg. 487–491.
3. Clemen, R.T.: Making Hard Decisions: An Introduction to Decision Analysis. Duxbury Press, 1996.
4. eCitizen. http://www.ecitizen.gov.sg, September 2002.
5. European Commission, DG Information Society. Web-based Survey on Electronic Public Services: Summary Report (Results of the first measurement: October 2001). http://europa.eu.int/information_society/eeurope/news_library/index_en.htm.

6. Gams, M., Bohanec, M.: Intelligent systems applications. Informatica 25(3), 2001, Pg. 387–392.
7. Jackson P. Introduction to Expert Systems (third edition). Addison Wesley Longman Ltd., 1999
8. Klein M., Methlie L.B. Expert Systems: A Decision Support Approach. Addison-Wesley Publishers Ltd., 1990
9. Urbančič, T., Križman V., Kononenko I.: Review of AI Applications, Jožef Stefan Institute, Ljubljana, Report DP-7806, 1998.
10. Vintar, M., Leben, A. The Concepts of an Active Life-event Public Portal. In: Traunmüller, R., Lenk, K. (Eds.), Electronic Government, Proceedings of the First International Conference, EGOV 2002, Aix-en-Provence, France, September 2002. Springer-Verlag. Pg. 383–390.

Knowledge Management Requirements and Models for Pan-European Public Administration Service Delivery

Konstantinos Tarabanis[1] and Vassilios Peristeras[2]

[1]University of Macedonia, Thessaloniki, Greece
kat@uom.gr
[2] United Nations Thessaloniki Centre, Thessaloniki, Greece
per@untcentre.org

Abstract. In this paper we study certain aspects of the important topic of pan-European public administration service delivery. Specifically we describe the requirements posed by pan-European public administration service delivery and in particular, we present the types of knowledge and meta-knowledge required for this purpose. We then present in detail conceptual models –object models and interaction models – that represent this domain. Implementation directions that employ Web services and Semantic Web services are finally sketched.

1 Introduction – Motivation

Within a country, citizens and enterprises need to interact with national public administrations. All EU member countries are currently initiating e-Government action plans in order to facilitate these interactions electronically. However in many cases within the European Union, there is a specific need for citizens and enterprises to interact electronically with a national public administration other than their own. In these cases many barriers currently exist, causing serious drawbacks both to the realization of the common internal market and to European citizen's mobility. There are services provided by public administration agencies that clearly should be open to cross-border users since access to them by people from different countries is common. The phrase 'pan-European public administration service delivery' refers to this type of services.

Towards this direction European initiatives exist for which the long-term vision is to "ensure that all citizens, enterprises and administrations will have access, where needed, to the pan-European e-services of any EU public administration in a seamless way, regardless of whether the service or any information or documentation associated with or needed as pre-requisite to the service, is under the responsibility of a local, regional or national public administration, or a European institution or agency" [1].

In this paper we study certain aspects of pan-European public administration service delivery. Specifically we briefly sketch the requirements posed by and in particular, the types of knowledge required by pan-European public administration service delivery. We then present in detail conceptual models –object and interaction models - for this domain.

M.A. Wimmer (Ed.): KMGov 2003, LNAI 2645, pp. 37–47, 2003.

2   Requirements for Pan-European Public Administration Service Provision

The basic requirements for pan-European public administration service delivery have been developed as part of earlier work [2] and are stated here in summary.

Multi-agent setting of public service provision.
Even in the case of providing public administration services within a single country, the workflow for realizing specific PA services very often cuts across the boundaries of a single agency. Thus, more PA agencies are required to participate in the "macro-process" execution than just the PA responsible for the overall service. These associated PA's provide constituent services contributing to the main service. Providing public administration services within the context of several countries requires multiple agent participation by its very definition. In addition, multi-PA agency participation and more so that from several countries, introduces more demanding coordination requirements of the macro-process execution on the part of the responsible PA. In order to address these macro-process coordination requirements, specific types of control knowledge and meta-knowledge are required [3] at both the country and European level respectively.

Transparent public service provision for the PA customer.
Transparent public services provision for the PA customer is posed as the requirement that both the inputs needed for the delivery of a service as well as the outcomes produced by the service are respectively given and received in a transparent as possible manner for the PA customer. That is, the PA customer will only need to provide the input that cannot be automatically accessed from its relevant source and also the consequences of the delivered service will be automatically propagated to its relevant destinations. While this requirement has been considered in a single country context, its importance in a multi-country context in compounded by the complexity of such service provision due to the differences amongst public administration systems demonstrated for example, by the significant potential for error in cross-border public administration service transactions and the high degree participation of human intermediaries (e.g. lawyers). In order to achieve this transparency requirement, forms of control knowledge and meta-knowledge need to be employed [3] with which the knowledge management strategies of "pull" of the input and "push" of the outcomes can be achieved.

3 Control Knowledge and Meta-knowledge for Pan-European Public Administration Service Provision

The control knowledge and meta-knowledge needed to address the requirements posed in the previous section can be considered in two parts, one that does not include the issue of country differences and the other that does.

In the case of service provision with the participation of multiple agencies assumed from one country, achieving intelligent coordination and input-output transparency of the macro-process requires types of control knowledge (see Fig. 1) such as the following:

- pre-conditions for provision of a service,
- consequences of a service together with the affected party, both within the agency but also in other agencies,
- controls that apply in any of the steps involved in the provision of the service together with the agency responsible for applying these controls,
- inputs of a service together with their source,
- outputs of a service together with their destination.
- Other example categories of control knowledge needed include:
- the Service Organization responsible for a particular Service
- the Evidence Type required for a particular Service
- the Outcome Type resulting from a particular Service
- the Service Organization responsible for a particular Evidence Type
  - this type of meta-knowledge facilitates the "pull" strategy
- the Service Organization interested in a particular Outcome Type
  - this type of meta-knowledge facilitates the "push" strategy

In the case of service provision with the participation of agencies from several countries (Fig. 1), additional knowledge is needed in order to *reason with* the distinct bodies of control knowledge that address the requirements for each country. The knowledge needed for this case corresponds to meta-knowledge, since it can reason about the control knowledge of each national public administration system. For example, meta-knowledge is needed:

1. to reason with term correspondence
   a) at a language level (i.e. corresponding terms in different languages) and
   b) at a conceptual level
      i. identical terms,
      ii. one term wider than the other together with the definition of the associated surplus,
      iii. one term narrower than the other together with the definition of the associated deficit,
      iv. one term overlaps another together with the definition of the non-overlapping regions
2. to reason with cases where the same service is provided differently in different countries, that is, cases where any of the above corresponding pieces of knowledge differ – e.g. different consequences for the same service, different preconditions for the same service etc.

In the following sections, broker actors are considered to embody the control knowledge and meta-knowledge described in this section for pan-European public administration service delivery

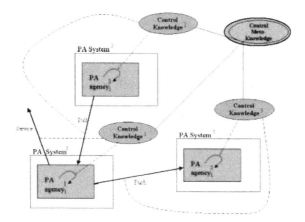

Fig. 1. Control knowledge and meta-knowledge for multi-country public administration service provision

4 Proposed Object Model for Pan-European Public Administration Service Provision

In this section we present the object model that has been developed in order to represent the control knowledge and meta-knowledge that was described in the previous section for pan-European public administration service delivery. Our model is based on the Government Common Information Model (GCIM) [4] that was developed as part of the e-government initiatives in the United Kingdom. The GCIM model is presented in Fig 2.

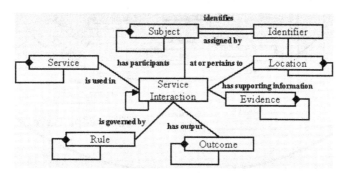

Fig. 2. The GCIM model

In the center of the GCIM model lies the "Service Interaction" object, which embodies the aspects of the particular service instantiation. Based on its purpose, the view of the GCIM model is focused on the transactional aspects of service provision by public administration.

For our purposes, we need to enhance this model in order to cover not only the transactional but also the planning aspects that are needed for pan-European public administration service delivery as presented in the requirements section. The distinction between knowledge and operational levels are a common model feature and references can be found in the object-oriented design and patterns literature [5]. As a result, we propose an enhanced object model in which an outer planning or knowledge layer has been added as shown in Fig. 3. Thus, the overall model is layered into two sections:

- the operational (transactional) layer and
- the knowledge (planning) layer.

According to the GCIM model, the operational level of the model consists of objects Subject, Identifier, Location, Evidence, Outcome, Rule, Service, Service Interaction and relationships amongst them modeling transactional aspects. At this stage of development, our knowledge layer consists of category objects such as Outcome Type and Evidence Type and their relationships amongst each other as well as with the operational entities of GCIM (see Figure 3).

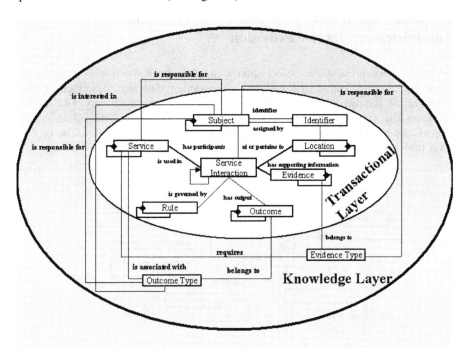

Fig. 3. The enhanced model covers the planning aspects for pan-European public administration service provision

In addition to the objects included in the GCIM model, we add the following:

Evidence Type characterizes each instance of evidence, thus maintaining metadata information for the instances of evidences that participate in a specific Service Interaction.

Outcome Type characterizes each outcome, thus maintaining metadata information for the instances of outcomes that result from a specific Service Interaction.

In addition to the relationships included in the GCIM model, we add the following:

Requires between Service and Evidence Type, as a service requires a specific set of evidences types in order to be provided according to the rules.

Is responsible for between Subject and Evidence Type. This relation demonstrates the fact that for each type of evidence needed for a service provision, there is a responsible organization that holds the relevant information. This organization has to be known and accessed by the service provider in order to "pull" the evidences needed for the specific service.

Belongs to between Evidence and Evidence Type. Each specific instance of evidence needed for a service provision belongs to a specific evidence type. The service repository will document information regarding the types and not the particular evidences belonging or linked to individuals.

Is associated with between Service and Outcome Type. Each service is associated with outcomes types as post conditions, consequences as well as outputs, of the service after it has been provided.

Is interested in between Subject and Outcome Type. This relation describes the interest of consequence receiver organizations for outcomes produced by the execution of the service.

Belongs to between Outcome and Outcome Type. The logic here is similar with the aforementioned relationship between Evidence and Evidence Type. Each service outcome either output or consequence belongs to an outcome type. A specific outcome type can be an outcome for one service and a consequence in another.

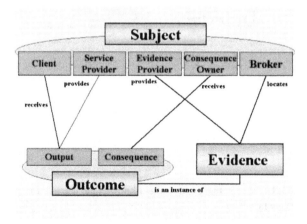

Fig. 4. Subject-Evidence-Outcome detailed model

In the enhanced model the GCIM object "Subject" models five different actors –roles, namely Client, Service Provider, Evidence Provider, Consequence Receiver, and Broker Actor. Additionally the Outcome object can be further specialized to Output and Consequence. Outputs are the final "products" produced by the Service Interaction and received by the Client who initiated the Service Interaction. Consequences are all the by-products of the Service Interaction (e.g. information that interests other Service Organization Subjects). As the relationships amongst these objects are of interest to the whole model, we present a more detailed schema in Fig. 4.

While the enhanced model presented to this point covers aspects of the control knowledge described in the previous section, the control meta-knowledge required at the European level has not yet been described. Thus, for effectively realizing this control meta-knowledge, the following relationships are added (see Figure 5):

Is responsible for amongst Client Subject, Evidence Type and Location

Is interested in amongst Client Subject, Outcome Type and Location

These two triadic relationships have been included, in order to realize the transparent "push" and "pull" strategies at a European level. The first relationship facilitates the "pull" function as it documents which evidence provider X is responsible for providing evidence type Y for a PA customer at a location Z. It is through this relationship that the service provider organization through its access to this control meta-knowledge will be able to locate the relevant organization for pulling the evidence types needed for the particular service execution.

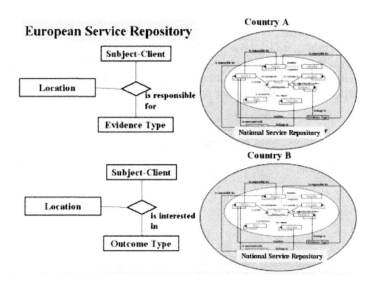

Fig. 5. The enhanced model covers the control meta-knowledge needed for pan-European public administration service provision

The second relationship facilitates the "push" function. It documents which consequence receiver organization X is interested in outcome type Y, for the citizen at a location Z. Through the instantiation of this relationship, the service provider organization would be able to locate the consequence receiver organizations, and could effectively exercise an automated "push" function.

5   Proposed Interaction Model for Pan-European Public Administration Service Provision

The Interaction Model that follows constitutes a generic representation of interactions that occur during the process of service provision at a pan-European level, amongst the various actors and the roles these actors carry out. A description of the model follows:

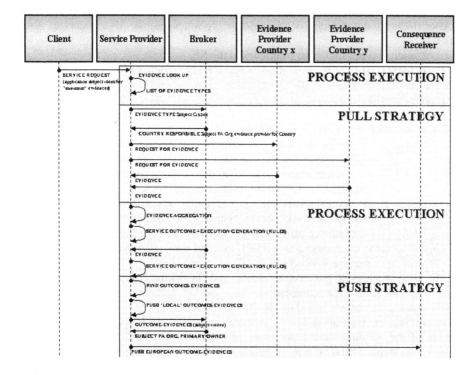

Fig. 6. The Interaction Model for pan-European public administration service delivery

Participating Roles
- ClientService ProviderBroker
- Evidence Provider Country x,y
- Consequence Receiver*Description of Steps*

1. A client requests a service from a service provider providing a minimum set of evidences, which can initiate service provision. This set consists of the following categories of evidences:
- Evidences needed for identification purposes
- Evidences needed during the service execution that can not be pulled automatically
- Evidences that will be needed later for guiding the "pull" process
- Evidences that will facilitate the "push" process after the service execution.

The less evidence the client provides to the service provider, the more transparent to the client the service becomes. In a "best case" scenario the client provides just a means of identification and an application for the service that is requested. This "minimum" set of evidences is service-specific.

2. The service provider (SP) with the evidence brought by the client decides whether the specific service can be initiated. If the answer is yes then the service provider looks up the list of evidence types that are related to the specific service.

3. After finding the complete list of evidence types needed, the SP categorizes it in two types:

3.1.   evidence types that exist internally in the SP,

3.2.   evidence types that exist in other service organizations located in the same or different country,

4. SP collects evidences

    3.3. internally

    3.4. from other organization in the same or different country

        3.4.1.   SP looks up with the help of the Broker, where the specific evidence type for the specific client can be found

        3.4.2.   the Broker returns information regarding the responsible country and organization for the evidence type needed.

        3.4.3.   SP contacts with the help of the Broker the proposed Evidence Provider and asks for the evidence type needed

        3.4.4.   the evidence provider organization sends the evidence needed.

    3.5. SP checks all evidences needed and informs client in case there are evidences that cannot be pulled

    3.6. SP aggregates all gathered evidence, and checks the completeness of the list of evidence for the requested service.

5. SP executes the service based on the Rules

6. During Service Execution more evidences may need to be pulled from one or more of the aforementioned two types of evidence "sources" (Step 3). If this is the case, steps 3 and 4 are executed iteratively, until the service execution finishes.

7. The service execution process finishes and an outcome is produced.

8. SP identifies output that has to be handed to the client and consequences that have to be forwarded to other organizations.

9. SP provides the client with the output

10. Consequences to be forwarded fall in two categories:
    –   For internal use
    –   To be forwarded to organization(s) in the same or different country

11. SP forwards consequences

11.1.   internally

11.2.   to other organization in the same or different country

11.2.1   SP looks up with the Broker where to forward consequences

11.2.2.   the Broker returns information on the responsible organization for each consequence type

11.2.3.   SP forwards consequences to the proposed Consequence Receiver organizations with the help of the Broker.

11.3.   SP informs Client for consequences that have been pushed and for those that could not be pushed.

6   Future Work – Implementation Directions

We plan to further elaborate on the models presented in this paper, testing their applicability and analyzing further the relationships and interactions amongst the various participating actors.

In order to realize the pan-European service delivery requirements (multi-country setting, transparent public service provision), we need to implement the control knowledge and meta-knowledge concepts presented in this paper. For this, Web services technology appears as fertile ground for such an endeavor. Due to the component-based and software-as-a-service perspective they introduce, they can handle complex information flows and successfully cope with multiplicity, diversity and incompatibility of infrastructure and systems. As an example utilizing a UDDI registry for cataloguing services based on their I/O characteristics, is a simple yet powerful technology for enabling the broker actor of our proposed architecture, to locate specific services.

However, and although the Web Services technologies support service discovery (UDDI) and configuration (WSDL), they cannot effectively address highly complex services with extended workflows. The majority of pan-European public administration services belong to this latter type of services. The technologies mentioned above are considered to lie at the syntactic layer. This layer provides means to define vocabulary, structure and constraints for expressing metadata about Web resources. However, formal semantics for the participating objects, processes and other primitives are not provided. Such semantics are required at the broker level especially for coordinating cross-country macroprocesses in the web.

In order to provide Semantic Web Services [6], current approaches employ a new type of mark-up that is backed-up with a vocabulary for representing and communicating knowledge about some topic and the set of relationships that hold among the terms in that vocabulary. The latter constitutes an ontology and its main function is to explicitly represent specifications of a business domain   (public administration in our case). The broker, as described above, should have access to a semantically enhanced infrastructure of this type.

A proposed formalism in this respect is the Ontology Interchange Language (OIL) and the DARPA Agent Markup Language (DAML). These two have been brought together to form DAML+OIL [7], a language now being proposed as a W3C standard for ontological and metadata representation.

While DAML+OIL can be used at the content level, for the explicit description of Web Services another DAML-based formalism has been recently proposed: DAML-S [8]. DAML-S provides the ontology structuring mechanisms within which Web sites declare and describe their services. In other words, DAML-S proposes an upper ontology for services. The model that is employed provides essential types of knowledge about a service automatic discovery, invocation, inter-operation, execution and monitoring. These tasks coincide to a large degree with the tasks required by the broker actor for public administration macroprocess execution, as described in this paper.

Acknowledgements. This work has been partially funded by the IST-2000-28759 project "InfoCitizen" and the IST-2001-35217 project "EU-Publi.com".

References

1. European Commission (IDA), Consultation: document for a future policy paper on Pan-European government e-services. 2002: Brussels.
2. The InfoCitizen Project, Deliverable 1.2.: Chapter 4.Integration to Pan-European Approach. 2002. p. p. 65–81.
3. Tarabanis, K. and V. Peristeras. Towards Interoperability amongst European Public Administrations. In 13th Database and Expert Systems Applications Conference (DEXA). 2–6 September, 2002. Aix-en-Province, France.
4. Office of e-Envoy UK, e-Services Development Framework Primer v1.0b, 2002, available at http://www.govtalk.gov.uk/documents/eSDFprimerV1b.pdf, as accessed in 13 Noe 2002
5. Fowler, M., Analysis Patterns. Object Technology Series. 1997: Addison-Wesley.
6. Fensel D., C. Bussler, and A. Maedche. Semantic Web Enabled Web Services. In ISWC 2002. Vol. pp.1 –2:LNCS 2342, Springer-Verlag, Berlin Heidelberg. 2002
7. W3C, DAML+OIL Reference Description,, 2001, available at http://www.w3.org/TR/daml+oil-reference, as accessed in 10 Nov. 2001
8. DARPA, DARPA Agent Markup Language Web Services (DAML-S) Version 0.7 Specification, 2002, available at http://www.daml.org/services/daml-s/0.7/, as accessed in 10 Nov. 2002

Requirements Engineering for Knowledge Management in eGovernment

Paolo Bresciani[1], Paolo Donzelli[2], and Angela Forte[2]

[1]ITC-irst, Istituto per la Ricerca Scientifica e Tecnologica,
Via Sommarive 14, 38050 Trento-Povo (Italy)
`brescian@itc.it`

[2]Presidenza del Consiglio dei Ministri, Dipartimento per l'innovazione e le tecnologie
Via Barberini 38, 00187 Roma
`{p.donzelli, an.forte}@governo.it`

Abstract. EGovernment aims at exploiting *Information and Communication Technologies* (ICT) to provide better quality services to citizens and businesses, mainly through electronic delivery channels. Different strategies have been suggested to implement eGovernment; all recognize as fundamental, to deal with, and exploit, continuous ICT evolution, to transform the public administration into a learning organization, characterized by a high sharing, reuse, and strategic application of the acquired knowledge and lessons learned. An interesting role can be played by techniques, methods and approaches recently suggested by requirements engineering (RE), being most of the reusable knowledge located at requirements level: from ICT components requirements, to business and organizational models. The paper presents an advanced agent- and goal-based RE framework, designed to support capturing and formalizing the knowledge embedded in the organization. An on-going project concerned with the introduction into a complex administrative organization of a Electronic Record Management System is described.

1 Introduction

EGovernment [1,2] aims at exploiting *Information and Communication Technologies* (ICT) to provide better quality services to the government customers (citizens and businesses), mainly through electronic delivery channels (internet, digital TV, easy web, mobile phone, etc.).

Although there are differences among strategies adopted by different governments, it is possible to identify a common roadmap towards government implementation, characterized by four main milestones: (1) Establish a government–wide communication infrastructure, to enable cooperation among the different public sector components, both at central and local level, and as a necessary step to (2) create a virtual corporate IT infrastructure, upon which (3) activate channels for service delivery. Fundamental for the success of the first three steps, and recognized as fundamental to efficiently manage eGovernment evolution (e.g. to deal with and exploit continuous ICT evolution), it is to (4) transform the public administration into

M.A. Wimmer (Ed.): KMGov 2003, LNAI 2645, pp. 48–59, 2003.

a learning organization, characterized by a high sharing, reuse, and strategic application of the acquired knowledge and lessons learned.

A learning organization [3] is an organization skilled at "modifying its behavior to reflect new knowledge and insights". The basic idea behind it consists in creating a *knowledge chain* (for knowledge collection, production, customization and delivery), suitable to support and improve the whole organization functioning. The critical point for applying such a concept to eGovernment is to find the materials suitable to feed the knowledge chain: a) to identify the fragments of knowledge that could be efficiently reused but, above all, accepted; b) to represent and formalize such fragments so to be tractable (stored, analyzed, understood, customized, and eventually transferred).

A modern public administration can be considered as an ecosystem where different entities, from central government units to local authorities, and public sector agencies, interact, cooperate and sometimes clash to achieve both general and private goals. While, as a whole, such entities act as the owners of the eGovernment process, each entity is granted a considerable level of political and economical independence, being entitled, for example, to make its own choices in technological, organizational and strategic terms. Transform such a structure into a learning organization is a difficult task: the kind of knowledge suitable to flow among the different entities has to be carefully identified and planned in order to be not only practically and economically feasible, but also acceptable by the various actors, so becoming a support to the evolution of the whole system.

In such a context, an interesting role can be played by techniques, methods and approaches recently suggested by *Requirements Engineering* (RE) [4,5,6,7].

RE is concerned with managing desired properties and constraints of software-intensive systems and with goals to be achieved in the environment. Traditionally, the focus has been placed upon the final system and its, more or less, direct users. Recently, the scope of the attention has been enlarged until encompassing the application context. The software system and its application context form in fact a larger social-technical system that has to be treated and analyzed as a whole: the overall needs of such social-technical system are the ones that RE has to fulfill. Consequently, appropriate organization modeling techniques are typically advocated to capture high-level organizational needs and to transform them into system requirements, while redesigning the organizational structure that better exploit the new system. While doing so, RE can also provide the means to capture, formalize and package the resulting knowledge, turning it into materials suitable to feed the knowledge chain, at the basis of the public administration learning organization. Most of the reusable knowledge, in fact, can only be located at requirements level, where the term "requirements" does not refer only to requirements for ICT components (e.g. from the classical system requirements, to user manuals, to procurements guidelines etc.), but also to organization structure and business models (to better employ the new technology), to technology transfer approaches, to human resources management (e.g. training and updating programmes), to final users needs.

The remainder of this paper is organized as follows. Section 2 introduces the concept of public administration as an ecosystem and discuss specific needs knowledge management and transfer may have for such systems. Section 3 discusses the role that RE, and specifically the recently proposed RE techniques based on concepts such as those of Agent, Goals and Dependency [4,5,6,7], may have in this context. Section 4 introduces a specific goal and agent-based requirements engineering framework (REF), by briefly describing its main characteristics. Section 5 elaborates some of the aspects introduced in Section 3, by showing some extracts from an on-going project aiming at introducing an Electronic Record Management System within the main administrative and decision-making processes of a main government unit: a first step towards a paperless knowledge workplace. Finally, Section 6 concludes by discussing some of the observed benefits, mainly in terms of knowledge management.

2 The Public Administration as an Ecosystem

Recently, different questions have been raised regarding the strict correlation between politics, public administration and ICT [1], among these, (1) the possibility of modernizing the public administration through the ICT; (2) the identification of strategies suitable to control the ICT application; (3) the impact of ICT on the political institutions; (4) the relationships between the innovation potential offered by the ICT and the changes that are transforming the public sector not directly related to the ICT, as, for example, the transfer of responsibilities towards local authorities. In an attempt to establish a government characterized by a strong interaction between political and social components, such a devolution process aims at establishing an auto-regulative and co-evolutive relationship among all the involved entities.

Borrowing from biology, we can assimilate the public administration, the citizens, the businesses, and, in general, all the social components to an ecosystem: an entity that encompasses all the subjects acting in the same area and interacting with the external environment, in such a way that the flow of energy (i.e., knowledge in our context) leads to a well-defined structure. The term ecosystem allows to stress the strong interdependency among components, but also to highlight the existence of an "universal law" that tends to optimize entities' freedom and wealth distribution. In particular, for the public domain, the presence of a decisional center enables to identify the "right", also if for a limited extension of time, for the whole society [8].

These are complex organizational issues, and the current shape of the public sector structure plays a controversial role, not facilitating such a transfer of powers. Various socio-political and administrative thesis recognize the ICT as an important accelerating factor in the process of government decentralization and see in the eGovernment a powerful implementation tool to support this new concept of public administration [1,2]. Although, at an initial stage, the application of ICT does not change the traditional government ways of operating, the eGovernment sets the basis for more advanced integration and exchange models: from a more active involvement of the citizen, not only user of services but generator of proposals, to the electronic democracy, where the citizen becomes a critical element of the political decision making process. The current debate about the public sectors options and the available technologies is the symptom of an innovation process that is clearly generating uncomfortable feelings, by which, however, the research towards models more suitable to satisfy the new socio-organizational needs through the eGovernment could be activated. As will be discussed in the next Section, knowledge representation and reasoning support tools recently suggested within the context of RE could be beneficial in dealing with such complex issues.

3 The Role of RE to Support eGovernment

RE deals with the definition, formalization, and analysis of the requirements that a potential system must have. Recent approaches [4,5,6,7] also suggest that RE must face, as well, the "problem of introducing the system"—an already existing or yet to be built system—into the organization. New developments in ICT have made new systems highly pervasive and strictly intertwined with their application context, so that, introducing a new system may have different and strong impacts (positive, but also negative—thus, to be analyzed as potential sources of problems) on the organization itself; these impacts may have a level of importance similar to that of the introduction of new human actors or positions and related responsibilities. Thus, defining and analyzing the requirements of a new system cannot anymore be considered as a stand-alone activity, rather has to be strongly interrelated with the deep comprehension of the target organization and of its evolutionary process, posing on the requirements engineers a completely new set of issues.

The impact of the new system on the organization is much more relevant when the system is tighter incorporated in the workflow of data and knowledge interchange that characterize the complex lattice of relationships inside the organization, and has to be dealt with by means of an approach in which the system and the other (social) components (i.e., individuals and teams) of the organizations can be tackled in the same way. EGovernment, in particular, specifically requires the adoption of such a perspective. Public administrations, and their organizational environment, are characterized by the presence of very diverse kinds of actors (e.g., citizens and businesses, employees and administrators, politicians and decision-makers —both at central and local level), each of them with its own objectives and goals. Thus, in general, eGovernment applications have to operate in a social environment characterized by a rich tissue of actors with strong inter-dependent intents. Due to this complex network of interrelated objectives, synergies and conflicts may be present. Being able to clearly identify the set of involved actors, their objectives (i.e., goals), and the way they depends on each other in order to achieve such goals, most likely by exploiting possible synergies or trying to avoid potential conflicts, is of utmost importance to obtain a clear and complete comprehension of the organizational setting into which the system has to be introduced.

This level of knowledge, situated between the high-level needs and goals an organization wants to achieve and the technological solutions, not only results fundamental in identifying the right system, but represents also the kind of information more suitable to be spread within the public administration, likely to be accepted and eventually reused by the different components of such an ecosystem. Being able to cope with such a level of knowledge, i.e. to capture, formalize and make it easily available, is therefore crucial to support and accelerate the eGovernment process.

Among different RE methodologies, only few center their attention on notions like those of Agent (or Actor), Goal, and Intentional Dependency [4,5,6,7] that can support the analysts in dealing with, and reasoning about, the kind of knowledge described above [9,10,11], making it available to foster the eGovernment process. In such a perspective, we present our RE methodology, called REF [7,9,12,13], that, by exploiting the characteristics just mentioned, we believe is particularly suited to be applied to eGovernment applications in general, while creating reusable fragments of knowledge.

4 REF

REF [7,9,12] is designed to deal with, and reason about, socio-technical systems. The basic idea is that REF has to provide the analyst with a powerful tool to capture high-level organizational needs and to transform them into system requirements, while redesigning the organizational structure that better exploit the new system. Moreover, while doing so, REF can also provide the means to capture, formalize and package the resulting knowledge, turning it into materials suitable to feed the knowledge chain that could be at the basis of the public administration learning organization.

The framework tackles the modeling effort by breaking the activity down into more intellectually manageable components, and by adopting a combination of different approaches, on the basis of a common conceptual notation.

Agents (elsewhere the term Actor is used) are used to model the organization [4,6,7,14]. The organizational context is modeled as a network of interacting agents (any kind of active entity, e.g. teams, humans and machines, one of which is the target system), collaborating or conflicting in order to achieve both individual and organizational goals. Goals [4,6,7,15] are used to model agents' relationships, and, eventually, to link organizational needs to system requirements. According to the nature of a goal, a distinction is made between hard goals and soft goals. A goal is classified as hard when its achievement criterion is sharply defined. For example the goal *document be available* is a hard goal, being easy to check whether or not it has been achieved (i.e., is the document available, or not?). For a soft goal, instead, it is up to the goal originator, or to an agreement between the involved agents, to decide when the goal is considered to have been achieved. For example, the goal *document easily and promptly available* is a soft goal, given that as soon as we introduce concepts such as "easy" and "prompt", different persons usually have different opinions. Another characteristics of soft goals is that they can often be seen as a kind of modifiers or quality attributes associated to a hard goal; thus, in the previous example, the soft notion of easily and promptly modifies the precise objectives of having the document available. Distinguishing goal modeling from organizational modeling, and then, further distinguishing between hard goal modeling and soft goal modeling, is a key aspect of REF, and helps to reduce the complexity of the modeling effort. The proposed framework, therefore, supports three inter-related modeling efforts: the organizational modeling, the hard goal modeling and the soft goal modeling.

During Organization Modeling, the organizational context is analyzed and the agents and their hard and soft goals identified. Any agent may generate its own goals, may operate to achieve goals on the behalf of some other agents, may decide to collaborate with or delegate to other agents for a specific goal, and might clash on some other ones. The resulting goals will then be refined, through interaction with the involved stakeholders, by hard and soft goal modeling. The Hard Goal Modeling seeks to determine how the agent can achieve a hard goal placed upon it, by decomposing them into more elementary subordinate hard goals and tasks (where a task is a well-specified prescriptive activity). The Soft Goal Modeling aims at producing the operational definitions of the soft goals that emerged during the organizational modeling, sufficient to capture and make explicit the semantics that are usually assigned implicitly by the involved agents [16,17,18] and to highlight the system quality issues from the start. A soft goal is refined in terms of subordinate soft goals, hard goals, tasks and constraints. Soft goals refinement has to be reiterated until only hard goals, tasks and constraints are obtained (that is, until all the "soft" aspects are dealt with). Constraints are associated with hard goals and tasks to specify the corresponding quality attributes. So, for example, the soft goal to make a document easily and promptly available, beside spawning the hard goal to make a document available, will lead also to a set of constraints (e.g., types of access channels, number of hours after which a document is available, etc.) specifying the concepts of easy and prompt. In other words, for each soft goal, the resulting set of constraints represents the final and operationalised views of the involved quality attributes, i.e. the quality measurement models that formalize the attributes for the specific context [16,17].

During Soft Goal Modeling the analysts and, above all, the stakeholders tend to (and somehow are forced to) clarify very early in the project concepts that are usually left blurred until implementation imposes to make some choice. Thus, soft goals become a knowledge representation vehicle that: 1) encourages the interaction between the analysts and the stakeholders, and among the stakeholders themselves; 2) leads towards a common terminology; 3) supports reasoning about trade-offs; 4) allows freezing temporary solutions, and formalizing final decisions. Soft goal models, in addition, allow the analysts and the stakeholders to early detect clashing requirements, which usually are hidden behind generic and left-implicit assumptions, providing, at the same time, an operational and cooperative way to resolve them, by reconciling the different stakeholders' points of view.

In a nutshell, we can say that REF provides a significant series of tools to identify, define, verify and transfer relevant pieces of context knowledge, taking into account the needs and points of views of the various involved actors, both as knowledge providers and knowledge users.

5 The Case Study

In order to illustrate REF potentials, we adopt as a case study some extracts from an on-going project aiming at introducing an Electronic Record Management System (ERMS) within the Italian Cabinet Office. The impact of such a system, on the common practices of the communities and the sub-communities of knowledge workers who will adopt it, is quite relevant. Indeed, ERMS is at the moment used by more than 300 employees and handles a flow of about 200.000 document/year, but it is expected to reach about 2000 users and 2 million documents/year.

A ERMS is a complex Information and Communication Technology (ICT) system which allows efficient storage and retrieval of document-based unstructured information, by combining classical filing strategies (e.g. classification of documents on a multi-level directory, cross-reference between documents, etc.) with modern information retrieval techniques. Moreover, it usually provides mechanisms for facilitating routing and notification of information/document among the users, and supporting interoperability with similar (typically remote) systems, through e-mail and XML [19]. An ERMS represents the basic element for a knowledge workplace, i.e. a working environment where a knowledge worker can easily access and gather information, produce knowledge and deliver results through a multitude of channels (from personal computers, to laptops, PDAs, mobile phones, etc.). It is, in fact, a necessary step for introducing more sophisticated document management tools, such as workflow technology and digital signature, both fundamental mechanisms for a paperless and ubiquitous working environment. Several factors (international benchmarking studies, citizens demand, shrink budgets, etc.) called for the decision of leveraging new technologies to transform the organization's bureaucratic structure into a more creative, and knowledgeable environment. The initial organization model expressing such a situation is shown in Figure 1. Circles represent agents, and dotted lines are used to bound the internal structure of complex agents; that is, agents containing other agents. In Figure 1, the complex agent *Organization Unit* corresponds to the organizational fragment into which it is planned to introduce the new ERMS, whereas the *Head of Unit* is the agent, acting within the *Organization Unit*, responsible for achieving the required organizational improvement (modeled by the soft goals *exploit ICT to increase performance while avoiding risks*, and *cost/effective and quick solution*).

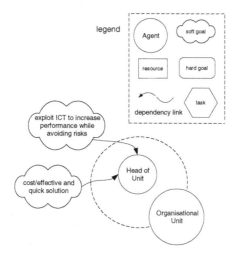

Fig. 1. Introducing the ERMS: the initial mod

Goals, tasks and agents (see also next Figures) are connected by dependency-links, represented by arrowhead lines. An agent is linked to a goal when it needs or wants that goal to be achieved; a goal is linked to an agent when it depends on that agent to be achieved. Similarly, an agent is linked to a task when it wants the task to be performed; a task is linked to an agent when the agent is committed at performing the task. Again, an agent is linked to a resource when it needs that resource; a resource is linked to an agent when the agent has to provide it. By combining dependency-links, we can establish dependencies among (i.e. two or more) agents.

As mentioned, the soft goals modeling process allow the analysts and the stakeholders to operationalise all the soft aspects implicitly included in the meaning of the soft goal. Thus, for example, Figure 2 describes how the soft goal *exploit ICT to increase performance while avoiding risks* is iteratively top-down decomposed to finally produce a set of tasks, hard goals, and constraints that precisely defines the meaning of the soft goal, i.e. the way to achieve it.

Figure 2, in other terms, represents the strategy that the *Head of Unit* (as result of a personal choice or of a negotiation with the upper organizational level) will apply to achieve the assigned goal. Again, the arrowhead lines indicate dependency links. A soft goal depends on a sub-ordinate soft goal, hard goal, task or constraint, when it requires that goal, task or constraint to be achieved, performed, or implemented in order to be achieved itself. These dependency links may be seen as a kind of top-down decomposition of the soft goal. Soft goals decompositions may be conjunctive (all the sub-components must be satisfied, to satisfy the original soft goal), indicated by the label "A" on the dependency link, or disjunctive (it is sufficient that only one of the components is satisfied), indicated by the label "O" on the dependency link (see Figure 4). According to Figure 2, the *Head of Unit* has to increase personal performance, to increase productivity of the whole unit, and also to avoid risks due to new technology.

In Figure 2, the items in bold outline are those that the *Head of Unit* will pass out, having decided to depend on other agents for their achievement. For such a reason, they are not further analyzed, instead they will be refined as further agreement between the *Head of Unit* and the agent that will be appointed of their achievements. The results of this analysis allow us to enrich the initial organization model in Figure 1, leading to the model in Figure 3, where some details have been omitted for the sake of clarity. In Figure 3 some new agents have been introduced: the *Archivist* and the *Employee*, which have to be more productive, the *Information Technology*, which has to guarantee security and the *ERMS*, upon which the identified goals, tasks and constraints will be placed. From Figure 3, we can also see that the *Head of Unit* has decided to delegate the soft goal *cost/effective and quick solution* to the *Information Technology* agent, which, on its turn, will have to achieve other goals coming from the external environment, such as, for example, *apply public administration standards*. At this point, the analysis can be carried on by focusing, for example, on how the *Employee* will try to achieve the soft goal *be more productive*. On the other side, to be more productive, the *Employee* will define its own strategy, eventually reaching an agreement with the *Head of Unit*. Such a strategy is shown by the soft goal model in Figure 4, where we can see how in order to be more productive the *Employee* will ask that the system will be *easy to learn* and will *make collaboration easier* with the other employees, which are dealing with the same document.

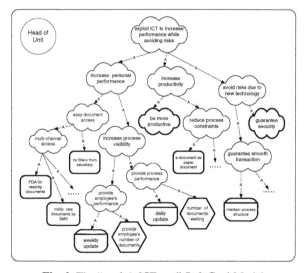

Fig. 2. The "*exploit ICT ....*" Soft Goal Model

Fig. 3. The evolving organization model

For sake of brevity, only a partial refinement of these soft goals is shown. The soft goal *easy to learn* will spawn, among other items here omitted, the constraint *adopt known technologies* (i.e. technologies which the employee is already used to), whereas the soft goal *make collaboration easier* will lead, through further refinement, to a series of hard goals implying specific capabilities (e.g. either a teleconference or an IP-based collaboration tool) and access channels (e.g. mobile phone, laptop, etc.).

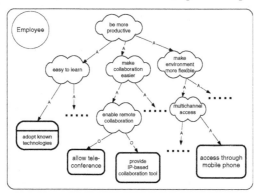

Fig. 4. The *"be more productive"* Soft Goal Model

6 Discussion and Conclusions

The described application example, as other similar ones [9], demonstrates the feasibility of the suggested approach, and the benefits it offers during the early phases of requirements engineering process, when the analysts and the stakeholders have to cooperate to understand and reason about the organizational context within which the new system has to function, in order to identify and formalize not only the system requirements, but also the organizational setting that better exploits the new system's capabilities.

A large amount of information is discovered in these early phases and have to be properly organized in order to be fully beneficial to development activities. In such a perspective, each type of model produced within the framework (soft goal, hard goal and organizational model) plays a particular role as a knowledge handling tool, by providing a specific knowledge representation vehicle that the analyst can use to interact with the stakeholders. For example, hard goal models allow the stakeholders to make explicit the tasks they will have to perform and the resources they will need. In addition to this, soft goal models bring quality issues into the picture and support the stakeholders while reasoning about their own concepts of quality, highlight possible conflicts, and support negotiation towards a feasible solution, in terms of tasks and constraints. So, while soft goal and hard goal models as a whole lead to system requirements, soft goal models, as by product, allow the analysts to freeze the knowledge acquired and produce models of the quality attributes of interest (for example, the model of employee's performance). The organization model, finally, represents the organization requirements, providing the management with a clear view of how the business process will be changed, or affected, by the introduction of the new system, and allowing the stakeholders to understand and validate their role within the organization, by making explicit the interactions with the system or with other agents in which they will be involved.

Once the project is over and the system deployed, the knowledge acquired during the requirement engineering process does not extinguish its role. On the contrary, made easily accessible and reusable through the different models into which has been captured, such a knowledge offers potential benefits also in the post-deployment phases, supporting system maintenance and evolution and use.

The clear links established (through the different models) between organizational goals and system requirements, in fact, allow the analysts and ICT managers to quickly identify the effects that changes in the organizational goals or new technology trends may have upon the system requirements. The possibilities offered to our context by a new access technology, for example, could be easily evaluated by observing the corresponding goal models (i.e. Figures 4 and 5): the new technology will be judged valuable for the system (and the organization) when capable to overcome some of the limits found during the previous analysis, or, in other terms, to enable the stakeholder to better achieve his goals. At the same way, a change in an organizational goal may easily be translated into requirements changes.

The framework models improve and support also knowledge transfer and sharing across different projects. In particular, fragments of knowledge, pieces or information, or system components may be reused in different application contexts. For example, the outcome of the framework, i.e. the requirements expressed as refinements of high-level goals, can be easily generalized and exported to different government units, contributing to improve the sharing and reuse of the knowledge captured, produced, and formalized during the very early stages of an ICT system development. In other terms, they represent the fragments of knowledge that may used to create the knowledge chain necessary to transform the public administration into a learning organization.

The last advantage we foresee that could be exploited by adopting REF is during the very use of a knowledge management (KM) system in the organization. Of course, the KM system so developed is in principle compliant to the knowledge workers needs; nevertheless, still it may be not easy for the users to totally understand the structure of the system, and the role it plays, as an agent—among others in the organization—with the capability of collecting and being the "communication channel" for the knowledge flow. As well, it may not be easy to appraise the value of the retrieved knowledge, if no context on the sources is provided. It is clear that both the roles of the KM system—as a repository and as a communication channel—and the value of the retrieved knowledge tightly depend on the social network, which is the source of the knowledge and in which the system is embedded. Having a clearly understandable representation of such social network, of its dependencies, of the motivations that stimulate the knowledge providers, and of their relationships with the system and among them, may represent a useful support to understand the real meaning and the value of the provided pieces of knowledge (and, thus, also to locate the most relevant ones). All these is already available in the REF diagrams developed during the RE process. Providing them, in appropriate formats, to the final system users, may represent an opportunity to improve the socio-technical system—as a whole—understandability, as well as its usability, providing, at the same time, the occasion for an evolution of the organization performances.

References

1. Frissen P.H.A. "Politics, Governance and Technology", Edward Elgar, Northampton, MA, USA, 1999.
2. Margetts H. "Information Technology in Government", Routledge, London, UK, 1999
3. Garvin, D. A., "Building a learning organization". Harvard Business Review 71(4): 78–91, 1993.
4. Yu, E. "Why Agent-Oriented Requirements Engineering" Proceedings of 3rd Workshop on Requirements Engineering For Software Quality, Barcelona, Catalonia, June 1997.
5. Yu E., Mylopoulos, J. "Using Goals, Rules, and Methods to Support Reasoning in Business Process Reengineering". International Journal of Intelligent Systems in Accounting, Finance and Management. (5) (1),1996.
6. Bresciani, P., Perini, A., Giorgini, P., Giunchiglia, F., Mylopoulos, J. "A knowledge level software engineering methodology for agent oriented programming". Proceedings of the 5th International Conference on Autonomous Agents, Montreal, Canada, May 2001.
7. Donzelli, P., Moulding M.R. "Developments in Application Domain Modelling for the Verification and Validation of Synthetic Environments: A Formal Requirements Engineering Framework", Proceedings of the Spring 99 Simulation Interoperability Workshop, Orlando, FL, March 1999.
8. Sen A, "Development as Freedom", Mondadori Ed., Milano, Italy, 1999.
9. Donzelli P., Setola R., "Handling the knowledge acquired during the requirements engineering process", Proceedings of the Fourteenth International Conference on Knowledge Engineering and Software Engineering (SEKE), 2002.

10. Mylopolous, J., Castro, J. "Tropos:A Framework for Requirements-Driven Software Development", Information System Engineering: State of the Art and Research themes, Brinkkemper, J., Solvberg, A. (eds), Lecture Notes in Computer Science, Springer Verlag, 2000.
11. Giorgini, P., Perini, A., Mylopoulos, J., Giunchiglia, F., Bresciani, P. "Agent-oriented software development: A case study". Proceedings of the Thirteenth International Conference on Software Engineering and Knowledge Engineering (SEKE), 2001.
12. Donzelli, P., Moulding M.R. "Application Domain Modelling for the Verification and Validation of Synthetic Environments: from Requirements Engineering to Conceptual Modelling", Proceedings of the Spring 2000 Simulation Interoperability Workshop, Orlando, FL, March 2000.
13. Donzelli, P., Bresciani, P., "Goal Oriented requirements Engineering: a case Study in eGovernment", proceedings of the 15th Conference on Advanced Information Systems Engineering (CAISE'03), Klagenfurt, Austria, 16–20 June, 2003 (to appear)
14. D'Inverno M., Luck, M. "Development and Application of an Agent Based Framework" Proceedings of the First IEEE International Conference on Formal Engineering Methods, Hiroshima, Japan, 1997.
15. Dardenne, A., Van Lamsweerde, A., Fickas, S. "Goal-Directed Requirements Acquisition" Science of Computer Programming, Vol. 20, North Holland, 1993.
16. Basili, V. R., Caldiera, G., and Rombach, H. D., "The Goal Question Metric Approach", Encyclopedia of Software Engineering, Wiley&Sons Inc., 1994.
17. Cantone, G., Donzelli P. "Goal-oriented Software Measurement Models", European Software Control and Metrics Conference, Herstmonceux Castle, East Sussex, UK, April 1999.
18. Chung, L., Nixon, B., Yu, E., Mylopoulos, J. Non-Functional Requirements in Software Engineering, Kluwer Academic Publishers 2000.
19. http://www.w3.org/XML/

Abort or Retry – A Role for Legal Knowledge Based Systems in Electronic Service Delivery?

Ronald Leenes

School of Business, Public Adminstration and Technology,
University of Twente, The Netherlands
`r.e.leenes@bsk.utwente.nl`

Abstract. Electronic service delivery is closely tied to legal decision making. Legal decision making is by nature complicated. It involves the (strict) application of rules, but it also inevitably leaves room for discretion. If the ambition of electronic service delivery is taken seriously, this means that (some) legal decisions have to be taken by computers. Legal knowledge based systems (LKBSs) capable of performing this task have been around since the early nineteen nineties. These systems, although successful, never really broke through and are somewhat forgotten. With the advent of e-Government and its focus on electronic service delivery, legal decision making systems are desperately needed. This paper argues that legal knowledge based system technology is neglected undeserved and that it offers opportunities for serious electronic service delivery.

1 Introduction

One of the central elements of electronic government is electronic service delivery. Governments aim to make their services more accessible to the public by removing time and space limitations, and by tailoring services to the needs of the public. ICT plays an important role in this respect because it enables services to be offered 24x7, independent of the location of the user. Furthermore, IT systems could cater for the needs of citizens and businesses by offering intelligent access to information and by helping them to apply for particular services. They could also play a role further on in the process by making decisions and by actually delivering the decisions electronically.

This all sounds familiar. It is the mantra that has been recited ever since the first steps towards electronic government were set in the middle of the nineties. Since then, progress with actual electronic service delivery has been relatively slow. Most governments are online nowadays and many offer fairly adequate information services. Some provide the electronic intake of services, although this often only means that citizens can fill in 'dumb' online forms. That is, static forms without real time checks on the input. True transaction services, where the user is guided through the application process, the decision is taken without human intervention and where the result is presented either by electronic means or by ordinary mail, is few and far between. This begs the question: why?

M.A. Wimmer (Ed.): KMGov 2003, LNAI 2645, pp. 60–69, 2003.

This simple question has, of course, many dimensions since there are many dimensions to electronic government and electronic service delivery. We also have partial answers. To name but a few: the development of electronic services is an organisational problem more than a technical one (Bellamy and Taylor, 1998), there is hardly any political pressure to implement service delivery reforms (Hoogwout, 2001) and development is very fragmented in the sense that the wheel is reinvented in many places (Leenes and Svensson, 2002).

But apart from these context factors, also the nature of electronic service delivery in the public sector itself is non-trivial. By service delivery in the public sector we mean: The performance by government of its basic legal functions (providing documents, orders and permits), of its welfare functions (providing benefits, subsidies and services) and the provision of information about these functions (Raad voor het Openbaar Bestuur, 1998). These functions are legal in nature because they relate to decisions taken by public bodies on rights or obligations of citizens and businesses. In making these decisions, government is ultimately bound by law. Therefore, (most) service delivery involves legal decision making. Legal decision making is considered to be difficult because it involves both flexibility and rigidity. Flexibility is required because rules and facts have to be interpreted and interests have to be balanced. Rigidity is required because of standards such as the principles of legal certainty and the legality principle (the Rule of Law).

The development of electronic services implies the development of computer applications capable of making legal decisions. This brings about questions about the possibilities of automated legal decision making and the role these systems can play in electronic service delivery. These topics are addressed in this paper.

The outline of the paper is as follows. In the next section I discuss the nature of legal decision making in some detail. Section three will discuss a technology aimed at legal decision making that may be suitable for electronic service delivery: rule-based legal knowledge based system technology. In section four the issues raised in the discussion on legal decision making will be discussed in relation to two relevant domains for electronic service delivery. Section 6 discusses the role legal knowledge based system can play in electronic service delivery and section 7 draws some conclusions.

2   Legal Decision Making in Public Administration

When a citizen applies for a public service such as a benefit, a permit, or a grant, the administration has to decide on this request on the basis of legal rules and the facts of the case. Usually these decisions are taken by so-called *street level bureaucrats* (Lipsky, 1980) who work in what is coined *human service organisation* by Hasenfeld (1983). The combination of legal decision making by street level bureaucrats in human service organisations presents a particular kind of decision making procedure. To understand the possible role for computer applications in electronic service delivery, we have to look at this particular setting in more detail. I will briefly address the organisational setting, legal decision making and the legal context.

Hasenfeld describes human service organisations as organisations that deal with people. These organisations have a number of features in common. The fact that they deal with people inevitably implies a moral dimension in decision making. They usually operate in a turbulent environment where the organisational goals are vague, ambigious and problematic. Effectiveness by objective measures is hard to establish and the measures taken by these organisations are often not undisputed. The picture sketched here applies to many organisations in the welfare sector. In other sectors, such as the building and housing sector, or taxation, these features are less prominent. But even here, some of the characteristics of the human service organisations are present. Most agencies involved in public service delivery are *selection bureaucracies* (Gastelaars, 1997). This type of organisation is focussed on rules and regulations. Authorities and powers are outlined in more or less detailed procedures. Selection bureaucracies are focussed inwards and the employees are strongly attached to their organisation. Application of rules and procedures to individual cases often leads to problems because, no matter how strict the rules are defined, there are always cases that do not fit the rules. The street level bureaucrat therefore has to have a certain room for discretion to decide individual cases as she sees fit.

Part of the discretion attributed to street level bureaucrats derives from the moral dimension innate in human service organisations. Another, although intertwined, source is the legal material the street level bureaucrats have to apply in their decisions. Rules and regulations are drafted in natural language, which introduces specific problems. Three types of problems are particularly relevant in the light of electronic service delivery: vagueness of concepts, open texture and the overall problem of (legal) interpretation. Legal concepts are often vague or evaluative. Article 24 of the Dutch Unemployment Act, for instance, stated that an unemployed person should avoid staying unemployed as a result of "insufficiently trying to obtain commensurate work". The concepts of "sufficiently trying" and "commensurate work" are vague and open to discussion among experts in the field. What amounts to appropriate work in a particular case, depends on all sorts of fuzzy factors that have to be weighed in order to reach a decision. Usually part of the vagueness is reduced by policy guidelines for the street level bureaucrats, but inevitably discretion remains.

The second source of problems is the open texture of concepts. The meaning of a concept may be clear at a specific point in time. But for every concept a moment may arise when a case presents itself that clearly falls within the borders of the concept, while there is reason to exclude the case as an instance of the concept in question. Or, a case may fall outside the borders of a concept, while there is reason to mark it as an instance of the concept. A classical example in the Netherlands arose when a windsurfboard collided with a yacht. The question arose whether a windsurfboard was to be considered to be a vessel, in which case the Water Traffic Act (Vaarwet) applied and the windsurfboard was to be held liable for the accident. Otherwise, it would not be liable. This decision was in a way arbitrary, because one could argue either way. All things considered, a decision has to be made and from that moment on there again is clarity with respect to the borders of the concept. When problems relating to the open texture of concepts arise, there clearly is room for discretion.

Both problems arise in the process of legal interpretation. Every rule and every concept has to be interpreted in the light of the case at hand. The same goes for the facts of the case. The interpretation of rules and concepts not only involves linguistic factors, but also the purpose of the rule, the context in which the rule is embedded, the history of the rule and the domain in which the rule functions and other factors. These factors make legal decision making a process in which flexibility has to be incorporated.

A third important dimension that makes legal decision making special is the constitutional context in which it takes place. Government agencies are ultimately bound by law as a consequence of the legality principle (the rule of law)[1], although the law in some instances only states policy goals as Lenk *et al.* (2002) note. Their decisions have to be based on legal grounds and decisions have to be justified by referring to the proper legal grounds and the appropriate facts of the case in the (written) decision itself. Furthermore, legal principles such as legal certainty and equity before the law aim to make the legal consequences of actions predictable. Citizens should be able to determine their rights and obligations on the basis of the appropriate legal sources (legislation and secondary material) and base their actions on this knowledge. These factors aim to keep the discretion of legal decision makers within bounds.

As will be clear from this short introduction, legal decision making by street level bureaucrats is finding a proper balance between the mechanistic application of legal rules and doing justice to truly special cases. This is the field in which electronic service delivery has to be embedded.

In most cases handled by street level bureaucrats, the problems sketched above play no role at all. Most cases are simple in the sense that it is clear that they fall within the scope of the applicable rules and that there is no room for discretion, because this would be unjust to the other cases. These are called the 'clear cases' in legal theory. Briefly stated, clear cases are the cases where: the rules are clear, the facts are clear, the rules and facts match and the decision is acceptable (Leenes, 1998;Smith, 1994). The others are called 'hard cases'. In hard cases, experts may argue over the rules, facts, the applicability of rules to the facts and/or the acceptability of the outcome. Stated in different terms, in hard cases two experts may arrive at different decisions.

The distinction between clear and hard cases is important for electronic service delivery. It seems plausible that computer applications can be built to handle clear cases. But what about the hard cases? How is a computer application going to handle cases that have no indisputable outcome?

3   Legal Knowledge Based Systems

The idea that computer applications could be developed to perform legal tasks stems from the 1950s. But only in the second half of the 1980s, real progress was made in the development of these applications, commonly denoted as legal expert systems.

These systems embody a representation of legal knowledge. They are capable of reasoning with this representation to derive legally valid conclusions. This makes them suitable for legal decision making. What sets them apart from traditional computer applications is that there is a separation between the knowledge base and the inference engine (and the user interface). The knowledge base contains a representation of the legal knowledge relevant to the system's domain of operation. In one of the prominent subclasses of legal expert system, the rule based systems, the legal knowledge is represented as a (large) set of if-then rules and text segments. The if-then rules may embody both legal and practical knowledge necessary for decision

---

[1] In the Netherlands at least, but the same, no doubt, holds for most (European) countries.

making in a particular domain. The inference engine is a general (re-usable) component that operates on the if-then rules. It can check whether the conditions of rules are met, and if so, conclude that the consequent of the rule is valid. It traverses the if-then rules to carry out its reasoning tasks. It will request the interface component to ask for user input by means of questions whenever necessary to proceed, and it will present its conclusions to the interface component. The interface component takes care of the actual question and answer 'game' between system and user. Inference engine and interface component together are also capable of producing justification of the results reached by presenting the applicable rules together with the relevant user input (Why and How functions).

Expert systems can be built on the basis of expert knowledge. But in legal domains it turned out to be possible to turn to the legal sources underlying a particular domain. The legal sources, primary legislation, can be represented in the form of if-then rules closely following the organisation and formulation of these sources. This kind of isomorphic representation of legislation in rule based knowledge systems appeared to have important advantages over other forms of knowledge representation (Bench-Capon and Coenen, 1992). The close correspondence between the sources of legal decision making and the representation in machine usable form eases the construction of knowledge bases, but also the validation, maintenance and use of the resulting system.

One of the first mayor experiments with the construction of a large isomorphic legal knowledge based systems (LKBS) was the Tessec system (Twente Expert System for Social sECurity), a system for the adjudication of social security legislation by case workers in Social Welfare offices. Various evaluations of Tessec and a similar system of a later date, the MR-Systems, show that the quality of the decisions made by these systems to be higher than that of the street level bureaucrats in the field of social security (see Svensson, 2001 for an overview of these studies). Johnson and Sutherland (1996) report similar improvements in decision making by legal expert systems in Australia.

Legal knowledge based systems are capable of making legal decisions by applying legislation to the facts as provided by the user. But what about the distinction between clear and hard cases and the need for discretion in decision making? The relative success of Tessec and similar systems, relates to the context in which they operate (Svensson, 2001). The social security domain is well structured. It contains concise and extensive rules that determine the legal consequences of most situations that can arise in the field. The legislator went at great length to completely regulate the field. Most lacunae left by the legislator are filled in by lower legislation (by-laws and policy guidelines). The resulting set of rules is binding upon the street level bureaucrats, which make them authoritative sources suitable for implementation in a LKBS. And, finally, the field is complex, which makes it difficult for the street level bureaucrat to administer. The same complexity makes it relatively easy for a machine to outperform the street level bureaucrat. Much of the problems ascribed to legal decision making in the previous section are tackled, either by the legislator or by the administrations. This does not mean that all cases are treated as clear cases. In this particular domain decisions are made by a case worker who uses the legal expert system. The case worker has the option to ignore or alter the expert system's advice, and indeed appears to do so when the need arises (Linden-Smith, 2001). Linden-Smith also observes that if hard cases in this domain do not receive the attention they deserve, this is not the result of IT systems, but much more of a trend towards more standardisation and rationalisation in the domain. This trend may in effect be enhanced by the use of ICT. This finding seems to be in line with observations that the powers of the street level bureaucrat diminish over time and through the introduction of ICT in the work processes as Snellen (2002) observes.

How do legal knowledge base systems handle vagueness, open texture and discretion? Legal knowledge based systems operate on a model of the domain within which they operate. They use pre-formulated rules and can do no better than the rules they have at their disposal. They are closed systems and therefore incapable of detecting new (and therefore possibly hard) cases and making weighed judgements not perceived at the time of construction of the system. Vague concepts are problematic for legal expert systems because it is often not possible to construct computational models to determine their applicability to actual cases. Humans are better in making decisions in these cases. They are more suited to use fuzzy and incomplete decision models. For instance, in the Dutch social security there is a concept "common household", which includes married couples, but also all sorts of arrangements of people sharing a household, such as students sharing a flat. Determining whether a particular case is an instance of a common household is not too difficult once one gets the gist of the idea of a common household. But the construction of a (rule based) model for this concept is a different story. It may therefore be easier to ask the user of the system whether the subject is part of a common household by providing some information about what this is supposed to mean, than to design a rule based model that can be evaluated by the expert system. The lesson here is that a balance has to be struck between reasoning by the expert system and reasoning by the user.

The bottom line is that legal expert systems are useful in domains where the risk of processing a hard case as clear one is low (Smith, 1994).

Although the technology to build legal decision making system has been around for quite some time now, and these systems turn out to perform relatively well, there are relatively few systems in use or in development. Worse, there is even mention of an AI-winter that also touches on legal knowledge based systems (Svensson, 2001). Why? Are most domains dominated by hard cases, or is it a mere unfamiliarity with the technology that prevents public administrations from using it?

4   A Field Trip

To start with the latter question, there indeed appears to be an unawareness of LKBS technology among the people involved in the development of electronic service delivery. While doing a study for the Dutch Ministry of housing, urban planning and the environment (VROM) on tools for electronic service delivery (Leenes, et al., 2002), we discovered that LKBS technology was unknown to most people involved at the ministry. At a conference on tools for electronic service delivery organised by the same ministry in November 2002, only one of the projects on display made use of advanced technology to implement electronic service delivery. The rest of the 30 projects mainly used hard coded 'dumb' online forms. These projects represented the forerunners in the domain of building and housing and were sponsored by the ministry. Among them was the city of Enschede[2], which is also largely unaware of the possibilities LKBS technology offers. The development of electronic service delivery primarily takes place at the local level in the Netherlands (Leenes and Svensson, 2002). This makes the chances that smaller projects with less resources than the Enschede project make use of advanced tools, is remote. Although these observations are nowhere near systematic or complete, it is my impression that there is a knowledge gap between those involved in LKBS development - traditionally the universities in the Netherlands - and the developers of electronic services - mainly the municipalities and software developers. A notable exception is the Dutch Tax and Customs Administration (DTCA) (Engers, et al., 2001) which has a research program (POWER) aimed at developing legal knowledge based systems for Tax legislation.

With respect to the question of the applicability of LKBS technology in real legal domains relevant to electronic service delivery there is little data. In the aforementioned study for the Ministry of VROM (Leenes, et al., 2002), we have performed a quick scan for two domains: "building and housing" and "living and care". The first domain contains a large number of services relating to the construction of private houses, home improvement, the acquisition of a (both private and rented) house, and services such as logging permits and housing permits. The second domain overlaps the first one, but the principal services are primarily aimed at the elderly and disabled. This includes services such as meals-on-wheels, home care, adaptations in the house to cope with a handicap, wheelchairs and other tools for the physically challenged. If we compare the two domains we see notably differences. The first domain largely builds on objective measures and quantities, such as income, age, price of the house, physical dimensions of a design for a building and type of tree to be felled. There appears to be little vagueness in the terms involved in the rules in this domain. In the latter domain, much more vague concepts exist. Many services depend on the level of inadequacy of the house of the citizen involved or the severity of a handicap. Consequently, vagueness and discretion play a much larger role here than in the former domain. The street level bureaucrat in this domain has to make an assessment of these evaluative concepts in interaction with the citizen.

Although these two domains are different in nature, they both contain many services that have a clear foundation in legislation that can be implemented in legal knowledge based systems. There seem to be few principal obstacles for LKBS use in 'hard' domains such as "building and housing", whereas the use in 'soft' domains such as "living and care" seems more troublesome.

5   Levels of Service Delivery

In the previous sections, I have discussed some of the problems involved in legal decision making. The background of the discussion so far has been decision making by street level bureaucrats about rights and duties of clients (citizens, businesses). Discretion in the application of rules to cases, and language related aspects of rules and regulation turn out to be obstacles to system development. Building systems that

---

[2] One of the three SuperPilots sponsored by both the Ministry of the Interior and the Ministry of housing, urban planning and the environment, to boost the development of electronic services.

correctly decide cases on domains where these factors play a decisive role, may be hard to almost impossible. That is, unless we are willing to sacrifice that hard cases are treated properly. If all cases are treated as clear cases, as is done in some domains such as speed limit violations in the Netherlands, then automated legal decision making is possible for many domains. Legal rule based system technology in these cases is a promising technology for the development of electronic services. But, since we are probably not willing to sacrifice legal principles, such as proper consideration, for the sake of introducing IT in decision making, the problems discussed come to play in implementing electronic service delivery in the public sector since many public services inevitably involve legal decision making. The role for legal knowledge based system technology in electronic service delivery may therefore, at first sight, be limited.

If we take a broader perspective the picture changes a bit. There is much more to electronic service delivery than legal decision making. This, in fact, is just one of the last steps in a process. Also in the stages before and after legal decision making there is room for support by electronic means.

It is useful to break down the interaction between citizen and public administration in phases to see where support by IT systems can be given. Chronologically the following steps can be distinguished:

1. Search: This phase consists of an iterative process of browsing general information to select possible relevant services and matching services to one's case by consulting the conditions and requirements listed for the service.
2. Intake: Once the citizen thinks she may be eligible for a service, the actual formal application has to be filled in and submitted to the administration.
3. Decision making: The application is processed by the proper administration and a decision is made on the basis of the application of rules and procedures of the service to the applicant's data.
4. Explanation: The decision is presented to the citizen in a way described by law. This may or may not include stating the relevant facts and grounds on which the decision rests.
5. Objection and appeal: Finally, the citizen can object to the decision at the administrative authority that took the decision or file court appeal to the decision.

The implementation of electronic service delivery at present in most cases focuses on steps 1 and 2. The concepts of 'life event' and 'care pathways' are generally used to guide the citizen in selecting relevant services. Often the user has to do the matching of her situation to the requirements of the various services herself. The intake often consists of 'digitally remastered'[3] paper forms. That is, relatively dumb forms the applicant has to fill in. Since the user often has to decide for herself that application for a service may be useful, she also has few clues about the relevance of the forms or the outcome of the process. The user has to do most of the thinking in the process. This seems odd to me. One of the reasons to develop e-government in the first place, is the notion that lay-people have trouble in effectuating their rights and meeting their obligations. IT was thought to be one means to improve on this situation.

The technology discussed in this paper can play a role in this respect. Even if legal knowledge based system are incapable of making legally binding decisions, they still may be able to assist the users in the steps before and after decision making.

---

[3] To use a nothing-new term from the CD industry.

Legal expert systems can, for instance, be developed to help people decide whether it makes sense to apply for certain services, such as benefits or subsidies. This allows for tailor-made advice applications, instead of one-size fits all systems we see nowadays. Or, systems can be built to help people fill in forms. These systems can explain why questions are asked (the standard why function available in most expert system shells) and intelligently select relevant questions. Even the construction of complaint assistants by means of LKBS technology is feasible.

The essence of these systems is not that they offer legally binding decisions, but that they can give reasoned legal advice that is valid within a margin. How broad or small this margin is depends on the particular domain, the effort put into the construction the system and the legal status the government involved is willing to attribute to the advice.

6 Conclusion

Electronic service delivery does not meet the goals set in many policy documents. This has many reasons, most not related to IT at all. In this paper I have discussed one of the core aspects of e-government, and hence of electronic service delivery, legal decision making. Legal decision making is generally difficult. This is precisely the reason why qualified personnel is used to make these decisions. One of the implications of e-government seems to be that IT systems will take over legal decision making in part. I have discussed some of the difficulties this will pose. I have also tried to show that, apart from legal decision making, there are other stages in the interaction process between citizen and government that can be supported by IT systems. At present the accomplishments on this terrain are not satisfactory. A reason for this in my view is that there is a knowledge gap in the field of electronic service delivery development with respect to useful tools and techniques. Legal knowledge based system technology is neglected as a promising tool to realise the full potential of electronic service delivery. A necessary first step in bridging this knowledge gap is raising the awareness of the possibilities of legal knowledge based systems among the people involved in the development of electronic services. This paper aims to be step on this path.

References

1. Bellamy, Christine, and John A. Taylor. *Governing in the information age, Public policy and management*. Buckingham ; Bristol, PA: Open University Press, 1998.
2. Bench-Capon, T. J. M., and F.P. Coenen. "Isomorphism and legal knowledge based systems." *Artificial Intelligence and Law* I (1992): 65–86.
3. Engers, Tom M. van, P.J.M. Kordelaar, and E.A. ter Horst. "Power to the e-government." In *2001 knowledge management in e-government kmgov-2001*, edited by Maria A. Wimmer. Linz: Universitätsverlag Rudolf Trauner, 2001.
4. Gastelaars, Marja. *'human service' in veelvoud een typologie van dienstverlenende organisaties, Bibliotheek beleid en management*. Utrecht: SWP, 1997.
5. Hasenfeld, Yeheskel. *Human service organizations*. 11th print. ed. Englewood Cliffs, N.J.: Prentice-Hall, 1983.

6. Hoogwout, Marcel. "Leuker kunnen we het niet maken, maar willen we het wel makkelijker? Waarom overheden geen haast hebben met het verbeteren van de dienstverlening." In *Klantgericht werken in de publieke sector: Inrichting van de elektronische overheid*, edited by Hendricus Petrus Maria Van Duivenboden and Miriam Lips, 149–66. Utrecht: Uitgeverij LEMMA BV, 2001.
7. Johnson, Peter, and Peter Sutherland. "The impact of technology on decision making and administrative review." Paper presented at the Australian Institute of Administrative Lawyers Conference, Canberra, Australia 1996.
8. Leenes, R.E., and J.S. Svensson. "Size matters – electronic service delivery by municipalities?" In *Electronic government - first international conference, egov 2002, aix-en-provence, france*, edited by R Traunmüller and K Lenk, 150–56. Berlin/Heidelberg: Springer, 2002.
9. Leenes, R.E., R. Winkels, and C.N.J. de Vey Mestdagh. "Kennisarchitecturen voor elektronische overheidsdienstverlening (knowledge architectures for electronic service delivery)." Den Haag: Ministry of housing, urban planning and the environment, 2002.
10. Leenes, Ronald E. *Hercules of karneades, hard cases in recht en rechtsinformatica (hercules of karneades, hard cases in law and ai and law)*. Enschede: Twente University Press, 1998.
11. Lenk, K, R Traunmuller, and Maria A. Wimmer. "The significance of law and knowledge for electronic government." In *Electronic government – design, applications and management*, edited by A Grönlund, 61–77: Idea Group Publishing, 2002.
12. Linden-Smith, Tina van der. *Een duidelijk geval: Geautomatiseerde afhandeling*. Vol. 41, *Iter-reeks*. Den Haag: SDU Uitgevers, 2001.
13. Lipsky, Michael. *Street-level bureaucracy dilemmas of the individual in public services*. New York, N.Y.: Russell Sage Foundation, 1980.
14. Raad voor het Openbaar Bestuur. *Dienen en verdienen met ict: Over de toekomstige mogelijkheden van de publieke dienstverlening*. Den Haag: Raad voor het Openbaar Bestuur, 1998.
15. Smith, Tina. *Legal expert systems: Discussion of theoretical assumptions*: Universiteit Utrecht, 1994.
16 Snellen, I. Th M. "Entrapment in knowledge management: The fate of street level bureaucrats." In *Knowledge management in e-government: Kmgov-2002*, edited by Maria A. Wimmer, 38–49. Linz: Universitätsverlag Rudolf Trauner, 2002.
17 Svensson, J.S. "The use of legal expert systems in administrative decision making." In *Electronic government - design, applications and management*, edited by Åke Grönlund. Hershey, PA: IDEA Group Pub, 2001.

E-knowledge Management in Public Administration: An Agenda for the Future

Ignace Snellen

Erasmus University, Postbox 1738, NL-3000 DR, Rotterdam, The Netherlands
snellen@fsw.eur.nl

Abstract. Knowledge Management has always been a constant concern in public administrations. Many ICT enabled applications of Knowledge Management have become available to support managers and street level bureaucrats with their policy development and policy implementation tasks. In a democratic constitutional state citizens are entitled, as well, to profit from the growing possibilities to influence policies and to monitor the performance of governments. It is time for a systematic development of an agenda of e-Knowledge Management for citizens in the future information society.

1 Introduction

Knowledge Management (KM) always has been a constant concern within public administrations.

More so than in private enterprise. One of the reasons for this is that, at least in constitutional states, the equality before the law principle is adhered to. Equal cases have to be handled equally. This principle gives special importance to "precedence". A decision taken in a former case will normally be decisive for the outcome in a later similar case. To enable public officials to take former cases into account, public administrations have to store those cases into their memory. So, this knowledge about cases has to be assembled, stored, and made available, when it is necessary to do justice to the case at hand. The same reasons apply for the storage of jurisprudence in public memory systems.

Besides, public administrations function within a legal environment, in which not only the content of decisions has to be based upon legal rules and regulations, but in which also the way in which those decisions are reached have to answer to the principles of due process. Legal control of the procedures according to which the decisions are reached is not possible without the possibility to retrieve the factual procedures that were followed, and without the knowledge of the criteria that have to be applied. Thus, Knowledge Management is not only required to know which rules and regulations to apply, but also to be able to reconstruct afterwards whether the right procedures were followed.

In Germany an illuminating distinction is made between "Dienstwissen" and "Fachwissen", i.e. between the knowledge that is built up within public administration ("Dienst") about factual situations and the knowledge that is related to the professional execution of administrative tasks ("Fach"). Both kinds of knowledge are essential prerequisites for a democratic, and legally well functioning, public administration, and to attain effective and efficient policies.

M.A. Wimmer (Ed.): KMGov 2003, LNAI 2645, pp. 70–75, 2003.

Weggeman makes a distinction between three dominant ways of operationalising Knowledge Management: 1) KM supported by ICTs, 2) KM through human talent development, and 3) KM through the design of a knowledge friendly organisation. In this paper the focus is upon the use of digital Information and Communication applications (ICTs) for different forms of Knowledge Management.

2 A Knowledge Management Framework for Public Administration

In this paper I will not make an inventory of all possible applications of Knowledge Management in public administration, but limit myself to applications of ICT on *policy development* and *policy implementation* as fields of Knowledge Management. The question I try and answer in this paper is, what agenda items could be raised to extend and improve the use of ICTs as instruments of Knowledge Management for policy development and policy implementation. Public managers, public servants and the citizens are seen as the three groups of possible stakeholders in the agenda items and as users of those ICTs.

The correctness or legality of the acts and activities of public authorities requires:
- a constitutive legal basis for the existence, the jurisdiction and the policy making of those authorities;
- a regulatory basis for their administrative decisions, their law maintenance and their inspection activities;
- a discretionary basis for their ex ante and ex post evaluations, their monitoring and their control..

Every public authority has to take care that all segments of the organisation are fully aware of those legal requirements, their content, and the possibilities and limitations they entail.

This a first dimension of Knowledge Management in public administration.

As far as the control activities with respect to public authorities are concerned, a distinction could be made between:
- democratic control by the media, interest groups, political parties and representative councils of the citizenry and the citizens themselves;
- political control by parliaments and other bodies of people's representation, to check whether the decisions of the legislature are implemented;
- legal control by courts, ombudsmen and other judicial bodies, of which the assigned function is, to judge the right rule-application by the administration;
- business control by managers, who are responsible for the "faits et gestes" of the employees as well as the clients of the organisation they manage;
- historical control by future generations against a common cultural background of a nation, a region, a city or a community.

This is a second dimension of Knowledge Management in public administration.

3 Leads for Knowledge Management in Policy Development and Policy Implementation

Most steps in public policy development and policy implementation require knowledge imputs. It is a task of Knowledge Management to see to it that the requisite knowledge is available at the time and in the form, necessary to realise successful and legitimate policies.

For policy development and policy implementation, each, different points of contact for Knowledge Management can be explicited and possible applications of ICT to facilitate Knowledge Management indicated.

In this paper the following points of contact for Knowledge Mangement with respect to Policy Development and Policy Implementation are distinguished:

Knowledge Management requirements for Policy Development (PD)

PD 1. data, information and knowledge about (cumulative) problem situations of segments or categories of the population, that require action of the public authority. *Datamining* in statistical data repositories, analysis of the data created by *"informating"* (Zuboff 1988) and the development of so-called *"profiles"* of categories of a population are obvious methods to detect those problematic situations. *Geographic Information Systems (GIS)* may be strong tools to analyse and visualise the situation.

PD 2. insight in the causes of a problematic situation. The development of a causal "policy theory" may be supported by sophisticated ICT applications such as are used in social scientific research *(SPSS)*. *GISs* may appear as strong analytical tools for the development of policy theories as well.

PD 3. feel for the most promising "intervention variables" to be derived from the policy theory. *Simulation games* may facilitate to get a feel for the likely candidate intervention variables, and the facility of an ICT equiped *"decision room"* may help to test the acceptability of the choice of interventions with the policy partners.

PD 4. the effectiveness of possible policy instruments has to be assesssed, apart from the choice of the intervention variables. In principle three kinds of policy instruments are to be considered: financial instruments, communicative instruments and legal instruments. The effectiveness of all three instruments could profit from the application of ICTs. *Websites* are an obvious example of the facilitation of communicative instruments through ICT. *Textblocks* (Snellen 2001) may facilitate legal instruments and *spreadsheets* financial instruments.

PD 5. ex ante evaluations, and the estimation of probable policy effects, are furthered by systematic feedback from former policies, that may become facilitated by ICT applications such as *datamining, spreadsheets, and GISs*.

PD 6. ex post evaluations and the determination of the outputs and outcomes of policies are greatly helped by the development of *performance indicators* and *benchmarking*.

Knowledge management requirements for Policy Implementation (PI)

PI 1. Information on the workflow and its different steps. Through electronic *workflow management systems* the public servants and their managers may keep an eye on the task sequences, on the steps that are still ahead, and on deadlines that have to be met.

PI 2. Information on the procedures which are prescribed in all kinds of general and specific legal rules and regulations, and in organisational policy documents. All kinds of software (such as *advisory systems, expert systems* and *processing systems*) have been developed to assist the public servant in reaching a correct decision.

PI 3. internal information about clients, based upon former interactions with those clients. *Electronic files* and *databases*, shared between the departments of an organisation, are playing an ever growing role in contacts of the officials with the clients.

PI 4. external information about clients, provided by outside organisations via the intermediary of an information office, which verifies the information the client is giving. In a former presentation (Snellen 2001) I refered to the role of the Dutch Routing Institute for (inter)National Information Streams (RINIS) with respect to *front end verification.*

PI 5. information about the general circumstances, in which a policy has to be made a success, and a client has to be supported, such as the employment situation, the level of schooling, or the kind of organisational support, that is available. *Geographic Information Systems (GIS)* may play an important role in this respect.

PI 6. information about the legal situation of the clients and their entitlement to permits, support or subsistance, as has to be retrieved from laws and regulations. *Advisory systems, Expert (support) systems* and *Processing systems* are the kind of decision support tools that are used for these purposes.

PI 7. management information about the workload, and other working conditions, of the employees of the public organisation. Next to *workflow management systems*, different kinds of ICT tools for Human Resource Management, such as absenteism registration, labour turnover statistics, exit interviews et cetera, are applied for this purpose.

PI 8. management information about the correctness as well as the average content of the decisions of the employees. *Relational databases* can be instrumental to give management a daily, weekly or other periodical overview of the results per employee. ICT applications in Call Centers are notorious in this respect.

PI 9. management information about the organisational consequences – a.o. in terms of personnel or finances – of the decisions that are being taken. The feedback reporting time about the consequences of the organisational activities is becoming ever shorter. *Spreadsheets* are a common tool to get in advance a systematic overview on those consequences.

PI 10. management information about the consequences of the decisions for tasks and activities down the interorganisational chain of services and provisions. Common approaches like sharing of databases and solutions like the above mentioned RINIS make it possible to take the repercussions for other public organisations, down the value chain of services or provisions, into account. Apart from that, applications of *Computer Supported Cooperative Work (CSCW)* may come into play.

4   ICTs in E-knowledge Management for Public Policy

The overriding impression is that the citizen is an underprivileged user of e-Knowledge Management (e-K.M.), while mangement and officials are ever better served. Management and public officials are well served by a whole array of e-Knowledge Management tools, but that the citizen is almost completely neglected. However, a viable agenda for the future to serve the citizen with e-Knowledge tools in public administration could be as follows:

I. Geographic Information Systems.

As far as policy development is concerned, the citizen could be served by Geographic Information Systems (GIS). GISs make it possible to combine geodata about physical environments, in which people live, with statistical data about their social situation such as levels of schooling, criminality, unemployment, health, life expectancy and so on. These data are essential imputs in policy development. A coupling of the geodata and the statistical data with the administrative data, that are created during policy implementation, are of the utmost importance for a possible democratic influence by the citizens. (Snellen 2001) The administrative data, generated within public administrations during policy implementation, give evidence about what public officials and their managers in fact are performing for a group or a sector in society. Comparison of the geodata, the statistical and the administrative data with the help of GIS makes it crystal-clear whether the public authority has been responsive to the (accumulation of) problems in the area covered by the GIS.

"A condition for effective influence by citizens and their interest groups is access to the data that are available within the public service. In most countries freedom of information is rather limited. It may be restricted to documents on which a policy is based. As policy documents, they will generally be fashioned to the knowledge interest of the policy-maker." "...access to the (raw) data available within the public domain is for the citizen – especially in the information society – much more important than the information in policy documents, which is edited with a certain purpose or view-point in mind. However, opposition to the transparancy of the workings of politics and public bureaucracies is massive." (Snellen 2002)

During the implementation of policies GISs can be helpful in demonstrating in what kind of environment they have to be made a success. Citizens and their organisations may use the GISs to improve the adequacy of the policies concerned.

II. Software programs.

Workflow system programs are in use to guide the officials through the bureaucratic maze of the case handling and to give their managers an overview of the caseload of each employee, of the kind of decisions each of them is taking, and of the progress of the activities. It would be worthwhile to enable the citizen to have, as well, a view on the progress of his/her case. Reference can be made to the postal services like UPS that give their clients insight in the handling process and give them an exact indication of the location of their mail. Comparable programs would be feasible all over the public administration.

Another program that deserves our attention is the creation of a personal data safe at the disposition of the citizen, in which all the personal data of the citizen – as far as he/she likes it – are stored. If every authority, that uses those personal data, is obliged to give notice of the use to the personal data safe, the citizen keeps a complete and up-to-date overview on his/her own privacy.

A third move in terms of software programs, that might substantially improve the situation of the citizens in their contacts with the authorities, would be if the advisory systems and expert systems that are developed as decision support tools for the officials are made available to the clients. This would enable clients to try and find a "winning profile" for the entitlement of a subsidy or any other kind of support. Especially underprivileged clients need this kind of help. Software programs are also more and more becoming into use to help the official to find the right (and best immunized) justification of the administrative decisions he/she takes. So-called "text building blocks", pre-fabricated motivations of positive or negative administrative decisions, are developed to assist the official in the decision making process. The more this decision behaviour of the official has become routinized the more important it is for the citizen to have access to the software programs by which the justifications of the administrative decisions are made. This kind of e-Knowledge Management for the citizen will put both public authorities and citizens on a more equal footing.

And finally, software programs that provide citizens with scores as to performance indicators through monitoring and benchmarks enable them to keep horizontal overview and guidance on the efforts and results of governmental policies.

5 Conclusion

In a modern constitutional state e-Knowledge Management is playing a major role in the management and functioning of public administrations. Especially public managers and public officials are supported by ICT applications for e-Knowledge Management. Almost every step in policy development and policy implementation is guided by e-Knowledge Management and the number of applications is still growing.

Citizens, however, have to manage almost without assistence in this respect, although the possibilities to strengthen their position in interactive policy making, monitoring and control are growing. It is time for a systematic development of an agenda of e-Knowledge Management for citizens in the fuuture information society.

References

1. Snellen, Ignace: ICTs, Bureaucracies, and the Future of Democracy. Communications of the ACM, januari 2001/Vol.44, No. 1, p. 45
2. Snellen, Ignace: Entrapments in Knowledge Management: The fate of street level bureaucrats. In: Wimmer Maria A. (Ed.): Knowledge Management in e-Government. KMGov-2002. Universitätsverlag Rudolf Trauner, Laxenburg.
3. Snellen, Ignace: Electronic governance: implications for citizens, politicians and public servants. International Review of Administrative Sciences, Vol. 68, No. 2, June 2002
4. Snellen, Ignace: E-government and E-democracy: Practices and Problems. In; Manolopoulos Y. and Evripidou S. (Eds): 8th Panhellenic Conference in Informatics. Proceedings Vol. 2, Nicosia, November 2001
5. Weggeman, Mathieu: Kennismanagement: leidinggeven aan kenniswerkers. In: Van Duivenboden H. a.o. (Eds): Kennismanagement in de publieke sector. Elsevier bedrijfs-informatie bv, 'sGravenhage, 1999, p.45–63.
6. Zuboff, S.: In the Age of the Smart Machine. Basic Books 1988.

Key Success Factors for Electronic Inter-organisational Co-operation between Government Agencies

Luiz Antonio Joia

Brazilian School of Public and Business Administration – Getulio Vargas Foundation and
Rio de Janeiro State University
Rua Presidente Carlos de Campos 115/503, BL 02, Rio de Janeiro, RJ, Brazil, 22231-080
luizjoia@fgv.br

Abstract. Electronic Government has proven a watershed in the domain of Public Administration, despite being difficult to pin down precisely. Indeed, the Government-to-Government arena is one of the least studied aspects of this newly established field of knowledge, despite its importance in fostering co-operation and collaboration between government agencies, mainly with respect to the management of their knowledge, in order to increase the effectiveness of Public Administration. This paper aims to present the key success factors needed to implement government-to-government endeavours effectively. The research design used in this article was largely drawn from a Government-to-Government case study successfully implemented in Brazil.

1 Introduction

The main scope of this article is to present some key success factors for building Government-to-Government (G2G) enterprises successfully. It also aims to show how public agencies themselves can benefit when they are electronically linked to others, thereby innovating and streamlining their working processes, in order to achieve greater agility and efficacy at reduced cost.

In order to pinpoint the key G2G success factors, a specific successful case study was examined, namely one involving the Brazilian Central Bank (BCB) and the Brazilian Justice Department (BJD). In-depth analysis of this case enables us to appreciate the barriers surrounding G2G enterprises as well as the associated causes involved and possible solutions thereto.

The BacenJud system developed by the Brazilian Central Bank was analysed in a more detailed manner. This paper shows how this G2G project made it possible for both the Brazilian Central Bank and the Brazilian Justice Department to achieve greater agility and effectiveness regarding the processing of legal demands made by the Brazilian Justice Department, thereby handing down its sentences at reduced cost. Furthermore, this study studied the factors that had a clear nationwide impact on the success of this endeavour in the realm of the Justice Department.

Therefore, this paper intends to answer the following research questions:

- From the case study analysed, what are the key success factors in the implementation of Government-to-Government processes between public agencies in Brazil?
- How did the G2G project impact the efficiency of the former interaction between the Brazilian Central Bank and the Brazilian Department of Justice?

M.A. Wimmer (Ed.): KMGov 2003, LNAI 2645, pp. 76–81, 2003.

2 Case Study

The Brazilian Federal Constitution grants very few institutions right of access to the bank accounts of both citizens and companies or, indeed, the power to freeze financial assets of either. One such institution is the Justice Department, which intervenes by means of judicial orders handed down by the judges of several courts nation-wide.

As required, a judge can either freeze or liberate the bank accounts of both citizens and businesses and even declare the bankruptcy of a company. Judges are further empowered to suspend a decreed bankruptcy or request financial information about organisations and citizens under scrutiny.

When it issues orders relating to information about the financial assets of either citizens or institutions, the Justice Department sends them directly to the Central Bank, which then forwards the orders to the specific recipients, namely either an institution or the Brazilian Financial System. It is almost impossible for the Justice Department to know precisely where the request should be sent.

As there was already a computerised system in the Central Bank linking it to the Brazilian Financial System, it was relatively easy to meet the Justice Department's requests. However, the increasing demand for this kind of information made by the Justice Department obliged the Central Bank to involve several employees on a full-time basis and expend considerable financial resources just to deal with this requirement. Over the years, the number of claims has increased dramatically. In the meantime, the Central Bank's Legal Department issued an opinion alleging that the Central Bank had no constitutional duty to assist the Justice Department with these specific demands. However, in order not to jeopardise its relationship with the Justice Department, the Central Bank decided to rethink its *modus operandi,* in order to continue giving assistance to the Justice Department. Consequently, the Central Bank acknowledged the need to redesign this working process, by streamlining it and achieving greater efficiency and responsiveness at reduced cost. At a time when the Federal Government has reduced the public spending budget and society is demanding greater efficiency, efficacy and accountability from the public agencies, it was of paramount importance to achieve this.

2.1 An Innovative Process

By 1999, the Central Bank realised it was no longer feasible to process this operation manually, i.e., receiving claims on paper and feeding them into the communication systems linked to the National Financial System. In 2000, the Central Bank received 300 claims per day, totalling 71,775 claims in that year. A team of 23 people working full-time on this task was unable to meet the Justice Department's demands in time, thereby causing problems in terms of efficacy. The Bank was spending approximately US$1 million/yr. to process these requests, including wages, equipment and so forth.

The Bank soon realised that there was a pressing need to develop an information system where the Justice Department itself could formulate its requests that could then be forwarded directly by the Central Bank to the financial institutions.

The Bank looked into the possibility of a revised information flow, seeking to take advantage of the deployment of the existing Internet access in most Brazilian courts. A web-based system was developed in order to centralise the interaction of the judges with the Bank so that they could file their requests directly. A web-based system was selected such that the judges would not have to install any specific software on their desktops, thereby reducing costs involved in the process.

2.2 Process Architecture

From the moment a court signs an agreement with the Central Bank, it designates a professional in charge of managing the system on its premises. This manager is supposed to conduct operations including: adding users; altering data; changing passwords; granting permission to judges to access the system and withdrawing this permission when necessary. These operations are done through the system itself, which has a dynamic interface, according to user profile. Users can then access a restricted site on the Internet and after their identity is verified, the system offers web templates to allow them to fill out their requests. These are recorded directly in the Central Bank's corporate database.

At 7 p.m. every day, all requests received during the course of that day are processed and forwarded to the financial institutions as electronic files. Each institution then replies directly to the judge involved. The process allows the institutions to standardise their answers and send them directly to the judges' e-mail addresses.

3 Findings

3.1 Perceived Benefits

This new process has brought several benefits both to the Brazilian Central Bank and the Brazilian Justice Department; the main benefit being the marked improvement in efficiency in processing and answering requests. Under the former system, it used to take an average of 5 days from the moment the request was made and delivered to the Financial System, though, at times it could even take as long as 20 days. Such delays can render a legal request worthless, as it gives the suspects sufficient time to remove monetary assets from the banks. Using the new process, a maximum of 24 hours is needed to prepare, transmit to the Central Bank and receive the answer to a request from the Financial System.

The agility attained by this new process derived not only from the reduced turn-around time in handling requests, but also from the opportunity given to the institutions to make or buy their own software in order to answer the claims automatically, as the e-mails of the judges are also supplied to the financial organisations [3]. Another improvement in process performance arose from the tracking capabilities available in this new workflow. In the event the request is not answered in due time, the judge is aware of who must be contacted and can follow up and demand an immediate reply.

In financial terms, the new process reduces costs both for the Central Bank and for the Justice Department. For the Central Bank, the main costs are related to the infrastructure needed to complete the process. For the time being, the former infrastructure still remains in place, as some requests still have to be processed manually, though now that the new structure there is no further pressure to improve the structure. Whereas requests used to cost the Central Bank nearly US$10.00 each, an automated request costs less than US$0.80. Costs to the Justice Department, were also reduced, as it is only necessary to establish Internet access in every court. The costs involved in traditional mail and personnel to handle the legal requests have also been eliminated.

3.2 Key Success Factors

From researcher observations and analysis of the questionnaires, we may deduce that the key success factors associated with a G2G enterprise are as follows:

a) Security
As the Internet has become a very important link between governmental agencies, it is of paramount importance to avoid security flaws, such as information violation by 'crackers', breakdowns in communication and so forth. Losses caused by such problems are more than just financial, as they can cause loss of confidence and acceptance by users and even involve the interruption of a given communication link [1].

In G2G processes, the issue of security is even greater, as confidential information can leak and be made public. Most of this information is protected by laws of secrecy under Brazilian legislation.

Thus, as was shown generically above, it is clear that security is one of the key success factors for a G2G endeavour. An authentication failure can allow any person to issue a legal request and expose the private life of citizens and relevant organisational information to all and sundry. Several courts insisted on seeing how the process worked before actually deciding to join the network proper.

b) Organisational Culture
Another factor that influences the success of an electronic governance model is the culture of the public agency in which it is developed. New processes of electronic governance, at different levels within the Public Administration, demand changes in organisational culture [2].

The influence of the culture is even more relevant when two different public agencies are working together, concurrently. The changes required in the organisational cultures in order to integrate different internal processes demand very clear prior definition of leadership and respective function. This role, itself, demands that a clear path be followed and precise judgement so as to make innovative workflows feasible [4].

Hence, as seen above, the success of the use of a new process depends on the culture within the organisations involved, in this case, the culture of the courts nation-wide. It was observed that the courts that already had a culture of using computerised processes assimilated the new *modus operandi* very rapidly and naturally. On the other hand, courts without Internet access or that barely used information systems in their daily activities have resisted greatly in joining the G2G process.

c) Training

New technologies, new processes and new models of electronic governance require the acquisition of new knowledge not just by the persons involved directly in the process, but also by the persons in charge of administrating them. Consequently, public agencies must assess their human capital carefully, as it is mandatory to train personnel before deployment of G2G enterprises [4].

When the process involves more than just one public agency, all players must implement training efforts, in order to leverage the knowledge of the personnel in the agencies involved equally.

Insufficient training can lead to misuse of the electronic processes hindering the potential benefits that might be attained by this new model.

Although the system was developed based on a user-friendly environment via a web interface, the Central Bank felt it necessary to make presentations to judges across the country, in order to explain how the system worked and explain the best practices associated with this new workflow.

In October 2001, the Central Bank started to make presentations to the judges in the courts in a state where only 10 judges had joined the system and a mere 8 requests had been generated until that moment. In the two months following the presentations, 130 judges joined the system and nearly 100 requests were generated. Interviews made by the researchers have shown that the use of the G2G process by trained people is increasing, proving the efficacy of the training strategy.

Thus, by consolidating information from all the observations, interviews and questionnaires, it can be seen that Access and Information Security, Organisational Culture and Training were the key success factors in this G2G enterprise.

4 Conclusions

From the case study analysis and interviews, it is possible to conclude that:
- Responsiveness to a G2G process is far greater than that obtained in traditional processes. This agility, itself, is of paramount importance in deploying more effective and efficient public policies;
- G2G processes are a valid alternative for Brazilian Public Administration, which is facing the dilemma of cutting back its operational budget to make the control of the governmental fiscal deficit feasible and to comply with citizen expectations regarding public agencies;
- The security issue in a G2G process is a critical factor, as breakdowns arising from it can cause losses not only for public agencies, but for society as a whole;
- To overlook the organisational culture of a public agency by concentrating efforts on a technological facet of a G2G project may cause the undertaking to fail. Nonetheless, public administration is ruled by the same legal agenda and must comply with similar procedures and rules. However, each public agency has its own identity, values and culture, leading it to develop different workflows, sometimes far different from workflows addressing a similar process in another public agency. To analyse the culture and values of a public agency is of paramount importance to the success of a G2G enterprise;

– Although technology offers people a user-friendly interface and, in some cases, the technology is already being used in the public agency, a G2G enterprise involves a *modus operandi* that is new for most of the people involved. It is necessary to show the benefits this new process can bring and the best *praxis*, as important steps for proper implementation of G2G projects.

It can be also inferred that the paper deals with e-governance [6], as it taps digital support for public choices and workgroups among several public administrators of different ranks. This is important as, according to [5] it is the least researched facet of e-government.

All the research questions presented earlier in this paper have been dully answered, as the key success factors and the barriers, causes and possible solutions associated with G2G processes have been addressed. Further, the profound influence of electronic inter-organisational co-operation between public agencies to deploy a knowledge management initiative within the government can be seen, i.e., G2G processes are the bedrock upon which knowledge management initiatives must be built.

References

1. Endler A. (2001). "Governo Eletrônico – A Internet como ferramenta de gestão dos serviços públicos". Available at: http://read.adm.ufrgs.br/read14/artigo/artigo1.pdf on 12/26/2001.
2. ITAC (2002). "Electronic Government – The Government of Canada as a Model Knowledge-based Enterprise". Position paper by the Information Technology Association Canada, Ontario, 15th October, 1999, available on 01/06/2002 at: http://www.itac.ca/
3. JUDNET. Troca de informações entre o Poder Judiciário e o Sistema Financeiro Nacional (Sistema JUDNET). Available on 12/18/2001 at: http://www.ditech.com.br/judnet.htm.
4. Kieley B. ,Lane G., Paquet G. & Roy J. (2002) "E-government in Canada – Services Online or Public Service Renewal". in A. Gronlund (ed.) E-Government – Design, Applications and Management, Ideas Group Publishing, Hershey et al, pp 340–355
5. Kraemer K.L. & Dedrick J. (1997) – "Computing and Public Organizations", *Journal of Public Administration Research and Theory*,7, 1: p.89–112.
6. Perri 6 (2001) - "E-governance. Do Digital Aids Make a Difference in Policy Making?", In: *Designing E-Government*, Prins J.E.J. (ed.), Kluwer Law International,p.7–27

Big Vision, Small Steps: A KM Strategy within a US Agency's Policy Content Management Environment

Duane Degler

IPGems, Columbia, MD, USA
ddegler@ipgems.com

Abstract. The US Social Security Administration (SSA) provides retirement and disability benefits to about 50 million Americans. Nearly 60,000 staff members and over 14,000 state employees rely on the Agency's policies to know how to process benefits claims accurately. In the last two years, SSA has begun to improve the systems that support creation and distribution of policy and procedural content. Many of these improvements demonstrate important concepts for end user information access. Alongside this has been the recognition of a need for more sophisticated knowledge management spanning the authoring and the end-user communities. This case study discusses the developing knowledge management strategy, in light of the experiences and lessons that are being learned from the ongoing implementation of a content management environment.

1   Background

The US Social Security Administration (SSA) manages both the retirement benefits system for American workers and the benefits system to support people who have become disabled. The work is carried out in conjunction with benefits assessors within each state – it is the states that actually make the benefits decisions for disability, as the benefits are tied to other state-sponsored programs. This creates unusual information-sharing relationships.

SSA provides retirement and disability benefits to about 50 million Americans. Nearly 60,000 staff members, and over 14,000 state employees, rely on the Agency's policies to know how to process benefit claims accurately. In the last two years, SSA has begun to improve the systems that support creation and distribution of policy and procedural content. The improvements have been prompted by many factors:

- Anticipation of a dramatic rise in the number of people SSA will serve, due to the aging "baby boomer" population, as well as an increase in the public's expectations of the service to be provided [1]
- Upcoming changes in the staff profiles within the Agency, as a result of increasing retirements and other changes in the US economy and workforce [1]
- An increasing amount of policy and general instructional content being created; much of that content is being created for the SSA Intranet by operational staff, outside of the traditional policy content creation systems
- Changes in content management technologies, such as the increasing move toward web-based services and XML

M.A. Wimmer (Ed.): KMGov 2003, LNAI 2645, pp. 82–93, 2003.

– Commitment throughout the US government for standardization and sharing of content and public services, generally known as the e-Gov initiative [2].

The planned improvements encompass a wide range of content management activities, including moving from a document-centric to a content-centric framework, database conversion to XML, introducing the ability to trace and manage links, better tracking of change control and the authoring process, and improvement of end-user interfaces.

Some people involved in this work have recognized that the Agency needs to think more broadly about the issues that it faces, and that this thinking leads to the need for a knowledge management strategy that builds on the content management foundation. Over the course of 2002, a few interested managers, staff and consultants have been formulating ideas around Agency knowledge management. They come from backgrounds in executive management, policy content, knowledge management, IT strategy, user-centered interaction design, business analysis and modeling, and web/technology development.

What follows is a summary of the organizational needs that create the requirement for knowledge management, a brief tour of some of the content management activities currently underway, and an overview of the knowledge management approach that is being analyzed for inclusion within the content management environment.

2   The Need to Respond to Changes in Public Expectations

What is known in the US as the "baby boomer" generation – those people born between the late 1940's and the early 1960's – will increasingly be nearing retirement age. The growing number of disability benefits claims, which have a more complex and demanding process of review by SSA and state staff, exacerbates an overall increase in workload.

Claimants and their families also expect to interact with SSA and the US government as a whole in new ways. People are increasingly using the Internet to find information, complete applications, and manage their personal and financial accounts. They expect their interactions with government web sites to be simple and clear, and they expect that the information they find will be understandable to them, no matter what their literacy level or primary spoken language. They expect a higher level of integration and cross-reference between different parts of the government, for both information and services.

This combination of factors puts significant demands on the people who create and manage content within the Agency.

3   The Effect of Increasing Knowledge Worker Retirement

At the same time that there is an increasing demand on services, there is soon to be a dramatic decrease in knowledgeable staff. It is estimated that over 50% of SSA staff will become eligible for retirement over the next five years. Many subject expert specialists who are responsible for writing policy and instructions are senior, more experienced staff, so the potential retirements within this group could be well over 50%.

Strange as it may sound, the loss of Agency knowledge may be felt less in the direct writing of policy and procedural content. The loss of experience is likely to be more subtle, more focused on changes or refinements to existing policy and to the alignment of policy with other operational requirements, and thus more difficult to address. Some people within SSA have recognized that it is increasingly difficult to find the answer to questions like "why was this written the way it was, and what will be the effect of changing it?" What is lacking within the existing content management processes is some method for finding the insights and discussions that led to the policy decisions that were then documented – i.e. the knowledge behind the content.

From the perspective of the end users of policy content, there is a rapid increase in the amount of information available to staff from a variety of sources, and yet a decreasing base of experience that can effectively filter and interpret the information they receive. Historically, it has mainly been left to individuals or working teams to "contextualize" information. This requires a high level of user experience and knowledge. Moving forward, other approaches need to be explored to help support the information consumer.

Historically, government departments and agencies have been seen as weak in their management of content and knowledge [3]. As it is becoming increasingly necessary to support the content authors and end users with a more sophisticated knowledge framework, a strategy has taken shape.

4   Overview of the Policy Content Management Environment

It has been recognized that there is a need to think holistically about content management and the systems that support content within SSA. Planning for the policy content management environment encompasses the full policy content lifecycle, including policy planning and development/authoring, change management tracking/reporting, a standard content architecture, sharing content between systems and between government agencies, user interfaces for direct access to content by the public and SSA employees, and a framework for evaluation of content use and its effectiveness. A number of projects over the past two years have led to interesting insights and some fundamental building blocks. The successes of these projects have proven certain concepts that are now being expanded into the broader improvement effort. The current project activities are described below.

The value and user satisfaction of providing information in the context of the user's job tasks has been illustrated by the recent launch of a web site that acts as a portal for users requiring Medicare and legal information as part of the appeals process following the denial of claims. The application is used by a wide variety of people, from senior judges in their 70's to junior administrators and researchers in their early 20's. The common aspect of their needs is that they do not have enough time to find the information they need to process cases when questions arise. There are hundreds of resource sites and internal instructional materials available to them, but all these resources require that they know the subject and content source in order to be successful. The application that was developed took a different approach: it asks them a few simple questions about the case in front of them, then uses that contextual starting point to rapidly deliver relevant information.

Subject experts are increasingly interested in entering web content directly, but they require that the content editing interface needs no special technology skills or training. Pilot work in this area (as part of the Medicare project discussed above) has been successful, particularly in the application of user-centered design methods to help make the content entry application easy to use by a range of subject experts across the country. The subject experts have been able to respond promptly to user needs and to manage large amounts of new material as it moves through the content development lifecycle. This project is a step closer to the goal of more subject experts being able to be involved in a flexible and sustainable process.

It was recognized very early that managing the content development and change process was a critical feature for the growing content management environment. Initial designs for a workflow/tracking system were devised with the long-term strategy clearly in mind. The approach taken to identify and track content relies on document metadata to associate content with organizational change initiatives for better management of implementations.

The architectural thinking for the content management environment has been based on an understanding of best practices in multi-tier, web-based architecture. The goal was to outline a sustainable, standards-based architecture that would allow for growth and change in the technical environment, and also to be scalable in order to meet the needs of an increasing number of types of content being stored. The approach being developed also aims to be in alignment with overall government standards for content management, including the conversion of the underlying content into the XML format, with the ability to create links to other XML content repositories.

Throughout all software development efforts, a key part of the process has been to gain a detailed understanding of both user and organizational needs through the techniques of user-centered design (UCD), supported also by the analytical requirements techniques of the unified modeling language (UML). Significant changes are planned for all user interfaces relating to policy content. One aspect of all these design activities is, of course, the need to meet the government requirements for access by the disabled. This provides further challenges and opportunities during the design of user interfaces for content-rich, context-aware sites.

5   The Critical Importance of Metadata as a Knowledge Enabler

The future backbone of SSA's growing content management environment is a robust structure for capturing and using metadata. This metadata structure also serves as the foundation for implementing knowledge management enablers within the policy authoring and end user communities.

What do we mean by "metadata"? Our working definition is: a structured collection of data that enables any individual element of content to be categorized and described, in order to be managed and then located when required by a user or application. In practice, useful metadata falls into two categories that work together to provide an extremely rich association with the real-world contexts users face:

- **Topics**: the categorized descriptions of the real world (SSA's organizational environment) to which content relates (this might include claim types, public life events, SSA office locations, job roles, etc.)
- **Properties**: the stored data elements about the content itself as it relates to the process of creating and managing it in the electronic environment (this might include the creation date, version, author's name, when it was last updated, file format, etc.).

The important concept from a knowledge perspective is the critical need to tie content to the real world of the end user [4]. An individual's knowledge and experience is applied in the context of what he or she is doing. If knowledge and experience need to be enhanced by further information, then the method for accessing that information needs to be both efficient and relevant to the situation. Metadata is the technical facilitator for delivering that contextually relevant information [5, 6].

As described above, one current SSA web application has proved the efficacy of allowing people to access a wide range of content using context-based navigation. Work is continuing on techniques for increasing the richness of the metadata available (moving from four contextual topic dimensions to twelve or more) while at the same time simplifying the mapping of content to relevant topics throughout the content authoring process. The techniques aim to draw on, and support, content management standards such as metadata protocols (Dublin Core, SCORM, etc. [7, 8]), ontology and XML topic map definitions [9, 10], link bases, and content-focused query languages. Further work is intended to capture and analyze the patterns behind how people use the context-relevant information, in order to learn more about the specific value of content in different organizational circumstances.

Another key aspect of using metadata to support the end user is to help them see the life history of a particular item of content, and to see the relationships that it has to other items of content (via the history of its creation, the linking relationships it carries, and the aligned subject expertise of the groups involved in its creation). The insights from metadata help when interpretation of content's relevance may be required, and when unexpected circumstances occur that require a greater degree of discretion outside the scope of the content.

One of the classic knowledge management application, directories that connect people to each other and provide an opportunity to begin collaborations [11], would be enhanced by rich metadata availability. There is great value in knowing who has been involved in content creation for various topic areas, where they are now, and how they might be able to help when questions arise. This serves the dual purpose of supporting less experienced content authors, and helping more experienced people feel valued and involved, which may encourage them to delay retirement.

6   What Is the Role of a Knowledge Management Strategy?

The knowledge management strategy aims to improve SSA's ability to know what it needs to know to support its overall mission, particularly in a public environment where the needs for knowledge change over time.

The focus on a knowledge strategy provides guidance to the efforts of defining Agency metadata and developing tools to support content management, and also provides direction for the long-term creation of content. The goal is for the topics (by which content is described throughout its life) to be directly aligned with the organization's articulation of its goals, values, and knowledge, and that the topics remain relevant to the Agency over time [12]. This allows not only the content to remain relevant, but for the ideas and decisions behind the content to be traceable. The quality of the defined topics directly affects SSA's ability to turn information into knowledge.

The ability to trace how policy evolves over time is particularly important for the future creation of policies that are not in conflict with existing policy. Tracing where policy came from and how it gets used over time helps authors and other participants during the creation process. People write more effective, relevant content when they understand both the organizational goals and the user's needs in the context of the external public environment.

The knowledge strategy is also a bridge to SSA's management information (MI). Over time, the content the people use needs to be tied directly to performance in the core mission of providing benefits to the public. The value of content is not measured in isolation, but in how effectively it supports broader work performance as represented in MI. This will become increasingly important, but potentially also more difficult to find correlation, as the Agency emphasizes "self-service" for beneficiaries. Self-service focuses on claimants and third parties using Internet forms and web applications to apply for benefits and manage their benefit accounts, without interacting with – or having the knowledgeable support of – SSA's trained field staff.

One final point about MI is that each year the Agency's goals are evaluated and targets are set for performance [13], thus placing a demand on the policy and procedural content to be kept directly relevant to evolving staff performance requirements. The creation and use of new content must be guided by the Agency goals, and existing content must be evaluated to be sure it remains in line with the Agency's direction. To regularly assess the relevance of content would be a huge – and impossible – task given the hundreds of thousands of individual items of content within SSA. The collaboration between knowledgeable people and refined, contextually aware technology begins to make this alignment with Agency performance goals more possible.

7 Knowledge Management Opportunities

Strategic guidance toward a knowledge management goal, in harmony with the development of a more robust content management environment, presents a number of opportunities to support SSA's overall service vision for 2010 [1].

7.1 Supporting How SSA Plans for Change

Two things can trigger change: external mandate (legislation, executive directive, or court judgment) or internal recognition of a need to change some aspect of service delivery to improve performance. In both cases, certain things need to be assessed and discussed that can be supported by a policy knowledge management approach.

- What will be the impact of any potential change on the ability to deliver a quality service? Can this be understood by assessing the level of change that might occur in the procedures that people follow on the job?
- How best to notify the public of pending changes, and effectively open up two-way communication as the change is being developed and implemented?
- Who should be involved in the analysis and planning activities? Who has the right mix of experience in the affected subject areas?
- How long will it take to prepare the staff, the systems, and the policy/procedural materials to implement a required change [14]? What can we learn from similar change efforts, and from other types of changes to content in this subject area?

7.2 Prompting Collaboration

Collaboration in the planning and content authoring activities requires both subject expertise and end-user contextual experience. How best to find the appropriate people to be involved in a content change process? It is valuable to have an indication of who has been involved before, what sort of role they played, and the experience they brought. It is also valuable to know who from field operations could support collaboration by providing an important user perspective, experience with the context in which policy is used, and insights into how best to communicate new policy as part of the implementation process.

7.3 Encouraging Broad-Based Communities of Practice

One outgrowth of collaboration that is increasingly important is the development of communities of practice. This is particularly true where subject matter is very complex, as is the case with assessment of disability claims, or where there are unique requirements put upon a small community, such as where state or circuit court requirements deviate from a national norm. Creation of knowledge-rich, supportive collaboration environments aims to encourage ongoing communication between participants, and the formation of communities. These communities then give value back to the organization by developing, refining and critiquing policy issues in light of real world experience [15].

7.4 Learning From an Archive of Collaborative Conversation

The concept of a "history file" goes back to the early days of paper policy documents. Such a file creates a historical reference of the drafts and dialogues associated with the creation and publication of a policy document. Increasingly, the history file has become fragmented, as parts of the authoring process are managed electronically in unstructured environments like e-mail and personal word processors, while other parts may be done face-to-face with incomplete notes and references. In future years, trying to understand the context and compromises in decisions will be extremely difficult, if not impossible. Many knowledge management and content management vendors are struggling to find solutions to this problem. Strategically, one important step is to create a supportive environment for collaboration, discussion and content workflow that people *will actually use* [16]. This creates a further opportunity to mine that resource in the future, an activity that is expected to be made more effective by the use of the rich metadata environment that allows better understanding of the information that is available and the context in which it was created.

7.5 Understanding How Content Is Used in Order to Encourage Best Practices

Topic-based alignment between content and organizational job performance creates an opportunity to "suggest" appropriate content and support when performance problems appear. But how are performance problems identified?

Evaluating the use of web-based content is still somewhat rudimentary, although it has improved greatly in the past few years with the introduction of more effective software tools, such as for Customer Relationship Management (CRM). However, the adoption of such tools outside of the e-commerce environment, particularly in government, is hampered in part by the need to think about how to use the tools very differently for a vastly different user environment. Another challenge is to align the information gained from such tools with the behavior and interfaces of the legacy software applications that still dominate the working environment of front-line staff.

There is tremendous strategic value to be gained from recording and understanding how people use content to perform their job tasks, and to begin to identify patterns of performance among experienced people [4]. The intent is then to use these patterns to identify best practices, which then help applications use metadata to deliver relevant, proactive content to support less experienced staff. Additionally, usage and performance data helps the organization understand how people learn over time, which supports refinement of the content itself (valuable for less experienced authors) and potentially refinement of the instructional processes for new employees. This is particularly valuable in light of SSA's upcoming increase in newer, less experienced staff as a result of the wave of retirements anticipated among experienced staff.

7.6 Evaluating How Content Relates to Decisions and Performance

In the long-term, as the public and SSA staff will increasingly use more sophisticated software applications to interact with the Agency, there will begin to be an increasing refinement in the management information available to understand performance at a public, staff, and Agency level. Part of the knowledge management strategy is to encourage the alignment between Agency MI and the MI gathered on the development and use of content. The approach to creating this alignment is to build consensus on the common definitions of key indicators and performance measurement categories that reflect real world organizational performance [17]. These common indicators then become one or more of the topic dimensions of the content metadata definition (and in fact, help drive consensus for other topic definitions). Alongside the development of consistent, aligned MI repositories will be more effective reporting interfaces, to allow correlations between performance and content to be more easily interpreted.

8   Some Foci for Managing Implementation

The effectiveness of any strategy can only truly be determined in the way that it is implemented. In order to best manage implementation and development activities over the years, it is important to identify some of the barriers that are likely to arise in the environment [18]. Identification of these areas of risk allow for tactics to be developed that reduce risk. In particular, the participants in strategy development are assessing where the culture of the organization or the technology available in the marketplace may not yet be mature enough for true knowledge management. Some of the risks that have been identified are summarized below.

8.1   Human Challenges

Ownership and Involvement. As with any KM strategy, success is contingent in part on creating a culture of shared ownership and common purpose. How best to assess issues of proprietary "ownership" boundaries for the content, the metadata, the applications, and the resulting data from users that powers the knowledge technologies? The approach being taken is to engage users at every opportunity. Contrary to some of the literature [19], we are finding that hoarding information may be less of a barrier than is the limited time people have available, as the brain drain from retirement has already begun and remaining experienced staff are very stretched. However, the key facilitator for removing barriers to involvement appears to be having tools that are simple, easy to use, save time, and bring user benefits.

Encouraging and Supporting Use. Encouraging people to use technology remains a constant challenge. Will the leadership from the user-centered design community help both technology developers and content authors overcome barriers? The indications from previous projects are positive. Project teams and end users are more engaged, and producing positive results. Keeping the focus on the users is an integral part of the Agency software development lifecycle, which helps keep this in project plans. Alongside encouraging people to use technology is monitoring the risk of giving them *too much* technology – i.e. asking them to use a number of different, incompatible systems to complete their work. If the KM applications are not well integrated (or embedded) with their daily working tools, they are not likely to be well used.

Alignment with Goals. The need for organizational consensus around the alignment with goals and targets will drive the definition of metadata topics, and support the correlation of use with performance [19]. It is often challenging to align high-level organizational goals with individual and departmental job performance measures. Applications are being designed to allow categories for metrics to be managed directly by business leaders, without having to recode [18]. One approach being explored is to actively engage a range of stakeholder groups in this area, including executive strategic planners, people involved in the ongoing refinement of SSA MI and reporting standards, and managers in the field. The latter hold the responsibility of translating goals into front-line performance, and thus have a wealth of experience on successes and failures to create alignment.

Setting Information Priorities. Individuals and organizations put value judgments on the importance of information. To what degree will these affect knowledge priorities? It appears that it will be important to continue monitoring content priorities in terms of the resulting end-user performance that supports the overall goals of the agency. Agency managers are also encouraged to focus on areas of greatest risk from knowledge loss.

Using MI Effectively. One of the key challenges is the critical need to help management use insights they gain effectively, rather than punitively. How can the educational and cultural task be supported? It is recognized that educating management on the implications of introducing new computerized tools and resources is a far longer and more complex task than training end-users. However, it is clear that helping managers use information and MI to support the cultural shift in the knowledge community is extremely important for success [19].

8.2   Technology Challenges

Creating Usable Systems. Users and stakeholders have repeatedly identified ease of use and suitability to user tasks as critical factors for success, in user focus groups, interviews and discussions. While this is not a technical challenge, per se, it becomes an important consideration for any project that falls under the knowledge management umbrella. This may affect the way project teams are made up, schedules and activities undertaken, and the nature of evaluations carried out during and after implementation.

Setting Technical Priorities. Just as there are ongoing value judgments related to content, there are priorities and budget considerations within the Agency relating to the adoption and implementation of technology. How best to keep the knowledge management activities on the organizational agenda? It remains important to identify the value of knowledge management activities to the organization. Current discussions around how to do this include identifying areas where user performance improvement can be measured, holding briefings on the KM initiative's links with Agency goals and targets, opening a dialog about KM with participants in the e-Gov initiatives, and monitoring research and publications within the KM community.

Integration. Does the organization have the capability to integrate the required KM technologies into the existing technical environment/architecture? How does this affect the priorities for implementing parts of the overall strategy? As with all large organizations, there are many "legacy" systems, processes, and collections of content. Analysis and modeling of the environment are undertaken regularly for individual projects. It has been identified that using a standard approach to this activity should help support management's ability to identify integration opportunities and barriers. Following on from an earlier point about users having to learn and use too many applications, integration planning will have to look at opportunities for reducing the number of applications (some of which are redundant) and focusing on user tasks.

Meeting the Scale of the Task. Is it possible to find good examples of implementations (in government or the private sector) that can scale to the size of this task? Among other activities, a benchmarking study was carried out in 2002 that compared aspects of SSA KM to other government and private organizations. The findings were taken into consideration as part of the process of exploring the organizational requirements for the KM strategy. It has been recognized that ongoing discussions need to be maintained with other government and commercial organizations to learn from large-scale implementations elsewhere. It has also been important to look at modular technical approaches to allow change and migration over time, if that becomes necessary.

Alignment with Standards. To provide the greatest long-term sustainability and the ability to share with other parts of the government, the underlying tools must be based on known standards. However, are they mature enough to be implemented, and are the tools that are available commercially to support standards really "standard"? Two ongoing activities are being pursued to date: to maintain discussions with standards and government working groups, and also to approach new technologies with pilots that are tasked with assessing robustness and ability to scale up over time.

9   Conclusion

SSA has begun to address the alignment of content management activities with a growing strategy for knowledge management. Initial pilot projects are showing promise. Identifying where KM provides benefits to the Agency, and continuing to manage risks and challenges as they arise over time, creates an environment that allows the KM approach to successfully support long-term Agency and public needs.

References

1. Social Security Administration (SSA): 2010 Service Vision and Strategic Plan. http://www.ssa.gov/strategicplan2000.doc.
2. E-Government Act of 2002. http://www.estrategy.gov/it_policy_documents.cfm.
3. Matthews, W.: Knowledge Management's 'Worst.' Federal Computer Week. April 25, 2002. http://www.fcw.com/fcw/articles/2002/0422/web-know-04-25-02.asp
4. Degler, D. and Battle, L.: Knowledge Management in Pursuit of Performance: the Challenge of Context. Performance Improvement Journal, 39(6), July 2000, 25–31
5. Auffret, M.: Content Management Makes Sense – Part 1: Delivering Increased Business Value Through Semantic Content Management. Journal of Knowledge Management Practice, December 2001. http://www.tlainc.com/articl28.htm
6. Tannenbaum, A.: Metadata Solutions. Addison-Wesley, Pearson Education, New Jersey. (2002)
7. DCMI (Dublin Core Metadata Initiative). http://dublincore.org/
8. SCORM (Sharable Content Object Reference Model). Advanced Distributed Learning (ADL) Initiative. http://www.adlnet.org/
9. Topic Map standard: ISO 13250:2000-2002. Originally published May 19, 2000. http://www.y12.doe.gov/sgml/sc34/document/0322_files/iso13250-2nd-ed-v2.pdf
10. Berners-Lee, T., Hendler, J., Lassila, O.: The Semantic Web, Scientific American, May 2001.http://www.scientificamerican.com/2001/0501issue/0501berners-lee.html
11. Hansen, M.T., Nohria, N., Tierney, T. 1999: What's your strategy for managing knowledge? Harvard Business Review. 3–4:105–116
12. Zack, M. H.: Developing a Knowledge Strategy: Epilogue. In: Bontis, N. and Choo, C.W. (eds.): The Strategic Management of Intellectual Capital and Organizational Knowledge: A Collection of Readings. Oxford University Press, New York. (2002)
13. Government Performance and Results Act of 1993. http://www.whitehouse.gov/omb/mgmt-gpra/gplaw2m.html
14. Malhotra, Y.: Why Knowledge Management Systems Fail? Enablers and Constraints of Knowledge Management in Human Enterprises. In: Holsapple, C.W. (Ed.): Handbook on Knowledge Management 1: Knowledge Matters. Springer-Verlag, Heidelberg, Germany, 577–599. (2002)

15. Wenger, E., McDermott, R., Snyder, W.M.: Cultivating Communities of Practice: A Guide to Managing Knowledge. Harvard Business School, Massachusetts. (2002)
16. Preece, J.: Online Communities: Designing Usability, Supporting Sociability. John Wiley and Sons, Chichester. (2000)
17. Sure, Y., Staab, S., Studer R.: Methodology for Development and Employment of Ontology-based Knowledge Management Applications. In Sigmod Record, December 2002. http://www.acm.org/sigmod/record/issues/0212/SPECIAL/3.Sure.pdf
18. Lindgren, R., Hardless, C., Pessi, K., Nuldén, U.: The Evolution Of Knowledge Management Systems Needs To Be Managed. Journal of Knowledge Management Practice, March 2002. http://www.tlainc.com/articl34.htm
19. Storey, J. and Barnett, E.. Knowledge Management Initiatives: Learning from Failure. Journal of Knowledge Management. 2000, Vol. 4, number 2, pp. 145–156

Vigorous Knowledge Management in the Dutch Public Sector

Daphne de Groot

Ministry of the Interior and Kingdom Relations
Daphne.Groot@minbzk.nl

Abstract. Knowledge has become a critical asset. Organisations which take good care of their knowledge resources have a competitive advantage over those that do not – a principal that applies in government organisations no less than in commercial. Within society as a whole, government is also a competitor – for example, on the labour market or with national non-government organisations (NGOs) over policy. Accordingly, government also needs to be careful to manage its knowledge effectively. This study discusses the ways in which Dutch central government has tried to come to grips with the concept of knowledge management in the public sector.

1 Introduction

The increasing complexity of society due to information and communication technology (ICT), globalisation, integration of products (e.g. multi-media) and services (e.g. bank assurance) and the proliferation of specialist professions and products has made ours a knowledge-based world. According to the Ministry of Economics, indeed, the Netherlands is 'rapidly developing into a knowledge-intensive economy. An increasingly large part of our income has to be earned by supplying knowledge-intensive services and by manufacturing and marketing knowledge-intensive products. "Knowledge" is becoming a key production factor' (Ministry of Economics, 2000).

Where once data, and later information, were the most important factors in managing an organisation, now the key control mechanism is knowledge (Weggeman, 1997; Davenport and Prusak, 1998). And yet the concept of knowledge management is not a concept which directly fits the essence of public administration. Rather, knowledge management is a concept imported from the trade and industry, and governed by principals such as effectiveness, economic efficiency and output. Knowledge management is therefore ultimately aimed at optimising knowledge within the organisation to increase productivity and profit.

In the public sector, by contrast, even though the principals of efficiency and effectiveness are well established, knowledge management must answer to different priorities (Van Duivenbode and Lips; in Van Duivenbode, Lips and Frissen (eds.), 1999). Profit and money-making are not prevalent in public management. Rather, concepts like justice and equality, legitimacy and responsibility predominate.

M.A. Wimmer (Ed.): KMGov 2003, LNAI 2645, pp. 94–99, 2003.
© IFIP 2003

2 Knowledge Management in the Public Sector

Due to the complexity of the policy-making process, the information on which it depends comes partially from within the organisation itself, but also in a large part from outside. Civil organisations, special interest groups, universities and research institutions all contribute knowledge out of which policy is developed. The problem is that in a complex society vast quantities of knowledge are available, but not always the right knowledge, inside as well as outside the governmental organisation. From the internal perspective, this superabundance is a liability because knowledge resides above all inside people's heads and therefore in large governmental organisations it is hard to access people's knowledge. The result of this is, that:
- (Crucial) knowledge is available only to small group of people.
- Knowledge is often not available to the people who need certain knowledge.
- Employees are overloaded with irrelevant information.

To handle these problems different government departments have attempted to develop knowledge management instruments. As these attempts make clear, knowledge management has become an important controlling device within the public sector. The Ministry of the Interior and Kingdom Relations, therefore, has tried to understand the possibilities of knowledge management for central government.

3 Vigorous Knowledge Management

The Ministry of the Interior and Kingdom Relations has a coordinating role within the public sector in the Netherlands. It consequently plays an important part in constructing a governmental vision of knowledge management. Without this broadly based vision the outlines of any knowledge management system are likely to be fragmented, leading to an insufficiently comprehensive application of the concept to government. The coordinating role of the Ministry of the Interior and Kingdom Relations with respect to knowledge management in the Netherlands can be defined according to three imperatives:
1. Developing a policy vision, which accommodate knowledge management initiatives for the entire central government.
2. Taking the lead by creating a framework of knowledge management for the entire central government while allowing departments to develop their own individual knowledge initiatives.
3. Monitoring development across central government and letting 'a hundred flowers blossom' without imposing a single rigid definition of the concept.

In their article about knowledge management in the public sector, Van Duivenbode and Lips (in Van Duivenbode et al., 1999) conclude that the public sector needs 'diversity in its approach to the concept knowledge management, with attention focused on the culture of the organisation, the routines of the organisation and the environment of the organisation, as well the organisation itself, the employees as the role of ICT as a facilitating instrument of knowledge management (p. 334, translation by the author). According to Van Duivenbode and Lips, this means that knowledge management in the public sector requires a multiform approach.

The Ministry of the Interior and Kingdom Relations came to its position on government knowledge management by taking the lead in developing a framework in which knowledge management initiatives could be pursued. To create this framework, the Ministry organised a conference in which several other ministries presented their initiatives in the knowledge management arena. It emerged that several different approaches to knowledge management were being pursued simultaneously in central government, leading to considerable misunderstanding. A second conference was therefore organised in which task forces were formed around specific issues, like resource management, organisational structure and information and communication technology. But rather than seeing these issues as the focal points around which knowledge management should be organised, it was argued that knowledge management should instead be a combination of people, organisation and technique.

In order to get a more public administration perspective on where the focus of knowledge management should lie in the public sector in the Netherlands, the Ministry of the Interior and Kingdom Relations defined a research mandate to investigate the feasibility of a 'conceptual' knowledge management framework, in which the different components of the public sector could be positioned. Based on the work of Van Duivenbode, Lips and Frissen (1999), it was felt that there was a need for a more flexible, multiform concept, especially for central government – but grounded in a recognisable and practical framework.

Based on interviews with key players in the field and approximately 40 working studies about knowledge management from ministries, a conceptual framework was created. The creation of the framework is a crucial step in structuring the understanding of the application of knowledge management in general and specifically in the public sector.

Table 1. The framework consists of the following configurations

Responsive knowledge management	Reflexive knowledge management
Motive: business-related motives	Motive: policy motives
Definition of knowledge: informative knowledge	Definition of knowledge: interactive knowledge
Definition of management: business management	Definition of management: policy management
Model: business-related model	Model: policy model
Scope: hidden projects	Scope: high-profile projects
Approach: strengthening of knowledge management	Approach: strengthening of knowledge use
Instruments: responsive instruments	Instruments: reflexive instruments
Integrative knowledge management	Innovative knowledge management
Motive: strategic motives	Motive: administrative motives
Definition of knowledge: experience-based knowledge knowledge	Definition of knowledge: new
Definition of management: strategic management	Definition of management: administrative management
Model: strategic model	Model: administrative model
Scope: massive projects	Scope: radical projects
Approach: strengthening of knowledge sharing	Approach: strengthening of knowledge creation
Instruments: integrative instruments	Instruments: innovative instruments

In short, the different knowledge management configurations contribute to the following goals:

- Responsive knowledge management, used in order to optimise knowledge management with a view to the ideal of the digital organisation.
- Reflexive knowledge management, used in order to strengthen knowledge use with a view to the ideal of the professional organisation.
- Integrative knowledge management, used in order to promote knowledge sharing with a view to the ideal of intelligent organisation forms.
- Innovative knowledge management, used in order to increase knowledge creation with a view to the ideal of flexible organisation forms.

The conceptual framework offers an understanding of how knowledge can work. To stimulate this process of recognition and determination, an initial proposal for a diagnostic and intervention instrument is sketched below (Ministry of the Interior and Kingdom Relations, 2001)

Step 1   Assess the nature of the setting applicable to the government ministry, or rather ministry units, by first assessing the nature of the knowledge base: how unequivocal is this knowledge base? Are issues measurable: can facts be gathered? Are the facts controversial: is it clear what facts are important? Can the significance of the facts be determined: are the facts self-explanatory?

Step 2   Assess the nature of the setting by evaluating the stability of issues: is the existing setting under discussion? Do the issues attract much political, parliamentary and/or media attention? Is there little time for administrative action? Are the existing policy structures under discussion?

Check 1: In taking both these steps consider the question of whether the setting in which the ministry or the unit finds itself is a 'split' setting. It may be that specific issues or knowledge field belong to different settings. The wider the knowledge management horizon and the more ministry units covered, the more likely this is.
Check 2: In taking both the above steps consider whether the knowledge base and/or issue stability will be subject to change in the short or medium term.

Step 3   Combine steps 1 and 2 and identify the type settings (a quiet setting: a setting in which it is relatively clear what the policy players have to do and in which there is sufficient time to work on the issues; an unquiet setting: a setting in which the knowledge field is clear, but in which the issues are or become unstable, thereby necessitating rapid action; an expert setting: a setting in which experts call the shots because the issues are complex and expert views differ; and/or an open setting: a setting in which much is unclear at any given time, experts are in disagreement and existing policy structures are under discussion – possibly at a fundamental level).

Step 4   Choose the type(s) of knowledge management applicable to the setting(s), that is responsive, reflexive, integrative or innovative knowledge management. Choose the correct motive, definitions, models, scope, introduce different, appropriate knowledge management projects.

Step 5   Create a project structure or team(s) or determine the duties of existing directorates or departments in accordance with the type of scope, so that the project is given organisational legitimacy.

Steps 6   Work on the implementation of the project or projects from the correct organisational embedding. The more open the setting the more 'force' will be necessary (in other words, more documents, more meetings and so forth). In quieter settings this can be done much more unobtrusively.

Check 3: Monitor whether the nature of the setting changes and, if so, go back to step 1.

4 Experiences with the Conceptual Framework

If we examine the usefulness of the managerial diagnostic and intervention instrument in implementing knowledge management in central government, we see that the framework on which the instrument is based is very useful, but the method of implementing differs from the steps described earlier. Two ministries have used different approaches to applying the framework. The Ministry of the Interior has focused primarily on the outline of the responsive knowledge management and the Ministry of Social Affairs and Employment initially filled in the four configurations on behalf of their internal positioning and definition.

4.1 Ministry of the Interior and Kingdom Relations

The focus of the Ministry of the Interior and Kingdom Relations has been on the issue of responsive knowledge management. The Ministry sees it as its main task to enlarge the responsive capacity of the public sector, for which legal knowledge is the most crucial element. Policy is often based on legal functions, such as laws, (international) treaties, etc. The Ministry has conducted a research project, therefore, to find ways in which legal knowledge can be made more accessible, usable and deliverable (O&I Management, 2003). The study concluded that it is hard to store legal information in such a way that it can be used comprehensively by policy makers with its original context intact. Even 'hard' explicit information like legal information can only be understood in its proper context. The researchers therefore proposed a central implementation of legal knowledge management from a shared services point of view. That means that the technical management would be organized centrally, but the content managed locally.

In conclusion, just to enlarge the responsive capacity of government by making legal information accessible is not enough. Responsive knowledge needs a human, organizational and contextual perspective.

4.2 Ministry of Social Affairs and Employment

The Ministry of Social Affairs and Employment used the conceptual framework to gain insight into the task of the Department Research and Development. In a study (Ministry of Social Affairs and Employment, 2002) for each of the configurations priorities and functions were identified. For each of the configurations instruments were then defined for each target group and each main task. No attempts were made to implement the framework according to steps of the diagnostic and intervention instrument to effectuate it in policy-making. Unfortunately however, before the implementation of the framework could be effected, the Department Research and Development was dissolved with no real use of the instruments having been made.

5 Conclusion

Due to the diverse character of the public sector, effective knowledge management demands the development of a multiform conceptual framework that can be employed by ministries to design their knowledge function. The framework as presented in the paper proofed its significance by helping to understand knowledge management in the public sector. The diagnostic and intervention instrument, in which issues and facts dictate the setting, has not worked; the managerial approach in a policy environment has not proven its value yet.

References

1. Ministry of Economic Affairs. *Pilot project: Balancing with knowledge*. Department of General Technology Policy. The Hague, June 1999
2. Ministry of the Interior and Kingdom Relations. *Vigorous knowledge management*. Department of Public Information Policy, The Hague, 2001
3. Ministry of Social Affairs and Employment. *Knowledge management in research and development*. Department of Research and Development, The Hague, 2002
4. Davenport, T.H. and Prusak, L. *Working knowledge. How organizations manage what they know*. Harvard Business School Press, 1998
5. O&I Management partners. *Juridisch kennismanagement voor de Rijksoverheid*. Department of Public Information Policy, The Hague, 2003 (in Dutch)
6. Van Duivenbode, Lips and Frissen (eds.) *Kennismanagement in de Publieke Sector*, Elsevier bedrijfsinformatie bv, The Hague, 1999 (in Dutch)
7. Weggeman, M., *Kennismanagement: Inrichting en besturing van kennisintensieve organisaties*. Scriptum management, Schiedam, 1997 (in Dutch)

MPs and KM: How Strict ICT Policy Has Enabled Development of Personalized KM Services in the Parliament of Finland

Olli Mustajärvi

The Parliament of Finland, FIN-00102 Helsinki
olli.mustajarvi@eduskunta.fi

Abstract. The Parliament of Finland has launched active development of KM services. The cornerstones of the development have been the following characteristics: strict and centralized ICT-policy, ambitious visions and focused development plans, determined building of applications and services, open standards (e.g. SGML) in information production and utilization and openness in Parliament's web services. The KM projects of the Parliament have assessed the effects of KM on work cultures, produced a vision for practical KM activities, made concrete functional targets and means of action, and provided a basis for further KM development. The MPs have piloted the electronic workplace for the committee work, mobile services and first parts of MPs' personal toolbox. Perhaps the most interesting results are connected with the personal missions of MPs. The final result of this development is personalized KM and ICT services for MPs.

1 Introduction

National parliaments utilize information and communication technology (ICT) widely and diversely. This can be noticed clearly for instance in the biennial ICT conferences of Nordic Parliaments 1988-2000 and in the annual ICT conferences of ECPRD (the European Centre for Parliamentary Development and Research) 1990-2001. However, there are only a few reports, which describe the utilization of KM in Parliaments.

MPs utilize ICT for administration, communications and information management, both information gathering (research) and dissemination (publishing). "Using ICTs to do an existing job better is not however sufficient. MPs must respond to the use of ICT by those outside Parliament, including developments such as on-line democracy." [2].

E-government and e-democracy are complex information intensive and wide areas so we must use the modern solutions and innovations of ICT. Perhaps the most important "tool" is Knowledge Management [1]. The following definition of KM has been accepted in the Finnish Parliament's KM project [3]:

"Knowledge Management consists of systematic development and management of the knowledge, competence and expertise possessed currently by the organisation, and that being acquired by it in future. To be capable of managing knowledge, an organisation must be aware of what knowledge it has, where this knowledge resides,

M.A. Wimmer (Ed.): KMGov 2003, LNAI 2645, pp. 100–105, 2003.

and how to access the knowledge in question. Practical measures within knowledge management are especially knowledge acquisition, processing, storage and distribution. Increasing the effectiveness of knowledge dissemination and sharing is the only way for an organisation to increase remarkably its knowledge."

2 The Case Environment

The Finnish Parliament has 200 MPs and employs 600 civil servants. The unicameral Parliament was established in 1906. It enacts legislation, decides on taxes and state expenditures. It oversees the ministries and their subordinates and approves international treaties. Parliament also participates in the national preparation of EU affairs (www.eduskunta.fi).

ICT era started in Parliament in 1985 when the strategy for the development of IT systems for parliamentary work was accepted [4]. From the very beginning development and utilization of ICT has been based on information processes.

Among other things this innovative development enabled close integration on session hall systems with the plenary session work in 1992 and the rapid adoption of Internet-based www-technology in 1995 when production databases were connected directly to www-servers. With the help of Parliament's www-service citizens can see very accurately and without delay what is going on in Parliament: for instance the agendas of sessions and committee meetings, MPs' speeches, voting results and all parliamentary documents are available in Internet –Parliament is really in a glass cage. Parliament's web-service has often received recognition for its advanced and wide content of information, for instance [9]. A structured document standard (SGML/XML) was adopted for document production, which means that knowledge produced by Parliament is now available in an easy-to-use form for in-house and external use.   This forms a base for managing and utilization Parliament's own information, a part of its KM [10]. In addition, structured legislative documents have enabled the semiautomated consolidation of the Finnish jurisdiction database. This database is open to all and can be used without costs (service was opened in 2nd Feb 2002, www.finlex.fi).

2.1 MPs and ICT

MP Suvi Linden has researched how MPs do their job and manage information in "the new ICT world" [7]. The results of research were that when the use of ICT increased the ICT services and tools became more useful, even necessary. At the same time there were more and more people involved to work with MPs –so active MPs build networks by the help of ICT.

2.2 ICT Policy

The organisation of ICT in Parliament has been centralized. Some benefits have been achieved, for instance common ICT standards, an effective way to utilize knowledge and bulk discounts on purchases. On the other hand centralized policy can cause some disadvantages, for instance ICT department does not fully understand business processes and it can be unclear who owns ICT applications.

Centralized services are for instance infrastructure, the main parliamentary applications, the purchase of ICT ware and training.

3 KM in the Parliament

3.1 ICT and KM

Parliament has excellent preconditions for its KM. Intranet (The Fakta system) is a central distribution channel for all information. For the most part, all written material produced by Parliament is accessible through this network, mainly in the form of structured documents. In addition, most of the Parliament's ICT infrastructure is of a high standard and well-functioning

3.2 KM Project

The Parliament's KM project was carried out during the period September 2000-March 2001. The project objective was to produce a vision for practical KM activities, to make concrete functional targets and means of action, and to provide a basis for further KM development. MPs and their personal assistants were involved in this work in the capacity of clients, as one project team. The main results are set out in a reform programme in which necessary activities have been described [3]. The results of KM project have been published in a book "Developing and Implementing Knowledge Management in the Parliament of Finland" [11].

Most activities of the reform programme are directly connected with the MPs' and their assistants' work and services offered to them. MPs have piloted the new electronic workplace for committees. In the mobile pilot ICT services and electronic workplace has been utilized by means of different mobile devices [8].

4 MPs' Missions

In the KM project one project team was MPs' and their personal assistants' team (12 people together). In the team's opinion people's ability to manage an increasing amount of the information, information deluge, is the problem of KM. Thinking the solution to the problem, "...a team of MPs decided to propose a new approach where each MP individually defines his or her own personal mission. Subsequently, these definitions would be used as aids in various KM processes. A mission is an MP's personal description of the essentials and core interest areas in his or her work." [11]. Four MPs in the team described their personal missions in the mind-map form.

Every MP has responsibility to make her/his own mission. The goal is to make all missions according to the same framework, which would make it easier to utilize missions in production of shared profiled services. Missions are made on the voluntary base.

It is very interesting to think, what missions of groups (parliamentary groups, committees, citizens etc) could be and would it be possible to utilize them in the same way as personal missions?

5 Utilization of MPs' Missions

Among others, the MP's mission can be exploited in the following areas [3]:
− to organise MP's personal work
− database structures
− e-mail organisation
− paper document archives
− to facilitate co-operation between MPs and their personal assistants
− to describe MP's duties
− to make easier co-operation with MPs and civil servants
− for developing profiled information services for the Parliamentary groups or committees
− for making a common concept for all services

The earlier mentioned MPs' team has started to develop and pilot the utilization of MPs' missions. In the team there are four MPs and their personal assistants. According to the first discussions, the biggest problems are: How MPs could best use information systems and manage basic information management operations, what to do with the information deluge (e-mail) and the vast area of parliamentary affairs.

Perhaps the most interesting possibility to utilize missions is to create personal interfaces for information retrieval and management. These interfaces, the trees of information/knowledge, are in a mind-map form. Information has been organised in the trees according to the missions.

In this phase, the personalized interfaces have been implemented and updated manually by Parliament's ICT office in co-operation with information service because the available automated solutions were not suitable for Parliament's present ICT solutions.

At least in principle Parliament's information services must cover all activities of the society. When information services are divided into small components, it is possible to build personalized and profiled services by the help of these components, for committees, parliamentary groups and MPs. Both the producer and the user get benefit: The producer is able to produce customized services instead of standard services with the same resources and on the other hand users will have solutions to the information deluge (at least partial solution). Now, in this phase, it seems to be reasonable that only certain parts of personalized services will be realized in the near future, for instance parts of news services, document management and Internet information services. Profiled services have been piloted successfully for the Committee for the Future [8]. The purpose is to take these profiled services in use in every committee this year.

6 Outcomes and Lessons Learned

I think that the strict and concentrated ICT policy has made it possible to build a good base for common services (information systems, data bases, personalized and profiled information services, infrastructure etc). Would it be the same situation with decentralized policy? Probably it would quite different, departments would have their own information systems, there would be no common databases and so on. Many visitors from different government and private organizations have told that the situation in their organizations is much worse and for instance it is almost impossible to establish really useful www-services –because of all information was spread all over the organization.

How is this in a large scale? How should e-government services be developed in society, a centralized or decentralized model? At least in Finland the biggest problem in e-government is that almost all services have been developed vertically, every ministry has been very active but more horizontal cooperation would have been needed. I believe that we would have a much better situation if the government had strict, also horizontal ICT policy and there would be real leadership somewhere in government. Probably plenty of resources have been used inefficiently.

One interesting model for e-government services and platform have been developed in the research project supported by European Commission [6]. In the project it has been created also a new GovML description language (based on XML). It is interesting to notice similarities with the results of Eulegis project. Eulegis was started by the initiative of the Finnish Parliament and supported by European Commission. Eulegis developed a prototype by which all EU and EU national legislative databases could be connected for searching and utilizing purposes [5]. Perhaps something like this would be needed for the whole e-government strategy.

I think that this KM project and pilots have been really a good start to develop better services. Some piloted services and solution have been taken into production use after parliamentary election (March 2003). We have established a new MP team which will start to develop MPs' workprocesses and solutions to master information and knowledge. In addition to these eGovernment type activities we have to develop also eDemocracy activities and solutions. I think that the results of KM project form a good basis for more demanding eDemocracy progress.

References

1. Burden, P.R., MacIntosh, M. and Srikantaiah, T.K. Knowledge management : the bibliography. Information Today, Medford, NJ, 2000.
2. Campbell, A., Harrop, A. and Thompson, B. Towards the Virtual Parliament - What Computers can do for MPs. *Parliamentary Affairs*, *52* (3).
3. Eduskunta Eduskunnan tiedon ja tietämyksen hallinta [knowledge management in the Finnish parliament]. Eduskunta, Helsinki, 2001.
4. Eduskunta   Automaatiotyöryhmä   Eduskunnan   lainsäädäntötyöhön   liittyvän tietojenkäsittelyn kokonaistutkimus [IT strategy of the Finnish Parliament]. Eduskunta, Helsinki, 1985.
5. Eulegis-project. European User Views to Legislative Information in Structured Form (EC DGXIII/AD4002) -project documentation, European Commission, 2000.

6. Glassey, O., A One-Stop Government Architecture based on the GovML Data Description Language. in *2nd European Conference on e- Governance ECEG 2002*, (St Catherine's College Oxford, United Kingdom, 2002), MCIL.
7. Linden, S. Kansanedustajan työn tiedonhallinta vuorovaikutusympäristössään uuden tieto- ja viestintätekniikan valossa [MP's information management in the era of new ICT]. University of Oulu, Department of Information Processing Science, 1998.
8. Mustajärvi, O., The Information Needs of MPs as a basis for the New Electronic Workspace: A Finnish Case Study. in *2nd European Conference on e- Governance ECEG 2002*, (St Catherine's College Oxford, United Kingdom, 2002), MCIL.
9. Ronaghan, S.A. Benchmarking E-government: A Global Perspective. United Nations, DPEPA, New York, 2002.
10. Salminen, A., Lyytikäinen, V., Tiitinen, P. and Mustajärvi, O., Experiences of SGML standardization: The case of the Finnish legislative documents. in *Proceedings of the 34th Annual Hawaii International Conference on System Sciences*, (Maui (HA), 2001), IEEE Computer Society Press.
11. Suurla, R., Markkula, M. and Mustajärvi, O. Developing and Implementing Knowledge Management in the Parliament of Finland. Parliament of Finland, Helsinki, 2002. http://www.eduskunta.fi/fakta/vk/tuv/KM_Finnish_Parliament.pdf

GovML: A Markup Language for Describing Public Services and Life Events

Gregory Kavadias and Efthimios Tambouris

Archetypon S.A., 236 Sygrou Av., Athens, 176-72, Greece
{gkavadias, tambouris}@archetypon.gr
http://www.archetypon.gr/egov/

Abstract. The Governmental Markup Language (GovML) has been proposed by the IST eGOV project to define structures (or vocabularies) for governmental data and metadata. In this paper, the GovML data vocabularies for describing public services and life events are presented. Technically, GovML is a proposed format for XML documents. Its adoption by public authorities will allow users (citizens, businesses) of public services to exploit the potential of XML technology. For example, users will be able to access governmental information in a unified presentation style through multiple communication channels (web browsers, mobile phones, handheld devices etc).

1 Introduction

E-government is becoming increasingly important for all European Union Member States. A large number of e-government initiatives and projects are currently under way, aiming to enhance access and delivery of government services to benefit citizens, business partners and employees [3]. Public authorities are providing a number of public services online. At the presentation layer, public services are grouped based on users needs and intentions e.g. in life events. Consequently, there is a substantial amount of information describing public services and life events.

The main idea behind this paper is that the information describing public services and life events could be standardised. We believe that public organisations and consumers of public services could both benefit from a standard electronic format for the description of public services. Public authorities would have a common structure for describing all their services, thus production and management of governmental information would be eased, while interoperability with other agencies would be fostered. On the other hand, users would more easily navigate through different public services. The more structured the information is, the more easily a human can understand it and use its information to make knowledgeable decisions

In this paper the Governmental Markup Language (GovML) data vocabulary is presented as a proposed document structure for the public sector. GovML is the result of research work conducted within the IST eGOV project [9]. GovML aims to overcome the arbitrary principles applied to the structure and presentation of governmental content at an international level.

From a technical point of view, GovML data vocabularies are a tailored XML implementation, suggesting a common XML structure for public services descriptions

M.A. Wimmer (Ed.): KMGov 2003, LNAI 2645, pp. 106–115, 2003.

and life events. By adopting GovML, users (citizens and businesses) are given the opportunity to access governmental information through multiple access channels. Moreover, GovML is characterised by flexibility and extensibility, thus facilitating its maintenance and adaptation to potential new requirements.

The rest of this paper is organised into 6 sections. In section 2 some background information is given, while in section 3 the motivation for the invention of GovML is explained. In section 4 the methodology and its outcome (i.e. the specified vocabularies for public services descriptions and life events) are presented. In section 5 an overview of the technical implementation and the utilised XML schema mechanisms are analysed, along with an example and a usage scenario. Finally in section 6 the main conclusions are presented.

2 Background

2.1 The IST eGOV Project

The work reported in this paper was carried out within the eGOV project. eGOV is a two-years EC-funded RTD project within the 5th Framework Program of the European Commission. The main objective of the project is to specify, develop, deploy and evaluate an integrated platform for realising online one-stop government. The eGOV platform will allow the public sector to provide citizens with information and services, based on 'life-events'. This platform will be deployed and evaluated in Austria and Greece.

The main technical objectives of the eGOV project include the specification and development of:

- The next generation of online one-stop governmental portals and the supporting network architecture. This sort of portals will feature a number of advanced characteristics: access from different devices including WAP-enabled devices, personalisation, customisation, multilinguality, support of push services etc.
- The Governmental Markup Language (GovML), an open XML document structure aiming to support data exchange among public agencies and their consumers.

Qualitative, effective and efficient access to governmental information is a critical success factor of e-government. The eGOV project aims to address this requirement by providing an integrated platform for one-stop government, along with the supporting process models.

2.2 Life Event Approach to Access of Governmental Information

The concept of "life events" is an increasingly used guiding metaphor for accessing public services and information online. Within the eGOV project, life events are defined as follows:

"Life events describe situations of human beings that trigger public services." Examples of life events are: getting married, traveling abroad etc.

In a similar way, "business situations describe topics of companies and self-employed citizens that trigger public services or interactions with public authorities."

Examples of business situations are: founding a company, (re-) constructing factory premises etc.

Life events and business situations can be used as meaningful metaphors at the presentation layer, aiming to facilitate and enhance users' access to governmental information and services. This approach gives users the opportunity to disregard the complexity and functional fragmentation of the public sector [16]. For example, the "getting married" life-event, ideally should enable citizens to electronically handle all possible interactions with the public agencies.

3 Motivation for Work

Knowledge management can be perceived as "how an organisation can get its arms around all of the knowledge and information held in the hundreds of gigabytes of information in the organisation's computer systems, e-mail systems, word documents, spreadsheets and so on, in order to meet its objectives" [13].

Unless organized, information provided by public authorities cannot be retrieved and disseminated to the consumers of public services

Thus, the demand for knowledge management within public authorities necessitates the creation of standard templates for describing information provided by public authorities.

Most of public agencies at an international level, make an effort to offer a significant portion of their services online. In this respect, citizens and businesses can benefit from Internet technology, as they can be electronically informed and interact with the public sector. Provided with remote access to public information and services, consumers are given the opportunity to avoid queuing, losing time for moving to several public authorities, finding contact persons, etc.

Online information however, does not comply with a specific structure. Furthermore, it is not characterized by unified presentation style and principles. On the contrary, it is very common that each public authority applies its own format to the presentation of information, hence preventing users from a unique experience, whenever they interact with the public sector.

Apart from presentation of pubic information, another important issue in online one-stop government is interoperability. It is common in e-government projects that several governmental data need to be exchanged among public authorities. Each authority however, usually stores governmental information in a proprietary data format and storing system e.g. HTML, ASCII, RDBMS etc. Therefore data conversion must take place from the format adopted by one public authority to the format adopted by others, whenever exchange of data is needed. This data conversion can become a significant overhead to the Information Technology (IT) responsibilities of public authorities.

The evolution of mobile phones and handheld devices are another challenge when implementing online one-stop government through governmental portals. It is common that public authorities wish to provide their users with access to governmental information and services through multiple communication channels: web browsers, mobile phones, Personal Digital Assistants (PDA) etc. This allows governmental information and services to be available 24 hours a day, via multiple access devices from everywhere, even on the move.

4 Towards Identification of GovML Elements

The proposed Governmental Markup Language (GovML) addresses the common structure, presentation and interoperability challenges stated in section 3. The eGOV consortium consists of 10 partners coming from Austria, Finland, Germany, Greece and Switzerland. Partners represent a mixture of private IT companies, academic and research institutes and public administrations. All parties collaborated closely in order to determine the components of the proposed document structure, for the description of public services and life events. The steps that were followed towards the specification of GovML data elements are (Figure 1):

1. All partners performed an analysis of existing governmental portals and Web sites. Existing governmental sites at an international level [1], [2], [7], [14], [15], [17], [18] were investigated and best practices of online eGovernment were taken into account. The investigation focused on structure and presentation of the public sector content, from the users' point of view.
2. Public services provided by various public organisations were investigated. Each partner of the eGOV consortium investigated a number of public services that were provided not only online but also non electronically. Subsequently, the necessary elements needed to describe the investigated public services and life events were identified.
3. The contributions of the eGOV consortium's partners were assembled and the first version of the proposed GovML data elements was circulated among the partners.
4. All partners commented on the first version of GovML data elements and proposed refinements. All comments were gathered and evaluated. Thereafter a new version of the GovML data elements was produced and circulated to the eGOV consortium for consultation.
5. Iteration among steps 3 to 5 was realised until consensus was reached between all partners of the eGOV consortium.
6. The final GovML data elements were reported according to ISO/IEC 11179-3 standard [8].

The final GovML data structure consists of three vocabularies, two for describing public services and one for life events. Technically, each sub-vocabulary is characterized by a set of predefined XML elements. The three GovML vocabularies are analysed in the next paragraphs.

Generic description data vocabulary for public services
This vocabulary defines a common standard for the content of all public authorities at a national level. Such governmental content is created only once, at a national level. This type of content could be normally based upon a governmental law, so it can be adopted by all public agencies of a country. Examples of data elements are: title, procedure, required documents, etc.

Specific description data vocabulary for public services
This vocabulary caters for the creation of content related to a public service provided by a specific public authority. It can be considered as a specialization of the generic description vocabulary, because the values of some elements of this vocabulary

depend on the public authority, which provides the public service. Some of its elements are: name and address of the public authority, public servant contact details, delivery channel of the service, etc.

It should be noted that the generic and specific data vocabularies for public services have many common elements.

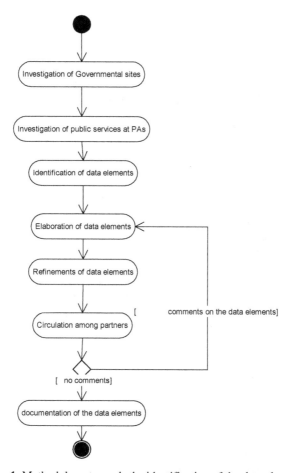

Fig. 1. Methodology towards the identification of the data elements

Data vocabulary for life events and business situations
This vocabulary defines a set of elements necessary to describe any every day life event or business situation. Elements of this vocabulary are a subset of the generic description data vocabulary for public services. The three GovML data vocabularies are listed in Table 1.

Table 1. GovML data vocabulary

	Public Services		Life Events
	Generic description	**Specific description**	**Description**
1	identifier	identifier	identifier
2	language	language	language
3	title	title	title
4	description	description	description
5	attention	attention	attention
6	faq-list	faq-list	faq-list
7	eligibility	eligibility	
8	required-documents	required-documents	
9	procedure	procedure	
10	periodicity	periodicity	
11	time-to deliver	time-to deliver	
12	cost-Info	cost-Info	
13	service-hours	service-hours	
14	employee-hints	employee-hints	
15	citizen-hints	citizen-hints	
16	related-services	public-authority-name	related-services
17	audience	Public authority department	
18	public-authority-type	e-documents	
19	law	delivery-channel	delivery-channel
20	result	cost	
21		contact-details	
22		service-code	
23		automation-level	
24		public-authority-address	
25		state	
26		service-name	

5 Implementation of GovML

5.1 XML Schema of GovML

From a technical point of view, the Governmental Markup Language (GovML) vocabularies are implemented using XML technologies. More specifically, in order to serialize GovML documents in XML format, an XML schema was implemented for the validation of their structure. The XML schema validation mechanism (http://www.w3.org/XML/Schema) was preferred from Document Type Definition (DTD) because it provides a richer set of data-types (including byte, date, integer etc) and allows users to derive their own data types and take advantage of inheritance of elements, attributes and definitions of data-types [10].

New XML documents describing public services or life events can emerge from the XML schema of GovML. Consequently, the appropriate XSL Transformations (XSLT) [19] should be applied for transforming GovML documents to the required format (HTML, WML etc).

XML schema can be easily extended, modified and maintained in the future according to consumer's needs. The full XML schema of GovML can be found in [2].

5.2 Example of a GovML Document

A GovML document describing a life event is illustrated in Figure 2. This document is valid against the XML schema of GovML. Data elements described in the third column of Table 1, are serialized in this sample GovML document. Hence this document is uniquely identified by the identifier element and the language of the document is characterised by the language element. In this example language is English (EN). Title and description elements are two descriptive fields. The attention field contains what the user should pay attention at and the faq-list is a list of the most frequent asked questions of users along with their answers. Related-Services includes public services related to the described life event along with their links in form of URI. Law is an optional element describing the governmental law related to the described life event.

```xml
<?xml version="1.0" encoding="UTF-8"?>
<govml:GovML xmlns:govml="http://www.egov-project.org/GovMLSchema/"
xmlns:xsi="http://www.w3.org/2001/XMLSchema-instance"
xsi:schemaLocation="http://www.egov-project.org/GovMLSchema/ file:///C:/temp/GovMLSchema.xsd">
    <description xsi:type="govml:SpecificLifeEventDescription">
        <identifier>ABC1234H</identifier>
        <language>EN</language>
        <title>Description of the life event "getting married"</title>
        <description>Getting married</description>
        <attention>This life event concerns only adults</attention>
        <faq-list>
            <item>
                <question>Is there a possibility to get married online? </question>
                <answer>Yes. Visit the national govermental portal</answer>
            </item>
        </faq-list>
        <related-services>
            <item>
                <title>Issuing a birth certificate</title>
                <uri>http://www.egovproject.org\birth# </uri>
            </item>
            <item>
                <title>Online payment</title>
                <uri>http://www.egovproject.org\online_payment#</uri>
            </item>
        </related-services>
        <law>Law with number FRC-234</law>
    </description>
</govml:GovML>
```

Fig. 2. Example of a GovM document describing a life event

5.3 GovML's Document Structure and XML Schema Complex Types

In implementation terms, the three GovML data vocabularies (generic service description, specific service description and generic life events description) are based on a number of XML schema complex types. Examples of such complex types are:

the *"address"* complex type used to describe the address of a public organisation and *"contact details"* used to describe the details of a contact person at a public agency.

Each of the three GovML data vocabularies has been built on a hierarchy of complex types. Hence GovML vocabularies are combinations of a number of complex types in a predefined order. A complex type named *"GovMLDescription"* serves as a base type that all data vocabularies (Generic and Specific service description and life event description) inherit from. The GovMLDescription base type is illustrated in Figure 3.

Language, title and description are mandatory XML elements for any type of GovML document.

GovML structures take advantage of re-usability and extensibility, which characterise XML schema complex types. As a result, GovML defines data structures, which are open, flexible, extensible end easy to maintain.

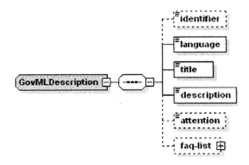

Fig. 3. *GovMLDescription* complex type

5.4 Lifecycle of a GovML Document According to eGOV Project

Certain processes at public authorities support the production and provision of GovML documents. In order to demonstrate the life cycle of a GovML document, a simplified scenario is described. It covers all stages, from document creation until its eventual depiction to consumers.

Supposing that a public authority is planning to provide citizens with the ability to obtain a birth certificate online. Firstly, a public servant is assigned with the administrator role. At a next step, the description of the public service should be generated in GovML. For this purpose, a web application named Service Description Tool (SDT) is utilised. SDT has been implemented within the eGOV project, to enable the management of GovML documents. SDT enables administrators of eGOV platform at public agencies to create, retrieve, update and delete XML documents via a user-friendly Graphical User Interface, following a sequence of predefined steps. Advanced XML techniques (i.e. indexing mechanisms based on Xpath expressions) are applied in order to enhance the efficient manipulation of GovML documents. SDT is a multilingual application, currently supporting English, German, French and Greek.

By using SDT, the administrator fills out the elements of the new GovML document. Their content derives from the related governmental law, rules at a national level and the regulations of the public authority (in case of a specific GovML). In this example, it is assumed that the administrator produces a specific service description. The element identifier aims to uniquely identify the GovML for internal management reasons (i.e. storage, retrieval etc). It is automatically filled in by the SDT. Language is an element of type xml:lang, illustrating the language of the document. It is also filled in by the system implicitly, after the administrator's language choice from the SDT. Title and description describe the title and a short description of the provided public service respectively. Eligibility element explains which citizens have the right to consume the public service i.e. who can apply for issuing a birth certificate. Required-documents element provides the list of transcripts that are considered prerequisite for the provision of the service; in our example these could be passport or identity card. Procedure describes analytically the steps that the consumer has to follow and periodicity illustrates how often the service is available. In this scenario it could have the value "every working day".

In a similar way the administrator fills in the rest of the data elements illustrated in the second column of Table 1 and stores the new GovML document via SDT. The new document is stored in the local repository of the public organisation, which contains all GovML documents of this organization.

The final step is to transform the document to a specific display format e.g. HTML or WML. This can be achieved with the utilisation of an appropriate XSLT script on the public authority side. The transformation mechanism is transparent to the users who are given the opportunity to access the desired information in multiple formats, for example HTML through a web browser or WML through a mobile phone supporting the WAP protocol.

6 Conclusions

In this paper the data vocabularies of Governmental Markup Language (GovML) were presented. GovML data vocabularies propose data structures for the description of public services and life events. GovML provides a uniform data structure that enables standardisation of public information aiming at the satisfaction of users by making information more accessible.

The better structured the information in a document is, the more easily a human can understand it, which in turn means that the human can make use of that information in order to make knowledgeable decisions. Hence, the standardization of governmental documents is a significant enabling technology for Knowledge Management.

It is anticipated that the wide adoption of GovML by public authorities will facilitate the exchange of information between public authorities and will enhance the experience of users (citizens, businesses) when accessing information provided by public organisations. For example, users will be able to access governmental information in a unified presentation style through multiple communication channels (web browsers, mobile phones etc).

Acknowledgements. The eGOV project has commenced on the 1st of June 2001 and is co-funded by the European Commission under contract IST-2000-28471. The authors would like to acknowledge the assistance of all partners of the eGOV consortium in deriving GovML. The partners of the eGOV consortium are: Siemens Austria (financial coordinator); Archetypon S. A. (administrative and scientific coordinator); TietoEnator Corporation; IKV ++, University of Linz; NCSR Demokritos; Hellenic Ministry of Interior, Public Administration and Decentralization; Municipality of Amaroussion; IDHEAP; Austrian Ministry of Public Service and Sports; and Austrian Federal Computer Center.

References

1. Austrian governmental portal, http://www.help.gv.at
2. Deliverable D231of eGOV project: GovML syntax and filters implementation
3. Deloitte Research, 2000, 'At the Dawn of e-Government: The Citizen as Customer', available at www.deloitte.com
4. E-envoy home page, http://www.e-envoy.gov.uk/
5. EzGov FlexFoundation, 'Realizing E-Government', White paper, available at http://www.ezgov.com
6. Greek governmental web site, http://www.polites.gr/
7. Hong Kong Special Administrative Region Portal, http://www.esd.gov.hk/
8. ISO/IEC 11179-3, Specification and standardization of data elements, Part 3: Basic attributes of data elements, 1994
9. IST eGov project http://www.egovproject.org
10. Mark Birbeck et al. Professional XML, Wrox Press Ltd, 2001
11. Maria Wimmer, Johanna Krenner. 2001. An Integrated Online One-Stop Government Platform: The eGOV Project. 9th Interdisciplinary Information Management Talks, Proceedings, pp. 329–337 (ISBN 3-85487-272-0)
12. OSCI, the German "de facto" standard for eGovernment, http://www.osci.de
13. Ramon C. Barquin et. Al 2001 "Knowledge Management, the catalyst for e-government", Management concepts.
14. Singapore Government Services, http://www.ecitizen.gov.sg/
15. Swiss governmental portal, http://www.admin.ch/
16. Tambouris, E., Gorilas S., Boukis G., 2001. Investigation of Electronic Government, in: Panhellenic Informatics Conference Workshop Track on "EGoverment", 8–10 November 2001, Zypern
17. U.K governmental portals, http://www.ukonline.gov.uk/, http://www.gateway.gov.uk/
18. United states governmental portal, http://www.firstgov.gov/
19. XSL Transformations (XSLT), http://www.w3.org/TR/xslt

Knowledge Management Applied to E-government Services: The Use of an Ontology

John Fraser[1], Nick Adams[1], Ann Macintosh[1], Andy McKay-Hubbard[1],
Tomás Pariente Lobo[2], Pablo Fernandez Pardo[2], Rafael Cañadas Martínez[2], and
Jesús Sobrado Vallecillo[2]

[1] International Teledemocracy Centre, Napier University, 10 Colinton Road, Edinburgh,
EH10 5DT, Scotland
{j.fraser, n.adams, a.macintosh, a.mckay-
hubbard}@napier.ac.uk
[2] Indra A.S., Avda. de Bruselas 35, 28108 — Arroyo de la Vega — Alcobendas, Madrid,
España
{tpariente, pfpardo, rcanadas, jmsobrado}@indra.es

Abstract. This paper is about the development and use of an ontology of e-government services. We identify the knowledge required to deliver e-government transaction services. Based on the SmartGov project, we describe the use of a domain map to assist in knowledge management and motivate the use of an ontology as a domain map. We describe the development of the e-government service ontology and give a few examples of its definitions. We explain why the SmartGov project has adopted taxonomies, derived from the ontology, as its domain map. We highlight issues in ontology development and maintenance.

1 Introduction

Delivery of complete e-government services requires public authorities to be able to:
- publish information that customers (citizens, private sector and other public authorities) can use
- gather information through usable forms
- react online to specific requests from customers
- manage the online exchange of items of high-value
- integrate services as much as possible

A large amount and wide range of knowledge is required to achieve this. The knowledge is applied by managers, service designers and those who operate and support the services, including information technology (IT) specialists.

This paper examines how such knowledge can be managed for the benefit of all the roles in the previous paragraph and, ultimately, customers. It is based on work done during the SmartGov project, the main deliverable of which is to be a knowledge-based software platform for design and delivery of e-government services.

First we examine the knowledge requirements in more detail and describe SmartGov. In particular we explain how a *domain map* and *knowledge units* are used

M.A. Wimmer (Ed.): KMGov 2003, LNAI 2645, pp. 116–126, 2003.

in SmartGov. We then motivate the use of an *ontology* as a domain map and explain how we derived the SmartGov e-government service ontology.

We acknowledge the difficulty in using the full ontology as a domain map and describe the use of *taxonomies* as an alternative. Finally we discuss our experiences, with reference to: the use of other ontologies; involving users; and maintaining ontologies.

2 Knowledge Management in E-government Services

2.1 The Knowledge Required

Delivering a service, whether online or offline, requires a great deal of diverse knowledge: about customers, their needs, their behaviour, applicable legislation, available resources, working practices, successes and failures, other services, *etc.*

Stages of e-government services are often distinguished. See, for example, [1-4]. The following examples of knowledge refer to some commonly identified stages:

publishing — one-way communication
Here, knowledge is required about how to present information clearly online, how to manage its publication and how customers are likely to use the information. Knowledge may be required about the design, completion and processing of forms, any of which may be supported by software. For example, if customers are offered a template that they can complete using software on their own computers, then knowledge about how to guide and constrain the completion process is required.

interacting — two-way communication
Here, knowledge is required of how to react "electronically" to requests from customers. This may include knowledge of how customers search for information and like to receive it; how to make bookings on behalf of the customer; or how to accept and maintain customer information. Issues of security may become important.

transaction — exchange of resources of nominally higher value than information
The distinguishing feature of this stage is usually the secure online exchange of items other than information, for example taxes, registration fees and licences. The knowledge required is concerned with the security and efficiency of the transactions. Efficiency is often achieved by smoothly interfacing the online system with back-office processing systems. People become more aware of issues such as trust, and the detail of the processes in which they are engaging.

integration — all aspects
"Integrate" is usually used here in the sense of integrating the provision of many, or all, of the offered services. This should lead to the blurring of distinctions in the eyes of the customer, *e.g.* which department provides a particular service or holds particular data, or where one "service" ends and another begins. Here knowledge is required of how to streamline and coordinate the design and delivery of services that already have all the required attributes from the previous stages.

2.2 An Example: The SmartGov Project

SmartGov is a project that aims to take some of the effort out of managing the knowledge. It is particularly relevant to the *transaction* and *integration* stages.

SmartGov will produce a knowledge-based core repository for government transaction services that is usable by public authority staff. It will store, in *knowledge units*, the kinds of knowledge identified above and make them available to those staff as services are being developed, deployed and maintained.

A knowledge unit is anything worth storing that may help things to be done better in the future: help, best practice guidelines, examples, stories, lessons learned, troubleshooting advice, or training material. They can be of any size. Here are some short examples:

> *A sensible choice of questions on this form can make it easy for people to fill in. I would suggest these: "What is your country of origin?", "Is English your first language?"*
> *People are often reluctant to fill in these details. This is a legacy from the days of the Poll Tax.*
> *Michael Marra in the Urban Sustainability (US) group has written a good guidebook for this. Look on the intranet under Local Guidelines.*

In SmartGov, we are accommodating unstructured knowledge units. We ask contributors merely to state which type of knowledge they are adding — guideline, lesson learned *etc.* — without analyzing the content of the knowledge unit any further. An area worth exploring in future is how to help users to structure their contributions for more fruitful sharing. In [5], for example, the use of terms such as *originating action, conditions, contribution* and *result* are proposed to describe lessons learned.

In SmartGov, the structure of the whole knowledge base is designed to reflect the domain of transaction services, as follows.

Knowledge units can be associated *directly* with the various components of electronic transaction services:

- transaction service element, *i.e.* a placeholder for data
- group of transaction service elements, *e.g.* the set of placeholders for company VAT registration data
- form, within which transaction service elements and groups are placed
- the whole transaction service

Knowledge units can also be associated *indirectly* with the transaction service components listed above, through a structure that defines the basic concepts and relationships of a domain. We refer to this structure as the *domain map*. Knowledge units can be associated with concepts and relationships in the domain map; the transaction service components can also be associated with concepts and relationships in the domain map. See Fig. 1.

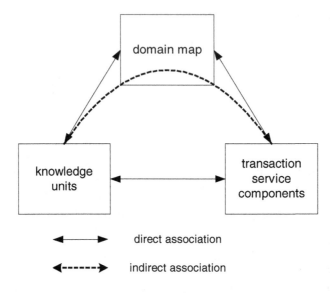

Fig. 1. Knowledge unit associations

The domain map, therefore, defines a conceptual framework with which to describe the components of a service and the knowledge associated with all aspects of the service from design to maintenance.

In SmartGov, the delivered platform — ready for use by public authority staff — will contain a defined domain map and existing knowledge units, with appropriate associations between them. There will also be a small library of template transaction service components, again with appropriate links.

Design of a new service entails the user making copies of service components and creating new ones. As this happens, the user is given access to knowledge units that are associated either directly or indirectly with the template components.

It is anticipated that new knowledge units will be added frequently by users, who can decide on associations between knowledge units and the other parts. The domain map may also change over time, but much more slowly.

As services get developed, therefore, the example knowledge units listed above might be associated directly with domain map elements such as:

knowledge unit	domain map elements
A sensible choice of questions…	ethnic origin, registration
People are often reluctant to…	tax, claim, benefit, budget
Michael Marra in the …	city, environmental provision

and with transaction service components such as:

knowledge unit	transaction service components
A sensible choice of questions…	*ethnic origin* group, *library registration* form
People are often reluctant to…	*home address* group, *council tax* service
Michael Marra in the …	*environmental assessment* service

Then, whenever a user of the platform is designing a registration form, the "sensible choice of questions" knowledge unit is available to the user if desired.

3   Ontology as a Domain Map

One of our activities in the SmartGov project has been to build an ontology for e-government services.

There are several key features of an ontology that are relevant in the context of e-government:

- An ontology precisely describes the important concepts in the domain of interest, and the relationships between them.
- The set of important terms and their definitions should be agreed between all participants within the domain, and thus form a basis for communication about the domain.
- The ontology can be specified independently from the specific application for which it is developed, enabling re-use for other e-government purposes.
- An ontology can be formalised and thus support communication between IT systems as well as between humans.

Fundamentally an ontology provides a reference for people to discuss and describe the ways in which they view and interpret a domain. So an ontology can be used to enhance understanding, or as a starting point for people to build models of the domain or a related domain. This was one of our motivations for building the e-Government service ontology, and the ontology forms part of our "framework for e-government services", which will be one of the later deliverables of the project. The framework will be of use to public authorities whether or not they have access to the SmartGov platform.

In general, we would want an ontology to represent the domain as accurately, unambiguously, completely and succinctly as possible. Then, given a particular concept or relationship, we could fully explore its meaning, in terms of associated concepts or relationships. We would, in effect, have a web that described the domain to whatever degree of simplicity or complexity we wanted, given any particular starting point. Such a structure would make an adequate domain map. This was another motivation for building the e-Government service ontology: we could use it as a domain map as shown in Fig. 1.

4   The SmartGov Ontology

4.1 Approaches to Ontology Development

A comprehensive review of ontology development methods appears in [6]. In general, methods are found to:

- take a task as the starting point
- either be stage-based or involve the evolution of prototypes
- involve two separate stages, to derive first an informal description of the domain, then a formal one
- contribute to an anticipated library of connected ontologies
- give some guidance on making choices at a variety of levels

Ontology developers also almost universally acknowledge the need for iterative refinement of an ontology.

More recently, interest in distributed development of ontologies is reflected in [7], who identified these different approaches to ontology development:

- inspiration: an individual viewpoint about the domain
- induction: description of a specific case within the domain
- deduction: extract general principles about the domain
- synthesis: build the ontology from existing partial characterisations
- collaborate to gain shared viewpoints, using an initial ontology as an anchor

4.2 Our Approach

Our approach has been a combination of induction, deduction, synthesis and collaboration. A few points are worth noting.

First, the objective of our ontology was to provide a conceptual framework at the knowledge level, rather than a "concrete artifact at the symbol level, to be used for a given purpose" [8]. This does pose problems in producing a usable domain map in SmartGov: we discuss this later in the paper.

In the sense that the aim of the SmartGov platform is to design transaction services, we did have a task as our starting point, *i.e.* the task of service design. However, we have tried to take heed of the advice in [6], that task-specific ontology development may limit the reusability of the ontology. Our intention, as stated in the previous section, has been for our e-government services ontology to be usable beyond the SmartGov platform.

We had already built a general view of the government services domain while gathering requirements for the SmartGov platform. We had access to staff at the City of Edinburgh Council (CEC) and in the General Secretariat for Information Systems (GSIS) in the Greek Ministry of Finance.

In addition, we were given access to the results of a wealth of interviews carried out within CEC in the last two years as part of Edinburgh's Smart City initiative to provide services through call centres, one-stop shops and online. From that material we extracted the most frequently-occurring terms and pruned them to a set that we considered to be representative of government services.

We studied the results of several other initiatives to categorise government services, such as [9, 10] and extracted terms from them.

We ran a workshop on social acceptance of e-government services, with members of staff at CEC and at Napier University, from which we took further terms that had not appeared elsewhere.

In total we had about 150 terms that described e-government services in general. We avoided being specific about particular services. Examples of the terms are CITIZEN, CONTACT, FORM, LETTER, PAYMENT, BENEFIT, LICENCE, RESPONSIBILITY, TRANSPARENCY, MANDATE and TRUST.

Then began the painstaking task of defining these concepts and relationships in terms of core concepts and of each other. We were greatly assisted in the task by our decision to adopt the Enterprise ontology [11] as a starting point. Its existing definitions — particularly in key areas of activity, organisation and market — proved a good basis for many of our definitions, some of which are shown later in the paper.

The Enterprise definitions of MARKET and related terms are based on the notion of SALE. We were somewhat surprised and heartened to find that many of these Enterprise terms translated very easily into the terms in our ontology to do with SERVICE. The Enterprise ontology was also influential in the mode of thinking that we adopted in producing our definitions.

Having created the natural-language definitions, we then formalised our definitions by producing a version of the ontology in the Resource Description Framework (RDF) [12]. This exercise tested the validity of our natural language definitions, several of which had to be revisited and changed. Some additional terms had to be introduced. We used the OIModeler component of the KAON tool set (see Acknowledgements) to generate the RDF.

Finally, feedback was sought from the public authorities and the previous steps were repeated. At the time of writing, this has only been achieved through discussion and workshops. Deployment trials of the SmartGov platform will yield more feedback and lead to further iteration through the ontology development steps.

4.3 Our Results

Below are some of the definitions from our ontology. A full list is available in the Results section of the SmartGov project web site (http://www.smartgov-project.org).

In the definitions below, a word in CAPITALS is defined in the e-government services ontology; a word in **BOLD CAPITALS** was already defined in the Enterprise ontology; a word with an Initial capital is a meta term; a word in *italics* is a fundamental concept that needs no definition.

The accompanying diagrams, which we produced using the KAON OIModeler, are visual representations of relevant parts of the ontology. We do not describe them in detail here: they are included to give a sense of the complexity of the ontology.

ENQUIRE: **ACTIVITY** in which a **LEGAL ENTITY** states their *desire* for INFORMATION

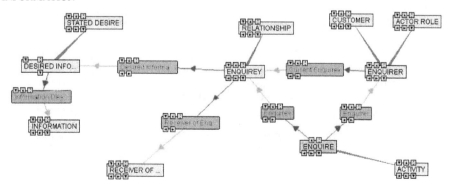

reward: a resource, authority or responsibility given by one legal entity to another on achievement of an activity for which the other legal entity has responsibility

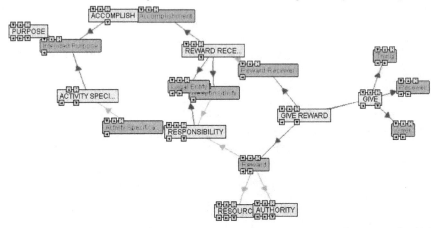

SENSE OF SECURITY: a Relationship between a **LEGAL ENTITY** and a State of Affairs in which the **LEGAL ENTITY** has BELIEF that the State of Affairs is SECURITY

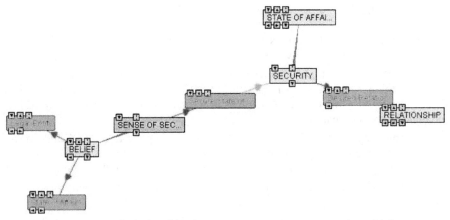

ACCOUNTABILITY: a Relationship between **LEGAL ENTITIES** in which one *must* JUSTIFY their **ACTIVITIES** to the other

APPLICATION: a Relationship between two **LEGAL ENTITIES** in which one states its *desire* for a **RESOURCE** or **AUTHORITY** from the other

FRONT DESK: a COMMUNICATION MEDIUM between a PUBLIC AUTHORITY and a CUSTOMER in which the Role of the PUBLIC AUTHORITY is played by a PERSON and the GIVING of INFORMATION is IMMEDIATE

NEED: a Relationship between a **LEGAL ENTITY** and a State of Affairs that is the *difference* between the *true* State of Affairs and a defined *standard* State of Affairs

5   The SmartGov Domain Map

As mentioned above, the ontology provides a conceptual description of e-government services. In general, it can be represented in RDF as a cyclic graph and is a complex, interwoven structure. This poses problems for its use as a domain map, both from the point of view of public authority staff maintaining the ontology, and from the point of view of the knowledge management system navigating the structure.

So, we decided to explore the use of a simplification of the ontology, in the form of a directed acyclic graph.

This graph was extracted directly from the ontology, starting from a set of relevant top-level concepts that adequately describe public authority service provision. These top-level concepts form the parents of searchable *taxonomies*, made up of concepts and structure taken directly from the ontology.

The top-level concepts are activities, actors, issues, legislation, needs, process, requirements, responsibilities, results, rights and service types.

The subsequent structure has been engineered to enable searchability and function. Each concept has an optimal number of children, which represent the domain as accurately as possible, while at the same time creating a logical search path to give an unambiguous route to the desired target. See Fig. 2.

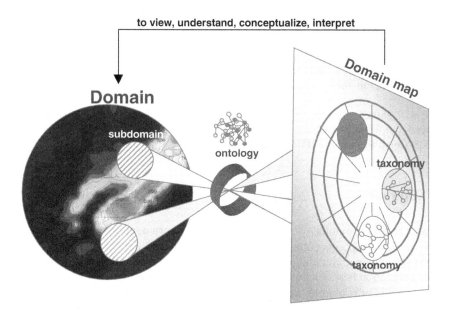

Fig. 2. Taxonomies as a domain map

6   Discussion

Using the Enterprise Ontology as a starting point proved invaluable. We did not need to reinvent the wheel and it set the style of the mode of thinking required to develop our e-government service ontology.

We are in little doubt that the existence of an ontology helps understanding, sharing and the process of building models. An apparent difficulty is the effort required to build and maintain the ontology. The people who matter — public authority staff — have constant operational duties and, even if they can spare the time, are not able to switch quickly into an "ontology" frame of mind.

Technically, too, maintenance poses extra problems. Most current effort in ontology maintenance, *e.g.* the Onto-logging project [13], is technology-based: how to maintain the integrity of the ontology when new terms are introduced or existing terms are changed. [14] describes the use of a taxonomic domain map (described as an ontology but, to our minds, not meeting the criteria for an ontology) to help people to browse multiple databases. The project has developed new ways of automating the construction and maintenance of their taxonomies.

There is, of course, another dimension: collaboration of people, either with or without the aid of technology. [7] describes a Delphi approach ([15]). We are currently considering whether Delphi-style methods might help us in ontology discussion and maintenance, particularly in view of the time pressure on staff mentioned above.

An additional problem for us is that, within the SmartGov platform, we are using an extraction of the ontology, not the full ontology, as our domain map. This means double maintenance — of the ontology and of the domain map — and the extra burden of keeping them consistent as public authorities want to change one or the other.

We will gather valuable evidence and experience of these issues as SmartGov is deployed, configured and evaluated in our participating public authorities. The project is due to finish in January 2004.

7   Summary

The main benefits from the use of the SmartGov e-government ontology are:

- The ontology supports communication by providing a shared vocabulary with well-defined meaning, avoiding ambiguities and misunderstandings. It can support communication between human agents and software agents.
- It is capable of providing flexible support for non-trivial e-transaction services. In the case of SmartGov it allows different aspects of the domain — knowledge units and transaction service components — to be interrelated to best advantage.

Acknowledgements. SmartGov (IST-2001-35399) is supported by the European Commission under the Information Society Technologies 5th Framework Programme (Key Action Line: On-line support for democratic processes).

We used the software tool OIModeler, which is part of KAON (The Karlsruhe Ontology and Semantic Web Framework), an open-source ontology management infrastructure developed by Forschungszentrum Informatik (FZI) and the Institut für Angewandte Informatik und Formale Beschreibungsverfahren (AIFB), Universität Karlsruhe. KAON is available at http://kaon.semanticweb.org/
Adrianos Evangelidis and Alexander Xenakis contributed valuable comments.

References

[1]   Bertelsmann: Balanced E-Government – Connecting Efficient Administration and Responsive Democracy. Bertelsmann Foundation Publishing House, (2001)

[2]   Howard, M.: e-Government Across the Globe: How Will "e" Change Government? Government Finance Review 2001 (2001) 6–9

[3]   Layne, K., Lee, J.: Developing fully functional E-government: A four stage model. Government Information Quarterly 18 (2001) 122–136

[4]   Papantoniou, A., Hattab, E., Afrati, F., Kayafas, E., Loumos, V.: Change Management, a critical success factor for e-Government. In: Proc. 12th IEEE International Conference and Workshop on Database and Expert Systems Applications DEXA 2001 (2001)

[5]   Webera, R., Ahab, D. W., Becerra-Fernandez, I.: Intelligent lessons learned systems. Expert Systems with Applications 17 (2001) 17–34

[6]   Jones, D. M., Bench-Capon, T. J. M., Visser, P. R. S.: Methodologies for Ontology Development. In: Proc. IT&KNOWs (1998)

[7]   Holsapple, C. W., Joshi, K. D.: A collaborative approach to ontology design. Communications of the ACM 45 (2002) 42–47

[8]   Guarino, N., Giaretta, P.: Ontologies and Knowledge Bases: Towards a Terminological Clarification. ISO Press (1999)

[9]   APLAWS. APLAWS Category List.[Online]. Available: http://www.aplaws.org.uk/products/product_acl.cfm

[10] LEAP. LEAP CUPID List. Life Events Access Project [Online]. Available: http://www.leap.gov.uk/xpedio/groups/public/documents/standards/000383.pdf

[11] Uschold, M., King, M., Moralee, S., Zorgios, Y.: The Enterprise Ontology. Knowledge Engineering Review 13 (1998)

[12] Miller, E. (1998) An Introduction to the Resource Description Framework. Corporation for National Research Initiatives [Online]. Available: http://www.dlib.org/dlib/may98/miller/05miller.html

[13] Cañadas, R.: Onto-logging Project Description. Indra, Archetypon, Deltatec, FZI, Insead, Meta4, IST-2000-28293 deliverable D0A (2002)

[14] Hovy, E.: Using an Ontology to Simplify Data Access. Communications of the ACM 46 (2003) 47–49

[15] Turoff, M., Hiltz, S. R.: Computer Based Delphi Processes. In: M. Adler and E. Ziglio, (eds.): Gazing Into the Oracle: The Delphi Method and Its Application to Social Policy and Public Health. Kingsley Publishers (1996)

Collaborative Knowledge Management and Ontologies
The ONTO-LOGGING Platform

Stelios Gerogiannakis, Marios Sintichakis, and Nikos Achilleopoulos

Archetypon S.A., 236, Sygrou Av., 17672, Athens, GR
{sgerogia, mms, nax}@archetypon.gr
http://www.ontologging.com/

Abstract. Corporate memories (stored information and internal processes) in both private and public organizations grow at an exponential rate. This growth is not only quantitative but also qualitative, in the form of increasing interdependencies between processes and information bits. Although the quantitative growth is relatively easy to handle, increasing information complexity is constantly pushing existing information systems to their limits. It is slowly becoming a self-proving fact that organizations will have to transition from the traditional model of searchable/updatable repositories of "facts and figures" to self-organizing, self-adapting corporate knowledge management systems. Ontologies and Semantic Web principles are the most promising relevant technology, now entering their mature age, allowing the creation of extensible vocabularies able to describe any semantic area. Project ONTO-LOGGING is an attempt to harness the full potential of ontologies as a flexible tool of knowledge management within any knowledge-driven organization, such as corporations and public ad-ministrations.

1   Introduction

Entering the third decade of the "information age", more and more private and public organizations are shifting their operational focus towards the service provision sector. Service provider organizations adapt their operational outcome to personalize treatment of individual customers (or citizens, in the case of the public sector). Fixed internal processes are modified in some degree to adjust to each particular case, in the form of dynamic adaptation of employee teamwork. The outcome of each process is not discarded, as it may be re-used in similar future cases. This is what is commonly referred to as *working experience*.

Increasing, or even maintaining at the same level, an organization's competence is a never-ending process of combining external stimuli with internally accumulated experience. All the different combinations of data cause the exponential increase of the organization's corporate memory, in the form of both structured (relational DB entries, spread-sheets) and unstructured (documents, memos, notes, etc.) data.

An interesting fact, about the proportion of structured and unstructured knowledge in an organization is contained in [1]. According to the author, almost 80% of an organization's knowledge is presented and stored in unstructured format, usually free text. What is even more interesting, in the author's arguments is that, on average, only

M.A. Wimmer (Ed.): KMGov 2003, LNAI 2645, pp. 127–138, 2003.
© IFIP 2003

20% of organizations' investments go in the management of that knowledge. This is especially important if we consider that, on average, EU public administrations have spent only 122 Euros per citizen on IT infrastructure [2]. Considering the volume and diversity of knowledge held in public authorities this figure is a far cry from private IT spending, although it is expected to increase by 6.8% in 2003 [3].

These facts show a lingering threat for the continuing effective operation of organizations, especially public authorities. Only a small part of accumulated knowledge can be immediately accessed and exploited via data processing software, while the larger part of an organization's corporate memory becomes increasingly chaotic and, hence, harder to locate and extract useful information from.

The rest of this document is organized as follows:

Section 2 provides some background on knowledge management in the organization. Section 3 gives a brief introduction to ontologies and their applications in the area of knowledge management. Section 4 provides a bird's-eye view of the ONTO-LOGGING platform, while Section 5 delves into a more technical description of the system. Section 6 presents the findings of the project so far in relation to existing technologies and relevant efforts. Finally, Section 7 summarizes the contents of this paper.

2   Knowledge Management

According to one definition, knowledge is

the fact or condition of being familiar with something (knowing something); this familiarity may have been gained through experience or association.

Knowledge may be recorded and stored in a variety of ways: in a person's brain, in corporate processes, in documents or electronic storage systems. In [4], knowledge is categorized in two general forms: *tacit* and *explicit*. The authors argue that, depending on the direction of knowledge transformation, knowledge creation can be categorized in *socialization, combination, externalization* and *internalization*.

Applying the previous definitions in the area of organizations, we may say that corporate knowledge (a.k.a. *corporate memory*) is an explicit and persistent representation of an organization's information and knowledge. Corporate knowledge is accessed, shared, re-used and updated by the organization's employees during the process of completing their assigned tasks [5].

Corporate knowledge requires solid foundations, as it is built upon (and around) the existing infrastructure of an organization. Figure 1 shows graphically the generic "knowledge pyramid" found in any organization, private or public [6].

Corporate knowledge is composed of hard and soft data. The different forms that knowledge comes in, result in ist uneven propagation among the different units and members of the organization. Knowledge distribution is the background process of sharing existing and new pieces of information among the organic parts of an organization, with a long-term result of increased productivity. It is interesting that, from the employee point of view, tacit knowledge is equally important with explicit knowledge in the workplace. [4]

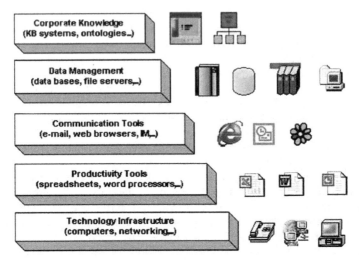

Fig. 1. Organizational knowledge pyramid

A knowledge management system (KM) should be, ideally, equally focused on both knowledge storage and knowledge distribution, preventing, thus, "corruption of knowledge", by keeping everyone up-to-date [5]. Related studies ([7], [8], [9], [10]), have shown that at an abstract level knowledge management systems are composed of four core processes which are interdependent.

- Generation of knowledge based on new facts and previous work
- Formal organization of collected information
- Development and refinement of existing material
- Distribution of existing knowledge

The task of creating an efficient KM system is still considered an open issue. On one hand, KM systems have to effectively formalize knowledge based on changing organizational needs. On the other hand, tacit knowledge is especially hard to capture and transfer, as organizations are reluctant to shift towards more human-centered practices.

3   Ontologies

As seen in the previous section, knowledge is distributed in many forms/formats and across many locations inside an organization. Ensuring seamless knowledge distribution requires a mechanism of unified description of knowledge sources, using a common vocabulary. Semantic Web principles in general and ontologies in particular are the technology that fits this purpose best.

The most quoted definition of ontologies is that *an ontology is an explicit specification of a conceptualization* ([11], [12], [13]). Ontologies provide formal semantic representation that describes a particular, real-world knowledge domain. Ontologies are the most promising technology for KM systems as they can be used as the back-bone structure, integrating access to diverse knowledge items. The main advantage comparing to traditional keyword based indexing/searching (relational DBMSs) is that ontologies are common-base, shared descriptions of domains. Therefore, they provide a set of a-priori assumptions about the intended meaning of used terms in communication.

Despite their advantages, ontologies are not the silver bullet for all KM problems. As real-world applications of ontologies have shown, there are two important problems that need to be overcome to harness their full potential. The first problem occurs when trying to model a semantically diverse domain, such as a public authority with different departments, using a single ontology. This approach results in large, monolithic ontologies that have proven difficult to employ for reasons of complexity and maintainability.

This problem has been addressed early on ([14], [15], [11], [12]) by adopting parallel development / operation of multiple, "compact" ontologies, each one focused on a particular knowledge domain of the organization. Mapping techniques between the terms in these ontologies have also been developed [14], providing a semantic link. This technique allows the unified access to diverse knowledge sources without the need to change the ontological commitments of the application or the individual.

This has introduced the second problem in the practical employment of ontologies. As a domain's needs and business processes change (because of natural evolution and/or administrative decisions), the domain ontology will also have to evolve so as not to be rendered irrelevant. However, having interdependent ontologies makes ontology evolution a complex process, as a modification in one part of the ontology may generate subtle in-consistencies in other parts of the same ontology, in the ontology-based instances as well as in depending ontologies and applications [16].

Although there has been a lot of activity in the semantic web and ontology area, the question of effective evolution strategies in multiple ontology environments is essentially open.

4   The ONTO-LOGGING Platform

Giving an outline of the platform, we may say that ONTO-LOGGING is:

- Motivated by increasing demand in both private and public sector for more effective KM systems,
- Adapting ist functionality based on the importance of documents as sources of knowledge in both corporate culture as well as public sector activities,
- Targeted at existing company infrastructures and technological background,
- Focusing on human-centered practices.

These high-level aims of the project are being realized by employing and extending Se-mantic Web standards (RDF, OIL, etc.) and combining innovation of open-source software with stability and reliability of commercial platforms.

The ONTO-LOGGING platform is a technological and functional pilot that leads the way for the next generation of commercial KM systems. The outcome of the process will be used as feedback to relevant standardization bodies, especially in the area of ontology management and interoperability.

The main characteristics of the system are

- Scalable, decentralized infrastructure
- Ontology representation and maintenance tools, supporting evolution of multiple ontologies
- Tight integration of the KM with the human resource management system of the organization, to provide personalized functionality

The ONTO-LOGGING system is focusing on all phases and aspects of the knowledge lifecycle in the organization, providing tools for both high-level/administrative and low-level/every-day work.

Beginning from the definition and design phase of a knowledge domain's ontologies, ONTO-LOGGING provides a number of graphical tools to assist knowledge engineers and domain experts in designing and combining together multiple ontologies.

Going to the aspect of every-day usage, a native application provides end-users with a familiar user interface to query and browse the knowledge repository and locate the de-sired information. A set of plug-ins for popular backend suites, like MS Office, is also being developed. These tools, being domain ontology-aware, integrate with the rest of the system, enabling one-click classification of documents during the authoring process.

Focusing on the human-aspect of such a system, a complete user-behavioral model has been developed within ONTO-LOGGING. This model allows the personalization of the system in both an explicit and an implicit way. On one hand, the user can explicitly state his/her preferences, while, on the other, usage patterns extracted by the system are used to both refine the domain ontology(ies) and to improve the way domain knowledge is presented to the user.

Finally, a network of collaborating software agents are employed, providing automated intelligent services in different system tasks, acting on behalf of system users. Knowledge propagation in the organization is handled automatically by agents, based on users' individual profiles. Distributed agents are also used in semantically intensive tasks, as ontology mapping or ontology modification. Agents automate the process by acting collectively on behalf of their respective knowledge engineers to achieve common consensus and reach the optimal solution.

5 ONTO-LOGGING Technical Description

ONTO-LOGGING has adopted a modular, 3-layered architecture for maximum extensibility. The system is divided in the storage layer, the middleware and the presentation modules. Figure 2 gives an outline of the system layers and components.

ONTO-LOGGING is attempting to utilize the best features of both commercial (Microsoft .NET platform) and freeware (Java) platforms.

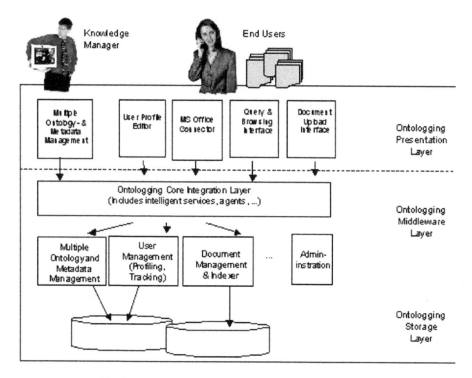

Fig. 2. ONTO-LOGGING architecture and components

Namely, the storage layer is based on the popular MS SQL Server, while middleware components are implemented in Java and reside inside the well-proven Jboss application server. The distributed system of collaborating agents has been implemented using the open-source JADE [17] platform. Finally, recognizing the need to provide non-technical end-users with a familiar look & feel, the systems front-end is implemented in the emerging .NET platform. ONTO-LOGGING makes a distinction between expert and normal users, allowing different operations for each type of user.

As seen in Figure 2, the middleware is logically separated in the back-office modules and the integration layer. Back-office modules are

- Document management (DMS): This is a commercial system, used for document storage and retrieval. The current version of ONTO-LOGGING has al-ready been integrated with Meta4 KnowNet and future versions will provide support for other commercial systems, like Lotus Notes.
- Ontology management (OMS): It is based on the open-source ontology server KAON [18], providing persistent storage and management for multiple ontologies, accessed by multiple users. Stress tests of this sub-system have shown that it can easily scale up to hundreds of thousands of concepts and instances per ontology.
- User management (UMS): This custom module maintains individual user profiles and preferences. It is also in charge of keeping track of user actions and extracting useful information from ontology usage patterns.

The integration layer components are physically placed inside the application server and provide an abstraction of the back-office component functionality. These interfaces are exposed in the form of published web services. This approach has two advantages:

- Ontology and content repositories are represented in a platform-independent way, thus making the system completely decoupled from the presentation layer. This makes possible future integration with third-party applications at almost zero cost.
- Clients need not be aware of proprietary data transportation protocols, as they do not maintain physical data connections

The integration layer is also host to the agent system's central containers.

The presentation layer is a suite of different productivity tools, integrated in a single working environment with a uniform look and feel. Presentation modules allow querying of the domain knowledge structure, as well as retrieval of individual knowledge items (docs, notes, etc.). Being a native application, allows the seamless integration of the presentation layer with the user's office applications, in the form of plug-ins. This capability allows single-click classification and storage of documents in the corporate memory, as they are created. The end-user environment is complemented by a set of dedicated semi-autonomous agents, acting on the user's behalf for tasks such as reception and filtering of interesting knowledge updates.

Figure 3 shows different components and the processes they live in.

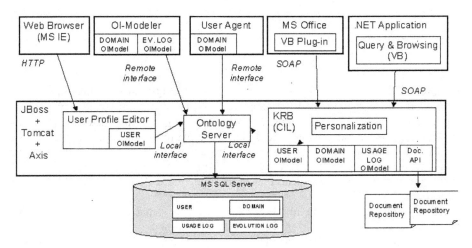

Fig. 3. Components and processes in ONTO-LOGGING

At the heart of the ONTO-LOGGING system, there are a number of ontologies, the structure of which dictates the functionality of the system.

The domain ontology(ies) are custom-made, created by the expert users of the system, using the provided visual modeling tools, capturing the domain knowledge structure. The user ontology models system users and their preferences, while the logging ontology captures user actions and is used by the user management system to infer useful information about system usability and implicit user preferences. The evolution and mapping ontologies allow system experts to apply evolution strategies and maintain mappings between seemingly irrelevant ontologies of different domains.

It is worth pointing out that the actual information pieces (documents) are managed separately from the corresponding ontology instances. Namely, documents are stored and managed by the DMS, while domain ontology instances by the OMS. Although this approach introduces a degree of complexity, it has two important benefits:

- Even if the domain ontology becomes corrupted or unusable for some reason, knowledge bits will still be available through conventional means, provided by the DMS.
- Integrating ONTO-LOGGING with an existing DMS already installed in the organization, or transiting to a new DMS can be done with minimal effort, as the integration layer abstracts away their functionality. In the same way, clustering and failover support can also be introduced.

6   Discussion and Related Work

The problem of effective knowledge management ontology formalization is still an open issue, despite several efforts and advances over the last years. Several research initiatives (OntoKnowledge [19], KnowNet [7] [20], RICA [6]) and standardization efforts (KQML, KIF, XML derivatives) have taken place, but most of these results have not yet been integrated with current commercial products. As a result, almost every new research KM installation seems like a one-off adventure, in which the KM system must be manually customized to the characteristics specific in each organization. This comes in contrast with market evolution dynamics, pushing towards a better integration of emerging formal ontology definition methods within commercial tools, in order to allow for the exchange of existing knowledge, between real-world applications.

ONTO-LOGGING does not re-invent the wheel but, instead, builds on top of foundations laid by various preceding efforts. The importance of ontologies in KM has already been stressed with the best way by OntoKnowledge project results. Issues such as ontology evolution based on changing organization dynamics have also been addressed. Moreover, OntoKnowledge's findings conclude that a KM system cannot be considered complete without a detailed user-modeling scheme. However, the focus of the effort is more on solution prototyping than integration with existing infrastructures.

Project RICA stresses the need for intelligent agents in the KM process of the organization, by employing semi/fully-autonomous agents for all tasks in the KM lifecycle. Although, this approach obviously has many advantages, it has one major disadvantage: there is almost no ad-hoc integration with legacy systems, as agent technologies are considered interesting for lab-work but still immature to be used "all alone" for time-critical tasks.

KnowNet is the most interesting of existing approaches as it addresses all issues of building an effective KM system: integrating with commercial products on the back-end, detailing user roles and processes in the organization, providing intelligent assistants for end-users. We feel that ONTO-LOGGING builds on top of KnowNet's achievements, providing better integration with commercial back-end systems, a more robust OMS and wider usage of collaborative intelligent agents, based on the widely-adopted JADE platform.

Focusing in the area of government and public administrations, so far they have been considered as non-areas for the application of KM principles, just because they are "public" [22]. However, this view is changing rapidly. It is now a widespread belief in relevant literature that public administrations are true knowledge-intensive organizations ([21], [22], [23]), with typical examples of ministerial departments, judiciary and regulatory agencies. Indeed, similar to private sector, human actors in the aforementioned authorities cooperate to process existing and produce new information, whether this is legislative actions or service provision to citizens.

Some interesting efforts, like smartGOV ([24], [25]) and eGOV ([26], [27]), show the way of things to come. The next generation of public administration information systems, shall provide the domain experts with the tools necessary to create dynamic, one-stop government portals for al aspects of a citizen's life. This will not be a trivial task as the amount of information found in public authorities is not only vast but also complex. Creating such an infrastructure cannot be a one-shot transition; instead, it will require a complete back-office infrastructure and well-organized, up-to-date domain knowledge, things that only a KM system can offer.

Of course, one cannot address issues and needs of the public sector by simply applying the same practices that have been proven successful in private organizations, as correctly argued in [28]. This is simply because not only the requirements are different but also because the mentality and culture are different. This is why usually simply porting successful systems from the private sector to public organizations usually fails or does not produce the expected results. The area of KM is no exception to this rule.

However, even if end-goals and internal processes change across domains, the technologies and the underlying infrastructures can still be re-used with minimal transition cost. We do not claim that ONTO-LOGGING will be the panacea for all of KM-related "ills" and issues of public organizations. We believe, though, that efforts like ONTO-LOGGING will smooth the way for the proliferation of e-Government services, acting in the back-office, enhancing productivity of public service employees. They will provide a solid foundation on which decision-makers and end-users (public servants) will be able to cooperate and transition more swiftly to the new technology era.

For example, Figure 4 shows how introducing KM systems, like ONTO-LOGGING, can transform processes in public organizations for the better. So far, editing a document involves creating/editing the document and either storing it in a public folder and notifying the interested parties or forwarding the document itself. This is not at all efficient because the creator of the document has to do additional tasks plus there is always the chance of notifying the wrong people (or not notifying the right people). However, in the case of ONTO-LOGGING, user preferences and semantic metadata allow the system to determine who is interested in what and act accordingly. The same Semantic Web principles also allow for more effective knowledge search and retrieval.

Of course, all this may sound greatly familiar, resembling existing document management systems. ONTO-LOGGING's difference compared to existing systems is that it employs the full potential of Semantic Web in the area of KM. We believe this transition will eventually lead to the creation of more flexible systems capturing the true logic of the knowledge doamin, able to adapt their internal logic to the changing environment instead of offering a set of fixed options.

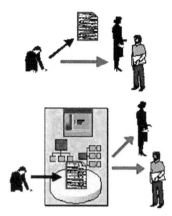

Fig. 4. Document edition/addition in the traditional and the ONTO-LOGGING "way"

7   Conclusions and Summary

The increasingly complex problem of organization knowledge management is far from solved, as it is not a linear problem, both in quantitative and qualitative terms. We believe that a solution for this problem will be two-fold. On one hand, make the organization accumulate new knowledge quickly and efficiently and on the other hand, aid end-users in their day-to-day tasks by preventing them from becoming knowledge-flooded or knowledge-starved.

ONTO-LOGGING is well placed in the area of KM, not only as a research effort, but also as an immediate ancestor of next-generation KM systems. These will combine the best from open-source efforts and commercial platforms, being based on open standards. ONTO-LOGGING is still an undergoing effort and is currently under evaluation deployment in test sites, under real operating conditions, at Indra Sistemas premises.

This paper provided an introduction to knowledge management in the enterprise and the most promising technology for this area, ontologies. Project ONTO-LOGGING is a re-search effort to harness the full potential of ontologies in KM systems, providing tools for both expert and non-technical users.

Acknowledgements. The ONTO-LOGGING project [29] has commenced on July 2001 and is co-funded by the European Commission under contract IST-2000-28293. Its duration is 2.5 years. The authors would like to acknowledge the assistance and co-operation between all partners. The partners of the ONTO-LOGGING consortium are: Indra Sistemas (administrative and financial coordinator), META4 (scientific coordinator), FZI, Deltatec, CALT-INSEAD and Archetypon S.A.

References

1.   McKay B: "Leveraging Corporate Knowledge Through Automatic Classification", Article on DominoPower, http://www.dominopower.com/issues/issue200002/autoclass001.html

2. McDonough F. A, Electronic Government in Europe and the US, Electronic presentation, http://www.hpcc-usa.org/pics/01-pres/HPCC_McDonough.ppt
3. RoperNOP Technology Reveals Encouraging Signs of Investment in the IT Sector, NOP World article, http://www.nop.co.uk/news/news_survey_barometer_14_01_03.shtml
4. Mentzas G, Apostolou D: Towards a Holistic Knowledge Leveraging Infrastructure: The KNOWNET Approach, Second International Conference on Practical Aspects of Knowledge Management, 29–30 October, 1998, Basel Switzerland
5. Gandon F: Ontology Engineering: A Survey and a Return on Experience, Rapport de Reserche No 4396, INRIA, France, March 2002
6. Aguirre J L, Brena R and Cantu F J: Multiagent-based Knowledge Networks, Special issue on Knowledge Management of the Journal Expert Systems with Applications, No. 20, pp 65–75, Elsevier
7. Apostolou D, Mentzas G: Managing Corporate Knowledge: A Comparative Analysis of Experiences in Consulting Firms, 2nd International Conference on Practical Aspects of Knowledge Management, October 1998, Basel, Switzerland
8. Mentzas G: Collaborative Technologies for Knowledge Management, presented at the "Business Process and Workflow Conference", October 1997, London, England.
9. Romaldi V: Collaborative Technologies for Knowledge Management: Making the Tacit Explicit, Proceedings of Informing Science + IT Education Conference, p. 1357–1365, June 2002,Cork, Ireland
10. Maier R, Remus U: Towards a Framework for Knowledge Management Strategies: Process Orientation as Strategic Starting Point, Proceedings of the Hawaii International Conference On System Sciences, January 2001, Maui, Hawaii.
11. Gruber T R: Toward Principles for the Design of Ontologies Used for Knowledge Sharing, International Workshop on Formal Ontology, March 1993, Padova, Italy.
12. Gruber T R: A Translation Approach to Portable Ontology Specifications, Knowledge Acquisition, 2, No 5, pp 199–220 (1992).
13. Z Cui, V A M Tamma and F Bellifemine: Ontology Management in Enterprises, BT Technology Journal Vol. 17, No 4, October 1999
14. Silva N: MAFRA – A Mapping Framework for Distributed Ontologies, Presentation at the 13th European Conference on Knowledge Engineering and Knowledge Management EKAW, Madrid, Spain, 2002.
15. Maedche A: Measuring Similarities between Ontologies, Presentation at the 13th European Conference on Knowledge Engineering and Knowledge Management EKAW, Madrid, Spain, 2002
16. Klein M and Fensel D: Ontology Versioning for the Semantic Web, Proc. International Semantic Web Working Symposium (SWWS), USA, 2001.
17. The Java Agent Development Framework (JADE), http://sharon.cselt.it/projects/jade/
18. KAON Ontology and Semantic Web Infrastructure, http://kaon.semanticweb.org/
19. Project OntoKnowledge homepage, http://www.ontoknowledge.org/index.shtml
20. Project KnowNet homepage, http://project.knownet.org/
21. Lenk K: Relating Knowledge Management in the Public Sector to Decision-Making and Administrative Action, 3rd International Workshop on Knowledge Management in e-Government (KMGov2002), Copenhagen, May 2002.
22. Barquin R. C., Bennet A and Remez S. G.: Knowledge Management: The Catalyst for Electronic Government, Management Concepts, USA, 2001.
23. Gabor A., Ko A.: Knowledge Management in Content Management at the Public Administration, 3rd International Workshop on Knowledge Management in e-Government (KMGov2002), Copenhagen, May 2002.
24. Georgiadis P et al: A Governmental Knowledge-based Platform for Public Sector Online Services, Proceedings of the 1st International Conference on Electronic Government-EGOV 2002, pp. 362–369.

25. Tambouris E et al: SMARTGOV: A Governmental Knowledge-based Platform for Public Sector Online Services, Proceedings of the KMGov2002 Workshop, Copenhagen, Denmark, May 23–24, 2002, pp. 173–185.
26. Wimmer M, Traunmueller R: Towards an Integrated Platform for Online One-Stop Government, ER-CIM News, Special Theme:e-Government, Issue 48, January 2002
27. Wimmer M, Tambouris E: Online one-stop Government: A working framework and requirements, In Traunm*ller (Ed.), Information Systems: The e-Business Challenge. Proceedings of the 17th World Computer Congress of IFIP, Kluwer Academic Publishers, Boston et al, pp 117–130 (ISBN 1-4020-7174-4)
28. Quirchmayr G, Tagg R.: An Architectural Concept for Knowledge Integration in Inter-Administration Computing, 3rd International Workshop on Knowledge Management in e-Government (KMGov2002), Copenhagen, May 2002.
29. Project ONTO-LOGGING homepage, http://www.ontologging.com/
30. Maurer H: The Heart of the Problem: Knowledge Management and Knowledge Transfer, Conference Proceedings of Enable 99, Espoo, Vantaa Institute of Technology, Finland, 1999, p. 8–17
31. Maedche A et al: Ontologies for Enterprise Knowledge Management . IEEE Intelligent Systems, November/December 2002. 2002/11/01

A Knowledge Engineering Approach to Comparing Legislation

Alexander Boer[1] and Tom van Engers[2]

[1] Dept. of Computer Science & Law, University of Amsterdam,
[2] Dutch Tax and Customs Administration, Utrecht, Netherlands

Abstract. In the E-POWER project relevant tax legislation and business processes are modelled in UML to improve the speed and efficiency with which the Dutch Tax and Customs Administration can implement decision support systems for internal use and for its clients. These conceptual models have also proven their usefulness for efficient and effective analysis of draft legislation. We are currently researching whether conceptual modeling can also be used to compare 'similar' legislation from different jurisdictions. Better insight in the process of modeling and comparing legislation from different legislators is expected to improve the capacity of the Dutch Tax and Customs Administration to react to future consequences of increased movement of people, products, and money between EU member states and increased harmonization between tax authorities in Europe. In addition, the discovery of the requirements of comparing models is also expected to result in a more principled, more robust, and language-independent methodology for modeling legislation. This paper discusses known problems and requirements of comparing legislation, and the expected results of comparing models of legislation.

1   Introduction

In the E-POWER project relevant tax legislation and business processes are modelled to improve the speed and efficiency with which the Dutch Tax and Customs Administration (DTCA) can implement decision support systems for internal use and for its clients. The conceptual models have also proven their usefulness for efficient and effective analysis of draft legislation, allowing the DTCA to give immediate feedback to drafts of the new income tax law of 2001 [16].

We are currently researching whether conceptual models can also be used to compare 'similar' legislation from different jurisdictions. Better insight in the process of modeling and comparing legislation from different legislators is expected to improve the capacity of the DTCA to react to future consequences of increased movement of people, products, and money between EU member states and increased harmonization between tax authorities in Europe. In addition, the discovery of the requirements of comparing models is also expected to result in a more principled, more robust, and language-independent methodology for modeling legislation.

Comparing similar regulations from multiple jurisdictions is not the same as comparing the legal systems to which the documents belong. Two countries may for instance contain almost a copy of the same crime description in their respective penal codes, but

M.A. Wimmer (Ed.): KMGov 2003, LNAI 2645, pp. 139–150, 2003.

it is also important to know whether both are backed up by similarly likely sanctions. Other notable differences are the degree of civil servant discretion, corruption, and different constitutional arrangements influencing when and how regulations are applied. In civil and common law systems, for instance, regulations usually have very different meanings and are written in completely different styles. Different jurisdictions, cultures, and languages, and the philosophical problems of comparing legal systems are the main subject of Comparative Law. Researchers in Comparative Law rarely compare written legislation directly.

But similar regulations are habitually compared in a number of contexts, and not all of them are perceived as equally complex and subjective. Regulations are compared for very different purposes, for instance:

Policy Comparison. Proposals for a regulation addressing the same problem are compared to judge which one is better according to preconceived norms of analysis.
Forecasting and Reconstruction. Two versions of the same regulation in time are compared to determine the effects (costs and benefits) of changes of legislation on behaviour, products, etc.
Migration. Two regulations addressing 'similar' things in different jurisdictions are compared to inform others about the effects (costs and benefits) of moving themselves, their property, products, or services over the borders of a jurisdiction.

Harmonization combines these purposes; It often aims to minimize the costs of migration, distinguishes the good from the bad legislation to repair the latter, and forecasts the costs caused by the changes it proposes in order to be able to minimize them. To harmonize legislation one has to quantify and prioritize costs and benefits for stakeholders with a variety of norms of analysis.

There are a number of initiatives for constructing international legal ontologies that expose the subsumption relations between legal vocabulary in multiple jurisdictions. Gangemi et al. [9] suggest, in a context of comparing versions of a regulation, that the problem of comparing legislation is a special case of the more general problem of ontology integration (cf. [4]). This paper discusses some the problems we run in to when we try to translate the problems of Comparative Law into those of ontology integration.

The next sections discusses how to establish 'similarity' between concepts, some concepts needed to describe and explain legislation itself, and the specific problems related to comparing knowledge models of limited scope. The expected results of comparing knowledge models of legislation will be discussed in the last section.

2   Similarity of Concepts in Legislation

Obviously, when two different legal cultures and systems come into contact, there is significant potential for misunderstanding. Translation of legal documents to a foreign language illustrates the nature of the problem. If legal texts are for instance conceived and drafted in Dutch, based on the concepts of Dutch law, and then translated into English, the result is an English text from a structural and linguistic point of view, but the text is semantically rooted in Dutch law and society. This problem is not unique for translation of *legal* texts, but it is especially obvious and acute in this context. In fact, the 'translation' problem between legal systems also exists for U.S., E.U., and British legal English, and communication between laity and professional in general. The translation must strike a balance between using the concepts the audience already knows, and teaching the definitions of unfamiliar legal concepts.

Translators use three general strategies to explain concepts and institutions bound to a particular legal system:

Literal translation. Take a dictionary, break a composite word into its constituent parts if necessary, and translate word for word. For instance, the Dutch term 'bestuursorgaan' becomes, according to the dictionary, either 'government organ', 'administrative organ', 'government body', or 'administrative body'.

Transfer to a similar concept. The Dutch concept 'bestuursorgaan' comes from general administrative law (a literal translation), which is applicable to all institutions labelled 'bestuursorgaan'. It regulates i.a. procedural requirements for administrative decisionmaking, appeals against administrative decisions, and delegation of decisionmaking competence. The concept 'public body' is used in a very similar sense in the United Kingdom and the English vocabulary of the European Union. A translator acquainted with these legal systems may therefore substitute 'public body' for 'bestuursorgaan'.

Periphrasis. Explaining an unfamiliar concept by a defining gloss using other concepts. Observing that translating 'bestuursorgaan' with 'public body' fails to convey the limits of the concept, a periphrasis (or circumlocution) may be more suitable: bestuursorgaan – an administrative body of a public legal person, including natural persons exercising public authority, bodies or colleges without legal personality, and bodies of a private legal person exercising public authority inasfar as they as they are making decisions based on a competence attributed by law, excluding the assembly of the States-General, assembly of a house of the States-General, the Judicial Organisation, the Council of State, the Court of Auditors, the National Ombudsman, etc.

Indiscriminate application of periphrasis results more verbose text that lacks a semantic grounding in the vocabulary of the target audience. Indiscriminate use of transfer, on the other hand, results in a text that is misleading from an information perspective. The most obvious procedure is thus to apply periphrasis until unambiguous transfer becomes possible. Whether transfer is unambiguous depends on the knowledge attributed to the intended reader and the purpose of the translation.

Intuitive 'similarity' can for purposes of Comparative Law be classified as extensional, immanent, or functional [19]. Concepts are the same in an *extensional* sense if their definitions are logically equivalent. Suppose that statements that harm someone's honour or dignity constitute insult, while untrue statements that harm someone's honour or dignity constitute defamation. Insult and defamation as described here are *immanent* concepts, abstracted from particular legal systems and the 'extensional' intersection (overlap or 'common ground') of specific definitions found there. In the *extensional* sense, the definition of 'insult' subsumes the definition of 'defamation'; All defamations are by definition insults, but not the other way around. Some western countries provide a civil remedy for defamation, while other countries (including the Netherlands) may treat the very same case as a criminal insult, arguing that establishing the truth criterium often leads to extra harm for the victim and is usually irrelevant because 'acting in the public interest' is a valid defense for both. Although civil defamation and criminal insult are different even with regard to the nature of the procedures to be followed and the legal consequences, they are *functionally* similar because they address a 'similar' problem. In this sense concepts can be functionally 'similar', even though the definitions are different.

Because the similarity is based on either the perceived causal effect of the concept on the 'similar problem', or the perceived intentions of the legislator (the intended causal effect), this notion of similarity is not very useful for automatic reasoning.

For Knowledge Engineering purposes, we want to separate extensional and immanent views of concepts from implicit value systems and assumptions about causal effects. The problem is, however, that comparative analyses made by scholars in Comparative Law that reveal 'interesting' differences between laws are usually based on functional 'similarity'. To create useful computerized support, these implicit underlying values that make things functionally 'similar' must be made explicit.

3   Concepts Describing the Role of Legislation

To explain why one regulation is better than the other, and how regulations affect the real world, we need concepts that explain the role that the text of the regulation plays in a jurisdiction. One example of generic legal concepts for the design of legal expert systems is the *Functional Ontology of Law* of Valente (cf. [17]), also one of the first to stress the importance of semantically grounding legal concepts in commonsense concepts.

The key concept for understanding legislation is the *norm* (e.g. [6, 17]); If you are describing two people playing what appears to be a chess game, for instance, and one player moves a pawn backwards, you may infer that it is not a chess game after all; The move contradicts the hypothesis that it is a chess game. If you are the other player, however, and you believe you are playing a chess game, then you will consider the move illegal – a violation of a norm. In this case you view the rules of chess as a prescription of what ought to happen during the game. The norm prescribes what ought to happen. Norms only regulate human behaviour; The eruption of a volcano may very well be undesirable, but it makes no sense to try to prescribe how it ought to behave. Norms are intended to change people's preferences between choices, to interfere with basic economic behaviour by changing the rules of the game. Norms are usually made explicit in a document (contract, regulation, jurisprudence, etc). The document often prescribes behaviour to agents assigned a certain role, for instance the owner and user of a road. Sometimes the document posits norms for the creation of artefacts – things made by agents, for example ships or tax forms. In other cases it constrains or defines procedures for actions or transactions by agents, for example a survey, hearing, or purchase, instead.

In deontic reasoning systems norms are treated as logical sentences describing situations that are *allowed* or *disallowed*. They mainly serve as an aid in establishing a preference ordering on situation descriptions to determine what one ought to do given a choice between situations. Because norms in legislation define a discrete metric with just two values (allowed, disallowed) there is no generic recipe for establishing a *total* preference ordering on situations that decides every choice one is confronted with in life, or that allows the DTCA to forecast the exact effect of legislation on taxpayer's choices for instance. Common decision-theoretic assumptions like preferential independence between disallowed situations do not necessarily hold for legislation. It is therfore in principle also impossible to predict the effects of legislation on choices. We have studied pragmatic automated normative reasoning in detail in earlier projects (generally [17, 2, 20]).

Deontic logics are logics of ideal worlds. Ideal worlds tell us little about what to do. If deontic sentences are interpreted as logical sentences describing an ideal world, they cannot be used to express what ought to be done in a sub-ideal world; This is the essence of the so-called Chisholm and good Samaritan paradoxes (e.g. [17]). It shows that deontic sentences can presuppose a sub-ideal world. Norms in legislation often express competing underlying values that may prove to be jointly unrealizable in some situations. In addition, some norms are (intended as) exceptions to other norms. In regulations these exceptions are often used for compactness; A so-called qualification model (a full, monotonic paraphrase, cf. [6]) of regulations is often much harder to understand and use. If explicit and intended, the exception relation is often marked in the text in some way. In principle the more specific regulation is superior, unless it is of lower order or of equal order but issued earlier. These principles impose a priority ordering on norms (not worlds) and go by the names *Lex Specialis*, *Lex Superior*, and *Lex Posterior* respectively in legal theory.

The situations constrained in the norms expressed in legislation are described in terms of a mixture of well-understood 'commonsense' concepts and the legal concepts discussed in the previous section, that are eventually defined in terms of 'commonsense' concepts. The application of codified norms by a judge to others is also regulated by norms. Norms intended for legislators also exist; European 'directives', for instance, impose a duty on legislators to change their legislation to achieve certain aims. Whether a legislator violates a directive again appeals to the perceived intentions of the legislator, or the perceived causal effect of the norms on the aims to be achieved – which is often impossible to establish.

We use the phrase 'norms of analysis' for norms used to distinguish 'good' from 'bad' norms (cf. generally [11, 10] in taxation context) that represent the values the legislator is committed to. Courts also appeal to 'values' or 'intentions' of the legislator to judge the propriety of applying a norm (generally [1]). These values can take the form of a continuous or discrete *metric*. To distinguish good from bad legislation, one has to deal with the additional problem of aggregation of norms in regulations, and the aggregation of the results of application of multiple norms of analysis. Tax neutrality is such a norm of analysis that postulates that taxation should not create avoidance behaviour. Tax neutrality is also a norm for distinguishing good and bad combinations of legislation in the context of migration; In this form it postulates that two jurisdictions that allow free movement between jurisdictions should try to minimize differences in tax pressure. The respective tax laws of both jurisdictions are 'tax neutral' towards eachother if they give no incentives or rewards for tax avoidance by movement between jurisdictions. The alternative is tax competition. Most general political values (like Pareto-efficiency, solidarity, liberalization, subsidiarity) can serve as a norm of analysis for distinguishing a good from a bad law. To operationalize norms of analysis, they have to assign a value to situation descriptions.

3.1 The Meaning of Harmonization

Having explained how we think legislation is supposed to influence human behaviour, we can explain what harmonization in the EU usually aims at:

Legal Convergence aims for similar legal responses to the same situations.

A 'similar' legal response can mean a lot of things: If a fine for a certain traffic violation in the Netherlands is higher than a fine in a similar situation in Portugal, they may still be qualitatively the same. It depends on the characteristics of legal responses that are we interested in and the metric we apply. For the jurist it is often enough to establish that both countries judge a situation as disallowed and give a fine to the actor held accountable for it. For the economist it is the amount of the fine that determines how it affects behaviour. Taxes are usually analysed as an 'interference' in economic behaviour, abstracting away completely from the way they are collected and why they are collected that way. The result of the analysis is operationalized as a quantitative value ordering tax systems according to, for instance, marginal or average tax pressure.

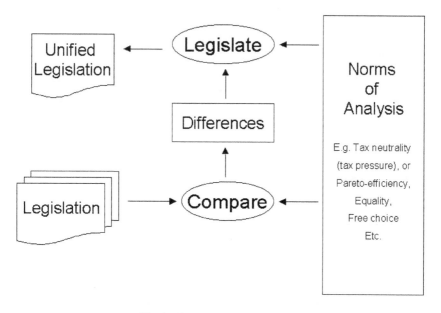

Fig. 1. The harmonization process

There are two general strategies for achieving legal convergence. The first is *unification*, or replacing 'similar' but different norms with one norm. In the EU this is achieved with a regulation, or CEN EN classified document. The other one is *standardization*, or issuing general norms prescribing what effects national legislation should achieve. In the EU this is achieved with a directive, or CEN HD classified document.

What should be standardized, and to what extent, is a question of which norms of analysis to apply. Figure 1 shows the relations between the differences detected, norms of analysis, and changes to legislation. Note that the norms of analysis play a role twice. Once in determining the differences that are 'relevant' and subject to unification, and a second time in determining what legislation is introduced as a replacement. A EU regulation is an example of unified legislation, and a EU directive posits norms of analysis legislators commit themselves to.

4   Models of Legislation

The UML models currently used by the Dutch Tax and Customs Administration very closely follow the text of tax legislation because that improves intercoder reliability for modelers. Liberal application of commonsense additions to the model is taboo because it is too subjective. For the design of decision support systems this need not be a practical problem, because software designers usually assume that 'extensional' commonsense connections, for instance the subsumption relation between senior and adult (all seniors are adults), will be transparent to the user of the system. But if you want to compare two models of different income tax laws, you must find a semantic grounding in shared 'commonsense' concepts to make them comparable.

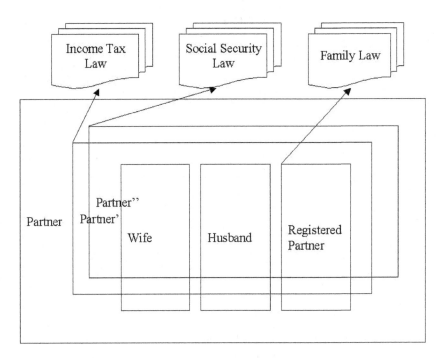

Fig. 2. Legislation and models of Legislation

For the computer, establishing that situations in two different models are similar or different requires a description of the situations using the same concepts, or a *transformation* model containing assumptions that explain the 'common ground' between concepts from two regulations. A relevant 'difference' may thus be a modeling error in the 'common ground model' assumptions. Figure 2 shows the number of different extensional assumptions that must be made to establish a 'similarity' relationship between different some interpretations of 'partner' to make them comparable. The Venn diagram displays three definitions of 'partner' from law, and the common sense concept. Since the assumptions can all be wrong, it is the responsibility of the modeler to judge whether differences are real or artifacts caused by interpretation. A new concept 'partner' can cover or overlap any of the 13 extensional spaces currently in Figure 2. Assigning the blame for a difference between norms is not a trivial task in the ontology integration perspective of [9].

In the current E-POWER method, modelers are required to model each fragment of law, and the partial definitions of concepts occurring there, separately. In the integration phase, the modeler may decide that two occurrences of the same phrase in different fragments of law, for instance 'partner', refer to the same concept. One of the purposes of making these choices explicit is to be able to communicate the differences between different meanings of a concept like 'partner' to the end user of decision support systems. This procedure is needed for integration of concept definitions in one field of law in one jurisdiction. To make models of regulations of different fields of law, and even multiple jurisdictions, comparable the same procedure is required. In this case we need more guidance for classifying concepts by a top ontology because we lose the guidance Dutch administrative law and guidelines for legislative drafting offers for classifying agents, actions, powers, procedures, and principles. To assign the blame for a difference it is also essential to know whose opinion is represented by an assertion in a knowledge base: a taxpayer, knowledge engineer, fiscal expert, the DTCA, fiscal court, or the Court of Justice of the EU?

UML is used because it is widely known among software engineers and supported by familiar CASE tools. UML can be used as a knowledge representation language [5], although it usually lacks a description classifier for verification. We have defined a translation of the exception graph we developed in the past [2, 20] to guide user dialog and knowledge acquisition and to resolve exceptions between norm descriptions to the description classifer paradigm (to be published elsewhere) for OWL (the draft Web Ontology Language; http://www.w3.org/2001/SW/) using the 'folding' procedure described in [12], so that unresolved differences between norms classify as truth-functional contradictions. The problem of comparing models is translated in this way into a problem of ontology integration (cf. [4, 14])

4.1 Comparing Models of Legislation

To compare legislation, we have to add four categories of knowledge about the comparison we intend to make. Initially, we have to make the choice of what legislation to compare. Since it is unfeasible to compare complete legal systems, we have to make an educated guess about whether regulations address similar situations, and whether they are the only regulations that address those situations. For the Dutch and Belgian Income

Tax Law that may seem fairly obvious; Mismatches mostly concern situations regulated in other laws that must be involved. Comparing the Dutch General Administrative Law with a British equivalent is however impossible; Since the latter does not exist it is better in this case to depart from a 'space' of interesting possible situations, and find pieces of legislation and court verdicts that address similar situations.

First, only situation descriptions covered by both models can be compared. The differences we are interested in, are inferred from 'similar' situations that lead to qualitatively different outcome valuations (e.g. different amount fine, marginal tax pressure) in the value system we are comparing with. We have to describe the space of situations that we compare and that the conclusions will pertain to.

Second, because we can only compare a limited space of possible situations, we have to make the assumption that the rest of the situation is static. The fact that a situation occurs in Amsterdam or London, or today or yesterday, or that it involves other persons is obviously not a relevant difference for the purposes of comparing legislation. But suppose that we want to compare the Dutch and British traffic code, which both regulate the 'same' traffic situations. We model the correspondences between Dutch and British to find out that the only thing that a formal reasoning procedure can prove to us is that every situation allowed in the Netherlands is disallowed in the United Kingdom, and there is no other meaningful comparison to be made. A useful and reasonable frame assumption to make in these circumstances is that "right in Netherlands is equivalent to left in England" for the purposes of the analysis, because driving right is normal in the Netherlands, and driving left is normal in the UK. This set of assumptions are the Ceteris Paribus (other things being equal) assumptions that have to be added to the ontology to make a specific comparison for a specific purpose. The assumptions state that the situation is valued similarly (in terms of utility, morality, etc.), and the situation is similarly likely (in that place, population, etc.).

In some cases we translate situations to accommodate general patterns of preference holding in a specific jurisdiction, to make them equivalent in valuation. This is intuitively right; Everyone agrees that although driving left may constitute a crime in a certain jurisdiction, the behaviour itself is morally neutral (as opposed to murder, for instance). These assumptions are added by the modeller to explain the links between legislation and the perspective we choose – in the abstractions we make – when comparing something.

Third, after establishing our space of situations, we have to choose and operationalize our norms of analysis as *metrics classifying the relevant situation descriptions*. This includes the preference ordering or weighing procedures for multiple norms of analysis that can themselves be seen as ceteris paribus comparatives; [7]. Obviously, because norms classify limited situation descriptions (ignoring all facts not asked for) they can conflict wrt. a specific situation.

Fourth, applying norms of analysis on a norm system requires *assumptions about behaviour*. The 'commonsense' perspective on income tax systems, for instance, treats it as a black box where your income in the input and the part of your money you may keep for yourselves is the output. What happens here is that the analyst who compares these black boxes makes a normality assumption about behaviour: all civil servants do what they ought to do and you have honestly submitted all relevant information.

In deontic terms, this means that an obligation $O(A \rightarrow B)$ no longer translates to $F(A \wedge \neg B)$ but to $A \rightarrow B$ for all norms irrelevant to the analysis. The norms become descriptions of behaviour instead of prescriptions. We have already remarked that the decision as to whether a legislator violates a directive (which is a norm of analysis) appeals to the perceived intentions of the legislator, or the perceived causal effect of the norms on the aims to be achieved. The assumptions about behaviour that we make capture these judgments.

The distinction between intented effect on behaviour and actual effect on behaviour becomes blurry if you make assumptions about the effect of norm systems on behaviour without validating them (confusing intentions with effects). That the two are different can be illustrated with a diesel fuel tax in two different countries A and B. Country a has a diesel fuel consumption tax of 50%, and country B has a diesel fuel consumption tax of 10% and an environmental diesel fuel tax of 40%. The intentions of the taxes are different. The consumption tax is intended to generate income, the environmental tax to encourage evasion behaviour by consumers of diesel fuel and as a bill for health problems (if health is publicly funded) and pollution caused by diesel fuel. Empirical research may support the hypothesis that both taxes cause the exact same evasion behaviour and generate the same income. From an economic viewpoint they are then 'similar'. At the same time they may be different because country B may have committed itself to spending the generated income in the environmental regulation to specific policies, but the economic analyst will have abstracted away that detail at an early stage.

5   Discussion

A number of international efforts to establish standards for legal XML have recognized the problem of mapping legal vocabularies to eachother and proposed standard ontologies of international legal vocabulary. The European LEXML consortium[3] has initiated the LEXML RDF Dictionary project, and the OASIS LegalXML working group [4] has a committee for a very similar dictionary project. The METALex consortium [3] [5] has a similar ontology subproject. These projects depart from the premise that a taxonomy of legal concepts is the obvious way to explain the relations between concepts from multiple jurisdictions. In [9] the regulation is thus represented as a 'local' ontology containing concept definitions and the problem of integrating two 'local' ontologies representing two different regulations is reduced to a problem of ontology integration. [9] do not account for norm conflict resolution strategies for establishing the validity of norms. We want to add such a component. In addition, we claim that the ontology integration view does not account for the purpose of the comparison. To account for the 'functional' similarities that human analysts see between concepts that the description classifier does not, we have to make the underlying assumptions and value systems explicit.

We understand from small experiments that the amount of external information from the legal system needed to explain in what way two regulations are different, is poten-

---

[3] http://www.lexml.de
[4] http://www.legalxml.com
[5] http://www.metalex.nl; The authors contribute to this consortium.

tially very large. Experimenting with comparative analysis on a somewhat larger and methodical scale will teach us whether these extra requirements increase explosively or level off at some point due to discovery of regular patterns.

When relevant differences are found, the modeler has to discover what caused the differences. It may be the legislation that is qualitatively different, but it may also point to a different interpretation of the modelers of both legislations, or a suspect assumption in the transformation model. An alternative problem may be that we are comparing the wrong set of legislation. Fortunately, all of these findings have the potential of improving legislation, or the models of it.

An implicit assumption underlying the notion of comparing knowledge models of legislation is that the knowledge models are complete declarative statements of the 'normative' reading of legislation, that have been integrated with, or translated to business processes afterwards. In large organizations like the DTCA, the relations between legislation, business processes, and IT infrastructure are sufficiently complicated to appreciate the advantages of principled normative models of legislation for designing and maintaining IT infrastructure and business processes. Being able to compare legislation is an added value of models that are valuable per se. Construction of a sizable transformation model is expected to result in an inventory of norms of analysis used for taxation legislation analysis and generic analysis of legislative quality and a core ontology of abstract legal concepts that are necessary that can also be used to evaluate the quality of theoretical legal core ontologies (such as [17]).

To make knowledge models of legislation with the purpose of comparing legislation from different jurisdictions is an additional effort that is not necessary to implement decision support systems. At the same time, if you fail to make the effort to ground your knowledge model in commonly understood concepts (concepts for which we can point out the 'extension', or the things to which it applies) it becomes as difficult to discover the interactions between different regulations in the same jurisdiction, or even one tax administration, as it is to compare regulations from different jurisdictions. Comparing with foreign law is useful for that reason alone: It is not convincing to show that the computer can make 'smart' commonsense connections between concepts in legislation that is very familiar to its users. The Knowledge Engineering approach to comparing legislation presented in this paper is a more systematic and transparent approach to analysing and documenting the development of legislation than the 'functional' approach a human analyst has to resort to. It has the potential to depoliticize the technical aspect of harmonization by separating it from the value systems applied.

Acknowledgements

E-POWER is partially funded by the EC as IST Project 2000-28125; partners are the Dutch Tax and Customs Administration, O&I Management Partners, LibRT, the University of Amsterdam (NL); Application Engineers, Fortis Bank Insurance (B); Mega International (F).

References

1. T. Bench-Capon and G. Sartor. Using values and theories to resolve disagreement in law. In J.A. Breuker, R. Leenes, and R.G.F. Winkels, editors, *Legal Knowledge and Information Systems (JURIX-2000)*, Amsterdam, 2000. IOS Press. ISBN 1.58603.144.9.

2. A. Boer. MILE: Turning Legal Information into Legal Advice. In A.M. Tjoa and R.R. Wagner, editors, *Proceedings of the Twelfth International Workshop on Database and Expert Systems Applications (DEXA)*, pages 787–791, Los Alamitos (CA), 2001. IEEE Computer Society.

3. Alexander Boer, Rinke Hoekstra, and Radboud Winkels. METALex: Legislation in XML. In A. Daskalopulu T. Bench-Capon and R. Winkels, editors, *Legal Knowledge and Information Systems. JURIX 2002: The Fifteenth Annual Conference.*, pages 1–10, Amsterdam, 2002. IOS Press.

4. D. Calvanese, G. De Giacomo, and M. Lenzerini. A framework for ontology integration, 2001.

5. S. Cranefield and M. Purvis. Uml as an ontology modelling language, 1999.

6. N. den Haan and J. Breuker. Constructing Normative Rules. In *Proceedings of JURIX'96*, pages 135–147, 1996.

7. Jon Doyle and Michael P. Wellman. Representing preferences as ceteris paribus comparatives. In *Decision-Theoretic Planning: Papers from the 1994 Spring AAAI Symposium*, pages 69–75. AAAI Press, Menlo Park, California, 1994.

8. Ewald Engelen. Financialization, Pension Restructuring, and the Logic of Funding. In *Proceedings of SASE 2002*, 2002.

9. A. Gangemi, D. M. Pisanelli, and G. Steve. A formal Ontology Framework to Represent Norm Dynamics. In *Proceedings of the Second International Workshop on Legal Ontologies (LEGONT)*, 2001.

10. Walter Hettich and Stanley L. Winer. Economic and political foundations of tax structure. *American Economic Review*, 78(4):701–712, 1988.

11. Walter Hettich and Stanley L. Winer. Rules, Politics, and the Normative Analysis of Taxation. Carleton Economic Papers 00-12, Carleton University, 2000.

12. Ian Horrocks and Sergio Tessaris. A conjunctive query language for description logic aboxes. In *AAAI/IAAI*, pages 399–404, 2000.

13. Murk Muller. The RDF Dictionary and the standardisation process in the legal domain. In *Proceedings of XML Europe*, 2002.

14. H. Pinto, A. Prez, and J. Martins. Some issues on ontology integration, 1999.

15. E. Rissland and T. Friedman. Detecting change in legal concepts. In *Proceedings of the Fifth International Conference on Artificial Intelligence and Law (ICAIL-99)*, pages 127–136, New York (NY), 1995. ACM.

16. Silvie Spreeuwenberg, Tom van Engers, and Rik Gerrits. The Role of Verification in Improving the Quality of Legal Decisionmaking. In Bart Verheij, Arno Lodder, Ronald Loui, and Antoinette Muntjewerff, editors, *Legal Knowledge and Information Systems (JURIX-2001)*, pages 1–16, Amsterdam, 2001. IOS Press. ISBN 1.58603.201.1.

17. Andre Valente. *Legal Knowledge Engineering: A Modeling Approach*. PhD thesis, Amsterdam, 1995.

18. Andre Valente and Joost Breuker. ON-LINE: An architecture for modelling legal information. In *International Conference on Artificial Intelligence and Law (ICAIL-1995)*, pages 307–315, 1995.

19. C.J.P. van Laer. The Applicability of Comparative Concepts. *European Journal of Comparative Law*, 2.2, 1998.

20. R.G.F. Winkels, D. Bosscher, A. Boer, and J.A. Breuker. Gencrating Exception Structures for Legal Information Serving. In Th.F. Gordon, editor, *Proceedings of the Seventh International Conference on Artificial Intelligence and Law (ICAIL-99)*, pages 182–195, New York (NY), 1999. ACM.

How Knowledge Management Can Support the IT Security of eGovernment Services

Markus Nick, Stephan Groß, and Björn Snoek

Fraunhofer Institut Experimentelles Software Engineering (IESE)
Sauerwiesen 6, 67661 Kaiserslautern, Germany
{nick, gross, snoek}@iese.fhg.de

Abstract. Safeguarding security for eGovernment services is an essential ingredient for the success of such services. For this purpose, isolated security efforts are not sufficient. Integrated concepts are required. In the publicly funded project SKe, we are developing such an integrated approach. One component of this integrated approach is a knowledge management-based solution to support the dynamic aspects of IT security. The component - an intelligent IT security console - supports the daily work of the IT security personnel and supports them in systematically recording and using experiences in their work process. The component is being developed in cooperation with an application partner and is also used in projects with industrial partners.

1 Introduction

eGovernment is becoming a more and more important issue in a number of countries. For example, in Germany there is the initiative BundOnline 2005 [9] that aims at making all services of the federal government (German: "Bund") online until 2005. In the USA, eGovernment is regarded as the next American Revolution that is expected by the public [24]. All these initiatives have in common that "safeguarding security and privacy is the top priority of the public for eGovernment services".

In the following, we refer with the term *eService* to such eGovernment services. An eService is the electronic counterpart of an interactive procedure between governmental organizations and their customers.

To ensure the security of eServices, integrated security concepts are needed that do not only address the technical issues of IT security but also relevant organizational, cultural, and social aspects as well as legal peculiarities of the implemented administrative procedure [25]. Furthermore, the security level has to be reasonable, i.e., a good solution has to be found that satisfies the often-conflicting goals of security and usability. Therefore, the success of modern eGovernment services dramatically depends on trustworthiness. So, reasonable security has to be ensured, which is one of the bases for user acceptance [18].

All this is in line with recent developments in the field of IT security, where a major change in the way of handling IT security happens. The IT security expert Bruce Schneier phrases this as "IT security is a process and not a product," which means that it is not sufficient to install a number of products to secure the IT of an organisation [21]. Case-based reasoning is a principle and technology that has the potential to enrich such processes [16].

M.A. Wimmer (Ed.): KMGov 2003, LNAI 2645, pp. 151–162, 2003.

Unfortunately, today's IT security concepts are not yet integrated as required for eServices. They cover only individual aspects and, furthermore, their relationships are not clarified. There is also a lack of (a) clarity about formal conclusiveness of a security concept, (b) the correctness of implemented security measures, (c) continuous monitoring of the measures, and (d) systematic recording of security incidents and experiences.

The presented work is part of a comprehensive approach being developed in the project SKe. The topic of SKe is to develop integrated security concepts and mechanisms for continuously ensuring and improving the required security levels during operation [20, 1]. In SKe, formal modelling of the eService process and its security aspects is used for identifying and verifying the required security properties of an eService [22]. However, to ensure the security requirements, the models require explicit preconditions and assumptions to be fulfilled. To ensure these preconditions and assumptions, a set of technical and organisational measures is derived. Another component of SKe, the electronic security inspector (eSI) supports the continuous monitoring of security measures that can be checked software-technically. By also collecting the experiences on the reaction on security incidents (events, breaches, threats, etc.) in an experience-based security database (eSDB or "experience base") and making them available through an intelligent IT security console, we provide fast and sophisticated support for the daily security-related work. Though the results of SKe can be applied to non-governmental eServices as well, the project is especially adapted for eGovernment services. For example, we cooperate with a governmental unit responsible for a financial eService of a major German city as application partner. The partner is involved in the development of the IT security console and will use the system in the context of a case study for the project.

In this paper, we focus on the intelligent IT security console and the experience-based security database (eSDB). Besides the development of the experience base, an overall process for the required security and knowledge-based activities has to be defined [4]. An integrated knowledge model ties together the formal security model with the experience-based security database.

The solutions for IT security console and eSDB have to be flexible and scalable with respect to different eServices and, therefore, different organisational infrastructures and different experience structures. This leads to different needs regarding "intelligent" support from the knowledge management (KM) system. Furthermore, a tight integration into the work process is required to make KM successful, i.e., a proactive, context-sensitive delivery of knowledge within the work process [3]. We use case-based reasoning (CBR) [2] as a principle and technology for knowledge management. Regarding CBR, the methods and technologies for IT security console and eSDB are also related to CBR-based diagnosis [12, 14], Textual CBR [13], and CBR maintenance [11, 19]. Furthermore, the work is based on our own methods and tools for experience base and CBR maintenance and evaluation [16, 17, 5]. The experience factory concept serves as organisational principle [6]. By establishing a feedback cycle and supporting this feedback cycle with the IT security console, we integrate the recording and usage of experience into the daily work process of the IT security personnel. With the comprehensive view on environment, knowledge model, and processes, intelligent IT security console and eSDB become typical applications of the rather new field of *experience management (EM)* [7, 23, 5].

The expected benefits of KM for maintaining the IT security of eServices are manifold: We expect to establish a feedback cycle for continuous learning and improvement of the IT security of eServices based on experiences. An experience-based security database (eSDB) is expected to speed up and improve the reaction to security threats and incidents. Furthermore, an eSDB is expected to improve the traceability regarding standard cases and non-standard cases. In addition, the systematic recording of incidents in the eSDB provides a good basis for preparing security audits. Last but not least, the systematic recording of experience allows maintaining a certain minimal acceptable level of security even when IT security personnel are not available (e.g., on holiday, illness, fluctuation).

The remainder of the paper is structured as follows: Section 2 describes the application of the KM method DISER [23, 5] for identifying the scenarios that are relevant for managing IT security experience. This resulted in the focus on experience on the reaction of security incidents and -as the core scenario- an experience feedback loop, which integrates the recording and usage of experience into the daily work of IT security personnel (Section 3). To translate this feedback loop into action, we are developing an intelligent IT security console in close cooperation with our application partner (Section 4). The plans for the evaluation of the IT security console are summarized in Section 5. The paper closes with a summary and conclusion (Section 6).

2 KM for IT Security in eGovernment Solutions

We applied the KM method DISER [23, 5] to develop a vision for KM support and CBR support for IT security personnel for eServices. Detailed results are documented in one of the SKe project deliverables [4].

In Phase 1 of DISER, starting with the major goal (as stated above) and existing knowledge such as the *baseline protection manual* as a kind of German standard from the BSI [8], we identified four subject areas. For these, an overall process for the required security and knowledge-based activities was developed [4], which consists of 14 scenarios and an integrated knowledge model that ties together the formal security model with the eSDB. The scenarios were mainly derived from or based on the IT security process from the baseline protection manual [8], and scenarios elicited in workshops with our project partners [4].

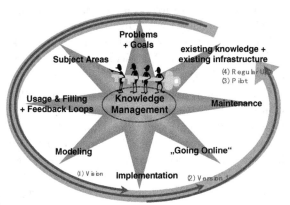

Fig. 1. An overview on DISER (=Design and Implementation of Software Engineering Repositories)

For the eSDB, this resulted in a so-called *experience feedback loop* for the systematic recording and application of IT security experience about the reaction on security incidents and 2 scenarios refining the feedback loop. For the 2nd Phase of DISER, which has the objective of systematically developing the design of the envisioned KM system and building a first version, this feedback loop was chosen as the core scenario. In the following, we focus on the experience feedback loop and its refining scenarios as basis for the IT security console.

3   Feedback Loop for Dynamic Controlling of IT Security

The feedback loop from the viewpoint of the IT security personnel is depicted in Fig. 2. We distinguish four phases in the loop: security status monitoring, diagnosis & decision support, reaction, and feedback. While the monitoring of the security status is a quasi-continuous task in order to keep the security measures effective, the other three phases are triggered by the recognition of potential security incidents and run sequentially for each of these incidents.

In the *security status-monitoring* phase, the electronic security inspector (eSI) monitors software-technically checkable objects using so-called sensors. The organisational security inspector (oSI) collects respective data on organisational measures or on measures that cannot be monitored by the eSI for other reasons. All states that cannot be classified as "OK" by eSI or oSI (i.e., people) are compiled in a list of potential security incidents. In the *diagnosis and decision support* phase, the status is determined for "unclarified" cases. Then respective reactions are proposed based on the experiences and selected by the person(s) responsible for IT security. Depending on severity and potential damage, a priority is assigned to each incident. The incidents to examine are put on a to-do list. In the *reaction* phase, the items on the to-do lists are handled by the respon-

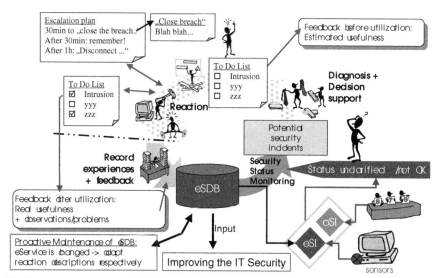

Fig. 2. A feedback loop for IT security experience, which is integrated into the work process.

sible IT security persons according to the priorities. Furthermore, regarding the escalation hierarchy for highly critical situations, automatic reactions are considered if the responsible persons are not available and do not or cannot react quickly enough (e.g., switching off the internet connection when eSI reports a breach and no-one is available because of a public holiday). In the *feedback* phase, experience on new or different reactions is recorded and feedback is given, e.g., if there was really a security incident, effect and success of the reaction, actual damage, and prevented damage. This feedback and new experience closes the loop by improving the diagnosis and decision support capabilities.

When an eService is changed, the proactive maintenance supports the identification of the relevant cases that have to be updated.

The systematic recordings on the security incidents can be used for identifying the need for improvements of the IT security and, as a consequence, introduce new measures or upgrade existing measures.

The feedback loop is an instantiation of the standard case-based reasoning cycle [2] at the organisational level [23] and shows a tight integration into the work process, which is an enabler for successful knowledge management [3].

4   An Intelligent, Experience-Based IT Security Console for eServices

The IT security console implements the core component of the SKe process, i.e., the feedback loop for IT security experience and its related scenarios. Its core task is the support of the IT security personnel in their daily work.

To ensure intelligent support within the daily work context of the user, we developed a process model and a graphical user interface that completely integrates the intelligent support (*iSupport*) into the work process (Section 4.1). This process model is based on the feedback loop from the previous section. To store experience in a standardized way, a representation schema is necessary to describe how the knowledge is recorded (Section 4.2). The schema allows distinguishing between standard and non-standard reactions on incidents. The maintenance process supports the merging of standard cases and related non-standard cases. The strategy for the maintenance process is adaptable to the needs of the environment (Section 4.3). Finally, the actual implementation is based on a product line architecture for experience management systems (Section 4.4).

4.1   How the IT Security Console Supports IT Security Personnel

We use a process model to describe how the IT security console supports IT security personnel. The process model is depicted in Fig. 3 using states (boxes) and transitions (arrows). Based on the process model, we developed a graphical user interface (GUI) for the IT security console. In the following, we describe the process and the opportunities for intelligent support in the different steps of the process and illustrate this with examples from the GUI.

After the login, the system presents the user his personal to-do list and the list of new, open incidents. An IT security manager can additionally view a list of all incidents in the to-do lists of the IT security specialists. New incidents can be reported by eSI (e.g., a port scan) or oSI or entered manually by the IT security personnel.

When a new incident in the list of potential incidents is assigned to a person by himself or by the IT security manager, further situation characteristics are added, which can not be determined automatically, e.g., cause. An iSupport proposes a set of categories. Another iSupport proposes

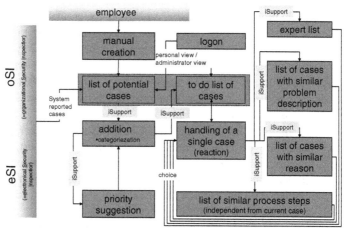

Fig. 3. The process underlying the IT security console

es the priority level based on similar existing cases. A third iSupport proposes reactions on the incident based on same or similar cases in the past. The user selects the reactions he regards as most useful for dealing with the new incident.

Prioritisation is relevant when there are more than 5-10 tasks in the to-do lists in the typical case for a certain environment. According to our experience from industrial projects, priority decisions are subjective and cannot be made consistently over a longer period of time neither by a single person nor by several persons. Therefore, iSupport standardizes the priority decisions.

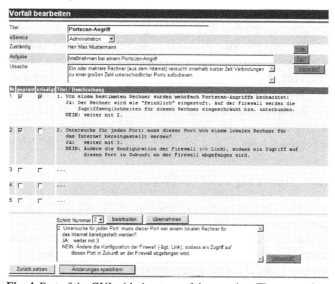

Fig. 4. Part of the GUI with the steps of the reaction. The orange buttons are for the iSupports "Help", "Goal", "Variant", and "Relatives".

To address the requirements of different environments (different eServices, organisational structure, and experience structure), we developed different variants for the presentation and modelling of the description of the reaction, which differ in their functionality and degree of formality. Based on example cases from and in discussions with our application partner, we identified structured text as the most adequate basis for representing the reaction. Variants of structured text for the reaction range from a simple single text field over text with a structure for steps to a decision tree-like structure. The representation of steps is necessary to provide support for planning and executing a reaction that takes longer to perform. The variants also differ with respect to their support for parallel execution. A further formalization is required for steps that can be performed automatically. Fig. 4 gives an impression of the resulting variant selected by our application partner, which supports parallel processing of single steps by the IT security personnel.

In the reaction phase, the system provides several iSupports, which are launched by simply pressing a button (see Fig. 4):

- *"Help" (Gr. "Hilfe")* supports persons who have further questions or who do not completely trust the answers of an IT system. As support, a number of experts for the current incident and reaction are identified. This is done by retrieving a list of similar cases from the experience base and presenting an overview of these cases together with the contact information of the person who handled the respective case in the past.

- *"Goal" (Gr. "Ziel")* aims at finding alternative reactions for solving the problem. For this purpose, a list of cases with same or similar cause and task is retrieved.

- *"Variant" (Gr. "Variante")* aims at identifying alternative causes for the problem. For this purpose, a list of cases with same or similar tasks is retrieved. When an alternative cause is identified, its reaction is also proposed as solution for the current case.

- *"Related" (Gr. "Verwandt")* aims at finding related information for a single step. For this purpose, the systems searches for cases and steps that are similar to the current step (e.g., in the port scan case for the step where the necessity for "open" ports at the firewall is checked, firewall configuration experience would we found). This iSupport requires a representation that supports steps.

The described process refines the feedback loop with respect to the user interaction of the IT security console and shows the integration into the work process as outlined by the feedback loop.

4.2   Modelling the Experience

To support the process model described in the previous section, the cases are structured according to the schema as depicted in Fig. 5. For the design of the schema, we had to consider the iSupports, feedback, and maintenance of standard cases (as a dynamic handbook for reactions on security incidents). Furthermore, the structure has to be open for further functionality such as version management.

The schema distinguishes between *standard cases* ("case", "step-position", and "step") and *concrete cases* ("case occurrence" and "step occurrence"). While standard cases provide a mature description for the reaction in a certain situation, concrete cases describe the application of standard cases for a concrete incident as well as non-standard cases. The application of a standard case can differ regarding the order of the execution of the steps, etc. Such concrete cases are accumulated over time for a standard case [15]. In a maintenance cycle, these concrete cases are used for improving the standard cases. This implements an experience-based improvement cycle for standardized reactions.

The core of a con-
crete case is the "case
occurrence" that in-
cludes the attributes of
the actual reaction in
the concrete case. Be-
sides the "editor" (the
responsible IT security
person), also "control-
ler" and date & time are
stored. The controller is
usually the responsible
IT security manager. A
yellow note allows the

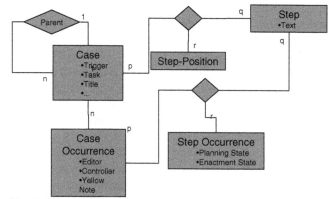

Fig. 5. Schema for experience on IT security incidents and reaction

editor to store some notes during the processing of the case (e.g., to whom a subtask was assigned). For our application partner, a yellow note is deleted after closing a case. Besides the general situation attributes (trigger, task, title), the steps of the reaction are modelled. The steps themselves are described textually. For the concrete case, the planning and execution is supported at the step level by providing a respective status for each step.

4.3   Maintenance Processes and Strategies

The maintenance processes deal with the question of when to update standard cases. For this purpose, there are two classes of concrete cases to be considered: (1) concrete cases that describe the unchanged application of the standard case, where the number of these cases indicates the validity of the standard case; (2) concrete cases that describe an application of a standard case with changes. In the following, we describe the options for the maintenance strategy and the meaning of "changed", i.e., when is a concrete case considered to have a "changed" reaction.

Basically, we distinguish between two extremes of maintenance strategies. The open and flexible nature of the described schema supports the range of maintenance strategies that is spanned by these two extremes:

1. Managed strategy: Changes to a proposed reaction are only recorded within the "concrete case". The standard case is not changed.
2. Unmanaged strategy: Each time when a proposed reaction is changed, a new standard case is recorded after finishing the handling of the incident. The new standard case is related to the old standard case via the parent relationship.

The managed strategy is the preferred strategy for handling cases where the standardization of the reaction is the major goal - for example, when the IT security personnel has a rather low level of expertise. In this case, a periodical or evaluation-triggered maintenance by the respective IT security expert is required [16]. This expert decides which histories are integrated in updated standard cases or lead to new variants of standard cases.

The unmanaged strategy is preferred when the IT security personnel are mainly experts and have a high level of expertise. However, this leads to a high number of new standard cases when changes are made frequently. Furthermore, unchecked new standard cases can also lower the quality of the experience base when error-prone cases are added as standard cases.

In practice, an intermediate strategy is expected to be most useful. For this purpose, evaluation-triggered maintenance is used with a triggering by, e.g., the number of available concrete cases with changes in the reaction (compared to the reaction description of the respective standard case) or changes in the execution order of the steps of the reaction. For this purpose, only semantical changes count as changes; e.g., syntactical corrections of text do not count. The editorial work of the expert prevents a decrease in the quality of the experience base. For the revision, the expert can also analyse differences in the order of the execution of the different steps. The different options for the triggering of the maintenance allow a flexible response to the maintenance needs of the different environments.

4.4   Architecture

The system's architecture is an instantiation of IESE's experience base product line architecture INTERESTS[1]. The product line architecture uses a stable relational data base system as basis. On top of the database management system, we have application logic and user interface. Application logic and user interface are enhanced with intelligent components. Scalability addresses components and database schema. The schema has to support the scalability right from the start, e.g., when replacing a simple "intelligent" search with a more advanced solution. The scalability addresses features and also the price. For example, for the database system, the product line considers MS Access as inexpensive commercial-off-the-shelf tool, PostgreSQL as open source product, and Oracle as advanced solution; for advanced intelligent search, the commercial case-based reasoning tool orenge from empolis is used as an advanced component [10]. INTERESTS itself also delivers the specific glue for "gluing" together the components with program code as well as the respective knowledge on how to model and how to plug the components together.

For the application partner, an inexpensive solution is being developed. This solution is based on MS Access as database management system, J2EE-based technologies for the user interface (i.e., JavaServerPages and JavaBeans), and our in-house CBR solution for similarity-based retrieval on structured text. An excerpt of the GUI is shown in Fig. 4.

---

[1]   INTERESTS = Intelligent Retrieval and Storage System.

5   Plans for Evaluation by Case Studies

For the evaluation, we distinguish three phases according to [17]. In the beginning of the usage of the system (i.e., Phase 1), we use our standard model for measuring indicators about the acceptance of the system [5, 16]. We combine measuring the usage of the system (i.e., number of queries per iSupport) and feedback on the utility of the retrieved experiences (i.e., the proposed reactions). Combining usage and utility allows obtaining a picture on the acceptance more quickly than just monitoring usage because -in the beginning- usage can also be high because the system is new and everybody plays with it. Furthermore, the utility feedback helps to obtain a better understanding of the users' real interests. Later, in Phase 2, application-specific issues can be added for a more detailed evaluation. Phase 3 focuses on the economic value of the system. For the IT security console, we are in Phase 1 and, therefore, will measure usage and analyse the utility feedback. These measurements will show if the feedback loop works.

6   Conclusion

We identified adequate IT security as an essential for eGovernment applications. In the SKe project, a comprehensive solution for ensuring the IT security of eGovernment applications is being iteratively developed and tested. Managing IT security knowledge is an integral part of the SKe approach. We are developing a so-called intelligent IT security console with special support for eGovernment web services as a means to use knowledge management for improving the IT security of eGovernment applications. This system supports the systematic collection and application of experiences on reactions to security incidents as well as the identification of standard cases and the proactive maintenance of the reaction in standard cases. Using case-based reasoning [2] as principle and technology, the system is able to provide intelligent support for several issues in the process of handling security incidents based on experiences in same or similar cases. For the system, we assured the integration of the intelligent support in the context of the work process [3] and developed a flexible schema and scalable architecture to allow an easy adaptation to the needs of different environments, i.e., eServices, organisational structure, etc.

The status of the work is as follows: Based on a design study using real-world cases from the application partner, the concept and user interface were reviewed by the application partner. Based on the design study, the most adequate variant for the representation of incidents and reactions as well as relevant opportunities for intelligent support were selected. A first version of the IT security console is being implemented and will be "fielded" in the first quarter of 2003. An evaluation program to demonstrate the usefulness of the solution will accompany the fielding. Furthermore, for the security department of a telecommunications company, we are coaching the development of a similar system from a simple case processing to a "real" KM solution.

Regarding the requirements and expected benefits, we draw the following conclusions: The role model supports the flexibility regarding the organizational structure. The IT security console can be adapted to different environments regarding the need for intelligent support (e.g., intelligent prioritisation is relevant for environments with a high frequency of incidents). For the modelling of the reactions, we identified for the application partner a rather simple variant that allows the planning of single steps and storing the execution status of each single step. However, for industrial partners, we are developing a more complex modelling for the reaction, which contains a solution log ("story") with positive and negative experiences. The schema supports different strategies for the maintenance of the reactions on standard cases/incidents. These maintenance strategies range from unmanaged to managed style. This supports the expected benefits regarding the traceability of reactions on standard and non-standard cases. The scalable architecture allows an inexpensive start. The evaluation program for the first version will show if the IT security console is able to establish the experience feedback cycle in practice. So far, representatives of the intended users expect a more efficient and effective handling of problems with the financial eService and are looking forward to the first version.

The next steps are the finalization of the first version and a case study with the application partner to show that the IT security console provides the benefits in the practical application. For the second version, we will focus on the proactive maintenance of the reaction descriptions regarding changes to the eService. Encouraged by the good feedback from the application partner and other projects, we expect that knowledge management can provide a number of benefits for ensuring the IT security of eServices in eGovernment.

Acknowledgements. We would like to thank the German Ministry of Education and Research (BMBF) for funding the SKe project (contract 01AK900B). Furthermore, we would like to thank our colleagues at Fraunhofer IESE, the project members from Fraunhofer SIT, TU Darmstadt, and from the knowledge-based systems group at the University of Kaiserslautern for the fruitful discussions and their support.

References

[1]   SKe - Durchgängige Sicherheitskonzeption mit dynamischen Kontrollmechanismen für eService Prozesse. http://www.ske-projekt.de/, 2001.

[2]   A. Aamodt and E. Plaza. Case-based reasoning: Foundational issues, methodological variations, and system approaches. *AICom - Artificial Intelligence Communications*, 7(1):39–59, Mar. 1994.

[3]   A. Abecker and G. Mentzas. Active knowledge delivery in semi-structured administrative processes. In *Knowledge Management in Electronic Government (KMGov-2001)*, Siena, Italy, May 2001.

[4]   K.-D. Althoff, S. Beddrich, S. Groß, A. Jedlitschka, H.-O. Klein, D. Möller, M. Nick, P. Ochsenschläger, M. M. Richter, J. Repp, R. Rieke, C. Rudolph, H. Sarbinowski, T. Shafi, M. Schumacher, and A. Stahl. Gesamtprozess IT-Sicherheit. Technical Report Projektbericht SKe - AP3, 2001.

[5]   K.-D. Althoff and M. Nick. *How To Support Experience Management with Evaluation - Foundations, Evaluation Methods, and Examples for Case-Based Reasoning and Experience Factory*. Springer Verlag, 2003. (to appear).

[6]   V. R. Basili, G. Caldiera, and H. D. Rombach. Experience Factory. In J. J. Marciniak, editor, *Encyclopedia of Software Engineering*, volume 1, pages 469–476. John Wiley & Sons, 1994.

[7]   R. Bergmann. Experience management - foundations, development methodology, and internet-based applications. Postdoctoral thesis, Department of Computer Science, University of Kaiserslautern, 2001.

[8]   Bundesamt für Sicherheit in der Informatikstechnik (BSI). *IT Baseline Protection Manual.* Oct. 2002. http://www.bsi.bund.de/.

[9]   Bundesministerium des Inneren (BMI). Die eGovernment-Initiative BundOnline 2005. http://www.bundonline2005.de/, 2000.

[10]   empolis GmbH. orenge (open retrieval engine) - empolis knowledge manager. http://www.empolis.comm/products/prod_ore.asp, 2000.

[11]   D. B. Leake, B. Smyth, D. C. Wilson, and Q. Yang, editors. *Computational Intelligence - Special Issue on Maintaining CBR Systems,* 2001.

[12]   M. Lenz, H.-D. Burkhard, P. Pirk, E. Auriol, and M. Manago. CBR for diagnosis and decision support. *AI Communications,* 9(3):138–146, 1996.

[13]   M. Lenz, A. Hübner, and M. Kunze. Textual CBR. In M. Lenz, H.-D. Burkhard, B. Bartsch-Spörl, and S. Weß, editors, *Case-Based Reasoning Technology — From Foundations to Applications,* LNAI 1400, Berlin, 1998. Springer Verlag.

[14]   L. Lewis and G. Dreo. Extending trouble ticket systems to fault diagnostics. *IEEE Network,* Nov. 1993.

[15]   M. Nick, K.-D. Althoff, T. Avieny, and B. Decker. How experience management can benefit from relationships among different types of knowledge. In M. Minor and S. Staab, editors, *Proceedings of the German Workshop on Experience Management (GWEM2002),* number P-10 in Lecture Notes in Informatics (LNI), Bonn, Germany, Mar. 2002. Gesellschaft für Informatik.

[16]   M. Nick, K.-D. Althoff, and C. Tautz. Systematic maintenance of corporate experience repositories. *Computational Intelligence - Special Issue on Maintaining CBR Systems,* 17(2):364–386, May 2001.

[17]   M. Nick and R. Feldmann. Guidelines for evaluation and improvement of reuse and experience repository systems through measurement programs. In *Third European Conference on Software Measurements (FESMA-AEMES 2000),* Madrid, Spain, Oct. 2000.

[18]   Organization for Economic Development (OECD). Update on official statistics on internet consumer transactions. http://www.oecd.org/pdf/M00027000/M00027669.pdf, 2001.

[19]   K. Racine and Q. Yang. Maintaining unstructured case bases. In *Proceedings of the Second International Conference on Case-Based Reasoning,* pages 553–564, 1997.

[20]   R. Rieke. Projects CASENET and SKe - a framework for secure eGovernment. In *Telecities 2002 Winter Conference,* Siena, Italy, Dec. 2002. http://www.comune.siena.it/telecities/program.html.

[21]   B. Schneier. *Secrets and Lies: Digital Security in a Networked World.* John Wiley & Sons, 2000.

[22]   C. R. Sigrid Gürgens, Peter Ochsenschläger. Role based specification and security analysis of cryptographic protocols using asynchronous product automata. In *DEXA 2002 International Workshop on Trust and Privacy in Digital Business.* IEEE Press, 2002.

[23]   C. Tautz. *Customizing Software Engineering Experience Management Systems to Organizational Needs.* PhD thesis, University of Kaiserslautern, Germany, 2001.

[24]   The Council for Excellence in Goverment. Poll "eGoverment - The Next American Revolution". http://www.excelgov.org/, Sept. 2000.

[25]   M. A. Wimmer and B. von Bredow. Sicherheitskonzepte für e-Government. Technische vs. ganzheitliche Ansätze. *DuD - Datenschutz und Datensicherheit,* (26):536–541, Sept. 2002.

Knowledge Enhanced E-government Portal

Jan Paralic[1], Tomas Sabol[2], and Marian Mach[1]

[1] Dept. of Cybernetics and AI, Technical University of Kosice, Letna 9,
042 00 Kosice, Slovakia
Jan.Paralic@tuke.sk
[2] Faculty of Economics, Technical University of Kosice, B. Nemcovej 32,
042 00 Kosice, Slovakia
Tomas.Sabol@tuke.sk

Abstract. There is a growing number of *e-Government portals* and solutions
available today. But what the users lack in particular is a customised assistance
– help that meets the individual situation and competence [13]. In this paper, a
system called Webocrat will be presented as an attempt to shift e-Government
portals toward this direction, providing knowledge management strategy as its
basis [11]. The Webocrat system applies a knowledge-based approach [5]. Information of all kinds produced by various modules is linked to a shared ontology representing an application domain. Such ontology serves as a means for
structuring and organizing available information resulting in improved search
capability and contents presentation.

1 Introduction

Knowledge can be simply defined as actionable information [12]. That means that
(only) relevant information available in the right place, at the right time, in the right
context, and in the right way can be considered as knowledge.

The knowledge life cycle defined in [9] hinges on the distinction between *tacit* and
explicit knowledge. Explicit knowledge is a formal one and can be found in documents
of an organization: reports, manuals, correspondence (internal and external), patents,
pictures, tables (e.g. Excel sheets), images, video and sound recordings, software etc.
Tacit knowledge is personal knowledge given by individual experience (and hidden in
peoples' minds) [12].

A considerable amount of explicit knowledge is scattered throughout various
documents within public and governmental organizations and people minds working
there. In many cases the possibility to efficiently access (retrieve) and reuse this
knowledge is limited [3]. As a result of this, most knowledge is not sufficiently exploited, shared and subsequently forgotten in relatively short time after it has been
introduced to, invented/discovered within the organization. Therefore, in the approaching information society, it is vitally important for knowledge-intensive organizations as public and governmental institutions to make the best use of information
gathered from various information resources inside the organizations and from exter-

M.A. Wimmer (Ed.): KMGov 2003, LNAI 2645, pp. 163–174, 2003.

nal sources like the Internet. On the other hand, tacit knowledge of authors of the documents' provides important context to them, which cannot be effectively intercepted.

Knowledge management [12] generally deals with several activities relevant in knowledge life cycle [1]: identification, acquisition, development, dissemination (sharing), use and preservation of organization's knowledge. Our approach to knowledge management in the e-Government context supports most of the activities mentioned above. Based on this approach, a Web-based system Webocrat[1] [11] has been designed and implemented. It is being now tested on pilot applications at Wolverhampton (UK) and in Kosice (Slovakia). Firstly, it provides tools for capturing and updating of tacit knowledge connected with particular explicit knowledge inside documents. This is possible due to ontology model, which is used for representation of organization's domain knowledge. Ontology with syntax and semantic rules provides the 'language' by which Webocrat(-like) system can interact at the *knowledge level* [8].

Use of ontology enables to define concepts and relations representing knowledge about a particular document in domain specific terms. In order to express the contents of a document explicitly, it is necessary to create links between the document and relevant parts of a domain model, i.e. links to those elements of the domain model, which are relevant to the contents of the document. Model elements can be also used for intelligent search and retrieval of relevant documents.

Existence of a knowledge model (ontology) in the center of the system is the key difference to approaches followed by other 5th FP projects like EDEN (they are strong in use of natural language processing techniques supporting communication between citizens and public administrations) or DEMOS (very elaborated approach focused on on-line consultation).

The rest of this paper is organized as follows. Sect. 2 describes the functional overview of the Webocrat system, following with Sect. 3 describing its architecture. Sect. 4 presents three from the knowledge management point of view interesting aspects of the Webocrat system. The first one is example of ontology for a specific e-Government application. The second one is an example of a new service required by users, offered using Webocrat in the first trial and its knowledge enhanced extension for the second trial. Finally, knowledge supported personalization offered by the Webocrat system is described in greater details. Sect. 5 makes a brief summary of the paper.

2   Webocrat System Functional Overview

From the point of view of functionality of the *WEBOCRAT* system it is possible to break down the system into several parts and/or modules [11]. They can be represented in a layered sandwich-like structure, which is depicted in Fig. 1.

---

[1] EC funded project IST-1999-20364 Webocracy (Web Technologies Supporting Direct Participation in Democratic Processes)

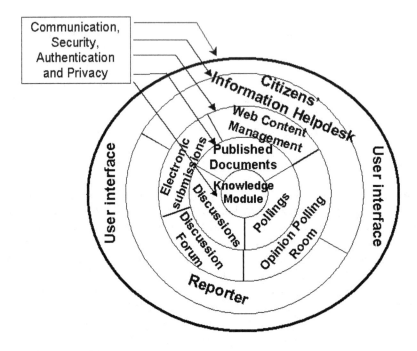

Fig. 1. *WEBOCRAT* system structure from the system's functionality point of view

2.1 First Layer

A Knowledge Model module occupies the central part of this structure. This system component contains a conceptual model of a domain. The purpose of this component is to index all information stored in the system in order to describe the context of this information (in terms of domain specific concepts). The central position symbolizes that the knowledge model is the core (heart) of the system – all parts of the system use this module in order to deal with information stored in the system (both for organizing this information and accessing it).

2.2 Second Layer

Information stored within the system has the form of documents of different types. Since three main document types will be processed by the system, the document space can be divided into three subspaces – publishing space, discussion space, and opinion polling space. These areas contain published documents, users' contributions to discussions on different topics of interest, and records of users' opinions about different issues, respectively.

2.3 Third Layer

Since each document subspace expects different way of manipulating with documents, three system's modules are dedicated to them. Web Content Management module (WCM) offers means to manage the publishing space. It enables to prepare documents in order to be published (e.g. to link them to elements of a domain model), to publish them, and to access them after they are published. Discussion space is managed by Discussion Forum module (DF). The module enables users to contribute to discussions they are interested in and/or to read contributions submitted by other users. Electronic Submissions module (ES) enables users to access special part of the document space comprising their formal or informal submissions to local authority. Opinion Polling Room module (OPR) represents a tool for performing opinion polling on different topics. Users can express their opinions in the form of polling.

2.4 Fourth Layer

In order to navigate among information stored in the system in an easy and effective way, this layer is focused on retrieving relevant information from the system in various ways. Two modules represent it, each enabling easy access to the stored information in a different way. Citizens' Information Helpdesk module (CIH) is dedicated to search. It represents a search engine based on the indexing and linking (to knowledge model) of stored documents. Its purpose is to find all those documents, which match user's requirements expressed in the form of a query defined by means of a free text, or a query composed from concepts from domain model, or by document attributes (like author, date of issue etc.).

The other module performing information retrieval is the Reporter module (REP). This module is dedicated to providing information of two types. The first type represents information in an aggregated form. It enables to define and generate different reports concerning information stored in the system. The other type is focused on providing particular documents – but unlike the CIH module it is oriented on off-line mode of operation. It monitors content of the document space on behalf of the user and if information the user may be interested in appears in the system, it sends an alert to him/her.

2.5 Fifth Layer

The upper layer of the presented functional structure of the system is represented by a user interface. It integrates functionality of all the modules accessible to a particular user into one coherent portal to the system and provides access to all functions of the system in a uniform way. In order for the system to be able to provide required functionality in a real setting, several security issues must be solved. This is the aim of the Communication, Security, Authentication and Privacy module (CSAP) [4].

Technical achievements comprise also a system designed to provide automatic routing of messages from citizens to the appropriate person within the public administration (ES module); tools for easy access to public administration information and to competitive tendering (WCM module) and personalization support (REP modules) that will be described in greater details in Sect. 4.

3 Webocrat System Coarse Architecture

Webocrat system has client-server architecture [7]. This is illustrated by a top-level system structure diagram, which is depicted in Fig. 2.

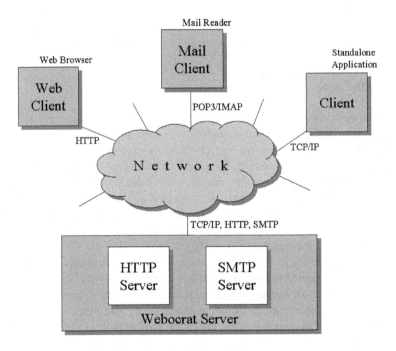

Fig. 2. Top-level decomposition of the Webocrat system structure

Three types of client software are expected in the Webocrat system – Web based clients, mail readers, and standalone applications (for the sake of simplicity they are called just clients). Mail clients are specialized in supporting of user alerting on events that could be of interest for these users as well as sending of replies to their electronic submissions. In order to provide users with mail messages, no special requirements are defined for mail clients – common mail user agents are perfectly usable.

Standalone clients represent specialised clients that are not intended for many users. Each of these clients focuses on a small set of functions provided by the system. Users working with these clients take special positions in maintaining the system and the information stored within it. At this stage of system design, three standalone clients are considered – ontology editor for building and maintaining a knowledge model, annotator for enriching documents, which should be uploaded on the Webocrat server by a set of links to elements from the domain model, and administrator tool for administering the whole system.

In addition to that, this type of client can represent an interface to an existing information system (i.e. the client is used by some software and not by people). For example, some external system can submit documents which should be published in the publishing space, together with information which (type of) users can access these documents, to what elements of the domain model these documents should be linked before their publication, etc.

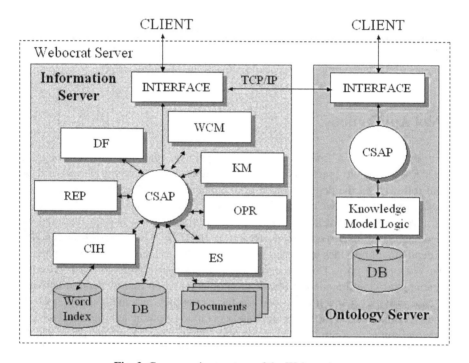

Fig. 3. Coarse grain structure of the Webocrat server

The most common type of client is a web client. The Webocrat clients are either a standard Web browser or any software, which uses the HTTP protocol to communicate with the Webocrat system. Web client is dedicated for main functions offered by the system – accessing information published in the publishing space, sharing ideas and opinions in various discussions, accessing of users' electronic submissions (e.g. a legacy system used at the local authority for recording and managing of the mail correspondence) and providing opinions on different issues by participating in some opinion polling. This type of client targets wide audience of users.

The Webocrat server itself is composed of several modules. The structure of the server is depicted in Fig. 3.

As discussed above, the Webocrat system consists of several modules that can be installed. Basically, these modules can be divided into two relatively separate parts splitting the Webocrat server into two separate servers – Webocrat Information Server and Webocrat Ontology Server. Since these servers can be installed on separate machines, which could be far away from each other (this covers also the possibility of their installation on the same machine), the communication between them is based on the TCP/IP protocol family.

This division of responsibilities for domain models and for documents containing information of interest for users enables easier maintenance of both domain models and documents and better utilization of available resources. As an example of this can serve a case where one ontology server is shared by several information servers (using the same domain model or working with different models). Another example, an extreme one, is not to use any ontology at all and relying only on full-text retrieval of documents – in this case there is no need to install the ontology server.

4 Pilot Applications

Within this project, a special attention is paid to the process of integrating *WEBOCRAT* tools into practical applications. Rather than separating phases of development followed by the deployment of pilot applications, the process of *WEBOCRAT* tool and methodology development is intertwined with deployment from early beginning (all pilot applications are splitted into two trial phases). The project started with detailed analysis of user requirements (result of this study has been published in [10]). Early deployment provides important feedback and drives their further development.

The Webocracy project uses a case centered and user-driven approach. The pilot applications provide the context for all the implementation and evaluation activities. Each case provides a specific test-bed for the technology and methodology enabling on-line (Web-based) support to services and operation of public administrations. Each case is configured according to the needs and "public context" of the particular user partner.

The first trials have been devoted to basic features of DF, WCM and OPR modules [2]. The second trials will involve all features on knowledge modeling technology, alerting and personalization.

In each phase, each of the user partners conducts trials concurrently. Wolverhampton City Council (WCC) is responsible for the design, specification and evaluation of the trials in the UK. The Local Authority Kosice - City ward Tahanovce (LATA) and The Local Authority Kosice - City ward Dargovskych hrdinov (LAFU) are responsible for pilot applications and trials in Slovak Republic.

The first trial in WCC did make use of DF and OPR modules, and involved partner agencies and citizens. First trial in LATA used WCM and OPR modules. LATA focused their pilot application on web publishing and content management. In LAFU the trial was focused on ES module [2].

4.1 Example of a Knowledge Model

The preliminary model for the pilot WCC's pilot application [6] identifies five main classes:

Locations are entities with a geographical location, and are either *areas* (such as the area served by a local authority, or the ward which elects a local representative), or *premises* (such as office buildings, schools or hospitals). Slots are used to describe the geographical relationship between locations (a school is located in a ward, a ward is part of a local authority area etc.).

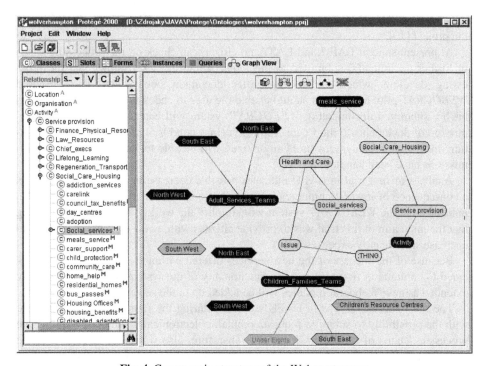

Fig. 4. Coarse grain structure of the Webocrat server

Organisations are the various public agencies, community groups and businesses that have a role in the city, and their departments or sections. This class also includes the various partnerships between these individual organisations. Slots are used to describe the hierarchy of organisation structures, and the relationships to areas served and premises occupied.

Activities describe either the provision of a service by an organisation (see Fig. 4), or the contribution of an organisation to a partnership. Slots are used to establish these relationships to organisations.

Issues are broad topics, which may be raised in discussion and consultation with citizens. These may not relate in a simple way to the structures or services of organisations. Slots will be used to identify the links between issues, services and organisations.

Persons are individual contacts - either *officers* or *elected representatives*. Slots are used to relate them to the activities for which they are the appropriate contact. Elected representatives are also linked via slots to the areas that they are representing.

4.2 Example of a New Service

Here presented service has been implemented as a result of one special requirement raised by LAFU within the user requirements analysis carried on at the beginning of the project [10].

At present state at LAFU and LATA no citizen can check on the processing status of his/her document(s) submitted to the Local Authority. User knows just the processing deadline, which is 30 days after document entry date. The proposed *WEBOCRAT* pilot application should enable the user to check the processing status of his/her submitted document(s). *WEBOCRAT* system will enable easy electronic submission of documents to the Local Authority. (In second trial after positive authorization, in first as a anonymous user) any citizen will be able to see how particular submissions have been handled.

Analysis of first trial in LAFU indicates possible decrease in overhead expenses as a consequence of lower communication costs but only by a negligible amount. It also indicates that the *WEBOCRAT* system will simplify the work at LA. It is worth noting that the main aim of this trial was to provide citizens with a new type of service, not to decrease significantly expenses of LA.

Because of the success of the new services offered within the first trial, LAFU decided to continue in first trial and the functionality of the system will be continuously extended as new Webocrat modules will be added up to the second trial.

The most successful was in LAFU's opinion during the first trial the CM module with the possibility to submit a request/complaint electronically and even tracking the processing status of submitted document. Therefore, also within the second trial the main focus will remain on this service, enhancing it significantly using functionality of the whole Webocrat system.

Current *WEBOCRAT* pilot application enables users to submit a complaint/suggestion electronically and check the processing status of the submitted document(s). No authorization is provided yet. Therefore all users can see all submitted documents as well as their processing status. For the second trial, authorization and fully personalized access will be provided. But the user will have a free choice whether his/her complaint/suggestion should be accessible form him/her only, or for other users as well.

Moreover, a number of standard forms will be provided using CM module and will enable citizens to submit them electronically using Webocrat system. The system will automatically route the form to the LA employee responsible for handling it. This should lead to a significant time saving when compared to the current practice, where all mails are coming first to a specialized person for that registering them and for-

warding to the superintendent of the LA, who distributes the mails to appropriate departments, more specifically to head of departments. Head of department assigns it
further to a particular employee for processing. *WEBOCRAT* system application by
means of the ES module will lead to a reengineering of this administration process
saving significant amount of time and effort.

In order to support intelligent retrieval (CIH module) within all electronic submissions, as well as various types of analysis (REP module), the following links to the
conceptual knowledge model should be created for each electronic submission (document).

A link to department that will be responsible for its processing,

A link to a clerk, who was assigned responsible for processing this matter,

A link explaining type of the given electronic document (e.g. a special form, request, application etc.),

A link explaining topics deals by this document (for informal submissions only).

For submission of pre-defined forms the Webocrat system will do all the linking
automatically. For informal matters employees (with Webocrat system support) may
do it.

Statistical analysis of documents submitted to local authority will be supported by
the REP module functionality. Based on the links to knowledge model it will be possible to analyze e.g. distribution of citizens' submissions into different topics resulting
in information about what areas are problematic or overloaded. The other possibility is
to analyze efficiency of processing electronic submissions by particular employees,
departments, etc.

4.3 Knowledge Based Personalisation

Since the system can contain a lot of information in different formats (published information, discussion contributions, etc.), it may not be easy to find exactly the information user is looking for. Therefore he/she has the possibility to create his/her profile
in which he/she can define his/her interests and/or preferred way of interacting with
the system.

When defining an area of interest, user selects elements from a domain model (or
subparts of this model). In this way user declares that he/she is interested in topics
defined by the selected part of the domain model.

The definition of user's area of interest enables alerting – user can be alerted, e.g.
on changes of the domain model, a new opinion polling, or publishing of a new document, opening of a new discussion, etc. User has the possibility to set alerting policy in
detail on which kind of information he/she wants to be alerted in what way (including
extreme settings for no alerting or alerting on each event taking place in the system).
The system compares each event (e.g. submission of a discussion contribution, publishing a document, etc.) to users' profiles. If result of this comparison is positive, i.e.
the user may be interested in the event, then the user is alerted.

Alerting can have two basic forms. The first alternative is represented with notification using e-mail services. User can be notified on event-per-event basis, i.e. he/she

receives an e-mail message for each event he/she is alerted on. Alternatively, it is possible to use an e-mail digest format – user receives e-mail message, which informs him/her about several events. The way of packaging several alerts into one e-mail message depends on user's setting. Basically, it can be based on time intervals and/or the size of e-mail messages.

The other alternative is a 'personal newsletter'. This does not disturb user at unpredictable time – user simply can access his/her newsletter when he/she desires to be informed what is on in the system. Moreover, he/she can access it from arbitrary gadget connected to the Internet. The personal newsletter has the form of a document published in the publishing space. This document is generated by the system and contains links to all those documents, which may be of interest for the user. Since the document is generated when user logs in, it can cover all information submitted and/or published since the last user's visit.

User registered in the system as an individual entity (i.e. not anonymous user) is provided with a personal access page ensuring him/her an individual access to the system. This page is built in an automatic way and can consist of several parts. Some of them can be general and the others are user-specific.

The former can serve as a starting point for browsing all published documents accessible to the user, all discussions he/she is allowed to participate in (in passive or active way), all running polls for which he/she is eligible, using search facilities of the system, read hot information, etc. The latter parts are devoted to user's personal newsletter, links to documents and discussions topics of which match the user's area of interest.

User can use his/her personal access page in an active way. For example he/she can make notes, which documents from those offered by the system he/she intends to read and/or in which he/she is not interested. Or he/she can store links to those documents he/she has found exceptionally interesting, or to which he/she would like to return later.

5   Conclusions

In this paper, a system called Webocrat has been presented as an attempt to shift e-Government portals toward a customized assistance and knowledge enhanced services. The Webocrat system applies a knowledge-based approach. The functional overview, as well as basic architecture of the system has been presented.

Webocrat approach is user-centered, focusing on pilot applications that are divided into two trials. At the time of writing the first trials, beta version of the full Webocrat system has been available for testing and the second trials have just started (scheduled for March – May 2003). First information about the real experience with full Webocrat system could therefore be provided at the time of the conference.

In this paper, three examples of the Webocrat potential from the knowledge management perspective have been described.

Acknowledgements. We would like to thank our project partners for helpful comments and stimulating discussions. This work is done within the Webocracy project, which is supported by European Commission DG INFSO under the IST program, contract No. IST-1999-20364 and within the VEGA project 1/8131/01 "Knowledge Technologies for Information Acquisition and Retrieval" of Scientific Grant Agency of Ministry of Education of the Slovak Republic.

The content of this publication is the sole responsibility of the authors, and in no way represents the view of the European Commission or its services.

References

1. Abecker A., Bernardi A. Hinkelmann K. Kühn, O. & Sintek M.: Toward a Technology for Organizational Memories, IEEE Intelligent Systems, 13 (1998) 40–48
2. Bocock, R., Cizmarik, T., Novacek E., Paralic J. and Thomson, P.: Specification of pilot applications and design of trials. Webocracy Technical Report R12.1, Technical University of Košice (2001)
3. Borghoff U. M. & Pareschi R. (Eds.): Information Technology for Knowledge Management. Springer Verlag (1998)
4. Dridi, F. and Pernul, G. and Unger, V.: Security for the electronic government. In Proceedings of the European Conference on E-Government, Trinity College, Dublin, Ireland (2001) 99–110
5. Dzbor M., Paralic J. and Paralic, M.: Knowledge management in a distributed organization. In: Proc. of the 4th IEEE/IFIP International Conference BASYS'2000, Kluwer Academic Publishers, London (2000) 339–348
6. Macej P., Novacek E., Thomson P., Paralic J. and Cizmarik T.: Conceptual Knowledge Models (Phase I). Webocracy Technical Report R12.2.1, Technical University of Košice (2002)
7. Mach M., Sabol T., Dridi F., Palola I., Furdik K., Thomson P., Cizmarik T., Novacek E.: Edited annual report for publication. Webocracy Technical Report R1.1.3, Technical University of Košice (2001)
8. Newell A.: The Knowledge Level. Artificial Intelligence 18 (1982) 87–127
9. Nonaka I., Takeuchi H.: The Knowledge Creating Company: How Japanese Companies Create the Dynamics of Innovation. Oxford Univ. Press (1995)
10. Paralic, J., Sabol, T.: Implementation of e-Government Using Knowledge-Based System. In. Proc. of the 12th Int. Workshop on Database and Expert Systems Applications, (W06: 2nd Int. Workshop on Electronic Government), Munich (2001) 364–368
11. Paralic, J., Sabol, T., Mach, M.: A System to support E-Democracy. Proc. of the First International Conference EGOV 2002, Aix-en-Provence, France, LNCS 2456, Electronic Government, R. Traunmuller, K. Lenk (Eds.), Springer Verlag (2002)
12. Tiwana A.: The Knowledge Management Toolkit. Prentice Hall (2000)
13. Traunmüller, R. & Wimmer, M.: Directions in E-Government: Processes, Portals, Knowledge. Proc. of the Int. Workshop "On the Way to Electronic Government" in Conjunction with DEXA (Munich, Germany), IEEE Computer Society Press, Los Alamitos, CA (2001) 313–317

A Collaborative E-authoring Tool for Knowledge Assets

Tang-Ho Lê[1] and Luc Lamontagne[2]

[1] Computer Science Department
Université de Moncton, 165 Massey Ave, Moncton, (N.B.)
CANADA, E1A 3E9
letangho@umoncton.ca
[2] Département d'informatique et de recherche opérationelle
Université de Montréal, C.P. 6128, Succ. Centre-Ville, Montréal (Québec)
CANADA, H3C 3J7
lamontal@iro.umontreal.ca

Abstract. The development of e-government enhances not only the public-agency relation but also inter-organizational cooperation between governmental agencies. In this context the promotion of knowledge distribution favors the application of existing techniques and approaches in Knowledge Management Systems. Especially, to exchange "knowledge in evolution" from different disciplines, one needs some groupware knowledge management tools to support knowledge worker communities via the Internet. To be effective, these tools should have visual features for several presentation issues like distributed tasks, evolution trace keeping, ontological discussion and action demonstration. In this paper, we provide an overview of our groupware tool, called Collaborative e-Authoring Tool for Knowledge Assets (CATKA) allowing to create, visualize, exploit and interchange two kinds of knowledge: declarative and procedural knowledge. We also detail the knowledge base updating technical issues for knowledge exchange process between knowledge workers to carry out an e-authoring project step by step, from the beginning to the final phase.

1 Introduction

In the current explosion of the Web, the development of e-government must include on one hand, the e-services that carry out the public-agencies relation, and on the other hand, the groupware to support inter-organizational cooperation between governmental agencies. For example, search and rescue operations, which imply several agencies, as the police, the Air force, the Coast guard , etc., actually need some kind of knowledge networks built with distributed tasks between these agencies. Several knowledge workers from distant sites must create this new multi-disciplines knowledge during a period of time. The procedures for such operations to follow may be revised several times and then disseminated to responsible workers. The development of such a tool pertains mostly to procedural knowledge. In the actual state of the Knowledge Management field, this kind of tools is also necessary.

From our point of view, the difficulties to realize such tools can be identified in terms of the lack of visual features for several presentation issues like distributed

M.A. Wimmer (Ed.): KMGov 2003, LNAI 2645, pp. 175–185, 2003.

tasks, evolution trace keeping, ontological discussion and action demonstration. According to [1], the need to better represent procedural knowledge is still poorly understood. Indeed, intensive research has been conducted over several years to devise formal methods to understand and to determine declarative knowledge based on ontology; for example, several proposals were made for ontology languages and ontology builder such as DAML, Protege 2000, Ontolingua, etc. But fewer research efforts were devoted to model and specify knowledge being procedural in nature, and to combine this with declarative knowledge. In this paper, we describe our groupware tool, called Collaborative e-Authoring Tool for Knowledge Assets (CATKA) allowing to create, visualize, exploit and interchange two kinds of knowledge: declarative and procedural knowledge. This tool was adapted from an e-learning project, realized during the last year, granted by the Human Resources Development Canada. First, we introduce some basic concepts related to practical Knowledge Management (KM) tools; then we present the modeling scheme for Procedural Knowledge used by our software. Finally, we detail the knowledge base updating technical issues for knowledge exchange process between knowledge workers to carry out an e-authoring project step by step, from the beginning to the final phase.

2 Basic Concepts Related to Practical KM Tools

KM tool developers and users have now reached maturity with some basic concepts included in these tools; for instance, the *granularity issue* for defining Knowledge Units (KU) that take into account the limitation of human cognitive capacity, the *visualization feature* allowing to visualize and directly manipulate KU on the computer's screen and the *modeling* of declarative and procedural knowledge. These essential concepts and features are further described in the following.

In the design of a Knowledge Management system, either as a process or as a product [2], one has to cope with the granularity problem. Indeed, if knowledge workers want to efficiently transfer the desired knowledge to one another, what would be its suitable volume? To answer this question, we believe that one must take into account the user's cognitive capability. Without determining this cognitive limitation, the transferred knowledge will be useless or/and not be reused. This issue is not clearly addressed in the current literature. We see two reasons for the difficulties to determine such a limitation:

- Because the knowledge is not well defined yet. Fundamentally, what is the knowledge we want to transfer? A declarative knowledge or a procedural one? The former concerns some concept definitions or some factual (short) information; the latter is essentially action(s) to perform some tasks (in the sense of an algorithm). In the both cases, to call them "knowledge" they must be self-understandable by the receiver. How one can ensure that?
- Because of the lack of a clear separation between information and knowledge. Consequently, instead of transferring the right knowledge, one may collect a bulk of information of all types. The receiver of this "knowledge", cannot consume it, has the impression that he/she lacks yet the desired knowledge and wants to know more.

One approach for the transfer of knowledge is to apply some research results already available from the Intelligent Tutoring Systems. In such systems, a knowledge object (i.e. a KU) corresponds roughly to a teaching subject. Several related subjects form a lesson, what we call a Knowledge Network (KN) that one can teach in a session during about one hour. Moreover, it is proven that the teaching of procedural knowledge will be more efficient if it is accompanied by demonstrations [3]. These demonstrations can be realized by animation files (e.g. by Macromedia Flash) or, if the memory space isn't matter, by some video films. Even in the context of ontological negotiation as proposed in [4], one must firstly frame out the underlying knowledge. To do this, a cognitive analysis will be necessary. From the light of Intelligent Tutoring Systems, we can design a KN as a task hierarchy consisting of just a small number of levels (from one to tree levels is ideal). That is, the KN is named as a global task, and its content can be detailed with some KUs as primitive tasks, which are arranged as a sequence (one level) or as a hierarchy of several levels.

While the ontology construction is based on the entities of the external world, the procedural knowledge results from our epistemological states of mind. This distinction leads to these two important consequences:

1. The ontology construction can apply the principles of *object oriented design* with class definition (a template to classify instances) in which the emphasis is put on the view of entities (expressed by nouns) and the relation between super and sub-classes as generalization/specialization. For example, we can have the superclass "Vehicle" and the subclass "Truck". However, the *actions* are designed as relations between two different class entities; for example, a "Car" being *driven* by a "Person". See more details in [5] and [6].

2. For procedure knowledge, the importance relies on the description of actions or the achievement of tasks. In order to make understandable this knowledge, *pedagogical principles* can be applied, e.g. one can specify the prerequisite (condition) for each knowledge progression step. Thus, as a result, one produces also a hierarchy of *domain knowledge concepts* which are a mix of entity concepts and procedural concepts. The latter can be expressed by verbs and by nouns derived from verbs (not like the entity nouns), for example, "*navigation* in the web site".

We observe another consequence of this distinction regarding the granularity problem of the Semantic Web: while it is difficult to define a manageable unit for an ontology (i.e. as a class, or as a hierarchy of classes, or as a knowledge base with some classes and their instances) it is simpler to define a unit for procedural knowledge, because each unit correspond to a task which already has its limitations. And then, as several related KUs form a KN, its volume is logically enough to describe any general task.

Although the above concepts and features can be realized in some manners for most software tools, a simple and effective tool stills to be desired. Especially, in the context of the knowledge exchange between knowledge workers (of inter agencies) where a small group works on a collaborative project via the Internet. This kind of groupware must be simple enough to not discourage the users in learning how to use the tool, while it is effective enough to allow users to continually visualize and work on the same knowledge bases (i.e. developing and updating their KU) over a period of time.

3 Declarative and Procedure Knowledge Modeling

The design of a Knowledge Management System is essentially the modeling of knowledge so that it is understandable to users, or at least, to provide them with the conditions for an adequate awareness.   As many authors in the Knowledge Management field, we make use of frames to model knowledge in the Collaborative Authoring Tool for Knowledge Assets. To clarify the terminology, we use the term "Knowledge Unit" (KU) to designate some knowledge about an *entity* or about a *process*. Thus, we distinguish two kinds of units: "Static" KU and "How-to" KU. A static KU is a declarative KU that contains concept definitions, labels, facts and information related to the underlying domain. The names of these KU form (or are derived from) the domain ontology. A How-to KU is task-oriented (i.e. procedural knowledge). It contains the procedure to follow through (actions or tasks) and refers to static KU when necessary. The description of a How-to KU focuses on a limited scope, and its attributes specify the underlying context, a situation or some conditions. This context allows users to become aware of the conditions to understand it (pedagogically called prerequisites). A How-to KU can also give some references (links) to other available documents.

Although a KU has limited scope, it is not confined to itself. In other words, a KU never exists in isolation and always relates to other KUs. Thus, a KN including several KUs linked together could provide a complete view of the knowledge related to a specific topic. The tool described below allows for the construction of KNs, independently of the application domain. Figure 1 on the next page illustrates an example of a How-to KU frame describing the creation task of Flash files. Figure 2 gives an example of a KN for an authoring project presented in the section 4; the blue node representing the related concept.

To each KU featured in a KN is associated a frame structure. The frame of a How-to KU has two parts with some attributes. In the first part, the following attributes are used for the KU identity:

Name: a term that abstracts the actions of the underlying KU.
Domain: an ontological hierarchy of the domain written as a sequence of terms (i.e. domain/sub-domain/sub sub-domain /...). The last sub-domain is where the actual KU is situated. For instance, in the computer programming domain, if the actual KU is "*for* loop", then the domain field can be specified as "Computer Science / Programming Languages / C++ Programming". This sequence simply is the path on the storage device to locate the actual KU. All together (i.e. the sequence plus the KU name), they form an index entry for the working domain.
Done by: refers to the knowledge worker who creates the underlying KU.

The second part models the procedural knowledge. This modeling takes into account the epistemological states of mind that is realized by describing the first three main attributes, which naturally correspond to what we already know, what we are learning, and what we will know afterwards:

Situation: a textual description of the conditions where the KU is applicable.
Actions: a textual description of some primitive actions or subtasks.

Results: anticipated states and consequences if the KU is applied. This final state will become the initial state (e.g. situation) in the next mind development phase of this individual. Two others attributes have a secondary role for annotation purposes:

Subtasks: a main task can be achieved by carrying out many subtasks; consequently, a hierarchy of tasks can be established and form a KN.

Remark: to highlight reminders suggested by the KU's author.

In the middle there are two optional fields, which may be necessary for the procedural knowledge:

Reference: a link to an existing document or to a web hyperlink (URL). Used to provide more explanation, or just to enlarge the underlying knowledge.

Demo: a reference to a multimedia resource (e.g. flash file, video, photo, graph, diagram, etc.). This link allows the activation of the multimedia resource from another window on screen. This on screen demonstration is an effective learning method applied for procedural knowledge according to [3] and [7].

The content of a KU is described in natural language and can be supported with multimedia resources (the file names are given in the Reference and Demo field). Thus, the underlying knowledge is represented by most available means corresponding to human perceptual senses. Moreover, with this knowledge modeling, several aspects of a specific context are mentioned: origin, environment, initial state and goal state. Some terms used in the attributes of the second part may be ontology terms that are defined in the related Static KU; consequently they are appropriate for further locating.

A KN is a directed graph where the nodes are KUs, each of them being related to some others by links of different types. In the current version, in addition to the subtask links, we implemented two other kinds of links: The *workflow links* reflect the order between KUs in an activity, a project or an organization. The *pedagogical links* connect prerequisite KU for understanding the actual KU. The required knowledge is called prerequisite knowledge, which is usually some Static KUs that provide users with explanations on the domain ontology (e.g. concept definitins). Existing KUs can be reused by integrating them into newly created KNs.

4 A Collaborative Authoring Tool for Knowledge Management

Our tool (CATKA) can be seen as an environment in which we can review how new terms emerging from the worker's creative knowledge are integrated within a knowledge hierarchy. This is of interest because an ontology reflects this hierarchy of knowledge [8]. In other words, we would like to intervene upon the emergence of a new term. This task can be seen as the "bottom-up" approach to construct ontology. This approach involves the capturing of the knowledge in evolution to keep trace of the domain progresses.

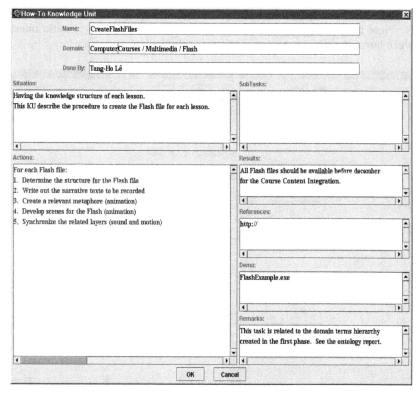

Fig. 1. Example of a Knowledge Unit Frame

In order to understand how it works, we should consider the Knowledge Creation Process (KCP) in a work context of a team. Through the internalization and externalization phases, new terms may be used to describe new concepts. These terms are necessary for knowledge interchange. However, since they were used for the first time, their meaning is well understood only by the team (a very small community). When the KCP comes to maturity with clear definitions of terms, more people may appreciate the new terms and they become popular and, by default, formal (i.e. implicit convention). For instance, we cite here several new terms that appeared in the web domain; most of them being already standard terms: webbot, cobweb, hover button, hotspot, thumbnail image, image map, rollover image, etc. In a KCP, knowledge workers propose new terms normally without taking into account the understanding or the impressions of a large community. So these new terms must be reviewed by a knowledge engineer to eventually justify them. This process consists of applying the consensus of the users community, if reachable. That is comparable to the proposition of [4]. In our CATKA environment, the content of the How-to units is considered as a corpus and each new significant term with its explicit meaning is recorded in a Static KU. When the number of KN reach a manageable size, a grouping task is necessary. We call it the sub-domain promotion (it seems like the promotion of an index level in the B-tree indexing). The knowledge engineer should name a sub-domain by a generic category term which conceptually covers all the underneath KNs. These category terms progressively form the domain knowledge hierarchy. The knowledge hierarchy is then updated in the domain attribute for these KNs. Note that, as opposed to conceptual graphs, there is no semantic interference between terms in different branches of the ontological tree.

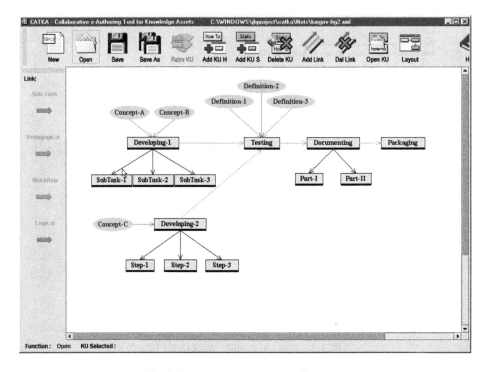

Fig. 2. Example of a Knowledge Network

5 Updating the Distributed Tasks of an E-authoring Project

During the summer of 2001, we conducted an e-learning project to improve the self-learning abilities of forty workers. The CATKA was used as a collaborative tool during the development of course's content and pedagogical material (animation Flash files). In the next steps, we will carry out some real applications in the context of inter-agencies. For this purpose, we generalize below the experience in a more general e-authoring project to well describe the distributed tasks.

To create and exchange "knowledge in evolution" between project members, the e-Authoring tool will allow for collaborative work on the Internet. In technical terms, to realize this tool, we have designed the visual interface for several presentation tasks like project issues, evolution trace keeping, ontological discussion and action demonstration. Put in others words, the e-Authoring tool allows the exchange of two kinds of knowledge: declarative and procedural knowledge. Finally, the updating of the project work in a client/server knowledge base system also allows for concurrent development by all project members, and this work can continue during several days/weeks. A member can visualize the recent development of others while elaborating his/her work. Moreover, the server updating does not interfere with the ongoing work of each member. To provide these features, our tool updates the collaborative work represented as a KN of several nodes (KU) basing on each member's distributed tasks. This approach is comparable to record's field updating in databases but with visual feature. Note that although some other groupware (e.g. MS-FrontPage) allows the collaborative work, the common document is totally blocked when editing by the user; all other users having to wait until the current user relinquish it. To show how the CATKA works, we summarize possible member's tasks as followed:

- The project leader sends the original KN of the initial plan to all members. In this KN, each member can recognize his/her distributed tasks, which are represented by some KUs according to the group discussion.
- Each member develops/updates his/her work by adding more KU around her/his distributed KU. Then, she/he sends the updated KN to the server.
- The server receives the member's updated KN, locks the original KN while updating. It updates the KN by importing (integrating) only the new KU to the identified node (KU) into its actual KN. And finally, it sends back the updated KN to the sender.
- A member, who has not updated his/her node yet, can request the recent updated KN before the development of his/her part. He/she always receives a new updated KN after sending her/his current KN. While developing, a member can locally save (at any time) the current KN and continue to work with this KN before sending it to the server.
- Only the project leader can add more distributed nodes (KU) to the KN located in the server and then send a notice message (specifying the added KU-names and their assigned developers) to all members so that on the next updating, members will recognize these changes.

The following scheme concretely illustrates these mentioned tasks:

Task #1. *Initial planning of KN*: The project leader builds the initial KN and distributes KU tasks to project members.

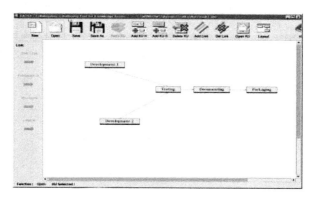

Task #2. *Development-1*: The server receives and updates the KN developed by the first developer.

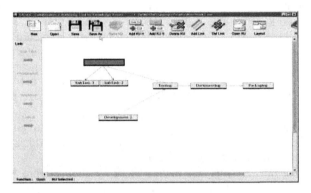

Task #3: *Development-2*: The server receives the KN developed by the second developer. The new added KUs of this developer are updated .

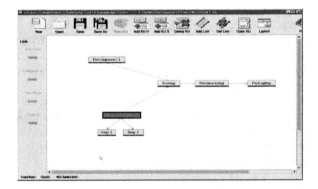

Task #4: *Requesting*: The tester requests the recently updated KN.

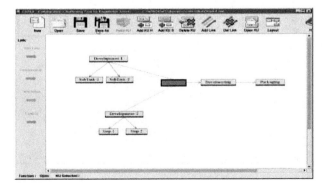

Task #5: *Testing:* The tester adds some Static-KUs (ontological terms definitions – rounded boxes). The server receives the updated KN from all members.

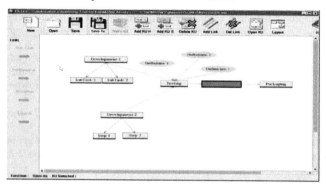

Task #6: Writing the Product User Guide. The writer does his work with more KU added. Other members may add mores KU to the KN (as illustrated in the figure 2) and the project leader finalizes the last KN before packaging.

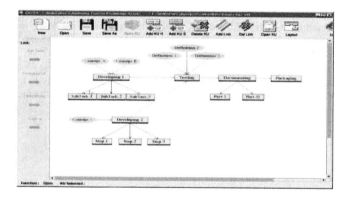

6 Conclusion

The development of e-Government reveals the need of groupware to support inter-agencies collaborative work. However, research efforts are still required to devise adequate formalisms for the management of procedural knowledge assets. In this paper, we provided an overview of an e-Authoring tool to exploit and interchange procedural knowledge represented as networks of semi-structured units. The "bottom-up" approach that can be carried out by this tool is appropriate to gather new terms for the construction of new domain ontology, which will be candidates for the discussion/selection of the underlying community. We detail the updating technique based on the distributed tasks of an e-Authoring project. At this point, we can conclude that group refinement of KN structures offers a simple and intuitive approach to the problem of knowledge interchange. For future work, the exploitation of the logical links created by the CATKA environment will help us to experiment with reasoning schemes, which can be applied to problem solving tasks.

References

1. Multiple authors in Research Challenges and Perspectives of the Semantic Web, Report from the joint European commission and National Science Foundation, Euzenat, J. (Editor), 3-5 October 2001, Sophia Antipolis, France, http://www.ercim.org/EU-NSF/semweb.html.
2. Apostolou, Mentzas, Abecker and Young, 2000. "Consolidating the Product Versus Process Controversy in Knowledge Management: The Know-Net Approach", in the Proceedings of Practical Application of Knowledge Management (PAKeM 2000), Crowne Plaza Midland Hotel, Manchester, UK.
3. Gagné, R.M., Briggs, L.J. and Wager, W.W., 1992. *Principles of Instructional Design*. Harcourt Brace Jovanovich College Publishers. Fort Worth, Texas, U.S.
4. van Elst, Ludger and Abecker, Andreas, 2000. Domain Ontology Agents in Distributed Organizational Memories, *Knowledge Management and Organizational Memories*, Rose Dieng-Kuntz and Nada Matta (Eds.), Kluwer Academic, U.S.
5. Noy, N. and McGuinness, D. L.: Ontology Development 101: A Guide to Creating Your First Ontology. 2001, Stanford Medical Informatics technical reports, SMI Report Number: SMI-2001-0880.
6. Lassila, O. and. McGuinness, D. L.: The Role of Frame-Based Representation on the Semantic Web, in Electronic Transactions on Artificial Intelligence, Volume 5, Number: 2001-03-07, 1403–2031 (Printed version) 1403-204X (Electronic version).
7. Lê, T.H., Gauthier, G. and Frasson, C., 1998. The Process of Planning for an Intelligent Tutoring System, in *Proceeding of The Fourth World Congress On Expert Systems*, Vol. 2, pp. 709–714, Mexico City, Mexico.
8. Chandrasekaran, B., Josephson, J. R. and Benjamins V. R., 1998. The Ontology of Tasks and Methods, in *Proceedings of KAW'98,* Gaines, B. and Musen, M. (eds.), Banff, Alberta, Canada. Foreword of Proceedings of SWWS'01, 2001. The First Semantic Web Working Symposium, Stanford University, CA.

Emergent Functions in Intranet Information Management

Ewa Zimmerman[1] and Björn Cronquist[2]

[1] Halmstad University, P O box 823, S-301 18 HALMSTAD, SWEDEN
Ewa.Zimmerman@ide.hh.se
[2] Kristianstad University, SE-291 88 KRISTIANSTAD, SWEDEN
Bjorn.Cronquist@mna.hkr.se

Abstract. Organizations and municipalities implements advanced information technology, intranets, in order to enhance information management within the organization. This technology is implemented with great reliance on the technology aspect. New functions emerge as a consequence of technology, functions not planned for. This paper puts focus one such function, the key persons responsible for publishing on intranets. A descriptive study shows that these persons do exist and describes some problems they appreciate.

1 Introduction

Organizations and municipalities today implement computer based systems e.g. Intranets for spreading information between individuals and departments. Organizations and municipalities acknowledge intranets as an information tool that they can use for distribution of their information and to enhance inter-organizational co-operation both within departments and between governmental agencies. One basic assumption is the belief that every member and citizen use and adopt the technology.

There is lots of information on the Internet and on Intranets, some is well organized and well structured, but much is pretty chaotic which creates real problems for people who need and rely on it. Knowing how to create information that people can use and rely on is within an area that has come to be known as *knowledge management*. Knowledge management supports the creation, archiving, and sharing of valued information, expertise, and insight within and across communities of people and organizations with similar interests and needs (Rosenberg, 2001). Following the implementation of intranets in municipalities new information architectures have emerged without being planned for. And new functions within these architectures have emerged. When we use the term emergent we refer to tasks and positions in the expressed environment that occurs without any considerations during and after the implementation process. The need for information in organizations today is vital for their survival and the need for access to the "right" information fast is growing (Castells 1996). This paper puts focus on one obvious and significant function in line with digital information distribution; the key-persons responsible for publishing information on the intranet.. The limitations in this paper are that we focus on the key person and his/hers tasks regarding the intranet and the situation connected to the publishing process. We are only briefly discussing the intranet content e.g. what kind

M.A. Wimmer (Ed.): KMGov 2003, LNAI 2645, pp. 186–191, 2003.

of information. We are not discussing intranet functions only the obstacles the study stress regarding the publishing process. Electronic networks like electronic mail, computer conferencing and groupware are expected to enable employees to work more flexible, exchange experiences and to collaborate more effectively (Orlikowski, Yates, Okamura, Fujimoto, 1999). A group communication technology suggests that the effects of the new technology are driven by the ability to implement it into the structure of the organization/ municipalities (Weick, 1990). If this had been achieved the emergence of the key persons never had been a problem.

2 Theory

2.1 Intranets

Intranets are built around the powerful idea that web technology can be used within the organizations to facilitate communication and to provide an effective knowledge repository. Therefore, the intranet must become a valuable resource to the employees to increase the efficiency and promote knowledge sharing. At its best, the intranet forms the core of information and knowledge management efforts in the organization enabling wider strategic goals to be met, (Robertson, (2002). To make the intranet part of the daily activities must be the primary goal; to become a normal part of employee's daily lives. If a strong demand can be achieved from the users, it will create a strong incentive to support the intranet and many complaints if it is not kept up to date. It is a "critical mass" of usage that is necessary to make the intranet viable in the long-term. There is no one feature, tool or set of pages that universally makes an intranet desirable to the employees. Instead, each organization and municipalities has its own, unique set of requirements and demands. Only by involving all users in the design and evolution of the intranet will these key features be uncovered.

We describe information as a message, in the form of documents, written communication with different purposes. Information is a message addressed to everyone or someone in the organization, and the information moves around in the organization through the traditional systems (paper format) and though the new systems (electronically) e.g. intranets, (Davenport and Prusak 1998).

2.2 Information Quality

A framework with four IQ categories, developed through empirical studies (Huang, Lee et al. 1999), could be applied here. The first category is *intrinsic IQ* that denotes that information has quality in its own right. *Contextual IQ* highlights the requirement that IQ must be considered within the context of the task at hand; that is, information must be relevant, timely, complete and appropriate in terms of amount so as to add value. *Representational IQ* and *accessibility IQ* emphasize the importance of the role of the systems and the systems must be accessible but secure. The systems must present information in a way that is interpretable, easy to understand, and concisely and consistently represented. These four categories should be considered in information consumer's perspective.

2.3 Approaches to Information or Knowledge Distribution

Information distribution can be described in four general modes (Dixon 2000).
1. Sending everything to everyone
2. Routing the material by the collector
3. Applying central control on distribution
4. Creating a pull system where information consumers decide what they want to see
Each of these systems has drawbacks. Sending everything to everyone generates an information overload and will hardly enhance the ability to get attention to and prioritize significant bits of information. Routing information might lead to placing decisions with people not qualified to make them. Applying central control generates needs of administrative support and will increase overhead by creating a central office. The fourth is, in our view, the most hazardous because it assumes that information consumers know what is available before they see the material. This can only be true for very formal and generalized artifacts of information.

Regardless of individual contexts it can be stated that in any organization, suffering from some degree of internal anonymity, the informal evaluation and transmission of information quickly creates gridlocks. Based upon thoughts and theories presented above following questions can be formulated. *How do the key person, the publisher perform their task, collect and distribute information using the intranet?*

3 Research Problem and Objective

The purpose of the research presented in this paper is to investigate the key persons and their roles in the organizational context of the intranet. The focus is on the difficulties that can occur when new functions in the municipalities are emerging. The emerging functions are new tasks concerning the collecting and distribution of the information, performed by these key persons.

Questions to be asked are to what extent the information published on the intranet is a dynamic source of knowledge creation (Nonaka and Takeushi 1995). To what extent it is valued and used. Are there other means of communicating information that are more trusted? Do the intranets function as an alibi for not having to inform but rather turning the responsibility to the information consumers to keep informed.

3.1 Research Design and Methods

We have examined municipalities in Sweden and performed interviews with the persons who have the responsibility to publish information on the intranets.

The research approach is descriptive and interpretative, and using a case study approach enables an understanding of the complex social phenomena that we are investigating. A case study allows an investigation to retain the holistic and meaningful characteristics of real-life cycles and organizational and managerial processes (Yin 1994).

The purpose with a survey investigation is to collect information that could be analyzed to identify patterns and to perform comparisons. The collected data should be used not only to describe but also to compare the answers. A survey can answer questions regarding, *what, where, how and when* but it is more difficult to answer questions about *why*. Our research is expected to answer both *how and why* and therefore the research strategy are two folded; the survey approach are used within a case study.

The main objective of the presented study was to obtain information from the persons responsible for the publishing process and about their opinions regarding their position in the organization. Our aim was not only to find out whether they were known by others in the organization, but also to discover how they performed there work. The survey contained questions regarding both general information about their working tasks but also the respondents personal opinion about some aspects of the publishing process were acquired. Briefly these questions refer to their background such as education, previous tasks, opinion about their current tasks and opinions towards the presumed users of the information.

The interviews where performed by telephone because the geographical distances. A survey interview could be described as a dialog between the interviewer and the respondents with the purpose to get information that the latter posses. The interviews were planned by choosing themes and questions related to the research area. The interview guide was built on four themes and underlying questions within those themes. The first theme focused on the identification of the person responsible for the intranet. The second theme focused on this person's background, education. The third theme had its focus on how the information was collected and published. Finally, the fourth theme concerned the opinion regarding the use of the intranet and its content. The interviews were performed by telephone and were written down during the interview, the respondent was allowed to express and discuss issues within the four themes relatively freely.

4 Results

The key persons expressed several difficulties in performing their tasks and some frustration was also expressed concerning this issues. Our study indicates that there is a lack of knowledge in municipalities concerning this important key person and their tasks. This function has emerged without being planned for and their performance has several obstacles that have to be solved. It has evolved with the technology which our results will show.

The first theme focused on the identification of responsible persons, the key persons. We started by identifying the key persons at the Swedish municipalities, we performed telephone interviews and asked to be connected to the responsible person for the intranet. Several of the respondents had no knowledge regarding which person to connect us to; this tells us that there is a lack of awareness of this function in the municipalities. The second theme focused on the key person's background and education. The result show that most of them had a technical education and they had been working with consultant activities, building web-sites, information secretary, culture worker and technical support. The key persons had a variety of background and educations; the connecting bound between them is that they have educations in other areas before they were given this position. The third theme focused on how the information was collected and published. Almost every key person expressed frustration regarding collecting information to publish. Administrative information such as handbooks, protocols, and work rules are always available on the intranet. The different departments are supposed to provide with information at a regular basis but this doesn't happen. Some of the municipalities have documented policies regarding the intranet and its content but most of them expressed a lack thereof. Finally, the fourth theme concerned their opinion regarding the use of the intranet and its content. Most of them expressed that they used e-mail to inform about new information; information in paper format was distributed to the managers in the different departments and the believed that most of the employees use the intranet. One of them said that she e-mailed a weekly letter to 350 middle-managers; it was printed and put on the bulletin board in the departments so everyone could read. The most expressed obstacles for achieving optimal use of the intranet was the accessibility to the computer technology. All municipalities expressed that there wasn't enough computers for the users and some of them had bad connections via modems. For example, one municipality had 9000 employees and only 1500 user names in the system. Our conclusions are that our study shows that there is a lack of knowledge in municipalities regarding implementation of intranets and the emergent functions that occurs. Several difficulties have to be over come if a successful use is going to be accomplished, for example, the accessibility to the technology must be increased.

5 Discussion

Designing and managing an intranet is not easy. Implementing the technical solutions is not enough. It can be viewed as a necessary but not sufficient prerequisite in supporting efficient and effective organizational information architecture. The overall purpose is to build foundation for timely and effective decisions and actions within the organization. One trivial but important aspect that often is neglected is the physical access to computer terminals during working hours.

New organizational behaviors develop as a consequence of implementing the technology. New tasks supported by employees forced to adapt to these new behaviors emerge within organizations without being planned for. One of these emergent roles is the key persons with publishing responsibilities. The importance of stressing this key person identified in our study is important. The very fact that they exists can be viewed as an indication of bad alignment between technical capabilities and organizational behavior. Old structures are just transferred to new media. The full potential and possibilities are not explored and developed.

Advanced information technology implies potential possibilities in achieving a useful and creative intranets supporting organizational communication. Acquisition and sharing of knowledge is a very important issue in modern organizations

6 Further Research

The mere existence of central functions for publishing on intranets and the anonymity of these key persons imply a weakness in fully taking advantage of the potential benefits of advanced information technology. The issue of information quality is an important aspect of information architecture. An extended study should address this issue. The usefulness of artifacts published and distributed by intranets should be studied. One hypothesis could be that published information merely functions as an alibi for making official decisions public. The responsibility to inform is shifting towards keeping informed. The publishers have done their part when putting documents on the intranet. It is up to the consumers to find it. Other functions made possible through intranet technology should also be attended. The Intranets could function as a facilitator for informal communication and communities of practice. In what way does technology influence communicative behavior? We hope that this paper will bring attention to these oft-neglected factors in implementation processes of intranets and encourage discussion about how to effectively address this issue.

References

1. Castells, M. (1996). Informationsåldern, Ekonomi, samhälle och kultur Band 1:Nätverkssamhällets framväxt, Daidalos.
2. Davenport, T. H. and L. Prusak (1998). Worknig Knowledge: How organisations Manage what they know, Harvard Business School Press.
3. Dixon, N. M. (2000). Common knowledge: how companies thrive by sharing what they know, Harvard Business School Press.
4. Huang, K., W. Lee, et al. (1999). Quality Information and Knowledge. New Jersey, Prentice Hall.
5. Orlikowski W.J., Yates, JA., (1994) Genre repertoire; The Structuring of Communicative Practices in Organizations. Administrative Science Quarterly. No 39 pp 541–574
6. Rosenberg, M., J., (2001) e-Learning – Strategies for Delivering Knowledge In the Digital Age. McGraw-Hill. USA.
7. Weick, K., (1995) Sensemaking in Organizations, Thousand Oaks, CA; Sage Publications Inc.
8. Nonaka, I. and H. Takeushi (1995). The Knowledge-Creating Company, Oxford University Press.
9. Yin, R. K. (1994). Case Study Research: Design and Methods, SAGE Publications inc.

Knowledge Management in Public Web Call Centres

Vincenzo Ambriola, Silvia Bertagnini, and Letizia Pratesi

Università di Pisa – Dipartimento di Informatica, Via F. Buonarroti, 2,
56127 – PISA (Italy), phone +39 050 22 12 {751, 784, 784}
{ambriola, bertagni, pratesi}@di.unipi.it

Abstract. The increased use of Internet has accelerated the evolution of call centres: from simple centres with few telephone lines to sophisticated web call centres that give users different instruments to search information. In this vision the success of a web call centre depends more and more on knowledge. Without enough knowledge, call centre staff cannot provide the level of service that users are demanding. Recently, the idea of using web call centres is gaining popularity in the public sector too. This paper presents and discusses the design of Pubblicamente, a newly created Italian web call centre.

1 Introduction

For a company a call centre represents the primary way of interacting with customers. Call centres are all about getting customers the information they need, as quickly as possible. To meet this goal, the knowledge resources of a call centre must be managed in a coordinated and integrated way.

A key ingredient in call centre success is knowledge. The greatest challenge of running a call centre is ensuring that customers are provided with the right information in a timely fashion.

A call centre is confronted with a number of considerable challenges. Staff members answer a wide range of customer questions, drawing on a large body of knowledge. With the high rate of staff turnover, the training required to impart this information can be a considerable burden on call centre resources. Employees are also expected to provide fast answers to customers, even though there is legal accountability for the information they provide. This is further compounded by the high stress work environment and the emphasis on reducing call-handling times. Knowledge management can be used to meet many of these challenges. These include reducing training time and improving the consistency and accuracy of information provided to customers.

The basic tenet is that work in call centres has to be conceptualized in terms of distributed knowledge. This means that only part of the knowledge needed to carry out any transaction is (or rather has to be) in the mind of the operator, and important knowledge may be distributed among colleagues in the organization, available and accessible cognitive artifacts in the work environment, and clients.

The most effective way of tackling the knowledge challenges of a call centre is to develop a knowledge base that contains all the information needed by the call centre staff.

M.A. Wimmer (Ed.): KMGov 2003, LNAI 2645, pp. 192–202, 2003.

In a call centre efficient processes must be put in place to ensure that the right knowledge is captured, managed, and kept up-to-date and knowledge management systems must be established to support these processes.

Classical call centres, focused on the effectiveness and efficiency of handling telephones calls, are now transforming towards web call centres. A web call centre is a system that integrates voice, e-mail, and web services. More than traditional call centres, a web call centre provides its users a rich set of interactive services that can be exploited by seamlessly combining the best of both traditional and new media communications.

To achieve these goals a web call centre has to communicate to a large set of users through different channels. For example, in case of need a visitor of a web site can interact with a special operator in many ways including e-mail, web callback, Voice over Internet Protocol (VoIP), and video. Each communication channel has access to a shared information system that thus becomes the most important resource of the entire system.

This work presents the design of an Italian web call centre. Section 2 discusses the nature and the characteristics of a web call centre. The newly created Italian web call centre Pubblicamente is presented in Section 3. Section 4 shows a comparison between Pubblicamente and similar web call centres. The paper ends with future development of Pubblicamente.

2 Web Call Centre Characteristics

The realization of a web call centre requires relevant investments in *technology*, to assure a rich set of services at a high quality level, and in *training*. A variety of new and emerging information and communication technologies are enabling this change in service delivery.

Some actions have to be carry out to implement a call centre such as:

- Consult with target groups to identify demand for particular services and types of access;
- Plan the type of delivery mechanism. This will help to identify *back office* functions that may need to be tied together to deliver services in the future;
- Clearly deliver the information system and more importantly, let target groups know of its existence;
- Define a structured and usable knowledge repository that can be used in a number of practical ways: publishing a selection of customer questions (FAQs) to the website, ensuring that on line information is accurate and comprehensive (this will reduce the number of calls in these areas), developing standard responses to a range of common e-mail or queries. Products even exist that will analyse incoming e-mails and automatically select appropriate responses;
- Monitor service delivery, manage its ongoing provision and identify areas in which it can be enhanced either through the addition of other internal services or through the joining up with others.

Adopting a wider range of contact media for dealing with citizens and business in the contact centre, which is ideally a highly structured environment for dealing with contacts, potentially makes it easier for citizens or business to be supplied with a consistent high-quality service [2].

2.1 Quality Control

To achieve appropriate and predefined levels of service it is necessary to implement a quality system. The main goal of the quality system is to define and control both the quality of the information given by the web call centre and the quality of its services.

The quality of the information given by a web call centre can be expressed in terms of three properties[1]:

- Consistency: similar documents are classified in the same way;
- Completeness: the presence of all relevant documents in each category;
- Accuracy: how properly a document is assigned to a category.

The assessment of information quality allows, in case of evident insufficiency, to activate corrective actions. Thesaurus characteristics, such as uniformity, precision, and dimension, are used to assess efficacy.

The quality of the service of a web call centre is assessed according to consolidated standard and parameters, such as:

- Efficiency: expressed in terms of productivity, response time, services utilization rank; efficient processes must be put in place to ensure that the right knowledge is captured, managed, and kept up-to-date;
- Effectiveness: the number of supplied services, users number, info update, service continuity, answer time;
- Quality: expressed as awaiting reply, processing reply,
- Transparency (with users), customer satisfaction;
- Accessibility: as navigability of web pages, accessibility to disabled people interaction, security, ease of use, reliability, utilities, standards.

3 The Project Pubblicamente

Progetto integrato call centre e servizi informativi per l'innovazione della pubblica amministrazione, started in December 2000 with an agreement between Formez and Dipartimento della funzione pubblica, is aimed to realize a web call centre (called Pubblicamente [3]) to deal with all major community inquiries about Local Public Administration (PAL) innovation sector, with a focus on high-volume inquiries such as access to government community support programs, access to government laws, regulations, procedures, PAL "help line" - to help the community identify the right source to particular information needs.

The goal of *Pubblicamente*, built using phone and Internet technology, is to become a single point of access to manage all enquiries relating to defined areas of information.

The web call centre also aims at establishing a well-defined interface between the expected users and the Formez experts.

---

[1] This definition is given by Information Quality and corresponds to the Centre for Information Quality Management (CIQM) definition.

3.1 Characteristics of Pubblicamente

Three operative sections, a Management Committee and other associations to exiting reality form the system:
- Scouting and operative coordinating group;
- Knowledge management and intermediation system;
- Front-office structure (help-desk and vortal)
- Management Committee to supervise development politics and services supply.

The scouting group researches and mapping exiting information sources, locates of information lack as to thematic areas, implements of knowledge base (KB), monitors of information demand.

To carry out its activity, t**SEQ**he scouting group is using an information system (KB-SI) with two databases (KB-BD and KB-SD) and a search engine (KB_MR) to search into the web.

In the first phase of Pubblicamente start-up plan the bases of *knowledge base* have been made. The KB is formed by first level information (data and documents) and second level information (external system). In the second phase the monitoring demand has been started to orient scouting group activities.

3.2 Functionality

Pubblicamente is organized in a public area and in a private area where it is possible to access a *database* of analysed and validated information. Both areas supply the following functionality: access to the glossary, navigate, through the glossary, inside a vertical classification of the thematic areas defined in the database, search, both in simple and advanced mode, driven by the glossary, send questions (only registered users).

In order to access the private area of *Pubblicamente* a user must be registered. After being registered, the user can submit a question to *Pubblicamente* by using one of the following channels: web site, telephone, e-mail, fax, mail.

The output channels used by *Pubblicamente* to reply are the same of the input channels plus the newsletter. Generally the answering time at first level operators is between 5 and 10 minutes. Questions forwarded to a Formez expert require an answering time that ranges between 24 and 48 hours. At the moment, non-registered users can have access only to not validated documents.

The operators that work at the *contact centre*, use two communications channels:
- The help-desk that manages incoming requests with standard methods, assuring appropriate answering time and monitoring the public interaction,
- The vertical portal (vortal) that allows direct interrogations and access to different communications channels and call centre sources.

The operators use a search engine to reply questions: the search engine does not deliver the complete solution, but provide structured and meaningful browsing and navigation methods. In fact it presents the correct items and the related pages.

3.3 System Database

Pubblicamente provides a flexible and high quality access to the widest range of PAL web resources by a structured *database* and a *quality system*.

System database is an on line information resource that is comprehensive, accurate and up to date, well structured, easy and efficient to use, supported by tools for searches and indexing, created and maintained by scouting group.

The database includes information (documents, magazines, web site pages, and public administration norms) of analyzed databases, FAQ and web site as *PARete* [4]. At the moment 3.523 documents and 424 institutional organizations (universities, departments, Public bodies, Local bodies) have been classified. The database is connected to others Formez databases, but to solve the problem of uniformity of the structures of databases they treat them as external sites.

The precise nature of the information to be provided, and the target audience of the information, has been determined by users needs and research on interest sites. *Pubblicamente* arise from such an approach would be driven by community information needs, rather than departmental information storage ownership.

To ensure that consistent responses are provided to operators, a repository of second level support teams and contact centre common problems and resolution have been developed. This information is an excellent source and will reduce the number of simple calls to contact centre. At the moment these repository is not on line, but only used by operators.

Develop Knowledge Management System. To collect information for the database the researchers have defined a taxonomic scheme [5], based on a top-down approach.

Taxonomic Scheme Definition. The taxonomic scheme is useful to structured search in areas and sub-areas or driven by glossary key words.

To develop the taxonomic scheme some activities have been carried out such as analysis of Formez web site and its thematic sections, analysis of others Central and Local Public Administration sites, analysis of others taxonomic scheme, individuation of interest areas and macro-areas, integration of all analyzed schemes in a unique taxonomic scheme, definition of relations between terms.EINBETTEN

At the moment there are 14 different thematic areas. The thematic areas could be modified: if there are not references in a thematic area, the scouting group begins to analyse this cause. There are two causes:

- Users information needs do not concern that area. Perhaps it is necessary include that area in an another one or erase it;
- The name of area is wrong and so only few documents can be catalogued.

This operation is periodically made by scouting group to provide a validated and revised research method, based on thematic areas.

The glossary. The taxonomic scheme has been analyzed to define glossary terms.

Usually there are difficulties to successfully retrieve information on advanced alternative methods in on line databases. For this reason, a thesaurus is used to locate information in data retrieval systems.

The thesaurus is a controlled particular sector terms vocabulary arranged in a know order, with specified types of semantics relationships. The structure of the thesaurus is [6]:

- Keyword: terms used to search the site by queries;
- Thematic area: the areas associable to keywords used for directory hand browsing;
- Definition: sharpening the sense of the term;
- UF (used for): keywords synonyms;
- BT (broader term): the super ordinate term, i.e. the one that identifies the following terms as broader terms to the heading term;
- NT (narrower term): the subordinate term, i.e. the one that identifies the following terms as narrower terms to the heading term;
- RT (related term): the terms in a logical relation to another keyword.

Keywords enable more precise retrievals. Thesauruses find their main application in large literature databases.

As the goal of Pubblicamente is to reach Public Administration, the scouting group has developed a specialised thesaurus ensuring the use of appropriate and homogeneous terms, classification schemes and topics covered. So the thesaurus is the basis for indexing and retrieving material.

To ensure appropriateness of the chosen terms, a methodology has been used. Some methods have been based on actual phrases, which occur in documents and should therefore reflect the preferred terminology of the authors of the articles. Pubblicamente thesaurus is, therefore, built out of the text and not added on. It will consist of key terms, which could usefully be used to search within any database [7].

List of words and phrases will be extracted by computerised analysis of original documents.

Schedule. Pubblicamente thesaurus has been developed in the following step:
1. *First definition* (July of 2001): development of the glossary by a bottom-up approach directed at sites, literature and documents about Public Administration. Each defined thematic area has been sound to find reference terms. The first version of the glossary has been confronted with key words found in the PA sites. Then a keyword glossary has been made and the keywords inserted in the thesaurus, with synonymous, related, broader and narrow terms. This first version has been circulated to a selected number of experts in the various fields for comments and suggestions.
2. *Evaluation of the method* (February 2002): the method has been evaluated considering if the used approach could create a complete thesaurus in all fields of Public Administration area;
3. *Thesaurus updating and maintenance* (after April 2002): based on the outcome of item 2, a second circulation is foreseen to a broader selection of experts with particular emphasis on new topics. A priority setting will be necessary before circulation. Periodically researchers insert new terms of glossary, basis on user demands and others research on interest sites and documents, and associate documents to them.

The population of glossary has to be made incrementally, inserting the complex terms definitions and then the missing definitions. The research could be made using research engines, on line vocabulary and norms definitions.

During the development of glossary, the related, narrow, and broader terms are consider keywords, thematic areas are not keywords and keywords must be inserted in the sub-areas (of main thematic areas).

In order to define terms form and meaning, the following editorial and conventional rules have been established:

- Abbreviations are synonyms, without punctuation and in lower-case;
- Composed names have only the first letter in upper-case;
- Foreign terms are not inserted.

An example. All the entries in the Pubblicamente database are catalogued by keywords listed in the thesaurus. Once selected a keyword, user can look for keywords that are related or more specific. Once he has found the relevant keywords, type them in the search engine form below the thesaurus.

Each subject field is expressed by a very broad concept, a top term. From these top terms chains of progressively more detailed descriptors develop downwards to most specific issues. Some issues at the same level of a particular structure may be related, but not dependent upon each other

If you click on a term in the combo box with thematic areas, the results page shows the thematic sub-areas and the term of glossary related to that area. To find information, you have to click on a term and a news page with documents and related sites, broader, narrow and related terms appears.

3.4 Information Quality

The analysis has been carried out on taxonomic schema. In order to define the quality of the taxonomy we need metrics to estimate the correctness of the hierarchical structure, the consistency of the terms, the degree of the hierarchy, the suitability of terms RT, UF, NT and BT. So we used the following metrics:

- Dimension, i.e., the number of areas, sub-areas, terms, organizations and resources;
- Terms distribution.

The metrics have been computed by some SQL queries (written in Microsoft Access). We use these metrics to monitor the growing rate of the collected material and the balancing of the taxonomic scheme:

- NUMKWperArea, returns the number of KW of each area;
- NUMBTperKW, returns the number of BT of each KW;
- NUMRTperKW, returns the number of RT of each KW;
- NUMNTperKW, returns the number of NT for every KW;
- NUMUFperKW, returns the number of UF of each KW;
- NUMBT, returns the events of every BT in the thesaurus;
- CorrispAreeNonSame, returns the number of KW, NT, BT, UF of each without duplicates;
- PopolamentoGauss, returns the number of areas with values in fixed ranges.

In order to analyze the dimension of the taxonomy and study its distribution we use a histogram having on the X-axis the data and on the Y-axis the measured values. The steps to build a distribution histogram are the following:

1. Define the population intervals to calculate the distribution;
2. Write on the X axis the term intervals;

3. Write on the Y-axis the number of areas, of unitary dimension, for the intervals defined on the X axis.

These histograms let us represent the number of terms BT, NT, UF, RT identified for each term KW, and obtain the indicators of generalization, specialization, synonymy and aggregation of the taxonomic scheme. Figure 1 shows the result of NUMKWperArea formula and NUMKWperArea histogram.

Thematic areas	N_KW		
area ambientale	48		
area culturale	16		
area economica	39		
area informativa	132		
area internazionale	10		
area istituzionale	23		
area legislativa	47		
area sanitaria	10		
area sociale	52		
area territoriale	32		
innovazione	23		
risorse	3		
	average	variance	standard deviation
	36,25	1176,386	34,29849

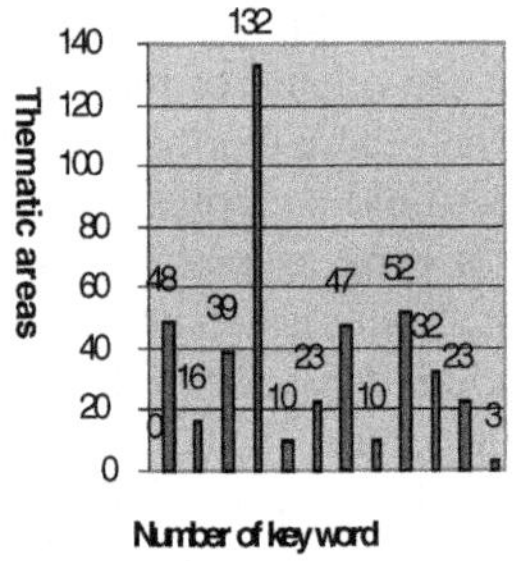

Fig. 1. NUMKWperArea, NUMKWperArea histogram

Further results for quantitative analysis of the taxonomic scheme are obtained:
- Applying the formulas for the average calculation, the variance and the standard deviation with respect to the query results;
- Comparing the histogram results with the average of the corresponding values;
- Analyzing the dispersion of the values.

In the initial phase it is recommended to have a uniform distribution of the terms in the thematic areas to be able to answer simple questions. Afterwards, as new requirements appears, it is possible to refine and expand specific areas.

3.5 Service Quality

To attain appropriate call centre levels of service and to assure usability and accessibility sites requirements, a system quality has been defined.

After identifying quality indicators and twenty-three levels of services, any indicators have been associated to corresponding level of service to control each considered aspect. Then each level of service has been specified, dynamically, according to the process phase. There are two phase:
- Start–up phase, i.e. initial supplying phase in which data are periodically analysing to define levels of threshold;
- Working phase, when used levels of service are defined according to call centre needs and are continually controlled.

Variables represent the levels of threshold. According to the phases, they will assume different values.

To define the right corrective actions if the service level is not observed is necessary define causes, detailing call centre interactions steps, associate statistical components to interactions steps, compute medium time of each step, define limit cases, compute the value of the levels of threshold according to each step medium time and limit cases.

Ishikawa's diagram [8] is used to analyze the causes when the service level is not observed. The level of threshold is on the horizontal row and the causes are on the transversal line. Then the causes are grouped in classes and ordinate, approach to major o minor probability to show up. So the right corrective actions have been defined.

Figure 2 presents an example of computed Ishikawa's diagram.

An example. We can analyze the level of service: *Daily Calling Percentage at first level by phone*. This value has to be less or equal to the following level of threshold:

$$Start\text{-}up\ phase:\ SI_s = C1\%\ of\ the\ total\ of\ calling \tag{1}$$

$$Operating\ phase:\ SI_f = C2\%\ of\ the\ total\ of\ calling,\ with\ C1 > C2 \tag{2}$$

We assume a higher value in the start-up phase because the users will use phone instead of the other channels. In the working phase, this value will decrease following the increase of the Internet requests. To decrease this value is necessary a good operator training, an important service dissemination phase and the observation of the other access channels levels of service. The following Ishikawa diagram analysis these factors, showing the violated level of threshold and the causes.

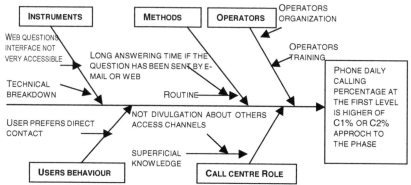

Fig. 2. An Ishikawa diagram

4   Comparisons to Other Similar Experiences

In several countries call centres are an important interface in the management of government relationships with citizen and business. In fact, citizens greatly value timely accessibility to government information that affects their lives. In fact, the vision of the citizen e-government center of the future is to allow citizens seamless access to government information at any time, from anywhere, in any form, and for free. Often a call centre is the first point of contact with government.

Some researches highlight that, in the next few years, government at each levels will be moving their low-tech call centres from back-office support to the front-line of the agency. In this migration, the call centres are being outfitted with the latest in high-tech hardware and software in both voice and data applications [9]. The focus is moving from only telephone calls to all forms of citizen access, including e-mail, fax-mail, kiosk, and the Internet.

We have analyzed some web call centre in the world to find similar characteristics to *Pubblicamente*, but *Service Tasmania*, in Australia, has the same key objectives, in spite of it presents a more articulated structure.

Service Tasmania [10] provides a flexible access to the widest range of web resources, primarily information and services from the State Government, but also from the Federal and local governments. The web site groups information and transaction services according to user needs, so that Tasmanians no longer need to know how government is structured to find what they want. Finally, if they do not find the required information on the site, they can contact a web call centre and receive back an answer by mail, phone, fax, or e-mail.

In order to improve the quality of the on line services, user behavior has been monitored and analyzed during three months, even using an help desk system operating via e-mail. The most frequently research keywords and the popular sections of the web site have also been identified . Also user preferences are analyzed and a special attention is devoted to unsuccessful queries.

The characteristics of *Service Tasmania* user-centric model are: the user sees government information as a simple and homogeneous collection of information that features a variety of browsing paths and discovery strategies (behavior), suitable for different kind of needs and capable to adapt to different user skill and education.

Pubblicamente and Service Tasmania supply a flexible access to the multitude of government information and develop a database to allow simple data insertion and maintenance operations. Although they operate in an environment where content continues to grow rapidly and where there is little or no control over development and quality content, major strategies have developed to enable the user to locate or discover specific content.

Both call centres use tools for automatic validation of the presence of sites after routine harvesting, and the exclusion of missing sites and annex of national and international standards, whenever possible.

Pubblicamente and Service Tasmania sites allow users to search information and services in a variety of ways.

Service Tasmania provides a navigation structure which allows user to search information and services with cross-linkages at various points to other views of the data, and with contextual free text searching available throughout.

The registered user of Pubblicamente can search information on the web site consulting the glossary, navigating with the glossary, in a thematic area or with simple and advanced research of information with insertion of glossary terms.

The development of these call centres is based upon a number of additional requirements of a technical nature including the capacity to cope with large amounts of data and a high site demand.

Quality assurance and standard adherence are fundamental to the operations of any call centre examined.

5 Conclusions

Call centres are all about getting customers the information they need as quickly as possible. To meet this goal, the knowledge resources of a call centre must be managed in a coordinated and integrated way.

In this paper we highlight the potential of call centres to meet PAL interest areas, but also the policy and management challenges they present.

This paper presents a framework that defines the essential characteristics of a web call centre such as:

- Use Web-based technologies wherever possible because these can be integrated into a single and consistent interface for users, which give greater efficiency;
- Give operator searching and browsing methods and support these with comprehensive meta-data, such as titles, descriptions and keywords;
- Search the raw information and shape this into a structured and usable knowledge repository;
- Use statistics to measure and track the success of the knowledge base.

In this work we have provided at least an example of a project to develop a PAL call centre that is suitable for other target call centre.

A further improvement of the project is expected from the introduction of XML to describe documents with meta-data and the development of a search engine on XML information.

References

1. Sebastiano Bagnara, "Euro-telework: Report on call centres",
    http://www.telework-irti.org/bagnara.htm
2. "Call Centres in the Scottish Public Sector"
    http://www.scotland.gov.uk/government/c21g/Call_centre_c21g.pdf
3. Pubblicamente web site, http://www.pubblicamente.it
4. PARete, http://www.di.unipi.it/parete
5. Marcello Giacomantonio, "Image Cataloguing and Didactic Management of a iconic file" (In Italian), *Quaderno di comunicazione audiovisiva* (in Italian)
6. Thesaurus on Advanced Alternative Methods (TAAM),
    http://ecvam-sis.jrc.it/cover/thesaurus.html
7. Marcello Giacomantonio, "Computerizing of Recording System" (in Italian), Quaderno di comunicazione audiovisiva, 8: 10–21, anno 3.
8. Ishikawa's diagram, http://mot.vuse.vanderbilt.edu/mt322/Ishikawa.htm
9. Purdue Research Foundation, "Government Call Centers Performance Benchmark Report, Final Results", http://www.amsinc.com/crm/govtcallcenterstudy.asp
10. Service Tasmania web site, http://www.servicetasmania.tas.gov.au

Knowledge Management for Organisationally Mobile Public Employees

Simon Lambert[1], Simona Stringa[2], Gianni Viano[2],
Jacek Kitowski[3], Renata Słota[3], Krzysztof Krawczyk[3], Mariusz Dziewierz[3],
Sabine Delaitre[4], Miguel Bermejo Oroz[4], Ana Conde Gómez[4],
Ladislav Hluchy[5], Zoltan Balogh[5], Michal Laclavik[5],
Mª Soledad Fuentes Caparrós[6], Maria Fassone[7], and Vito Contursi[7]

[1] Business & Information Technology Department,
CCLRC Rutherford Appleton Laboratory, Chilton, Didcot, Oxon OX11 0QX, UK
S.C.Lambert@rl.ac.uk
[2] Softeco Sismat SpA, Italy
[3] Cyfronet AGH, Poland
[4] Sadiel SA, Spain
[5] Institute of Informatics, Slovak Academy of Sciences, Slovakia
[6] Consejería de la Presidencia, Junta de Andalucía, Spain
[7] Comune di Genova, Italy

Abstract. Public organisations often face knowledge management problems caused by organisational mobility, the continual and pervasive movement of staff between units and departments. This can be a strength, but also introduces problems of loss of experience and reduced efficiency and effectiveness in working. The Pellucid project is developing a knowledge management system to assist in such situations. The project's three pilot applications are described, and an abstracted view of their knowledge management needs is developed. An outline of key parts of the technical solution is given.

1 Introduction: The Pellucid Project

Knowledge management has attracted great deal of attention in recent years. It is generally accepted that a large part of the assets of an organisation are knowledge assets [1], and much effort has been devoted to methods, both technological and social, for understanding and augmenting these assets and encouraging their better utilisation— [2] is regarded as a seminal work in the field, while many journals in both the business and IT domains (such as *Harvard Business Review* and *IEEE Intelligent Systems*) include articles on the theme.

Knowledge management is of as much interest to public administrations as private companies, though has perhaps attracted less attention. Pellucid is a project tackling knowledge management for public bodies under the European Commission's Information Society Technologies (IST) programme. It began in March 2002 and has a duration of 2 years and 8 months. It brings together academic and software developer partners with end-users from across Europe. Its specific motivation comes from the knowledge management issues arising from organisational mobility of employees—th

M.A. Wimmer (Ed.): KMGov 2003, LNAI 2645, pp. 203–212, 2003.
© IFIP 2003

e movement of staff from one department or unit to another, a pervasive situation in public organizations.[1]

In this context, knowledge management can be viewed as experience management, since that is what distinguishes the experienced employee from the novice, even if the novice comes from elsewhere in the organisation. The novice might in fact be highly experienced in other parts of the organisation, but lack experience of the new domain of work or the specific procedures that are relevant.

The objectives of Pellucid are to develop a customisable platform for knowledge management, and three pilot applications for validation and demonstration. By a platform is meant a set of methods, tools and reusable components that may be applied to develop further knowledge management applications. The project's approach begins with requirements capture, analysis and generalisation from the three pilot sites within the project, and the development of a general system architecture based on software agents, a paradigm particularly suited to supporting work processes [3]. The system architecture will then be populated, customised to the pilot sites and validated. At the time of writing, the knowledge management needs of the pilot sites have been thoroughly analysed, and the system architecture is undergoing its first implementation. Trials of a first functioning version of the Pellucid system, partially customised to the pilot sites, are planned to take place shortly; it is then expected that valuable feedback will be obtained and refinements will be made to the systems. At that point it will be possible to make a preliminary assessment of the experience of the Pellucid platform in practice.

The rest of this paper explains the nature of organisational mobility in general terms and as it appears in the pilot applications of the Pellucid project. The technical solution is outlined, including a sketch of the Pellucid platform and what will be involved in customisation of it.

2 Organisational Mobility in Public Organisations

Organisational mobility is the pervasive movement or circulation of staff from one unit or department within an organisation to another. This is commonplace in public organisations, which may deliberately encourage it as a form of career development— exposing employees to different working environments and domains of work as a way of building experience. It might also occur due to promotion, and the consequent need to bring in staff from elsewhere in the organisation to fill the newly vacant post.

It is clear that organisational mobility is not necessarily a bad thing: inasmuch as mobile employees bring fresh ideas or experience of other areas, then the organisation can be enriched. Nevertheless, inevitably these employees will find it harder to perform as effectively as more experienced (static) staff, due to their relative lack of specific knowledge. Time must be spent in gaining familiarity, and although there might be training available, and possibly an Intranet as a source of information, these are not sufficient in themselves. It is these problems that Pellucid aims to address.

---

[1] Organisational mobility should be distinguished from geographical mobility, in which individual employees work from different locations, possible widely distributed. In organisational mobility the working location will generally be fixed, but the position will be filled by different individuals over time.

The Pellucid project includes in organisational mobility the case of high staff turnover. Here the mobile staff are actually coming from outside the organisation, thus without even the knowledge of internal people, but the problems of knowledge management are similar.

3 The Pellucid Pilot Applications

3.1 Requirements Acquisition Methodology

The determination of the user requirements for the Pellucid platform has followed a previously defined methodology that allows the users to participate in the definition of the system from the very beginning of the project. This methodology is based on three steps.
1. Semi-structured interviews, to get the implicit information / knowledge from the users. This type of interviews is very useful in order to capture the vocabulary, the opinions and the general users requirements.
2. Analyses of relevant documents and users organisations, to get the explicit information/knowledge.
3. Scenarios, to capture end-users' needs in their context and focus on the specific aspects of knowledge management. Scenarios also provide a way to validate the results of the interviews and analyses, with the end users.

The results of these steps allow the identification of the requirements, of the knowledge management improvements and of the different actors involved in the process.

For each pilot application, each scenario has been described by gathering and analysing the information about the activities, the actors and their roles, the people interactions, the information sources and the information flows.

3.2 Pilot Application 1

The pilot application of the Comune di Genova (Italy) will address the support to organisational mobility among the several areas of the Traffic and Mobility Management Department of a large city Administration. The services managed range from the strategic traffic planning, to the definition and design of traffic circulation plans within the overall road network, to the simulation activities, to the design, installation and maintenance of traffic signs and signalling systems and to daily operation and management of technical systems and facilities controlling traffic and mobility within the road network.

Particularly, the Pellucid platform will be developed and tested within the process for the installation and maintenance of the traffic light plants. This procedure involves many actors and is constituted by several phases. It is possible to schematize them in the following ones:
1. Input: to point out the need for a new traffic light;
2. Preliminary analysis: to underline particular problems in the interested zone;
3. Verification: to collect information about pedestrian, traffic flows, accdents,..;
4. Design: to define in detail the plant;
5. Definitive evaluation: to verify all the aspects of the project;

6. Administrative procedure: to define the financial and administrative aspects;
7. Execution: to install the traffic light;
8. Testing: to verify the correct running of the system;
9. Maintenance.

It is not a very complex process because generally there is not overlap during the different phases, but the task is not straightforward because it comprises several aspects, both technical and administrative.

The main actors acting during this process are the Mobility and Transport Directorate of the Comune di Genova, the urban police, the area district, the public transport company, and the company that executes the works. There are not only internal actors to the organisation of the Municipality of Genoa but also external, and therefore the experience and the knowledge obtained by the technical staff during the job are very relevant in order to carry out the task more efficiently. A major source of knowledge management problems is the large number of actors involved, and the need for co-ordination among the several departments in order to get the optimal final result. Less experienced employees have less awareness of who they need to contact at what stage among the external actors, how this contact should be made (by email, by letter, whether there is a standard form for a letter, ...), and how long the actor normally takes to reply. These are all examples of knowledge that an experienced employee will have acquired, and they should be shared effectively.

3.3   Pilot Application 2

The Mancomunidad de Municipios del Bajo Guadalquivir (MMBG) is an organisation created by eleven local authorities with the main objective of contributing to the social and economic development of an area with 250,000 inhabitants in the southern Region of Andalusia (Spain). The particular problem of MMBG is the wide range of tasks that must be handled by its employees, from handcraft to IT related activities. This variety of areas in the working environment requires a high degree of flexibility among the employees, and expertise is scarce and very valuable. In this situation, the need for knowledge capitalisation and for reuse of previous experiences is very critical, as it would lead to an increase of the efficiency and would allow for a better use of the human and technical resources.

The pilot application that will be validated at the MMBG concerns the Management of publicly funded Projects among this complex organisation. This will include all the tasks to be performed from the very early stages of the project (definition of the idea, preparation of the proposal and submission to the funding authority) to the justification of the project's costs and activities, and the preservation of all the documents generated during the project execution.

The main problems to be addressed concerning the Management of Projects are due to the lack of integration among the departments involved in the different project phases, and to the non-existence of a solid information structure to provide support for external and internal issues, such as contacting potential providers or preparing a proposal. This is however not simply an IT issue; it reflects the varied and ill-structured nature of the work done. Thus staff find themselves without support—not only new employees but also experienced staff who can be involved in very different proposals and projects, so that they could also be considered as 'organisationally mobile employees'.

3.4 Pilot Application 3

The Consejería de la Presidencia integrates and co-ordinates several Regional Bodies in the eight Administrative Departments which compose the Andalusian Region. Due to their wide scope of application, the several processes performed by this Regional Ministry are large and complex, as they are intended to fulfil the needs of over 7 million inhabitants, and have to establish collaborative working with private and public organisations.

Although Pellucid will mainly concentrate on employees at middle and upper levels of the organisations, the so-called 'knowledge workers', the objective of the Pilot application of the Consejería de la Presidencia is to test the viability of Pellucid at low-level organisationally scenarios with common problems related to high staff mobility.

The testing environment for Pellucid among this pilot site will be the Call Center for Management and Resolution of Fixed Telephony Breakdowns of the Telecommunications Corporate Network of the Andalusian Regional Government, and more precisely, the induction of a new agent into this Call Centre.

Call Centre agents have to adapt in a very short time to a very specific working environment, getting a slight 'on-the-job' training support. These employees suffer from a very high mobility degree, and it has been proven that, due to their special working conditions, they use to keep their position 6 months as an average. This very unstable environment makes the need for:

- improving the learning process of new employees, what is very critical to achieve the needed homogenisation of behaviours;
- registering, keeping and exploiting efficiently the experience and knowledge of the agents before they leave the Call Centre or leave their jobs. This is critical to avoid the complete loss of their experience.

There is already available a Workflow Management System supporting the managing and resolution of the breakdowns, the Vantive System, but this system does not cover all the knowledge management requirements. Therefore, additional support will be needed from Pellucid for the complete process life-cycle, in order to guarantee the optimal integration of the new agent in the call centre, and thus the quality of the services provided.

4 Generalising Knowledge Management Needs

Although the selected procedures for each pilot application are quite different, all the involved employees have to deal with similar issues when performing their daily activities. Each procedure has to be accomplished by contacting several external and internal actors and by producing and evaluating documents, and all these, meeting the established deadlines.

This leads to a generalised set of knowledge management needs that are of wide applicability in many organisations.

1. *Contact management*, the capability to get in touch with the 'right person at the right time' when performing activities involving several actors.

2. *Document management*, that deals with knowledge about how to prepare documents and how to find and reuse existing documents.
3. *Critical timing management*, that deals with activity planning to prevent problems or failures due to possible delays by evaluating how critical activities are, which conditions can influence their accomplishment, which symptoms can warn about possible problems arising and are able to prevent problems.

In these three areas, what distinguishes the experienced employee from the newcomer is the knowledge that he/she has available at their fingertips: knowledge about who to contact and how for particular information or to get a job done; knowledge of what documents are available for reference and reuse, and how to create new ones; and knowledge of how long certain tasks are expected to take or certain organisations to reply to queries. Across these three needs, there is a common 'experience management' cycle with three steps.

1. *Capture*, the observation of employees' behaviour in relation to the work process, for example adding contacts with some comments, choosing one document rather than another.
2. *Capitalisation*, the creation of new knowledge based on the observation of all employees, making inferences to update (for example) the organisation of contacts for all employees.
3. *Return and reuse*, the optimised presentation of relevant information according to the activity the employee is carrying out. Another way to return the experience captured is to present a 'roadmap' (of documents/contacts), a plan of future activities with attached the list of contacts needed for each.

This cycle is seen as key to the effective operation of the Pellucid knowledge management solution, because it allows for continuous improvement of behaviour.

5   An Approach to a Technical Solution

5.1   The Architectural Basis

The Pellucid project is developing a customisable platform to aid with the knowledge management needs identified in the foregoing sections. This platform is based on software agents, arranged in a multi-level structure as shown in Fig. 1.

The three levels each containing a number of agent classes with defined responsibilities.

1. The *interaction layer* is responsible for managing the interaction with individual users, presenting information in a personalised and timely way and allowing queries and evaluations to be made.
2. The *process layer* is where the main knowledge management functionality resides, providing assistance on particular activities and roles and interacting with the workflow management system (if one exists).
3. The *access layer* is responsible for searching and retrieval from document repositories.

In addition there is the Organisational Memory, storing a history of the processes and interactions as a basis for continuous improvement of the knowledge management functionality.

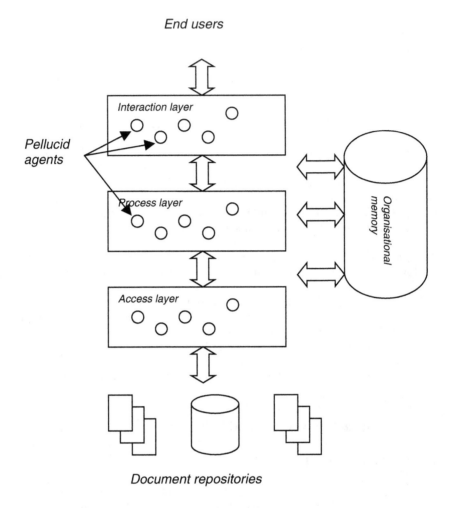

End users

Interaction layer

Pellucid agents

Process layer

Organisational memory

Access layer

Document repositories

Fig. 1. Block diagram of the Pellucid architecture

The three main elements of the Pellucid platform are described in more detail below.

5.2 The Use of Software Agents

Agent Oriented Programming (AOP) [4, 5] extends the abilities of Object Oriented Programming (OOP). Classes or objects in OOP are replaced by agents. In OOP an object can call another object by methods and has to know the definitions of the methods of another object. In AOP agents are communicating and acting by message exchange; this is an advantage compared to method calling in OOP which can throw exception. Inter-agent communication is based on content languages and agent ontologies for specific domains of communication. An ontology is a structured representation of the entities and relationships between them in a particular domain, and as such forms a common basis on which agents communicate and perform their reasoning.

Pellucid uses so-called Intelligent Agents based on FIPA standards for intelligent knowledge management. Using agents makes Pellucid component-based, more scalable and more customizable [6]. Designing the Pellucid system based on agents helps to focus on individual tasks which are solved by a single agent, together creating a complex system. The use of ontologies makes Pellucid customisable for different problem domains by changing the domain ontology; some parts of the ontology will remain unchanged, for example those relating to general organisational properties and processes.

5.3 Organisational Memory

Organisational memories [7] are motivated by the desire to preserve and share the knowledge and experiences that reside in an organisation. As such, they focus on capturing the knowledge, storing it, and making it accessible to analysis and reasoning processes. In the Pellucid context the role of the Organizational Memory (OM) fits tightly the above conceptual definition. It is the central repository of all data and knowledge captured, accumulated and created during the system lifecycle, and provides the raw elements for the agents' reasoning.

The OM contains two main item classes: facts and inferences. The first comprises all kind of data gathered thought the interaction with the users. The second includes the initial knowledge base and the results of reasoning and learning processes taking places in the Pellucid agents on the basis of what is present in the OM. Thus the OM is a living and evolving repository that will support experience capturing (the facts), capitalisation (facts are transformed into inferences) and reuse (from inferences).

The dynamic nature of the OM implies a continuous increase of stored data that are used by agents for knowledge base evolution. The conceptualisation process, together with time flowing, can be at the basis of the progressive and gradual reduction of data relevance thus allowing pruning to maintain the dimension of the OM within a sensible range. The OM permits data mining: uniformities and patterns in workflows and behaviours may be detected and fed back into the active knowledge management components, thereby dynamically enhancing their performance. Knowledge management systems must never be static, or they will become obsolete; such ongoing updating is very necessary.

The OM will not provide knowledge management functions itself, but only storage. Agents are responsible for knowledge management and interact with the OM module, which provides services to support the agents' activity. The OM is mainly composed of three parts.

- An *internal database*, which is the central storage system and provides the persistence functionality. Object-oriented database technology is under investigation for the effective implementation of this part.
- A *communication layer* able to interact with agents using FIPA's ACL, a language quite far from usual 'database query languages'. Communication will adopt the Pellucid ontology rather than typical database terminology.
- An internal *indexing service* to analyse stored data for index preparation and object cluster discovery. The external agents can modify indexing principles to follow the knowledge discovery process.

5.4 Document Search and Retrieval

There is an agent class, the Information Search and Access Agent (ISA), which receives requests for document search and retrieval from other components of the Pellucid system. The environment that the ISA is working in consists of the following elements [8].

Organisational repositories with information assets stored in documents, databases, filesystems, etc. These are needed by the organization to perform its standard activities.

- Document ontologies.
- Document metadata, that describe documents in the organization: (a) business-level metadata to express content, context and location of the documents, and (b) technical-level metadata, to express the way to accessing information from a particular type of the repository.
- Full-text search engine index, that optimizes search for documents described in terms of their contents.

Search capabilities are based on smart usage of metadata repositories and full-text search engine. Metadata repositories store descriptions of all documents in the organisation and the way to accessing, while full-text search engine maintains indices vital for providing the user with fast and precise response to his query.

The first method of searching (with metadata) is especially useful when locating documents strongly connected with workflow activities, since with every change of activity there is a need to provide the user with relevant information concerning this current activity. In this case the responsibility is to bring to the user a list of corresponding documents. They are selected by means of request context used for matching knowledge contained in document or domain ontologies and business-level metadata.

To searching and accessing documents, which are not strictly connected to any particular activity, searching with full-text search engines is more adequate. In this case query to ISA is expected to contain some hints concerning documents content specified by means of words or phrases, which should or shouldn't appear in the documents. This kind of request is realized with the help of indices prepared earlier with the document indexing engine. It is up to the agent to make decision about the way it performs the search; it could be a simple search in metadata repository or aggregated search in metadata and in indices repositories from the full-text search engine.

5.5 Customisable Platform

The Pellucid platform will consist of elements that are in some way or another reusable. The type of reuse will depend on the nature of the element itself: for example, the software representing an agent class might be stripped down into a template for future application, and/or provided as an example to be modified. Clearly this will depend on the experience gained during the project. The general reusable elements are expected to include the following:

- ontologies (general and domain-specific);
- user interface (Web application);

- system interfaces (to document repositories and workflow management systems);
- the agents themselves;
- the organisational memory.

The following table indicates a preliminary view of how the elements can be provided in the platform, and the corresponding kinds of customisation that will be applicable to them.

Table 1. Customisable elements in the Pellucid platform

Element provided in platform	How customised
Core (e.g. of ontology)	Expand/Populate/Possibly adapt
Template (e.g. of agent class)	Fill in/Populate
Prior case (e.g. of agent class)	Adapt
Building blocks (e.g. of organisational memory)	Assemble
Guidelines (e.g. for interfacing to document repositories)	Implement
Specifications (e.g. for interfacing to workflow management system)	Implement

Further investigation is needed to establish the best way of including each element in the platform.

References

1. Strassman, P.A., 'The value of computers, information and knowledge', 1996, available from website http://www.strassmann.com/pubs/cik/cik-value.shtml.
2. Davenport, T.H. & Prusak, L., Working Knowledge: How Organizations Manage What They Know, Harvard Business School Press, 1998.
3. Jennings, N. et al., 'Autonomous agents for business process management', Int. Journal of Applied Artificial Intelligence 14 (2) 145–189, 2000.
4. Ciancarini, P. & Wooldridge, M. (eds.), Agent-Oriented Software Engineering, Springer Verlag, 2001.
5. Jennings, N., 'Agent-based Computing: Promise and Perils', *Proc. 16th Int. Joint Conf. on Artificial Intelligence*, Stockholm, Sweden, 1429–1436.
6. *Review of Software Products for Multi-Agent Systems*, published by AgentLink, June 2002.
7. Abecker, A., et al., 'Toward a technology for organizational memories', IEEE Intelligent Systems, May/June 1988.
8. Słota, R., Krawczyk, K., Dziewierz, M., Kitowski, J., Lambert, S., 'Agent paradigm for accessing document repositories in Pellucid platform', EuroWEB 2002 Conference, Dec. 17–19, 2002, Oxford, UK, accepted.

Process-Based Knowledge Management and Modelling in E-government – An Inevitable Combination

Silke Palkovits[1], Robert Woitsch[1], and Dimitris Karagiannis[2]

[1]BOC GmbH, A-1010 Vienna, Baeckerstrasse 5/3,
{silke.palkovits, robert.woitsch}@boc-eu.com
[2]University of Vienna, A-1210 Vienna, Bruenner Str. 72
dk@dke.univie.ac.at

Abstract. As the processes in e-government are diversified and complex the need for an appropriate knowledge management strategy for governmental employees and citizens as well arises. In this paper an approach is introduced how to define and implement a process-based knowledge management tool which takes e-government processes and transform them into valuable knowledge measures.

1 Introduction

Today the expression "e-government" (electronic government) is a synonym for a modern and efficient administration. In the area of information and communication technology a number of new terms came up in the past few years. A huge amount of different, partly contradictory definitions can be found in the literature. As e-government has an internal as well as external administrative perspective, the following definitions may be most appropriate.

"Under the term electronic government we understand all measures of the public administration that have the aim to primarily external, but also internal service improvement concerning defined tasks or the satisfaction of customer needs".

What can be criticised on the above definition is the missing explanation of the important term "electronic". The following definition emphasising on the important of information and communication technology seems to be more suitable.

"E-government is defined as the redesign of internal and external governmental relations with the help of internet-supported flows, information technology and communication with the aim to optimise governmental services as well as to increase the involvement of private persons in the decision process"

E-government and Business Process Management with all its reorganisation and optimisation aspects became crucial topics in connection with the administration engineering in the past few years. Governments and public administrations are facing the same problems than business organisations with respect to the management of their knowledge.

In the following chapters process-oriented Knowledge Management and process modelling in e-government are described in detail. Later on these two approaches are combined.

M.A. Wimmer (Ed.): KMGov 2003, LNAI 2645, pp. 213–218, 2003.

2 Process-Oriented Knowledge Management

Rapid changes of the technological model and business models of today's public administrations demand critical changes within the organisation. Knowledge Management has become a serious management discipline[1] to co-ordinate the transfer of today's linear business processes (BP) to a web-based process view and to deal with the complexity of new technological models. Knowledge Management should "enhance customer value" (Beckman), "aim to achieve the company's objectives" (van der Spek) or "produce biggest payoff" (Hibbard).

This article introduces the concept of the EU-Project PROMOTE[2] where an overall framework for process-oriented Knowledge Management, starting with modelling knowledge intensive business processes in a web-environment and focusing on the knowledge management processes, such as identification, validation, distribution, usage and evaluation of knowledge, that have been developed.

Within the project three challenges have been defined. The first one resulted from the quotations above: "How can PROMOTE guarantee, that a knowledge management approach creates additional value to an organisation?" The PROMOTE approach therefore starts with the analysis of business processes to identify "knowledge intensive tasks" and to select activities where "an explicit control of knowledge" leads to a better performance of the business process.

This "explicit control of knowledge" is seen as identification, development, distribution, usage, storage and evaluation of knowledge (in the following summarised as "knowledge activities"). The second challenge is therefore: "How can PROMOTE support the explicit control of knowledge, in a transparent, well structured and platform independent way?". The PROMOTE® approach therefore introduces the so-called "Knowledge Management Process Model" that defines the knowledge interaction between knowledge workers in a process-oriented manner.

In this context knowledge is seen as "humanised information" (Karagiannis) where information can reside in "databases, on papers, or in people's heads" (Hibbard). This leads to the third challenge: "How can PROMOTE describe the location, the availability and security aspects of knowledge?"

The PROMOTE® approach therefore introduces the so-called "Knowledge Structure Model" that categorises knowledge resources (the categorisation is based on Topic Maps, the ISO13250 standard) and defines access rights.

The benefits of using a model based knowledge management approach like PROMOTE® are listed as follows[3]:

- On the basis of business processes, knowledge intensive activities that strongly influence time, quality and cost of a process are easily identified and supported via knowledge management processes.

---

[1] Wickli, A., Jonischkeit, R., Kunkler, B., Give your people canoes and compasses (translated), in Chemie und Fortschritt, Clariant 2/2000 in Muttenz, p28-31

[2] Karagiannis, D., Prackwieser, C., Telesko, R., The PROMOTE® project: Process-oriented knowledge management, in Proceedings of the 3rd European Conference on Product and Process Modelling, Lisbon, 2000

[3] Woitsch, R., Karagiannis, D.: „Process-Oriented Knowledge Management Systems Based on KM-Services: The PROMOTE® Approach"

- The integration of knowledge models with business process models and evaluation models supports an overall management view with consistent analysis, evaluation and coordination.
- The definition of a knowledge management approach by knowledge models is tool and method independent. To realise the approach several different knowledge management tools can be combined.
- With evaluation models like Balanced Scorecard models it is possible to evaluate the knowledge management approaches, successful approaches can be distributed through knowledge model documentation.

In the following chapter we briefly describe the characteristics of process modelling in e-government and the approach for a tailor-made modelling methodology developed in a project of BOC.

3 Process Modelling in E-government

The main characteristic of e-government applications is their complexity, as a number of actors (citizens, clerks, etc.) as well as business processes according to more or less defined roles and heterogeneous technologies have to be integrated. The modelling of processes with respect to electronic administration therefore is a big challenge. It is not enough to use traditional modelling tools for the Business Process Management in e-government, it is moreover necessary to be aware of the flows, the necessary resources, the responsible roles and the competencies of the authorities[4].

The approach of BOC is to develop a modelling tool which realises the most important requirements of e-government. Some of these requirements are the identification of actors and their roles, the definition of possible communication channels, the transparency of the flows, the standardisation of terminologies for an efficient and transparent communication, the holistic modelling from the portal to the back office and the integration of the citizen as service consumer.

In the course of a number of projects, BOC has developed a framework called E-BPMS which integrates business-oriented modelling approaches and approaches for the modelling information systems (IS) and IT infrastructures[5]. E-BPMS is ideal for the use in e-government as it provides a generic procedure model for the development of e-business applications. This framework is not restricted to a specific kind of e-business applications, but can also be used for business to business, business to administration, business to customer, administration to customer or administration to administration applications.

Basis for this E-BPMS framework is the modelling on four levels, to get control over the complexity of e-business applications. On the strategic level the business model is depicted. Additionally decisions about objectives, the common organisational structure and the core business processes are made. On the business level the business processes as well as the working environment are modelled and on

---

[4] Karagiannis, D., Palkovits, S., Prozessmodellierung in der öffentlichen Verwaltung – Ein ganzheitliches Rahmenwerk für E-Government, October 2002, for eGOV day 2003

[5] Bayer, F., Kühn, H., Junginger, S., Petzmann, A., E-BPMS: Ein Modellierungs-Framework für E-Business-Anwendungen, September 2001

the implementation level the organisational and technical realisation is executed. The aspects of runtime environment and the IT infrastructure are considered on the execution level.

With this tool, which is currently being developed within a project, the problems of modelling in e-government should be cleared up. With the integration of the perspectives of the organisation and the technology as well as the inside and outside perspectives, the consideration of the specific characteristics of administrative processes and the strategic reflections of the administrative development a holistic realisation of process modelling in e-government is guaranteed[6].

When modelling business processes in e-government two different steps are identified[7]. The first step is the design and the optimisation of the process models of the public administration. The focus is laid on the development of a tailor-made modelling methodology within a business process management tool. In the second step the addressed business type (business to business, business to administration, business to customer, administration to customer, etc.) has to be defined. With the use of information technology, new business models should be introduced to be able to realise the tight integration of the authorities with the citizen. The next few paragraphs mainly focus on the first part of the realisation.

For the success of a project it is important to select and develop the appropriate modelling methodology respectively. Starting from the E-BPMS paradigm different modelling types are defined according to the concept of life events[8].

On the strategic level questions like: Which processes and products/services should be realised?, Who are my participants and partners in e-government? and Do the strategies of the participants and partners match with each other? can be answered within a business model.

The business level contains a number of different model types. The life event map should give an overview of the different process models related to specific life events and business situations. The product model helps describing and managing the offered products and services. To structure the working environment within an authority, a ministry or a city an organisational model will be used. The skill profiles of the employees should be depicted here to guarantee the best management of each individual's knowledge. Business process models are the main point within the modelling in the public administration. How these processes are linked with Knowledge Management will be described later on in this paper.

Last but not least the IT level is described with the help of different models, like for example an interaction model depicting the process flow directly on the platform level. Security aspects like the digital signature can be modelled here.

When these processes and models are engineered within a public administration a defined knowledge management group analyses the processes according to the knowledge management approach described in a previous chapter of this paper.

---

[6] Palkovits, S., Europaweite Ansätze zur Modellierung im E-Government, Präsentations-unterlagen BOC ITC GmbH, May 2002

[7] Karagiannis, D., Kühn, H.: Metamodelling Platforms

[8] Wimmer, M.: Geschäftsprozessmodellierung in E-Government: Eine Zwischenbilanz, in: Computer kommnikativ 03/02, page 23

4 Knowledge Management in E-government

The introduction of Knowledge Management into e-government is done on two levels. The above mentioned process management phase ends with the definition of business processes and other process types. Knowledge Management is seen as an improvement of business process management in this case[9].

The organisational driven business process models turned out to be insufficient for a detailed analysis. In most cases a knowledge based business process has to be modelled on the basis of the business processes to focus on knowledge management aspects. Some activities that are in an organisational aspect not so interesting become more important in the context of knowledge management and therefore need to be re-designed. Some aspects that are interesting on an organizational aspect do not influence knowledge management at all and should therefore be removed. Each knowledge-based business processes is linked to the according business process and describes knowledge intensive aspects in more detail. Within a knowledge-based business process knowledge intensive tasks (KIT) are detected and analysed. The main problem is to rate the difficulty of the knowledge intensive task, as each knowledge worker tends to under estimate the difficulty of his colleague's activity.

This analysis is performed for each activity in the knowledge-based business process during a pre-analysis phase; the result is the distinction between KITs and non KITs.

On the second level the working environment model, where the organisational structure is depicted, is analysed in more detail introducing skill profiles. Skill profiles describe the competence of either a topic (from the semantic network) or of activities within a business process. Using this framework, it is guaranteed that the skills of a person are well designed and categorised. There is also the possibility to enter "Should-" and "Is skills" at each profile to analyse "skill gaps". The focus of this approach is not to identify skill gaps, but to identify experts who voluntarily enter the skill documentation. Skill profiles can be also directly imported from other data sources, like Lotus Notes or SAP.

5 Conclusion

We come up with the conclusion that knowledge management in the public administration is inevitable and should go hand in hand with the currently conducted administration engineering. Knowledge management is enlarging the scope of process modelling in E-Government to an extended and holistic approach.

To evaluate the implementation of a knowledge management system, an evaluation model will be defined based on the concept of the Balanced Scorecard. Criteria are linked to either the business process (in this case we speak of a business goal) or to a knowledge management process (this would be a knowledge goal).

The PROMOTE approach is open to be enlarged with whatever requirement coming up from different business fields. The specific requirements of the public administration can be easily adapted and implemented within this knowledge management framework.

---

[9] Abecker A., Hinkelmann K., Maus H., Müller H.J., (2002) *Geschäftsprozess-orientiertes Wissensmangement*, Springer Verlag, Berlin, Germany

References

1. Abecker A., Hinkelmann K., Maus H., Müller H.J., (2002) *Geschäftsprozess-orientiertes Wissensmangement*, Springer Verlag, Berlin, Germany
2. Bayer, F., Junginger, S., Kühn, H., A Business Process-oriented Methodology for Developing E-Business Applications, in Baake U., Zobel, R.N., Al-Akaidi, M. (Eds.): Proceedings of the 7th European Concurrent Engineering Conference (ECEC 2000), April 17–19 2000, Leister. Society for Computer Simulation (SCS), pp32–40
3. Bayer, F., Kühn, H., Junginger, S., Petzmann, A., E-BPMS: Ein Modellierungs-Framework für E-Business-Anwendungen, September 2001
4. ISO/IEC 13250, Topic Maps Information Technology Document Description and Proceeding Languages, 3.12.1999
5. Karagiannis D., Woitsch R.,(2002a) "Modelling Knowledge Management Processes to describe organisational knowledge systems", In *Proceedings of 15th European conference on Artificial Intelligence, WS Knowledge Management and Organizational Memories*, 21–26 July 2002, Lyon, France
6. Karagiannis, D., Palkovits, S., Prozessmodellierung in der öffentlichen Verwaltung – Ein ganzheitliches Rahmenwerk für E-Government, October 2002, for eGOV day 2003
7. Karagiannis, D., Prackwieser, C., Telesko, R., The PROMOTE® project: Process oriented knowledge management, in Proceedings of the 3rd European Conference on Product and Process Modelling, Lisbon, 2000
8. Palkovits, S., Europaweite Ansätze zur Modellierung im E-Government, Präsentations-unterlagen BOC ITC GmbH, May 2002
9. Stefanidis G., Karaginnis D., Woitsch R. (2002), "The PROMOTE approach: Modelling Knowledge Management Processes to describe knowledge management systems", In *Proceedings of the third European Conference on Organizational Knowledge, Learning, and Capabilities (OKLC 02)*, 5–6 April 2002, Athens, Greece
10. Topic Maps, *http://www.topicmap.com*, access 08.11.02
11. Wickli, A., Jonischkeit, R., Kunkler, B., Give your people canoes and compasses (translated), in Chemie und Fortschritt, Clariant 2/2000 in Muttenz, p28–31.
12. Woitsch R., Karagiannis D., „Process-Oriented Knowledge Management Systems Based on KM-Services: The PROMOTE® Approach", In *Proceeding of the fourth International Conference on Practical Aspects of Knowledge Management (PAKM 02)*, 2–3 December 2002, Vienna, Austria
13. Woitsch, R., Karagiannis, D., Renner, T., Model-based Process Oriented Knowledge Management, the PROMOTE Approach

Learning and Personal Development within the Public Sector by a Cognitive Narrative Cultural Approach

Theresia Olsson Neve

Department of Business Studies and Information Systems,
Mälardalen University College
P.O. Box 883, S-721 23 Västerås, Sweden
theresia.neve@mdh.se

Abstract. Many organisations suffer from "illness symptoms" because of high pressure and fast changing environments. There is no time for reflexion and perspective making, and learning within organisations falls short. However, if we cannot change the organisations outer pressure we must oppose the problem from inside, and it is assumed here that the narrative dialogue approach is one way to approach the problem for the employees within organisations. A 'Learning and Personal Development' Instrument has been developed in order to increase the individual's capability to describe his/her own situation within organisations. This instrument is based on ideas from the cognitive narrative area and the Socratic Question Technique. Interviews and seminars of a prototypical nature have been conducted within the health care and at universities in Sweden. The empirical results are positive for eliciting knowledge.

1 Introduction

Our society is characterised by a global economy, it favours immaterial things (ideas, information and relations), and it is highly connected. The interactive computer nets are growing exponentially and gives the communication new appearances and channels, and the capitalism has experienced a fundamental restructuring characterised by: more flexible management; decentralisation and network co-operation, both inside and between companies; reinforcement of the power of the capital; increased individualisation and diversification of the work conditions; govern interventions to selectively deregulate the markets and abolish the welfare states; and escalated global economic concurrence, because of geographically and cultural differentiated environments (Castells, 1996). This fast and changeable nature will affect a significant part of our society. Almost no individual, no operation, no part of the public or private sector will be uninfluenced. An overall disturbing trend is that stress symptoms among individuals in all different groupings become more ordinary.

The public sector is often responsible (according to the law) to supply the inhabitants in the society with health care, water, electricity, *etc.* But, if the individuals in the society, that are dependent on the quality of the service in the public sector (for example patients in the primary care), not obtain the care they need, the society will have "illness symptoms" which will be very costly in the end. It is a well-

M.A. Wimmer (Ed.): KMGov 2003, LNAI 2645, pp. 219–229, 2003.
© IFIP 2003

known problem that, for example, the health care suffers from scarce resources, high pressure, sick reporting, *etc.*

How can we prevent and manage this "illness symptoms" within organisations in the society? If an organisation is characterised by these problems but has this societal responsibility, how can we prevent it from falling apart?

One way to approach the problem is to focus on the dialogue and motivation for the employees within organisations (if we cannot change the organisations outer pressure, we must oppose the problem from inside). It is the individual's motivation, engagement, and ability to communicate knowledge and experiences to others that underlies the possibility for the individual (and especially the whole organisation) to learn, and learning is often a sign of mental health. The dialogue helps the employees to narrate, construct and validate their own and each other's experiences.

A 'Learning and Personal Development' (LPD) instrument has been developed in order to increase the individual's capability to describe his/her own situation within organisations. Interviews and seminars of a prototypical nature have been conducted within health care and at universities in Sweden. The method has similarities with Yin´s (1994) description of explanation-building, when analysing the data. The important characteristics for explanation-building are that the final explanation is a result of a series of iterations. Each interview started with questions worked up from theory and earlier practices. After each interview, the questions were evaluated in consultation with the respondent according to pre-defined evaluation criteria. It was important that the questions should teach the individual something about him/her self. It was also important that some of the answers were suited for being stored in a database. Thereafter, the questions were redesigned, and the procedure reinitiated.

The Socratic Question Technique, with its deductive and inductive reasoning, has been used as a framework for the research. This technique is believed to motivate the individual to interact with other individuals in order to contribute with knowledge, receive feedback, and receive new knowledge about him/her self and his/her colleagues. Cognitive psychotherapy frequently uses the Socratic question technique in the therapy-session and we find it interesting to make reference to the psychiatrist Carlo Perris and his definition of knowledge-growth: knowledge-growth (learning) is accomplished when "...a cognitive/emotional reconstructuring of view based upon one self, upon others and the reality takes place" (1989, p. 2112). The purpose of the Socratic question technique is to activate individuals and to encourage reflection and critical thinking; this is assumed to contribute to learning and personal development.

2 Knowledge Elicitation

The purpose of our research is to improve learning (Blackler, 1995, for example, is talking about *encultured knowledge,* which refers to the process of achieved understandings) and personal development within organisations. Even thou the application area is distinguished in the following two different examples, for example, the ecological approach as described in chapter 3 are not striving for huge amounts of data (which is often the case when building expert systems) but *personal unique knowledge,* the knowledge elicitation process described within the expert area is quite contiguous and useful as a contrast because we believe it represents much of how knowledge is looked upon these days. Modern social science often organises itself around the production of cumulative knowledge, and this knowledge about the world is kept outside the world itself instead of being in contact with and changing with the world (Alvesson & Deetz, 2000).

The procedure of capturing knowledge into an expert system is called knowledge acquisition. A knowledge engineer interacts with an expert in order to acquire, organise, and study a problem's knowledge (Durkin, 1994). The goal is to compile a body of knowledge on the problem of interest that can be encoded in the expert system.

To acquire knowledge from the expert is distinguished from the more general knowledge acquisition term and is called *knowledge elicitation* (*ibid*). This implies an interactive session between the knowledge engineer and the expert where the knowledge engineer, many times, interviews the expert. "The main vehicle for knowledge elicitation is face-to-face discussions between the expert who possesses the domain knowledge and the knowledge engineer who asks questions..." (Gonzalez & Dankel, 1993, p. 349) Case studies may also be used where the knowledge engineer study the expert when he or she is solving a problem.

The Knowledge Elicitation Cycle
Durkin (1994) explains the sequence of the knowledge elicitation cycle as to: (1) *collect* (an iterative style of collecting the information), (2) *interpret* (this involves a review of the collected information and the identification of key pieces of knowledge), (3) *analyse* (the key pieces of knowledge uncovered will provide insight into forming theories on the organisation of the knowledge and problem-solving strategies), and (4) *design* (now new understanding of the problem that can aid further investigations should have been formed).

Direct and Indirect Questions, Probes and Prompts
In the interview *direct questions* and/or *indirect questions* may be used. A direct question seeks answers that have a limited number of responses, for example: "What is the value of...?" Indirect questions are exploratory in nature and allow the expert to answer in a more independent way. *Probes* are also used in order to provide further information on the issue, for example: "Can you explain...?", "Can you discuss...?" *etc. Prompts* are questions intended to direct the interview in some direction. It has usually the form: "Can you discuss...?" or "Can we return to...?"

The Funnel Sequence
The *funnel sequence* is recommended in order to enhance effectiveness of these questions. This technique addresses a particular topic by first asking general questions to then move to more specific questions (figure 1, next page):

3 Knowledge Elicitation from an Ecological Perspective

An ecological approach according to the knowledge elicitation process is here defined as something that implies the importance of *studying individual's actions on the basis of interpretations of motives and intentions, social norms, feelings, plans, and mutual undertaking*. Castells (1997) defines the concept of ecology as follows: "By ecology, in my sociological approach, I understand a set of beliefs, theories, and projects that consider humankind as a component of a broader ecosystem and wish to maintain the system's balance in a dynamic, evolutionary perspective" (p. 113). We believe an individual's knowledge must be studied in the light of the individual's subjective world – i.e. individuals' actions can only be studied by interpreting their subjective contents of meaning. Here in this section, the main methodological difference between the presented approach in chapter 2 and the ecological approach will be described.

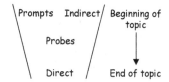

Fig. 1. Funnel Sequencing Technique (adapted from Durkin, 1994)

The Funnel Sequence in chapter 2 is described as a general-to-specific approach for eliciting knowledge and uses the types of questions introduced in the last few sections. Prompts and indirect questions are used to obtain a broad description of the topic. These are followed by probe questions in order to direct the interview toward the more detailed issues.

The ecological perspective has in general the same entrance. However, it starts with a more specific question (on the basis of a specific purpose). This question is then dealt with in an iterative manner (by using probe questions) and finally a specific knowledge description is received. What is added to the sequence in the ecological approach is a dimension where the subjective part of the individual are coped with by asking questions about his/her central references, by letting the respondent make comparisons with other individuals procedures, and raise unspoken questions the individual have up to an organisational level. Figure 2, next page, models the idea:

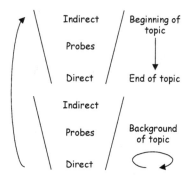

Fig. 2. The Funnel Sequence in a Broader Perspective

The human being is seen in this paper as a creature that performs actions *deliberately*, and that action is part of a complex system of actions with some kind of specific goals, purposes, tasks, or functions. Molander (1996) raises the question: "What constitute an actions *identity*?" Immediately he answers, "The identity is connected to the question *why* something is done" (the reasons the actor can give). This makes it extremely important to receive knowledge about the background of the topic.

3.1 Perspective Making and Perspective Taking

In the activities that constitute our form of life is *question-answer* one of the links that holds together the mutual understanding of what we do (Molander, 1996). Answers and opposite questions contributes to verification, modification and sometimes to a deepening of our *comprehension of what others and we are doing.* For example, Boland and Tenkasi (1995) are arguing for the importance of being able to create strong perspectives within a community, as well as the ability to take other perspectives into account. This improves the individual's capability to understand and influence the situation/environment in which he/she is a part.

By interacting with others in dialogues, we are aided in formulating thoughts and tacit skills (i.e. implicit personal knowledge difficult to articulate in language), as well as forced (or have the opportunity) to structure our thoughts and mental models and express them in an understandable way (in words and/or in images) for others. When we narrate our experience we also construct and validate the self, and in an externalisation-internalisation situation of knowledge, we learn (1) when we talk (when we express ourselves and/or explain something), (2) when we listen to others, (3) when we give feedback to others, and/or (4) when receiving it.

Before two individuals start to interact with each other, they have their earlier assumptions, experiences, values, *etc.* When a person asks another person something, this person replies and the conversation begins. They give each other feedback and their dialogue results hopefully in new understandings and knowledge for them both. When the individual articulate and externalise something he/she becomes at the same time aware of his/her personal knowledge that he/she have but earlier have taken for granted or have had implicit.

3.2 The Cognitive Narrative Dialogue

A dialogue is a conversation between two or more individuals with the purpose to help the individual to reflect and to widen his/her boundaries. "[It] is a dialectical movement between *examples* and different ways to talk about these examples to *put them in a greater wholeness.* The goal is not to break down the concepts in its "parts", but to *try them in usage in different contexts*" (Molander, 1996, p. 208, authors own translation).

The dialogue is a fundamental model for knowledge creation. The psychiatrist Carlo Perris' (1989) definition of knowledge creation is useful here: "[It is] the process which leads to a reach beyond the current state of clarity, competence and comprehension, or, in other words, that a cognitive/emotional reconstructuring of view based upon him/her self, upon others and the reality takes place" (p. 2112, authors own translation). An interpretation should occur in the knowledge process which leads to a corresponding image, both useful for the observer and the actor.

Bruner (1986) differs between two distinct modes of cognition, *the paradigmatic mode* and *the narrative mode.* The paradigmatic mode tries to establish reality by formal and empirical proof, and the narrative mode gives the ability to see possible formal connections before one is able to prove them in any formal way. It is more about verisimilitude than truth, and cognitive psychotherapy, with its focus on the Socratic question technique, falls within its scope.

3.2.1 The Socratic Question Technique

Many authors make references to Socrates when they want to discuss the "true" search for knowledge (see for example Selling, 1984; Perris, 1989; d'Elia, 1992; Hoppe Jakobsson, 1992; Molander, 1996; and Svenneby, 2002). Socrates represents some kind of symbol for the unbribable search for truth by continuously asking critical questions (Molander, 1996).

The goal with the Socratic question technique is to find knowledge and insight that the *participants already have*, even if they do not know that they have it. Questions, answers and reflection should make non-reflective knowledge and insight available. That this goal *never in full is achieved* is an important aspect of the dialogue. (*ibid*)

Molander (*ibid*) explains the characteristics in the Socratic Method as follows:

- The dialogue has a *concrete situation* as a presupposition
- Socrates behaves as *if he has no knowledge* in that way that he knows the answer of the central question
- Socrates turns to another person who *think that he/she knows*
- Socrates *just want to learn* and is a true knowledge searcher who "does not know for sure"
- However, Socrates does not pretend to be *totally ignorant*. This means that he has a *will to learn*; he listens, observes, ask questions, and so on. He is not a passive listener.
- Socrates questions uncover ignorance
- It is important that the dialogue partner will realise this ignorance by him/her self

The "resistance" an individual meets in dialogue is of great importance. As in cognitive psychotherapy, it is here assumed that the right questions will help individuals to relieve their knowledge (Perris, 1989). In general, questions should promote individual awareness and mutual comprehension and not lock the individual, not mislead, or give him or her incorrect associations.

Cognitive psychotherapy is a learning process in which the goal for the individual is to receive new knowledge about him/her self. It is an *active* process (where the therapist not only should listen to the patient passively with empathy and express an opinion "at an appropriate occasion"), *directive* process (the individuals' mental structures continually develop when his/her knowledge about him/her self and the world around grows), and *humanistic* process (if humans are regarded as, so called, "pilots", you see the individual as capable to take control over his/her behaviour and situations he/she confronts). This approach is characterised by *collaborative empiricism*, where two individuals cooperate in an investigating way (*ibid*). They collect facts and presents hypotheses, to thereafter analyse their acceptability; if they should remain or rejected and replaced. Note, it is important that the investigator not becomes the central character in the interview, which too often is the case (Fisher & Geiselman, 1992).

The statement in chapter 3, that the human being is seen as a creature that performs actions *deliberately*, and that action is part of a complex system of actions with some kind of specific goals, purposes, tasks, or functions, makes the cognitive theoretically traditions collected knowledge of how learning and change is possible as an *enabler to increase the understanding of knowledge and actions* in the knowledge elicitation process.

3.2.2 Cognitive Techniques

Cognitive techniques are used to change individuals' fundamental assumptions - i.e. preconceived hypotheses. They are used to make a map of thoughts of patterns, capture traps in thought, and find alternative ways of thinking.

Examples of specific techniques are (Freeman *et al.*, 1994; Malm, 1992; Wistedt, 1997; Hoppe Jacobsson, 1994; Perris *et al.*, 1988):

- *Clarify concepts*. To have an effective and fruitful dialogue, concepts and formulations must be clarified. The word "satisfied", for example, might be interpreted in a number of different ways. Questions like: "What do you mean by...?", "What does it mean to you...?", "In what way does it affect you...?", *etc.*, guides the respondent in the right direction.
- *Investigate sources of evidence*. An effective way to question the description is to investigate to what extent the description are confirmed or proved to the opposite or if it eventually exist some other interpretations. Questions like: "Could you give me an example...?", "How do you know that...?", "Has someone said...?" *etc.*, helps to investigate the source.
- *Reattribute*. To reattribute is to rewrite the situation. Examples of questions are: "Could it be interpreted in another way?", "What do you think I think?", "How do you think others see it?" *etc.*
- *Investigate alternatives*. To investigate alternatives is to try to have a perspective of the situation, questions like: "Is this the only way?", "How is this done by other individuals?", Could this be done in some other way?", could be used.
- *Cognitive repetition*. Cognitive repetition is to verify that there is a correspondence in the dialogue. Questions like: "Have I understood it right...?", "Could we sum up?", "What have we been talking about?" *etc.*, are useful to ask.

A concluding remark: the cognitive approach may be perceived like "common sense". There could also at times be difficult to perceive the difference to more "traditional" ways of, for example, interviewing. However, the techniques above should be used in accordance with the whole cognitive therapeutically frame (the whole culture): structure, collaboration, respect, focus, feed-back, open-mindness (for perspective making and perspective taking), asking right questions in order to 'deliver' knowledge, *etc.*, this to strengthen individuals at a deeper level.

3.3 The Ecological Knowledge Elicitation Process

The main purpose with the project is to develop the overall process around the management of knowledge within organisations (an Ecological Knowledge Management System): from (1) *management and organisational mobilisation* (with the important activities to define the knowledge management strategy, to define key performance indicators that will measure existing knowledge-exchanging activities, appoint knowledge managers in the organisation, *etc.*) to (2) *identifying knowledge-key individuals* (it is important to identify knowledgeable and interesting individuals who have a crucial importance of the organisations future development and who have the capacity of helping others to relieve their knowledge), to (3) *generate the knowledge*, and to (4) *package, spread and reuse it*. These parts will not be presented here in this paper when the specific 'Learning and Personal Development' (LPD) Instrument is in focus. However, three questions must be answered before the knowledge-eliciting activities starts: *what is the goal with the knowledge-elicitation activities?*, *what questions should these activities answer in general,* and *who will be the specific user of the externalised knowledge?* (Blair, 1984).

3.3.1   The 'Learning and Personal Development' Instrument Outlined

The extended knowledge elicitation process is described from a "knowledge-in-action" perspective. An individual's action is always part of a wider context, and it must always be understood in this context (Molander, 1996). A visual description of the procedure is presented below (figure 3). Two major streams may be recognised in the process: one knowledge-generating part (phase 1-4), and one part for developing the individual (phase 3-6).

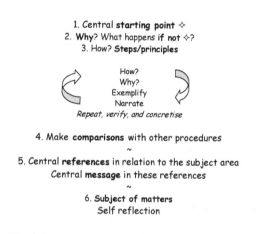

1. Central **starting point** ⬦
2. **Why?** What happens if **not** ⬦?
3. How? **Steps/principles**

How?
Why?
Exemplify
Narrate
Repeat, verify, and concretise

4. Make **comparisons** with other procedures

~

5. Central **references** in relation to the subject area
Central **message** in these references

~

6. **Subject of matters**
Self reflection

Fig. 3. The Ecological Knowledge Elicitation Process

Most important of all when asking questions according to a cognitive (psychotherapeutically) manner is that the opening question(s) should be as wide as possible and the questions in general should be value-neutral.

Step 1
(Phase 1) The procedure begins with a *central starting point*, for example with the question, *"how do you look at your work situation?"* The opening phase should be general enough to not mislead the individual in an incorrect direction, and specific enough to attract attention for him/her.

Step 2
(Phase 2) Thereafter, to verify that the topic is of significance and worth to handle, one should question what happens *if not*. This phase should be characterised by critical thinking and *de-familiarisation*, i.e. how to think and act dialectically and how to turn the well-known into the unusual (Alvesson & Deetz, 2000).

Step 3
(Phase 3) As a third phase, the issue will be dealt with in an iterative manner in different *steps* and/or *principles*. In general, the interviewer continuously repeats, verifies, and concretises the respondent's description by asking how and why, and

requesting him/her to exemplify and narrate the issue – *"tell me how you perform your tasks in different steps"*, *"how?"*, *"could you exemplify?"*, *"in what way?"*, *"do you mean that...?"*, *"is it correct that...?"*, *"have I understood you right when...?"* After this sequence some form of explicit knowledge description should be available.

The following example illustrates the procedure described above: A respondent were asked to explain how she proceeded in a particular matter, and from the beginning she found it somewhat ridiculous to discuss the issue (she thought this was widely known in the organisation). However, during the session a structure started to evolve, and finally when she saw her story in a formalised representation, she understood its value for others.

Ambrosini and Bowman (2001) have developed a similar method – a mapping process, based on cognitive and causal maps, semi-structured interviews, and metaphors. The mapping process (with focus on a special issue) raises questions like; 'What causes A to happen?', 'How does A happen?', 'Could you tell me an example about B?', and 'Could you narrate a story about the occurrence of C?' Since tacit knowledge has a cognitive dimension, is practical, context specific, and difficult to formalise (*ibid*), this approach will help individuals articulate the tacit and often taken for granted knowledge.

Step 4

(Phase 4) Fourthly, *reflection and comparisons* with others behaviour or procedures will take place. A good question to ask is, *"do you think your way of doing this is different from how others do it?"* (However, the word 'different' must not be parsed as negative).

The technique of Repertory Grids might be used (Kelly, 1963). These consist of a chart, in which "elements" usually placed in columns, are rated by adjectival phrases or simple adjectives known as "constructs" set in rows. For example, to the constructs 'trust' and 'honesty', a nurse may have the following directional relationships: "nurse to patient", "patient to nurse", "nurse to colleagues", "colleagues to nurse", *etc*.

Step 5

(Phase 5) An individual's *central references* will next be sought. One could for example ask if there is someone the respondent is inspired of or influenced by in a particular matter. This gives an opportunity to start to unwind some of his/her underlying assumptions. Individuals might not share their tacit knowledge because of a risk of loosing power and competitive advantage, but *by supplying ones references, the individual has the possibility to be understood, without revealing any specific valuable knowledge.* The questions: *"is there any central in your thinking that affects your actions when it comes to... (the discussed issue)?"* tries to create an understanding to why the individual acts as he/she does.

The psychoanalyst Erich Fromm used a similar technique in his studies of the German working class. His classical question: 'Name three people, living or dead, that you admire the most, and why?', has been used to interpret the ideal and characteristics the respondent values and aspires to in order to characterise him/her self (Rendahl, 1992).

At this point in the empirical tests, when steps 1-5 had been conducted, it was observed that the discussion of other issues and extraction of knowledge (steps 1-4) from the respondent became increasingly unhindered. The interviewer had attained an appreciation of the respondent, and he/she in turn received assistance in revealing underlying assumptions or mental models related to the knowledge to be elicited. This helped a number of individuals to further relate their behaviour to other actions.

Step 6
(Phase 6) The last step tries to raise unspoken questions the individual have in order to lift them to an organisational level – *"if you could ask you colleagues anything, what would you ask?"* The respondent is also requested to reflect about the question by him/her self: *"how do you do it by your self?"*

To sum up, instead of searching for "the right answer", the purpose is to have the individual to describe his/her version in such a way that others understand the description (what, *why* and how) and have the possibility to make their own interpretation of it.

4 Summary and Concluding Remarks

Gaines (2003) has, in his article "Organizational Knowledge Acquisition", a similar view as ours when discussing how to develop a model of organisational knowledge acquisition. He describes the recognition of knowledge as critical in distinguishing rational arguments from emotional ones, he explains some of the reasons of the failure of artificial intelligence, the nature of human behaviour, and so on.

Gaines continues to point out that it is better to perform actions in a way that is not 'wildly wrong' rather than to compute the 'optimum situation'. So far we agree with him. However, he continues to say that actual expertise arises naturally through positive feedback processes involved in proto-experts having greater access to learning experiences, and *models the expert as the central part* in the formation for interaction between the client community and professional community (consisting of case histories, theories and strategies). And here we question, is learning really promoted by this?

We believe expert-thinking, when it comes to learning, is erroneous and misleading. In a learning process one should first and foremost not talk about knowledgeable individuals as experts, but of leadership, assistance, and guidance.

For example health care is very much characterised by expert-thinking. The organisation is separated into different functions, like; physicians, nurses, assistant nurses, laboratory personnel, receptionists, almoners, therapists, physiotherapists *etc.*, where the physicians holds the highest order of rank (this was noticed in our interviews and seminars). The level of coordination and mutual adjustment among functions are reduced with hierarchical and expert-thinking, and as a result we believe it is central to re-investigate the learning situation from another perspective. We suggest the utilisation of the culture and techniques, as found within the cognitive narrative mode (i.e. cognitive psychotherapy), enables a passable way to start to deal with this problem. Besides, as have been discussed in the paper, the approach is more concerned about learning as a complex process involving skills like mental mapping, use of intuition and imagination, and problem solving, instead of a view of learning as more de-humanised.

References

1. Alvesson, M. & Deetz, S. (2000) Doing Critical Management Research. SAGE Publications.
2. Ambrosini, V. & Bowman, C. (2001) "Tacit Knowledge: Some Suggestions for Operationalization". *Journal of Management Studies*, 38:6, pp. 811–829, September.
3. Blackler, F. (1995) "Knowledge, Knowledge Work and Organizations: An Overview and Interpretation". *Organization Studies*, 16/6, pp. 1021–1046.
4. Blair, D. C. (1984) "The Management of Information: Basic Distinctions", *Sloan Management Review*, Fall.
5. Boland, R. J. & Tenkasi, R. V. (1995) "Perspective Making and Perspective Taking in Communities of Knowing", *Organization Science*, Vol. 6, No. 4, pp. 350–372, July-August.
6. Bruner, J. (1986) Actual Minds, Possible Words. Harvard University Press.
7. Castells, M. (1997) The Information Age: Economy, Society and Culture, Vol 2: The Power of Identity. Blackwell.
8. Castells, M. (1996) Informationsåldern: ekonomi, samhälle och kultur Bd 1: Nätverkssamhällets framväxt. Daidalos.
9. d'Elia, G. (1992) "Kognitiv terapi – inlärningsprocess som förändrar dysfunktionella tankemönster. *Läkartidningen*, Vol, 89, No, 48.
10. Durkin, J. (1994) Expert Systems – Design and Development, Prentice Hall.
11. Fisher, R. P., & Geiselman, R. E. (1992) Memory-Enhancing Techniques for Investigative Interviewing. Charles C Thomas, Springfield, Illinois, USA.
12. Freeman, A., Pretzer, J, Fleming, B. & Simon, K. M. (1994) Kognitiv psykoterapi i Klinisk tillämpning, Pilgrim Press.
13. Gaines, B. R. (2003) "Organizational Knowledge Acquisition", in Holsapple, C. W. [ed] (2003) Handbook on Knowledge Management. Berlin: Springer.
14. Gonzalez, A. J. & Dankel, D. D. (1993) The Engineering of Knowledge-Based Systems – Theory and Practice, Prentice Hall.
15. Hoppe Jacobsson, U. (1992) "Hur kan vi förstå alkoholisters handlande?" PhD. Thesis, Department of Education, Stockholm University.
16. Hoppe Jacobsson, U. (1994) "Den sokratiska dialogen", Compendium from Pro Vobis. Unpublished.
17. Kelly, G. A. (1963) A Theory of Personality: the Psychology of Personal Constructs. Norton, New York.
18. Malm, K. (1992) "Frågebank", Kognitivt Center, Danderyds Sjukhus. Unpublished.
19. Molander, B. (1996) Kunskap i handling, Daidalos.
20. Perris, C. (1989) "Det psykoterapeutiska arbetet en lärprocess som syftar till personlig kunskapstillväxt". *Läkartidningen*. Vol. 86, No. 22, pp. 2112–15.
21. Perris, C., Blackburn, IM. & Perris, H. (1988), The Theory and Practice of Cognitive Psychotherapy. Berlin; New York: Springer-Verlag.
22. Rendahl, J-E. (1992) *Arbetets drivkrafter: existentiellt värde och auktoritetsorientering: två dimensioner som belyser arbetets mening för de anställda i kriminalvården.* PhD. Thesis, Lund University, Sweden.
23. Selling, M. (1984) Om tänkesättet Sokrates, Own Publishing House, Lund, Sweden.
24. Svenneby, E. (2002) "Den sokratiske dialog og motstandermetoden", in Om samtal – en nordisk antologi, Holm, U. M. [ed].
25. Wistedt, B (1997) "Kompendium kognitiv psykoterapi", Psykiatriska kliniken, Danderyds Sjukhus
26. Yin, R. K. (1994) *Case Study Research: Design and Methods.* SAGE Publications, Inc.

Data Management and AI in E-government[*]

Tibor Vámos and István Soós

Computer and Automation Research Institute, Hungarian Academy of Sciences
H-1111 Budapest, Lágymányosi u. 11., Hungary
vamos@sztaki.hu

Abstract. Similarities and differences between large companies and e-government data management are discussed. The major issue of e-government systems is the human face, i.e. the citizen–administration dialog. Openness vs. individual and administration procedure security are delicate legal and technological problems. A regional experiment is reviewed that applies three languages: natural language of the citizen, formal one of the administration and quasi-natural one of the dialog. Natural language understanding is a special feature using subject-oriented closed-world vocabularies and scenarios. The combination provides a decision support especially dedicated to the citizen.

1 Introduction and Motivation

Data management problems faced by e-government generally do not differ too much from similar issues in large companies. This statement is not without controversy; however it reflects the authors' views. A modern government should be run, in many ways, like a large, well-managed company. This implies that the basic system tools in use should be similar to well-developed commercial data management systems that are already available, and that it would be a waste of money to develop any special system that has not stood the test of time and does not have a well-developed support system.

Even so, there are some differences that need special attention. These are issues related to privacy and user interface. A democratic government is basically an open one: the Latin expression 'res publica'—originally meant 'public affair' [**]—means anything owned by the people referring in Roman Law to all public ownership and best expressed by the concept of SPQR – Senatus Populusque Romanus; and, contrary to the underlying needs in the management of a private business, secrecy should only be required under very exceptional circumstances. On the other hand, due to the fact

---

[*] The project was supported by NRDP Grant No. OM-00510/2001

[**] originally res publica (see Cicero: De re publica libri VI, I. (39): "Est igitur, inquit Africanus, res publica res populi, populus autem non omnis hominum coetus quoquo modo congregatus, sed coetus multitudinis iuris consensu et utilitatis communione sociatus. eius autem prima cause coeundi est non tam inbecillitas quam naturalis quaedam hominum quasi congregatio; non est enim singulare nec solivagum genus hoc, sed ita generatum ut ne in omnium quidem rerum affluen\<tia>")

M.A. Wimmer (Ed.): KMGov 2003, LNAI 2645, pp. 230–238, 2003.

that the governments, especially local authorities, deal with their citizens' individual problems, too, it is imperative that they abide by strict privacy principles. Privacy is not the same as security in commercial systems; it is a delicate web of interaction and decision-making communications rather than a simple system closure task as required in company management or the management of government organizations dealing with national security.

In the aftermath of September 11 we are seeing just how delicate priva-cy really is. It essentially comes down to a conflict among different valid interests. The other side of the problem is the social support agenda. Why a certain people should be the recipient of money collected as tax is an open question for a community; for the beneficiaries however it is their own private problem.

The other difference is the nature of the user interface. Commercial systems, such as banks have well-developed user communications; how-ever these are based on rather simple rule sequences leading to narrowly defined results. E-government, especially at the local level, deals with a wide variety of its citizens' individual problems. These citizens are, for the most part, unable to formalize their queries into a machine understandable, unambiguous text; and oftentimes they are unaccustomed to the use of regular questionnaires. However, the introduction of e-government should not increase the alienation of the citizens from public administration.

Our project is a local government experiment in a region with about 120.000 inhabitants; at its center there is a university city; there are also several rural settlements in the region at varying levels of economic and cultural development. 70 localities (city and villages) are included. The project has two special emphases: it addresses the e-government issue from a certain sociological perspective and it experiments with advanced artificial intelligence tools. The two are rather closely related: the first is built on human relations and the second is the creation of a human face through artificial intelligence, the flexibility of which allows for the reproduction of more sophisticated human attitudes by machines and the creation of a machine support for human activity. This last aspect is of particular significance: By the automation of routine services more time and attention can be devoted to cases that require human attention. The possibility of personal consultation with a sophisticated system prepares the citizen for better understanding of his/her chances, as well as for the presentation of his/her case to the administration.

The major contribution of AI to the human face of machine-supported administration is the human-oriented dialog, i.e. the understanding of natu-ral language. It can serve as a tool for real dialog that not only checks whether both partners, i.e. the administration and the citizen, understand each other, but also helps them in the process. The citizen not only receives the resolution of his/her case, but can follow each step of the procedure, get all related regulations from the original legal text, as well as, comments and interpretations, all as a part of the dialog and in a language closer to his/her linguistic usage.

How the communication takes place is another human issue. Currently the citizen has to go to the administration office, in most cases several times, wait in humiliating conditions and spend his/her own precious time. The process itself can take an unreasonable amount of time, and be both an irritating and costly experience (in terms of economic loss) for the citizen. With intelligent machine-supported administration this all can be done from home, at any time of day and, possibly, in one short process.

2 Interfaces

The interface problem here is very different from the problems company wide systems face. A well-designed company system has uniform inter-faces and mostly standardized internal representations. For practical reasons this cannot be achieved in public administration. Different branches of government and of local administrative boards have different standards; they have some autonomy in choosing the software they use. All have their specific history, and receive their financial backing at different times. The platforms, operating systems, basic software products in use and procedural customs are all somewhat different; the unification would be a very costly investment, unrealistic in most cases; and it would be met with much resistance. This entails the need to develop practical standardized interfaces and gateways, and to investigate the possibility of legislating the use of the interface system in administrative practice.

The other interface problem is privacy and data protection. Existing laws forbid all forms of data unification, even within a same administrative board. Data unification means the collection of different personal data in the same file, e.g. taxation data with health records. This is regulated to prevent the different bodies of administration from getting an overall picture of the citizen that could then be used to intrude in his/her private life. The unification can only take place with the informed consent of the data owner, for whom even the context of the retrieval and transfer of the data should be accessible. Another directive requires either the deletion of the transferred data once the case has been settled, or the preservation of those in line with specific laws. Statistical surveys require special attention notably with regard to data purification of different kinds of statistics. The gateway service would need to have an automated system for the registration of all transactions to ensure data is not misused. This is a far more complex task than the sensitive controls of banking systems.

3 Languages

Our system uses three different versions (vernaculars) of the same language. The first is the language of the citizen, mostly poorly educated, unable to present his/her case in a concise, unambiguous and non-redundant form. This unfortunate fact is supported by the recent European review of literacy-related understanding and a similar study, a few years earlier, in the US. On the other hand, the language used in legal texts is difficult for any-one who does not have a background in law to understand, due to the strong requirements for a professional logical definition power. This is the second language, the formal language of the administration. Although this is a rather well formulated procedural communication tool based on legal practice, further refinement is required to make it into a strictly logical description of the case, avoiding all ambiguity; or, when ambiguity is inherently present in the case, to incorporate probabilistic logic into the description. This language is a schematic description of the procedural scenarios.

The third language is for communication with the citizen. Basically it is a popularization of the formal language using everyday expressions for a more user-friendly communication. Its first role is a retranslation of the citizen's claim, to check if the system understood it well and the applicant agrees with the interpretation. It is a more advanced form of Feigenbaum's Eliza dialogue. Its second role is to query for missing information. The third role is the communication of the result of the administrative procedure. This last role, when needed, must be both empathetic and convincing. Remember what the humorist George Mikes wrote about a letter from a British civil servant in his How to be an Alien!

4 Special Databases

The system has two kinds of special databases. The first contains specific vocabularies. These are semi-automatically selected from claim documents that the administration has handled in the past. The words are selected ac-cording to their relevance to the subject, stemmed and grammatically analyzed by the HUMORESK software of MORPHOLOGIC. A large Hungarian Language Corpus is used to further analyze the words. This Corpus was developed by the Szeged University in cooperation with MORPHOLOGIC. The Corpus also helps in the selection of non-regular words, especially names of persons and companies that are important for the understanding of the claim.

The vocabular2ies are broken down into different administrative subjects; this is the basis for direction and refinement in the interpretation. The text to be interpreted is analyzed by the weight of relevant, preselected words as stored in the subject-oriented vocabularies. The recognition of simple grammatical relations, such as the who's what genitive noun relation and the who what accusative verbal phrase, further helps in the understanding of the context. The vocabularies contain a thesaurus of synonyms, based on the earlier claim documents. This is of particular interest for a further socio-linguistic analysis.

5 Understanding, Case-Based Reasoning

We stop here for a moment. One of the main philosophical issues in discussions about AI is the concept of understanding. For us understanding means the perception or identification of a piece of information as it relates to con-sequences. In most cases, and the one we are dealing with here is similar, the understanding of a given piece of information entails the triggering of a specific response scenario. This is the role of our second category of data-bases.

The second category of databases contains the possible scenarios for regular claims and the related administrative actions. These scenarios are rather general, the head of the scenario graph is always the naming of the subject (social relief, complaint against somebody or some organization, construction permission, etc.) and branches lower down, as well as the nodes are also all well-definable, and follow the logical steps used at the given administrative department. The terminal expressions of the graph will often be vague, here the thesaurus and the question-answer dialogue are helpful.

The procedure is a typical case-based reasoning, combined, if possible with rule-based processes. The project, in putting its emphasis on better meeting human needs, puts its emphasis on the case-based problems; these are also more attractive from the point of view researchers in artificial intelligence. We have already experimented with two different subjects: children custody decisions after a divorce, and case-study support in US bank-ruptcy law.

Technically the task is the matching of the two databases. Given how the administrative subjects are well defined and have limited vocabularies, this has so far proved to be less difficult than the understanding of discretional texts. Most goal-oriented human communication is subject-limited and the professional procedures create closed linguistic entities. The real problem is the translation of the natural language of communication used by the unprepared citizen.

The basic trick for a workable system is the limitation of linguistic components. The analysis of hundreds of texts provided by the local authority showed this to be feasible. No specific subject used more than 2000 relevant words. By relevance we mean relevant from the point of view of under-standing. Filtering for relevance was done using word statistics and manual extraction. The vocabularies contain several vernacular-specific synonyms but the number of these is not too significant either. Although they change in time with the changes in linguistic fashion, their usage is more uniform and poorer than any sophisticated discourse. To account for this phenomenon, a learning routine is added. With official legal texts allowing no room for ambiguity, their vocabulary is also limited; it *must* reflect a closed conceptional world.

However, in the case of non-understanding by the system, the human dialog is helpful and this is the point where the machine process should stop and switch over to human communication. The machine filters all seemingly regular cases and helps the human expert concentrate on the truly problematic cases. This is the other contribution to the more human face of the machine-supported governance – as was earlier emphasized.

As was mentioned above, the nature of natural language allows for an interesting experiment. The language used by the claimant is full of information about the true status or nature of that claimant. The subjective psycho-logical impression that a skilled administrator will have of a given claimant will often be to the claimant's advantage; of course, this psychological impression can just as easily be the basis for unwanted, incorrect prejudices. A socio-linguistic analysis here is an attempt to help understand the emphasis needed for a given case all the while avoiding preconceptions.

Two simplified examples show how the much more complex systems work (see Annex).

The experiment is ongoing and is progressing well. A thorough information flow analysis of the whole administration, including all the departments of the self-government has been completed. Figures 1 and 2 show examples of information flow diagrams. Each procedure was analyzed in terms of discrete actions; on average there were 30 to 50, but some procedures required 100 discrete actions. The analysis included the active time of process handling, and the waiting times for delivery within the administration, request for data and other idle periods. The result was a factor of more than 100; the active process time of manual handling was a few hours, while the whole process lasted several weeks. This means that a complete electronic dialog and data acquisition process among the different administrative units can reduce the process time to an hour or less instead of long weeks.

The system would naturally be expected to handle voting and opinion polls, as well as inquiries related to the operation of the governance and chat groups on these subjects. The main software frame is an interactive portal including all usual services.

The work is based on written texts; technology for vocal understanding, as would be needed to understand the wide variety of utterances and texts, has yet to be developed.

The system is partly under installation. There are several vandal-proof terminals in units similar to telephone booths providing open access for less sophisticated procedures, while other terminals are located in telehouses, schools and libraries and come with supporting personnel. Participants in this experiment working with the local administration all have a terminal at home.

The first experiments, after successful laboratory tests, will be orga-nized between the system's designers and a group of local administration personnel. The laboratory tests are ongoing, the project as an experiment should be completed by the end of the first quarter of 2004.

The evaluation of the project has two levels. On the one level the socio-logical group of the Budapest University of Economy and State Administration is working on the second survey and they will close the project with a third one. On the next level the founding National Research Development Project regularly supervises the progress.

In its first phase the experiment is to provide support to the administration and get feedback from the citizens.

6 Conclusion

The feasibility of an active data management system for e-government is de-monstrated using advanced artificial intelligence. The experiment is carried out in a local government setting; i.e. an environment in which there is a significant amount of human contact involving direct, natural language communication with individual citizens. Certain legal and technical problems also arise; but they can be resolved.

Annex

Example 1

"Dear Mr. Major,
Forgive me for disturbing you and for coming to you with my personal problem but I am unable to help myself. We have no cash; we are disabled *pensioners*. Our pension is 15000 + 5000 Ft and we cannot pay the *rent* that the owner of our very humble home wants. We need some help..."
This is an extract from a longer letter to Mr. Major. The words in italics clearly show that this is a social problem; the claimants would like to get some regular money (rent) for their home or some other solution for their dwelling.

The system identifies the nature of the problem and tries to match it with a scenario in the case base:

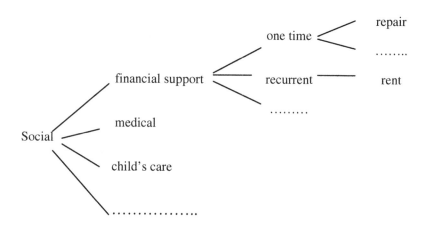

The structure is naturally more complex; the scenario-base contains all typical social problems.

The grammatical analysis identifies the relations: How many persons are involved, what is the relation (mostly family) of the persons, who owns what, who is in debt to whom, etc.?

The redundancy of the text and the use of some typical words, e.g. cash for money are characteristic for the claimant. The style suggested by the words and grammar used by the claimant also indicates his/her age.

If the scenario is clear, the translation is given with a related text, in this case:

'We understand that you cannot pay the rent for your home. Do you need any regular support above and beyond your disability pension or would you like to move into a social home?'

After clarification the final answer is also attached to the scenario:

'Unfortunately we are unable to raise your retirement pension due to both the current pension regulations and the budget of the community. On the other hand, you have now been added to a waiting list for social accommodation that is within your financial means. The expected waiting time is about two years. To meet your immediate needs you will receive a one-time extraordinary support of 2000 Ft.'

Example 2

"We *cannot sleep* because of the *horrible* people making *noise* under our window. It is being done by the *Yellow Submarine Disco* and it goes on *long in the night* and they leave all their *trash out* in the morning…"

The scenario is simple:

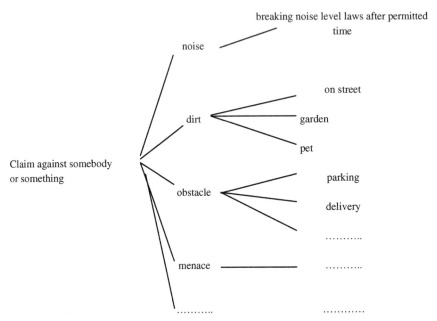

'Do you mean that the Yellow Submarine Disco breaks the noise level laws and that they leave their garbage on the street?'

Answer of the system:

'We will send the local police after 10 pm to measure the noise levels, and after 11 pm to check the levels again. We will ask the city's garbage collection company for a report. Following their report we will take measures as prescribed by our regulations and inform you about the result.'

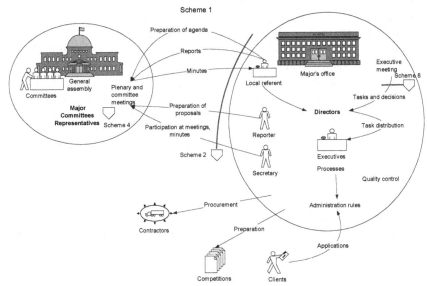

Fig. 1. General model of the self-government activity

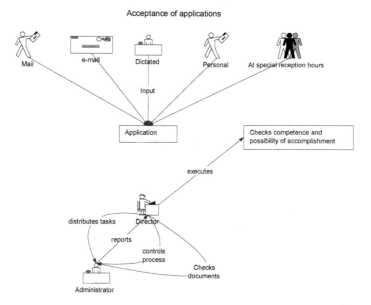

Fig. 2. General rules

Optimizing Cooperation in Spatial Planning for eGovernment

Angi Voss, Stefanie Roeder, and Oliver Märker

Fraunhofer Institut Autonome Intelligente Systeme
Team Mediation Systems
Schloss Birlinghoven; D-53754 Sankt Augustin
{angi.voss, stefanie.roeder,
oliver.maerker}@ais.fraunhofer.de
http://ais.gmd.de/MS/index.html

Abstract. As a reaction to societal, economic and technological changes, new forms of cooperation are applied in projects of urban and regional development. We argue that this trend can significantly be amplified by the use of information and communication technologies (ICT). Through ICT more persons can participate in a more open, fairer and more transparent way. More complex information can be analyzed, discussions can become more focused, the process is documented and becomes reproducible and comparable. Methods and media can be combined in a very flexible way to design more efficient and effective processes. To the extent that projects are stored in a knowledge base, knowledge management tools can exploit growing experience in order to continuously improve a methodology for cooperation in spatial development. Our approach aims at exploring the opportunities that new ICT offer for new cooperation methods in e-Government and planning - beyond the extension of traditional methods to electronic communication media. It acknowledges the need for experimentation and an evaluation, not only concerning isolated methods but the combination of methods based on knowledge management concepts.

1 Knowledge Management in the Context of Spatial Planning and E-government

This contribution focuses on the possibilities of ICT for cooperative planning processes in the context of e-Government. Mainly three concepts of knowledge management correspond with this thematic area:

First, **intellectual capital** is the basis for cooperative planning procedures, that involve multi-party-processes including public participation. Many stakeholders with various roles and different knowledge backgrounds are the source of the intellectual capital. The concept of "intellectual capital" generally refers to an organization's recorded information (and, increasingly, human talent itself). The term reflects the understanding that information is a growing part of every company's assets, and that such information is typically either inefficiently warehoused or simply lost, especially in large, physically dispersed organizations. The challenge is to find what you have

M.A. Wimmer (Ed.): KMGov 2003, LNAI 2645, pp. 239–249, 2003.

and use it. The terms "intellectual capital" and "intellectual assets" appear to have been popular for several years before the term "knowledge management" became popular (Caviedes (1991), cited in: [14]). In this case, the intellectual assets are those of municipalities and other involved stakeholders, as well as the public's, rather than those of companies and organizations (this circumstance will be further addressed in part 2 of this contribution).

Second, the combined knowledge management concepts of **learning organizations** and **process optimization** are the core elements of the developed methodology for process models (as explained in part 3 of this contribution). The goal of the process optimization concept is to optimize business processes with regard to time, costs and quality through knowledge management. Primarily, it attempts to overcome functional barriers. Topic-oriented networks acquire distribute knowledge across organizations and across business processes. The role of "learning" in business organizations gained awareness with the appearance of Peter Senge's "The Fifth Discipline: The Art and Practice of the Learning Organization" in 1990. Nonaka and Takeuchi's "The Knowledge-Creating Company" (Oxford University Press, 1995) also focused on organizational strategies for creating new knowledge as a competitive advantage (both books cited in: [14]).

Third, the concept of a **knowledge base** is important to the thematic area of cooperative spatial planning processes in e-Government. Knowledge base has traditionally referred to the data produced by the knowledge-acquisition and compilation phases of creating an expert system application. But that definition, too, is now often broadened to include every imaginable corporate intellectual asset. "The knowledge base is the absolute collection of all expertise, experience and knowledge of those within any organization." (Aegiss (1995), cited in: [14]). In the context of this contribution, a central goal is to build a knowledge base under the premise of a certain methodology (see part 4 of this contribution).

Not only the concepts of knowledge management but also the representation of the knowledge is a central question in the positioning of this contribution. According to the specifics of the thematic area, such as cooperative procedures and knowledge sharing as well as documentation, the described research addresses a groupware platform, thus the groupware platform is the medium of knowledge representation.

The second part of this paper describes the nature of the knowledge in the context at hand, and the necessity for the specific knowledge management concepts. The third part refers to how those concepts are to be addressed with ICT usage. The fourth part is a methodology for modeling and optimizing processes in the respective context and the fifth part concludes with some thoughts on further investigation of the problem.

2   Trends in Spatial Development

2.1   Towards Cooperation: Planners as Moderators and Municipalities as Catalysts?

In Germany today, municipalities are used to carry out urban and regional projects in a comparatively closed manner. Input from citizens and stakeholder is feared rather than welcomed when, by law, these groups are informed first about new development projects - goals, purposes, different options and their effects - and later about the draft of the proposed solution. In both cases, the information is presented at a particular time and place, imposing physical constraints on the participation.

The traditional planning style has deficiencies. Next to formal planning procedures there are informal - and not transparent - decision structures which lead to the loss of confidence between municipality and citizens. In particular when projects have a high potential of conflicts, citizens and groups of stakeholders may form coalitions and take actions to prevent the envisaged solution. This increases the time and costs for implementing the plan. Simultaneously, municipalities are confronted with more information, more uncertainty, less time, less money, and more actors. The complexity is hardly to manage anymore through isolated planning and analysis procedures. This leads to an imminent danger of masking crucial coherences, developments, trends and risks. Additionally, since some years, German municipalities have had to cope with decreasing budgets.

Innovative planning procedures are becoming more important. While traditional procedures aim at legitimating municipal planning, innovative processes focus on effectiveness and efficiency of municipal bargaining. Due to this trend the task of planners shifts from providing finished solutions for planning problems to moderating the planning process between the concerned parties in an innovative and cooperative way. Municipalities outsource parts of development projects to a third party with supplementary competences. In pilot experiments municipalities assume the role of a catalyst that joins the knowledge, resources and commitment of multiple actors, including investors, citizens and local stake-holders. The organization of communication processes between all concerned parties becomes a key factor of successful urban development.

2.2 The Impact of ICT on Sustainable Planning

The internet means information, communication, interaction and transactions almost at any time and from anywhere. Mobile devices achieve ubiquity coupled with new forms of communication, personalized and localized services. ICT is changing the way how companies interact with each other and their customers (e-business) and how governments inform and serve their citizens (e-government). Hierarchical structures are giving way to looser networks of more autonomously acting individuals.

Regardless of the increasing information overload, the term 'information society' is gradually being replaced by the term 'knowledge society'. The construction of knowledge, the availability and application of knowledge and a comprehensive knowledge management determine the way of life and working environment and therefore also modern society to an increasing degree [13].

The upcoming ways of handling knowledge are effective in particular to planning and implementing a sustainable development, which is involved in the solution of diverse social, ecological and economic problems. To account for the three dimensions of sustainability and the complexity of the problems to be solved, the role of networking information and knowledge of heterogeneous actors is to be emphasized. Institutional sustainability can be seen as an additional dimension to be considered in sustainable development. Co-operative structures and bottom-up approaches of planning form new processes for a democratic sustainability.

A spectrum of more cooperative planning approaches is emerging. Apart from a variety of data and information sources, the knowledge and experience of individual heterogeneous actors is especially relevant. This corresponds to planning theories which regard the development of a common problem viewpoint through the participation and integration of heterogeneous actors as a central prerequisite for mastering complex problems of planning [15], [17], [10].

A recurring theme in urban cooperation projects is the need for a high quality of process management, auditable and accountable processes, and a moderator as a neutral party. The required new skills may be contributed by external project steering offices. Among these skills, practical ICT competence may even become a competitive advantage.

2.3   Baseline for Cooperation and ICT in Spatial Development

In 2002 a new government-supported program called 3stadt2 was launched in Germany. Within the following 2,5 years five model cities will apply new cooperation styles between municipalities, investors, citizens and other actors in selected projects. Accompanying research aims at a systematic characterization of cooperative approaches as a basis for guidelines to optimize cooperation in urban development, to quantify the added values with respect to all dimensions of sustainability and thus obtain tangible arguments for this approach.

While valuable and important results may be expected from the 3stadt2 program, it is surprising that ICT is not taken into account explicitly. Indeed, up to now software in urban development projects has been dedicated to experts and is often lacking integration. For example, Batty (1995) [2] devised an integrated planning support system that is still being promoted because it combines manual and software-supported work [8]. His scheme includes urban IS, GIS (geographic information systems), spread sheets, expert systems, optimization tools and scheduling, but no software for group work like problem and goal definition, bargaining, delphi methods, brainstorming, group decision support, consensus building. As the German e-government initiative [3] is obliging municipalities to put information and services on the internet, installations of Lotus Notes, Microsoft Exchange or other software technology for information, communication and interaction in urban administrations are turning up.

Recent projects in Germany emphasize technical aspects of integrating cooperation support software. At CORP 2002 a Lotus Domino server was presented that shall offer web access to an urban information system, a library of documents and a discussion forum [6]. The data shall be transferred from Domino to relational data bases in order to perform automated analyses.

Our own work takes a socio-technical stance. It began with GeoMed (1996-1998), a European research project that proposed a web-based solution combining groupware for cooperation and participation with spatial visualization tools. Empowerment of all was one goal. The software had to be easy to handle so that all participants could analyze the available information to the individually desired depth.

Since GeoMed, we have continuously improved our software Zeno® for online mediation, e-participation and more generally for moderated electronic discourses. In the project KogiPlan (funded by the German Government from 2000 - 2003) the latest version of Zeno has been integrated into a platform for cooperative site planning [21], which additionally includes

– a geo-brokering system for collection of geo-data from heterogeneous sources
– SPIN!, a platform with a variety of methods for data mining [12]
– LoLa for mathematical optimization of spatial allocations [7]
– CommonGIS, for multi-criteria analysis and spatial exploration on the web [1]
– the GIS MapExtreme for high end visualizations

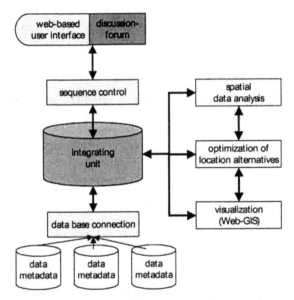

Fig. 1. KogiPlan software architecture for facility allocation

We apply and extend our software to investigate new methods of software-supported cooperation, online, offline and possibly blended with face-to-face meetings. We have accompanied public participation processes [9], carried out role plays concerned with group decision problems [19], [20], [16] and are compiling our experience into a methodology for e-moderation [11].

3 E-cooperation in Spatial Development

3.1 Opportunities

With the introduction of ICT, existing cooperative methods should not simply be copied to the new media without further modifications. Electronic techniques (synchronous or asynchronous, distributed or not, audio-, video or text-based media) can be used for different traditional methods in different phases of the process, and they can be combined in completely new ways, leading to new methods and workflows. Only if this potential of ICT is taken into account by restructuring the process itself, cooperative planning processes lead to informed high-quality decisions in less time.

- Through e-communication media, more persons can be involved more actively in a planning process. Independent of their location and time participants can read the material provided electronically. Groupware can facilitate their coordination, communication and cooperation, it supports distributed discussions, annotations, reviews, editing and polling.
- Highly connected information, in multiple media, with smart interactive visualization functions, can push information sharing to a shared understanding. All interested participants can interactively explore data prepared by planners and experts - analyze and visualize geographic data and criteria, compare options and their consequences, recognize dependencies, sensitivities, drawbacks and advantages.
- New e-cooperation techniques will combine offline and online elements. Software will enhance traditional face-to-face meetings, conferencing software allows to include dislocated persons or to conduct meetings exclusively over the internet. Shared workspaces and forums enable preparation and follow-up work from different places and at different times. Rigid workflows will give way to moderated, self-organized processes.
- Moderators will be able to combine methods in a highly flexible way in order to focus the discourse and to suitably react to any complications. Electronic questionnaires can turn into electronic interviews or group discussions, and vice versa the issues in a discussion can easily be reorganized into a rationale (a map of options and arguments) and be turned into an online poll. Monitoring software allows to observe ongoing collaboration processes, track interaction patterns, analyze the effects to the moderators' interventions, detect points of conflict or compromise, thus increasing process awareness and allowing to cope with higher complexity.
- To the extent that development processes are conducted or documented electronically, new participants will find it easier to catch-up and join an ongoing project. The processes become more transparent and auditable. When additionally collected in a knowledge base (or electronic warehouse), development projects become comparable, and analytic software can be used to extract patterns, recommendations, guidelines and classifications more systematically. This provides a basis for continuous methodological improvement and optimized use of cooperation methods in urban development.

3.2 Requirements for an E-cooperation Platform

An e-cooperation platform is an ICT solution for urban and regional development processes that provides information, communication and interactions services in a highly customizable way. It should be conceived as part of an infrastructure for e-government and comply to the respective standards [4]. To offer the opportunities described above, the following requirements should be met:

- Virtual offices: To satisfy the basic needs of groupwork - group calendars and directories, shared folders, electronic boards and access to telecommunication media such as web conferences, chat, forums, etc – virtual offices can be realized by shared workspaces on the web.

- Decision support for the appreciation of criteria and values: Informed decision making is tied to an understanding of the space of options. How do the different options affect the quality of the result and what happens if certain modifications are made, assumptions, weightings or priorities are changed? The quality of an urban design process can be measured by its performance on a number of indicators. These indicators will have to be developed by the community of actors, either in the current project or in preceding projects whose purpose was to develop longer term frameworks and concepts. Long-term indicators and indicators of project-specific values have to be considered together in order to avoid over-reactivity and opportunism. Tools to explore dependencies between indicators and perform sensibility analyses should be easy to use, highly interactive and visual.

- Annotation, review and feedback: It should be possible to comment on any piece of content, in particular reports and plans. The border between comments and discussions should be fluent. Comments may be private annotations, annotations that extend to informal discussions in different groups, or comments may be organized by a moderator as a formal review.

- Surveys: Surveys are a flexible instrument. They can be used very early as a questionnaire to identify important issues. Answers of key persons can feed into a dialog between this person and the planning group. Options identified during a discussion can be come the object of a poll that gives valuable hints on the distribution of opinions. And finally, the same instrument can be used to take an official voting. Whatever their function may be, surveys must be will integrated with the discussion facilities, there should be powerful tools to analyse and visualize the results.

- Semantic structures: any electronic content, like bits of information, parts of multimedia documents, pieces of communication, comments, components of models and plans, spatio-temporally referenced objects, should be embeddable in a semantic structure. The connections should support association between and automated reasoning about pieces of content. The connections may be labeled, they should be traversable in both directions and they have to be automatically be maintained when the network is manipulated. Nodes and links may be labeled according to dedicated vocabularies, but cooperating groups should be able to evolve the vocabulary and adapt it to their particular communicative needs [18].

- Tools for e-moderation: moderators of electronic discussions should be able to design a cooperative process in detail (participants, roles, beginning and end time, review and publication periods, obligations and rules, etc.). They must be able to monitor and control the discussion process, and to change the setting in a transparent way. Moderators and participants should be aware of the social context: individual contributions of a person, active, passive and absent participants, coalitions and opponents. There should be help to interpret the discussion and identify progress: controversies arising and being settled, chances for compromises, changes of opinions, opening and closing threads, etc.. Switching between methods should be easy, so that moderators can initiate a survey, a review, or a private discussion with selected persons rather spontaneously. Writing summaries, restructuring or editing argumentation structures should be easy.

4   A Methodology Based on Empirical Knowledge

While technological innovation is fast, a methodological understanding – especially on the modeling level – is coming forth only slowly. Due to the extremely complex and interdisciplinary task of planning, the demands upon a methodological framework are very high.

In accordance with the 3stadt2 project, we expect that a methodology for e-cooperation in urban development projects helps to design the cooperation within these projects so as to maximize effectiveness and efficiency. It has to consider the importance of flexible and dynamic composition of ICT-tools and methods, while providing support for a variety of tasks.

A methodology should provide a questionnaire which helps to characterize and consistently plan a project in several dimensions.

- Stages of problem solving: Multi-party problem solving processes roughly follow the phases (1) process clarification, (2) exchange of information, (3) clarification of interests, (4) exploration of options, (5) decision, (6) formulation of contract, (7) implementation [5]. A first group of questions must identify the stages to be covered by the project.
- Degree of cooperation: A project (or a phase in a project) may roughly be qualified as being closed, informative, consultative or cooperative. A second group of questions has to identify for each phase the degree of cooperation and the actors to be involved, possibly even a set of methods. The questions will be concerned with the budget and time frame, the degree of controversy, which aspects are open at all, what competencies and skills are required and available, etc.
- ICT support: The next questions try to elicit for each phase how it could be supported by ICT. A phase could comprise one or more activities, which could run in parallel or sequentially, depending on their input-output dependencies. An activity could be classified as a face-to-face meeting, a synchronous but distributed online conference, or asynchronously. More precisely, for each activity (electronic) media, software tools, and the period could be recommended. Questions in this group concern the number of participants and their spatio-temporal availability, the complexity of the problem and the task, the availability of mathematical models for optimization, simulation or prognosis, the need for accountability and documentation.
- Further groups of questions may elicit further external constraints in order to suitably embed the cooperation process into the organizational environment, and to provide more precise estimates for the expected costs and time.

With the help of the suggestions obtained in this way, a plan for the cooperation in the project has to be elaborated and accompanying measures have to be defined. Figure 2 shows in a simple visualization a part of the process planning procedure for two nearly similar processes. The problem solving stages are identified as well as their corresponding media/tools. Additionally the mode online/offline is indicated. The procedures in this example differ in the choice of Media/tools and in the mode. Figure 2 only illustrates a rough outline of the plan. This visualization does not show detailed information on time-frame, participants, etc., which also should be planned beforehand.

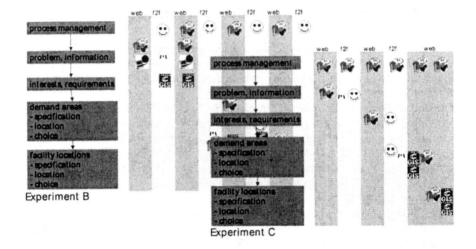

Fig. 2. Process outlines with stages of problem solving, ICT support and cooperation mode

During the project, the plan may be modified and further accompanying measures be undertaken. These deviations, together with the original plan, the "digital trace" and the electronic documentation of the project should be stored in a data repository. As this data base grows with every project, intelligent techniques (indexing, data mining, text mining, case-based reasoning) can be used to analyze, compare and cluster the projects, ultimately to provide hints for improving the questionnaire, and to enrich the guidelines with examples and templates.

5 Conclusions

The presented approach aims at exploring the opportunities that new ICT offer for new cooperation methods. Beyond the extension of traditional methods to electronic communication media, ICT offers new possibilities through flexible process patterns under the premise of a methodology which is based on knowledge management concepts. This approach acknowledges the need for experimentation and an evaluation, not only concerning isolated methods but the combination of methods in a development project. It is essentially socio-technical and requires the a joint effort of spatial planners, sociologists and computer scientists.

The interdisciplinary research may establish and build up the knowledge base upon varying processes. The further research could investigate requirements for a platform which allows for more intelligent techniques (indexing, data mining, text mining, case-based reasoning), to successfully classify the projects beforehand.

Acknowledgement. We want to thank all participants of the empirical studies and our colleagues of the Teams Mediation Systems and Spatial Decision Support SPADE of the Fraunhofer AIS. This contribution includes outcomes of the KogiPlan project funded by the German Federal Ministry of Education and Research (BMBF) under contract number VFG0003B.

References

1. Andrienko, N. and Andrienko, G. Intelligent Support for Geographic Data Analysis and Decision Making in the Web. Journal of Geographic Information and Decision Analysis, 5 (2). 115-128.
2. Batty, M. Planning Support Systems and the New Logic of Computation. Regional Development Dialogue, 16 (1). 1–17.
3. BundOnline, I. Implementation plan for the "BundOnline 2005" eGovernment initiative, Bundesministerium des Inneren, 2002.
4. BundOnline, I. SAGA. Standards und Architekturen für eGovernment Anwendungen, Bundesministerium des Inneren, 2002.
5. Gordon, T. and Märker, O. Mediation Systems. in Trenél, M. ed. Online-Mediation. Theorie und Praxis computer-unterstützter Konfliktmittlung, Sigma Verlag, Berlin, to appear 2002.
6. Gräf, A., Rinsche, S. and Streich, B., Basisdaten für die städtebaulichen Planung: UrbanIS – Konzept eines Informationssystems. in Computergestützte Raumplanung CORP 2002 / GEOMULTIMEDIA02, (Vienna, 2002), Department of computer aided planning and architecture, Vienna University of Technology.
7. Hamacher, H.W. and Nickel, S. Classification of Location Models, Universität Kaiserslautern, Kaiserslautern, 1997.
8. Kammeier, H.D. New tools for spatial analysis and planning as components of an incremental planning-support system. Environment and Planning B: Planning and Design, 26. 365–380.
9. Märker, O., Hagedorn, H. and Trénel, M., T. F., Internet-based Citizen Participation in the City of Esslingen. Relevance – Moderation – Software. in CORP 2002 – Who plans Europe's future?, (Wien, 2002), Selbstverlag des Instituts für EDV-gestützte Methoden in Architektur und Raumplanung der Technischen Universität Wien.
10. Märker, O., Morgenstern, B., Hagedorn, H. and Trenél, M., Integrating Public Knowledge into Decision Making. Use Case: Internet Public Hearing in the City of Esslingen. in Knowledge Management in e-Government – KMGov 2002. 3rd international Workshop jointly organised by IFIP WG 8.3 & WG 8.5, GI FA 6.2, (Copenhagen, Denmark, 2002), Universitätsverlag Rudolf Trauner, Linz, Austria.
11. Märker, O., Voss, A., Roeder, S. and Rottbeck, U. E-Partizipation im Kontext einer nachhaltigen Siedlungsentwicklungssteuerung. in Handbuch Regionales Flächenmanagement, Berlin, to appear 2002.
12. May, M. and Savinov, A. An architecture for the SPIN! spatial data mining platform. NTTS & ETK 2001 New Techniques and Technologis for Statistics (Eurostat). 467–472.
13. Mittelstraß, J., Information oder Wissen – vollzieht sich ein Paradigmenwechsel. in Zukunft Deutschlands in der Wissensgesellschaft, (Bonn, 1998), BMBF.
14. Murray, P.C. New language for new leverage: the terminology of knowledge management, 2002.
15. Rittel, H.W.J. On The Planning Crisis: Systems Analysis of the First and Second Generation, Institut für Grundlagen der Planung IGP, Stuttgart, 1972, o.S.
16. Roeder, S. and Voss, A., Group decision support for patial planning and e-government. in Global Spatial Data Infrastructure Conference (GSDI), (Budapest, 2002).
17. Selle, K. Was ist bloß mit der Planung los? Erkundungen auf dem Weg zum kooperativen Handeln, Dortmund, 1996.
18. Voss, A., E-discourses with Zeno. in Web Based Collaboration WBC, (Aix-en-Provence, 2002).

19. Voss, A. and Roeder, S., IT-support for mediation in spatial decision making. in International Conference on Decision Making and Decision Support in the Internet Age (DSIage), (Cork, 2002).
20. Voss, A., Roeder, S., Salz, S.R. and Hoppe, S., Spatial Discourses in Participatory Decision Making. in Environmental Informatics 2002, (Vienna, 2002), ISEP International Society for Environmental Protection, 371–374.
21. Voss, A., Voss, H., Gatalsky, P. and Oppor, L., Group decision support for spatial planning. in Urban Data Management Symposium UDMS2002, (Prague, 2002).

A Knowledge Management Environment for Knowledge Working Communities Fostering Local Development

Alberto Faro[1], Daniela Giordano[1], and Salvatore Zinna[2]

[1] Dipartimento di Ingegneria Informatica e Telecomunicazioni,
Universita' di Catania, viale A.Doria 6, 95125, Catania, Italy
[2] Direzione XXIV – Politiche Comunitarie, Relazioni Internazionali
e Programmazione dello Sviluppo Locale,
Comune di Catania, via S.Euplio 13, 95100 Catania, Italy

Abstract. The paper presents a case study dealing with an e-government system specifically designed and implemented for supporting knowledge working metropolitan communities and their internetworking to favour local development, where "local" doesn't have a bureaucratic meaning (city or county) rather it is centred on the notion of basic economic-productive community upon which the virtual community of the net-economy rests. The system provides knowledge-based services such as information on plans, programs and projects dealing with local development and supports several simultaneously working groups. Each group may access a common board, whereas authorized users may access an advertising service for communication and workflow synchronization, an advanced information retrieval service on relevant web documents and best practices, joint authoring of documents, peer reviewing and access to expert assistance. The first experiences indicate that the interface simplicity has been a key factor for the successful acceptance of the system.

1 Introduction

Although the role of knowledge management for supporting organizations has been widely recognized for many years [1], and recently, its importance for e-government has been pointed out (e.g., [2]), the effort in developing e-government systems in Italy has been mostly devoted to address citizens' papers requests. This has biased the public sector towards implementing front-office systems, with little knowledge inside, mainly to distribute certificates, forgetting that the effectiveness of the e-government systems highly depends on having an efficient back-office infrastructure provided with suitable knowledge management tools. In the shift from a "stand alone" administration to public administration networking at a metropolitan or regional scale, issues such as groupware support for knowledge working communities [3] and data standardization (ontology) for information systems integration [4] are crucial, yet this subject is widely underestimated. Moreover, although modernizing the public bureaucracy cer-

M.A. Wimmer (Ed.): KMGov 2003, LNAI 2645, pp. 250–261, 2003.

tainly impacts on improving the quality of life, an e-government policy to foster local development is important too, especially for those communities that need assistance in finding funds and developing proposals for innovating traditional sectors and activating new business. In this field, workers do not need automated tools to collaborate in a generic way, rather they need a CSCW environment in which the e-tools are integrated with respect to the specific working context and objectives.

Aim of the paper is to present a case study dealing with a web-based e-government system specifically designed and implemented for supporting knowledge working metropolitan communities and their internetworking to favour local development. The web system provides knowledge-based services such as information on plans, programs and projects dealing with local development, an advertising service for communication and workflow synchronization, an advanced information retrieval service on relevant web documents and best practices; it also allows joint authoring of documents, peer reviewing and access to expert assistance. It has a simple web user interface to facilitate interaction and supports several simultaneously working groups. Each group may have access to a common board, whereas authorized users may access all the remaining services per group, i.e., they can access and work only on the data belonging to a specific group. The paper is organized as follows: sect.2 explains why the territorial dimension of local development extends outside the conventional boundaries of the cities and industrial districts and points out the organizational change needed by this extended physical dimension pertaining to local development. This involves cooperation of many subjects on a multi-department and multi-disciplinary basis to develop the integrated and complex projects pertaining to the "space of places" where both the local and global flows of the net economy must intersect. Sect.3 outlines the functions and architecture of the web system that has been implemented to support this organizational change of the public sector in the Catania metropolitan area.

2   The Territorial Dimension of Local Development: The Space of Places and the Space of Flows

Currently, the Public Administration (PA) supports economic local development mostly by activating calls within National or European Development and Funding Programs and distributing the relevant information to the enterprises by means of Official Gazettes and sites that diffuse the calls and announcements. This approach to local development has the effect to enhance the transnational flows (of information and resources) and contributes to a global economy at a large scale. This coherently leads to a net-economy that increasingly develops in the "space of flows" [5]. As a consequence of the process of globalization and virtualization of the economy, the "space of places", i.e., where activities are located, looses importance to the space of flows. Metaphorically, places become shrinking points whose specificity simply derives from being the source or the destination of some large scale flow. Still organizations and enterprises keep functioning in a dual mode: a) the virtual mode, which is carried out through information exchanges with partners and clients via Internet (these

immaterial exchanges are followed by material exchanges through traditional infrastructures), and b) the physical mode, which relies on the services offered by the local
PA and by the companies that manage the territorial technological networks. In this
new scenario the PA cannot limit its action to provision of innovative services to make
bureaucracy lean and efficient, as are those traditionally associated to e-Government.
It must go beyond and adopt methods, organizational and administrative procedures to
enact all the initiatives relevant to these financial and work policies capable of providing the local system with infrastructures and networks (both physical and virtual) to
support economic development, thus giving to the space of places the importance it
deserves. The relationship between the space of places and the space of flows is ex-
emplified in fig.1, where two productive communities, in the agricultural and tourist
fields, are distributed on the territory. Both these communities, made up of private and
public companies, cannot work or produce independently of their local context which
is responsible of many competitive factors such as safety, energy and transportation,
advanced telecommunication services and access to public co-financing. Thus, while
enterprise compete within their productive and commercial networks (the space of
flows), the PA must contribute to economic development by supporting endogenous
growth (the space of places), by means of co-financing new investments in public
utilities and full utilization of the territorial goods: if economy takes place in the space
of flows, life is still carried out in places. Hence the notion of territorial areas as the
space of places whose value must be improved.

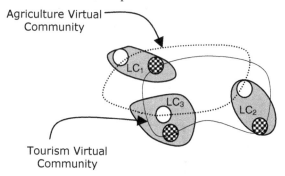

Fig. 1. Net society: a system of productive communities consisting of organizations (represented by nodes) that collaborate via Internet and receive basic services from the Local Communities (LC) to which they belong.

In the past, the Public Administration has pursued actions at the city level or at the
industrial area level. Today these actions seem to be too specific and limited to be
regarded as sustaining a suitable space of places. There is a "dimension", or a level of
scale in which the local productive context has its own organic characterization not-
withstanding its economic-productive diversification. This level is the intermediate
area between the city and the county, typically the metropolitan area. It is at this level
that the PA should be able to address effectively and coherently the territorial development needs. Thus novel e-government actions and the related knowledge management system should be designed to support local economic development, where "lo-

cal" doesn't have a bureaucratic meaning (city or county) rather it is centred on the notion of basic economic-productive community upon which the virtual community of the net-economy rests (for example, networks of tour operators or networks of import-export agencies). To understand why local development must be addressed starting from the above basic community, it is useful to think of the problems of people transportation, goods distribution, school and training, office supply and office automation, spending free time, enjoying environmental and historical heritage, or local crafts and low-tech and high-tech industrial areas. In all of the above cases the level at which the economic activity is carried out is neither the city nor the county: it rather has a local trait made up of the available resources and professionalism, besides the specific territorial vocation. In our case, the ideal dimension at which the e-government system should operate to pursue integrated development has been identified as consisting of the city of Catania plus nine surroundings municipalities plus the industrial area. In the above context the local government (PA) can take on the responsibility of complementing the process of globalization (i.e., large flows, small places) by creating a more comprehensive space of places where local flows can flourish (i.e., smaller flows, larger places), and actors who would be leaved out of transnational flows are supported in their activity. These "larger" spaces of places become on their turn more useful and attractive also for large scale activities. If the PA is involved in the process of creating a more comprehensive space of places, its projects must undergo a significant transformation: from sector interventions they become integrated and complex (multidisciplinary) interventions. The above strategic choice calls for an overall reorganization of the local government to introduce another organizational level centred on projects to be carried out in places.

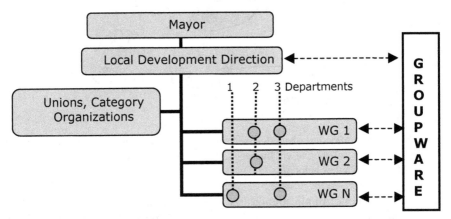

Fig. 2. Organizational change in the Public Administration: from department-centric to project-centric organization for local development. Resources from Departments (DP) participate to Working Groups (WG) if the intersection between DP and WG is labelled by a grey node.

This kind of reorganization is illustrated in fig.2 by using the organization chart adopted by the Catania Municipality to promote local development. It consists of a local development direction under the authority of the Mayor. This direction coordinates a set of working groups dedicated to develop projects and to monitor their implementation. Coordination is achieved also upon consultation of the Union and Category associations. Due to the complexity of the projects to undertake all the above actors and groups may utilize a groupware system whose features are illustrated in the next section.

3 A Knowledge Based System for Local Development: A Case Study

In the scenario of sustaining local development as outlined above, web based information systems must be conceived not only as a means to provide general information and certificates to the public but also as an environment that allows the users (i.e., citizens, enterprises and personnel of the public sector) to do the following: a) reuse meaningful experience that the system makes available under the form of expert assistance and best practices to solve specific problems; b) easily retrieve suitable information on how to fund their projects; c) develop their proposals by joint authoring and peer reviewing of documents; and d) coordinate the implementation of complex projects according to the workflow methodology.

To proceed in this direction the public sector needs to undergo a transformation from a bureaucracy organized in divisions that provide services at the city scale (e.g., development of sector projects, issuing certificates and so on) into an active system organized in groups dedicated to support the projects at the metropolitan scale from ideation to implementation, and with greater responsibilities, i.e., by assuming the role of project leader or partner depending on the nature of the projects. However, this integration of functions and competencies cannot be reached without specific automated tools that allow the personnel to contribute to departmental, interdepartmental and intercity groups despite the distance between the departments and the culture of cooperative work that is just beginning. By the joint use of web and groupware technologies it has been possible to implement a web based e-government system for supporting this process of organizational change, the knowledge working metropolitan communities and their internetworking, thus favouring local development. This system (www.cataniapolitichecomunitarie.it) has been implemented in PHP and is accessible to three categories of users (i.e., citizens, social and industrial organizations and public administration personnel). It provides the following four types of services:

1. Information services dedicated to local development and consisting of an area in the Web site that makes all the current and future projects visible to all the users. Information on significant events that explain the projects (i.e., what is their aim, who may participate and how to present a proposal) is also available.

2. Advertising services consisting of an advertising board, an event management facility based on a calendar and a messaging system supporting wireless communication; these are available for organizations and public administration personnel.

3. Information retrieval services allowing personalized and feedback based searching (e.g., project fund, technical recommendations, quality standards, personnel re-

cruiting etc.) assisted by intelligent agents; these are available to authorized organizations and public administration personnel.

4. Groupware system allowing: a) joint authoring of documents, b) access to expert assistance for developing projects via mailing and conferencing systems, c) online consulting of a best practice environment provided with a Case Based Reasoning (CBR) mechanism [6]. This is available to organizations and public administration personnel provided with full access authorization.

Service N.1 is a portal entirely dedicated to the projects for local development and differs from the traditional portals of the public sector usually dedicated to presenting divisions, functions and related services. It aims at providing all the interested parties with a shared representation of the territory and its projects organized along the temporal dimension (current and future) and by scope. As is shown in fig.3, the first section deals with the funds available for local development, the second one with the socio-economical aspects (i.e., who are the people resident in the area, what they are doing, what these people and organizations expect from the public administration in terms of structures and services), the other section deals with the master plan of the metropolitan area, i.e., the future projects related to the thematic fields (life quality, tourism, and so on) chosen by the Municipalities to steer development. The next two sections deal with the programs already activated to support both multi-sector and sector activities. The last section deals with international programs.

Home	Funds	Socio-Econ. Aspects	Master Plan	Integrated Projects	Sector Projects	International Relations

Fig. 3. Sections of the web site for local development

Passing from the emerging needs of the metropolitan area to the programs of the master plan to address such needs, and from these programs to the detailed integrated and sector projects and to the management of their implementation requires organizing the public sector as a network of working groups instead of more or less independent departments. This does not entail that classical public organization should be abandoned, rather at least another organizational dimension dedicated to designing the future projects and optimizing the current ones has to be added to the traditional dimensions (i.e., department, functions and services). The main difficulty is the interdisciplinary nature of the project groups and the distance between participants which involves a high cost of meetings and of collecting the documents and, more generally, the resources needed for supporting project and planning. Thus **Service N.2** addresses the need of supporting communication and synchronization among people involved in the groups. This has been obtained by the sections named "Board" "Calendar" and "E-Mail" of a groupware system accessible, as a reserved area, from the web site. In

these sections, people belonging to a given group may find the main facilities for communication and synchronization of their activity flows. These facilities are:
- an advertising system shared by all the groups, consisting of an advertising board to inform the entire design community about general events, conferences, deliverables, and deadlines, each coded by a different colour. The insertion of a message in the board is very simple to allow any user to insert personally her/his communication. As is shown in fig.4, this may be obtained by simply writing the message (few text lines) in the text box and then by pressing "Aggiungi" (i.e., Add). The message will immediately appear as a row in the message list ; this row will point out also the message author and her/his e-mail. Interested people can send an e-mail to the author's message to know details about the event. Currently, messages in the board may be extracted by date. Other retrieval methods (by author or by text) are planned in the next version.

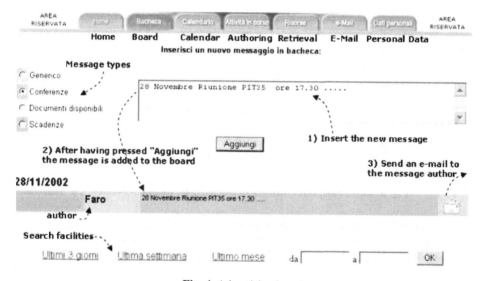

Fig. 4. Advertising board

- an event management facility allowing each group to visualize only their own calendar (fig.5). This system is conceived to synchronize project activities and it is especially needed when a group is organized in cooperating subgroups. In these cases it is suggested to organize each subgroup as a separate group, whereas coordination is achieved by another group whose members are the leaders of the subgroup and the leader of the overall group. The calendar is accessible to all the members of the group to read and post general events. Only the group leader can insert deadlines for delivering documents, de-allocating resources and allocating the ones received from the higher level leader. Any event posted in the calendar consists of a title and of a downloadable file that could be the agenda or the draft of the meeting, a document to be revised or voted by the members to become a group deliverable, conference programs, notification of allocation or deallocation of resources and so on. Posting an event and inserting the related document is very easy: first the user has to press "Inserisci un nuovo evento" (i.e., Add a new event), then she/he fills the form and chooses the document to be associated to the event by the classical browse window. The calendar dates in bold refer to days containing meaningful events. After pressing the event title, the user may download the related document. Only the author of the insertion or the group leader may delete the event inserted in the calendar. SMS services may be requested depending on the importance of the event. The system is also provided with an e-mail service to support communication between the group members; it may be augmented by videoconferencing for increasing communication efficacy.

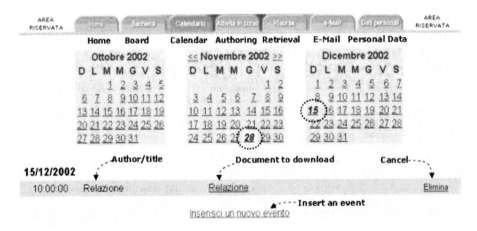

Fig. 5. Advertising and synchronizing activity flows by calendar events

The groupware can support several simultaneously working groups. Each group may have access to either its private communication area (i.e., service N.2) and to the communication area common to all the groups (i.e., service N.1) without closing the working session. This is obtained by controlling the access to the communication records contained in a single data base (in our case IBM DB2) by a double key: one identifies the section currently accessed and the other identifies the group to which the user belongs to. From the implementation point of view, this architecture based on a single database allows us to use the same indexing scheme for information and case retrieval for all the working groups, thus greatly simplifying implementation and updating of the services N.3 and N.4 which are illustrated in detail in the following.

Service N.3 deals with information retrieval and is based on the IBM Web-crawler agent [7] programmed to visit daily interesting remote sites and take away the more recent documents. These documents are stored in the local server so that the IBM Text Miner may start the indexing procedure that makes it easy for the user to retrieve documents according to a lexical search string. This string is based on the scheme $(Term_1 + \dots + Term_n)^*$, where $Term_i$ is a general word, the string $(Term_1 + \dots + Term_n)$ causes the engine to retrieve the documents containing $Term_i$ and $\dots$ and $Term_n$ in sequence, and the asterisk in the scheme means that the user may insert an arbitrary number of strings. As an example, the search string: "2002 tourism local + development" asks the engine to retrieve all the documents that contain the words tourism, 2002 and the two words "local development" in sequence. The engine considers two words having the same root as the same word, thus all the documents containing tourism and touristic are retrieved in response to the search string "tourism". In addition, to avoid remembering a lexical string that the user wishes to repeat in the future, the user is allowed to give a name to any search string.

Fig. 6. Information retrieval of web documents by mobile agents and text miner

Fig.6 above shows how, after the system has retrieved the Sicily Official Gazettes dealing with "agriculture and FSE" (i.e., European Social Funds), the user may open the document by simply clicking on the selected Gazette number. Let us note that the artificial agent stores the Gazettes on the local server for indexing reasons, however, after having indexed the documents, the system may delete them and maintain only their URLs. A relevance-feedback mechanism that allows the users to increase the search precision is planned for the next version of the system. This method has been tested off-line. It needs a client-side software to be installed on the end systems and a server-side software to be installed on the computer where the web site is running. Based on an indication of to what extent the found document fits the user request (e.g., high, medium, low), the system is able to refine the original search string. This technique may be used to classify the documents not only according to personalized strings but also to traditional taxonomies. As an example, if a group wishes to classify the documents according to the scheme: POP, POM and POR (these are typical EC programs), then the group has to create three classes and subsequently evaluate the documents by providing feedback until the classification contains few errors. Let us note that the search engine learns by user feedback why a document containing both POR and POM has to be considered belonging to both classes or to only one of these classes. This information is exploited by the search engine to refine the initial search string by autonomously adding other keywords that suitably correspond to the user needs. This is done by taking into account the other words of the document, usually the most frequent and the more rare ones, with respect to the evaluation of the users.

The above scheme is also adopted to retrieve best practices and other documents relevant for the problem at hand (e.g., meeting notes, project deliverables, etc.). This is obtained by storing these documents into the directory managed by the Text Miner which is in charge of indexing and retrieving them according to the search string issued by the users. To increase precision, any document may be described by a template subdivided in sections according to the Case Based Reasoning (CBR) paradigm [6]. For example, the best practices may be suitably subdivided into sections such as: Title, Problem, Solution, Where the solution has been implemented and Who was involved; similarly, the meeting notes may be subdivided in sections such as: agenda, participants, and so on. As a consequence, the search method allows also the user to express queries as follows: [$(Term_1 + \ldots + Term_n)$ in $Sect_k$] *. In this way, all the documents that are extracted share the search string in the same sections, thus greatly increasing precision [8]. To increase documents'recall it may be useful to link the documents by a similarity index defined as follows: $S_{ik} = (\Sigma S_{iks})/N$, where N is the number of the sections of the template describing the documents, and S_{iks} is the similarity between document i and k with respect to section s defined on the basis of the frequently and rare words they share [9]. The square matrix S_{ik} is then passed to a Kohonen-like neural network to classify the document in M classes [10]. The input neurons are equal to the number of documents, whereas the output neurons are equal to the class number M which is not known a-priori. The network starts from a tentative M and increases it until adding a new class does changes a little the previous classification. In response to a query the system retrieves the documents satisfying the search string and the ones contained in the classes to which these initially retrieved documents belong.

By the above tools the members of the group may communicate, synchronize their activities with the ones of the other groups, obtain assistance, via e-mail or videoconferencing, from a pool of consultants made available upon agreement with selected consulting companies, exchange best practices and documents relevant for their problems, but they still need to jointly author their projects. For this reason we have developed another section of the groupware dedicated to this task, i.e., **Service N.4**. Any member may insert a document into the system to be corrected by the other members until the final version is agreed by all. This is obtained by a simple and efficient semaphore mechanism that guarantees information consistency. Any document may be deleted only by its author or by the group responsible. After completing a document, the responsible of the working group may publish it in the board (see service N.2), or ask the system to send it with digital signature to a given destination address. In addition the system allows the responsible to store the documents into two directories, i.e., the directory managed by the Text Miner and the one belonging to the "Joint Authoring" section of another group. In the former case the document may be retrieved according to a search string issued by any partecipant of the group, in the latter case the document may be consulted by any partecipant of other groups. In particular the system allows the documents of each group to be exported to the higher level group, thus making possible to sustain the work of groups subdivided into subgroups.

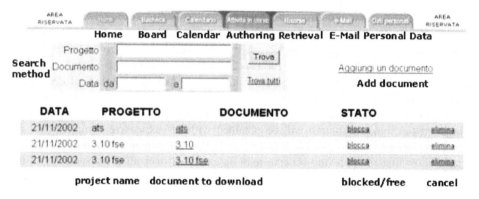

Fig. 7. Joint authoring of documents

4   Concluding Remarks

The major contribution of the paper is that of having pointed out the importance of the "space of places" and related local flows for supporting a net-economy traditionally believed to be mostly linked to global flows. This entails an organizational change of the Public Administration towards a project centric organization consisting of working groups supported by knowledge based web systems. Consideration of cultural and psychological aspects suggests that the transition from a departmental based organization to a net-organization for local development has to be performed step by step. For this reason, all the services described have been implemented, but some of them (i.e., the relevance feedback and the neural net based classification of documents) will be deployed only in a new version of the platform, thus proceeding incrementally. Another claim of the paper is that an information portal and related multi-channel access is not enough for the net-economy. Rather, advanced groupware systems augmented with intelligent agents and mobile facilities seem more suitable for it, especially if they are provided with a simple user interface that speeds up diffusion of the culture of cooperative work.

So far the system has been used for managing the web-site, for carrying out projects and developing project proposals at both local and international level. In particular, information to be published in the site is sent for immediate publication by the authorized components of the group to the web site manager by using the service implemented for the joint authoring of documents. This guarantees information freshness. Another relevant application of the environment has been the development of two joint projects among the Municipality, the University and external companies dealing with local development: one project regarded the elaboration of questionnaires on work conditions, another project dealt with the definition of an architecture for location information services at metropolitan scale (e.g., information on traffic conditions, parking, etc.). The system has been also successfully used for the preparation of proposals carried out by many actors such as the one dealing with the activation of e-learning facilities for enhancing the skills of the personnel working in the public sector. An application of the presented system for developing a joint proposal at European level is currently going on. All these experiences clearly indicate that the interface simplicity is a key factor for a successful acceptance of the system.

Standardization of the proposed environment by means of ontological definitions and related F-Logic based queries has been also developed in Protegè [11], and it is ready to be implemented in further versions. This will be activated when the advantages of the semantic search will be obtained without expensive computational resources. In fact, current experiments on the ontological implementation of the groupware show that the indexing scheme may be extended over all the documents in the local web without transporting them on a single server if fast computing systems are available, due to the high processing time needed by the ontological searches. Thus a deeper evaluation of usability and performance for this new environment has to be done before extending the current system. This might imply a re-definition of the ontological schema and the related queries.

References

1. Davenport, T., Prusak, L.,: Working Knowledge. Harvard Business School Press (1998)
2. iig, K.M.,: Application of Knowledge Management in Public Administration. KRI Inc., Arlington, USA, www.krii.com/downloads/km_in_public_admin_rev.pdf (2000)
3. Dawes, S., Préfontaine, L.,: Delivering Government Services. CACM, N.1.vol.46 (2003)
4. Hovy, E.,: Using an Ontology to Simplify Data Access. CACM, N.1.vol.46 (2003)
5. Castells, M.,: The rise of the Network Society. Blackwell Publisher Okford (1996)
6. Kolodner, J.,: Case Based Reasoning. Morgan Kaufmann (1995)
7. IBM : Using the Intelligent Miner for Text. IBM (1999)
8. Faro, A., Giordano. D., Santoro, C.,: Link based shaping of hypermedia document assisted by a neural agent. Journal of Universal Computer Science, N.7 vol.4 (1998)
9. Herch, W.R.,: Information Retrieval. Springer Verlag (2002)
10. Faro, A., Giordano. D.,: Concept formation from design cases: why reusing experience and why not. Knowledge Based Engineering Journal N.7/8 vol.11 Elsevier Science (1998)
11. N. F. Noy, et al.,: Creating Semantic Web Contents with Protege-2000. IEEE Intelligent Systems N.2, vol.16, 2001..

Empowering Society through Knowledge Records

Meliha Handzic

School of Information Systems, Technology and Management
The University of New South Wales, Sydney 2052, Australia
m.handzic@unsw.edu.au

Abstract. This paper focuses on the role of knowledge records in helping governments to achieve a wiser and fairer society. It presents a view of knowledge records as society's tools for establishing evidence, protecting human rights, supporting the rule of law, and preserving cultural capital. It also discusses the issues of quality and integrity of knowledge records, and suggests a plausible method to direct the development and implementation of proper knowledge records management systems in government agencies.

1 Introduction

Our current understanding of the level of penetration and impact of knowledge management initiatives in non-profit organizations, including government, is very limited. Preliminary empirical evidence from Australia reveals a relatively high level of awareness, combined with a low level of implementation of knowledge management in academia [8]; some promotional activities related to the creation of knowledge-enabled environments in major government agencies [20]; and initial efforts focused on delivering better electronic government services to the public [12].

So far, Australian federal agencies have been successful in implementing an initial "Government Online" strategy which ensured that all appropriate information and services are now available via the internet for those wanting to access them. "Better Service, Better Government" is a new strategy that maps out the next phase in the federal government's drive to move on from placing information and services on-line. Key objectives include greater efficiency, convenient access to services, better service delivery, integration of related services, building of user trust and confidence, and enhanced citizen engagements or "e-democracy".

This paper focuses on the role played by knowledge management, particularly the process of capturing and preserving society's knowledge, in helping governments ensure fairer and wiser society.

2 The Concept of Knowledge Record

The term "knowledge record" is a derivative of two terms: "knowledge" and "record". The word record denotes any kind of recording that is created and kept as part of conducting individual or institutional affairs. There is no one agreed definition of

M.A. Wimmer (Ed.): KMGov 2003, LNAI 2645, pp. 262–267, 2003.

knowledge. Rather, knowledge is defined differently from different philosophical perspectives. From the cognitive perspective, for example, knowledge is perceived as externally justified beliefs, based on formal models, universal and explicit, that operate through cognitive processes. On the other hand, from the constructivist perspective, knowledge is viewed as acts of construction or creation, creative arts, not universal, beliefs that depend on personal sense making [23]. Often, knowledge is defined in terms of relationships between data and information.

In theory, knowledge is described as deeper and richer information [3]; information combined with experience, context, interpretation and reflection [4]; valuable information in action [6]; and information that has been internalised by a person to the degree that he or she can make use of it [5]. However, in practice, the terms data, information and knowledge are often used interchangeably [10].

Based on Polanyi's [16] original work, knowledge is usually classified as either explicit or tacit [13], [14]. Explicit knowledge is described as formal, systematic knowledge that can be expressed or communicated without vagueness or ambiguity. It can be stored in books, manuals, databases and in other ways. Tacit knowledge, on the other hand, is considered as highly personal know-how that is derived from experience and beliefs and usually hard to articulate and communicate. Such knowledge exists in the individual minds of people.

Some taxonomies make a distinction between declarative, procedural, inferential and motivational forms of professional knowledge [17], as well as conditional, relational and pragmatic types [1]. Other schemes recognise individual and artifact loci, varying degrees of knowledge structure, and individual and collective levels of knowledge [7]. A pragmatic approach to classifying knowledge simply attempts to identify knowledge useful to stakeholders. Recognising knowledge as a complex and multifaceted concept, the objective of this paper is to take a closer look at one specific facet: explicit recorded knowledge, created in the conduct of society's affairs.

3 How Knowledge Records Empower Society

Individuals, groups and societies treat their knowledge in different ways. Eastern cultures seem to value more "tacit" knowledge that is kept in people's heads and transferred through socialisation. Western cultures, on the other hand, appear to focus more on "explicit" knowledge, captured and preserved in collective and codified repositories [14]. Based on this distinction, a widely adopted broad classification of knowledge management strategies comprises two classes: personalisation and codification [9]. The personalisation strategy assumes that tacit knowledge is shared through interpersonal communication. Codification assumes that knowledge can be effectively extracted and codified. In this approach, knowledge artifacts are stored and indexed in databases for later retrieval and use. As such, it can serve as evidence and proof of an idea, decision or action taken by either an individual, organisation or government.

Following the principles of codification, a comprehensive framework for building a society's cumulative "explicit" knowledge base has been proposed [15]. This framework suggests that the process starts with identifying critical documentable knowledge. This may include individual and group ideas, actions, decisions and transactions worth preserving. Once identified as such, these documentable "acts" are then codified, organised, stored and kept together with relevant meta-knowledge for as long as required. Typically, only a small portion of recorded knowledge has long term significance and becomes part of the society's cumulative memory and of concern to public authorities. Pederson [15] provides numerous examples of such knowledge records from the worlds' public archives available on the internet. The following paragraphs summarise and illustrate a number of representative Australian cases.

Example 1. Accumulated knowledge records can be viewed as an important societal tool for establishing facts and a way to validate human memory. Typically, they include personal documents; corporate knowledge bases; industry and government reports and statistics; technical and specialist literature; databases and internet resources; academic journals; scholarly and reference books; general knowledge compilations; popular books and magazines; and info-tainment. *Founding Documents* is one example of an important Australian project in social history realised as a partnership of eight government archives for the Centenary of Federation celebration. The project is available at http://www.foundingdocs.gov.au/.

Example 2. Knowledge records are also important in ensuring the protection of individual rights. Personal records are especially crucial to individuals seeking to establish their identity and ensure their entitlements. The intentional destruction of one's vital personal records can be extremely disruptive and often life threatening to those affected. The stories of Kosovars found at web pages of the United Nations High Commissioner for Refugees, and various government councils give a graphic insight into the experiences and deprivation suffered by people whose identity documents were systematically destroyed and who were forced to become refugees. Australian Government provides instruction and help to refugees through *Refugee Council of Australia* available at http://www.refugeecouncil.org.au/.

Example 3. Progressive societies demand that governments and individuals demonstrate great responsibility and accountability in the conduct of their public and personal affairs. Typically, governments enact laws and regulations that define the structures and sets of rules governing the relations and activities of all legal entities within their jurisdictions. Despite this, keeping those in charge honest still represents a major challenge for democratic societies. The Australian Government has recently awarded a major research grant to the *Records Continuum Research Group,* at Monash University to investigate the issue of accountability in public services. Their web site at http://rcrg.dstc.edu.au/publications/recordscontinuum/smoking.html contains numerous reports and analyses of recent crises, scandals and risks faced by the Australian public sector that all have their roots in inadequate knowledge records management.

Example 4. The capacity to construct and transfer culture has always been considered as an essential social function. Recorded knowledge has an important cultural value too. It links us to the ideas and activities that have lasting importance for symbolic or concrete reasons. Bodies of recorded knowledge constitute a society's "cultural capital". Cumulative layers of evidence legitimise and witness the development of significant ideas and activities within a society over time. One of the recent Australian contributions to preserving society's achievements is *Bright Sparcs,* available at http://www.asap.unimelb.edu.au/bsparcs/bsparcshome.htm. It is a register of over 3,000 people involved in the development of science, technology and medicine in Australia. The site also includes references to scientists' materials and resources

4 Issues in Knowledge Records Management

Because of the power of recorded knowledge as a resource of wisdom and justice in society, knowledge management must ensure that government's knowledge repositories are of high quality and integrity and also ensure their availability to the right people, at the right time, and in the right form.

Different perspectives on quality are provided by different proposed frameworks. Shanks and Tansley [19] define quality in terms of "fitness for purpose". Others consider accuracy, reliability, importance, consistency, precision, timeliness, understandability, conciseness and usefulness as desirable quality dimensions [2], [24]. The framework by Strong et al. [22], suggests four quality dimensions: intrinsic, contextual, representational and accessibility. The framework of Shanks and Darke [18] consists of syntactic, semantic, pragmatic and social quality goals and measures for stakeholders. Other frameworks include Wand and Wang [24], based on Bunge's ontology, and Kahn et al. [11], which is based on product and service quality theory.

The Australian standard for knowledge records management [21] lists several important characteristics that records should have in order to ensure society's need for evidence, accountability and information. First of all, a record's content should correctly reflect an idea that was communicated, or a decision that was made, or an action that was taken. As well as the content, the record should also contain metadata describing its structure, context and links to relevant other records. Furthermore, the record should be authenticated, that is proven to be what it purports to be, shown to have been created or sent by the person purported to have created or sent it, and verified as having been created or sent at the time purported. The record should also be reliable, so that its contents can be trusted as a complete and accurate representation of knowledge. The integrity of a record should be preserved by protection from unauthorized alteration. Finally, it should be useable, easy to locate, retrieve, present and interpret.

The failure to address the issues of quality and integrity of records in a government's knowledge repositories may lead to serious impairment of functioning of society and its institutions, the loss of evidence of the rights of people as citizens, the inability of societal watchdogs to call to account governments and individuals, the loss of collective and individual identity and memory, and the inability to authenticate and source critical knowledge. These issues pose a great challenge to governments.

5 Australian Standard Guidelines

The Australian Records Management Standard provides a methodology that specifically aims at facilitating the implementation of knowledge records management systems [21]. One of its first recommendations is to define and document relevant policies. A policy statement can be understood as a statement of intentions. It also sets out programmes and procedures to support those intentions. Then, the standard describes a step-by-step procedure for designing and implementing records systems, that includes preliminary investigation, analysis of activities, identification of requirements, assessment of existing systems, identification of strategies, systems design, systems implementation and post-implementation review.

Another Standard recommendation specifies required operational processes and controls. Theoretically, these processes include a linear sequence of capture, registration, record classification, access and security classification, identification of disposition status, storage, use and tracking, and implementation of disposal activities. However, in practice, some operations may take place simultaneously. Certain operations may depend on the existence of controls. Controls include the instruments needed for different operations, and factors that may affect these operations. The principal instruments include classification schemes, the disposition authority, and the security and access scheme. Additional ones include specific tools such as a thesaurus and a glossary of terms, as well as regulatory and risk frameworks, formalised delegation of authority and the registry of permissions.

Finally, the standard specifies the need to define responsibilities and authorities. The overriding objective of this recommendation is to establish and maintain the regime that meets the needs of all stakeholders. The likely authorities and responsibilities of senior managers include ensuring the success of the overall knowledge records management programme. Specialised professionals have primary responsibility for the implementation of policies, procedures and standards. Other knowledge workers may have a variety of specific duties, including responsibility for security, responsibility for design and implementation of information and communication technology based systems, or creation, receipt and storage of knowledge records.

6 Conclusions

This paper addresses the role of knowledge records in empowering society. In summary, it identifies accumulated knowledge records as important societal tools for establishing facts, and a way to validate human memory, protect human rights, support the rule of law, and preserve culture. It also recognizes the need for high quality and integrity within the knowledge records in government repositories, as well as allowing availability to the right people, at the right time, and in the right form. Finally, guidelines for developing and implementing knowledge records management systems that comply with the best national practices are outlined.

References

1. Alavi, M., Leidner, D.E.: Knowledge Management and Knowledge Management Systems: Conceptual Foundations and Research Issues. MIS Quarterly, 1 (2001) 107–136
2. Ballou, D.P., Pazer H.L.: Modeling data and process quality multi-input multi-output information systems. Management Science. 2 (1985) 150–162

3. Davenport, T.H., Prusak L.: Working Knowledge. Harvard Business School Press, Boston (1998)
4. Davenport, T.H., DeLong, D.W., Breers, M.C.: Successful Knowledge Management Projects. Sloan Management Review, Winter (1998) 43–57
5. Devlin, K.: Infosense: Turning Information into Knowledge. W.H. Freeman and Company, New York (1999)
6. Grayson, C.J., O'Dell, C.: Mining Your Hidden Resources. Across the Board, 4 (1998) 23–28
7. Hahn, J., Subramani, M.R.: A Framework of Knowledge Management Systems: Issues and Challenges for Theory and Practice. In: Proceedings of the International Conference on Information Systems, ICIS'2000, Brisbane (2000) 302–312
8. Handzic, M., VanToorn, C.: Penetration of KM Practices in a Non-Profit organisation: A Case of Academia. Working paper, UNSW (2002)
9. Hansen et al.: What's your strategy for managing knowledge?, Harvard Business Review, March-April (1999) 106–116
10. Huang, F.T. et al.: Quality Information and Knowledge. Prentice Hall, New Jersey (1999)
11. Kahn B., Stong D.M, Wang R.Y.: A Model for Delivering Quality Information as Product and Service. In: Proceedings of the International Conference on Information Quality, MIT, Boston (1997) 80–94
12. NOIE: http://www.noie.gov.au. (accessed 30 November 2002)
13. Nonaka, I.: The Knowledge-Creating Company. In: Harvard Business Review on Knowledge Management, Harvard Business School Press, Boston (1998)
14. Nonaka, I., Takeuchi, H.: The Knowledge Creating Company: How Japanese Companies Create the Dynamics of Innovation. Oxford University Press, New York (1995)
15. Pederson, A.: http://john.curtin.edu.au/society. (accessed 30 November 2002)
16. Polanyi, M.: The Logic of Tacit Inference. Philosophy, 1 (1966) 1–18
17. Quinn, J. B., Andeson, P., Finkelstein, S.: Managing Professional Intellect: Making the Most of the Best. Harvard Business Review, March-April (1996) 71–80
18. Shanks, G., Darke P.: Understanding Metadata and Data Quality in a Data Warehouse. Australian Computer Journal, November (1998)
19. Shanks, G., Tansley E.: Data Quality Tagging and Decision Outcomes: An Experimental Study. In: Proceedings of Decision Support in Internet Age Conference, DSIage2002, Cork (2002)
20. Standards Australia: Case Studies in Knowledge Management, Vol. 1, Standards Australia, Sydney (2002)
21. Standards Australia: Australian Standard: Records Management, Part 1&2, Standards Australia, Sydney (2002)
22. Strong D.M., Lee Y.W., Wang R.Y.: Data Quality in Context. Communications of the ACM, 5 (1997) 103–110
23. Van Krogh, G.: Care in Knowledge Creation. California Management Review, 3 (1998) 133–153
24. Wand, Y., Wang R.: Anchoring Data Quality Dimensions in Ontological Foundations. Communications of the ACM, 11 (1996) 86–95

Application of KM Platforms for Internal Operations

George Asimakopoulos, Vlasis Metaxas, Kostas Papadopoulos, and Elpida Metaxa

01 PLIROFORIKI S.A, 438 Acharnon St, 111 43 Athens Greece

Abstract. This paper deals with these issues and reveals specific matters that are substantial for the transformation towards true e-government from today's digital representation of legacy processes. These issues have already been coped with in organizations that have transformed from a service based to a customer based model, due to regulatory changes. First is the use of KM in order to manage individual service users rather than operations. The second area is issue management, a technique that governmental organizations utilize in order to cope with public security matters.

1 Introduction

This paper deals with issues and reveals specific matters that are substantial for the transformation towards true e-government from today's digital representation of legacy processes. These issues have already been coped with in organizations that have transformed from a service based to a customer based model, due to regulatory changes.

First of these issues is the use of KM in order to manage individual service users rather than operations. The second area is issue management, a technique that governmental organizations utilize in order to cope with security matters.

The importance of KM in the public sector is easy to understand, if we consider that governmental processes are mostly about exchanging information with citizens. The major issue is that this information is not connected. This implies that although the governmental structure is handling information about citizens, it cannot transform it to knowledge, because this information does not reach as a whole the appropriate civil servant, but only as small bits of information. In other words, governmental organizations can not view citizens as an integral being but just as a part of many different processes. Under this perspective, KM could shift the government from viewing administrative processes to viewing individual citizens, through aggregating all information sources. This means that issues as information overload, interoperability, interfaces etc must be answered by any technology that will be selected.

Of course speaking about customers in the public sector is excessive. On the other hand though, as shown in the introduction, the public sector must shift towards a citizen based model from today's process or services based one. So there is much expertise to gain from organizations that have already shifted from their service based model to an individual end user model. After all, both citizens and customers are users of benefits that are provided from some kind of organizational structure. From

M.A. Wimmer (Ed.): KMGov 2003, LNAI 2645, pp. 268–273, 2003.

this point of view, any KM solutions that have been proven successful in such environments may easily be reused in governmental KM transformation.

Another governmental field where KM is very important is security. Awareness gives private enterprises the ability to react efficiently to environmental and market changes and thus gain competitive advantage. This awareness is more difficult to gain as competitors accrete and information sources regarding competitors, markets and customers are almost infinite. In the governmental sector though awareness is needed in order to establish security, either regarding external threats either threats that rise from inland agents. The fact that sources of threats have changed and multiplied means that vast amounts of information must be processed. The fact that information sources regarding threats are virtually infinite implies that manual monitoring of security relevant developments is not adequate. Governments need mechanisms that automatically can process vast amounts of information and forward specific bits of this information to individuals that can react to specific situations.

2 Required KM Platform Characteristics

The platform on which the solution could be built on must process automatically any kind of unstructured and structured information. Given the uninterrupted growth of unstructured information which is doubling every three months (Gartner), efficient processes that manage and extract value from such information are solely dependant on the ability to automate the tasks that previously, have been performed with manual labor.

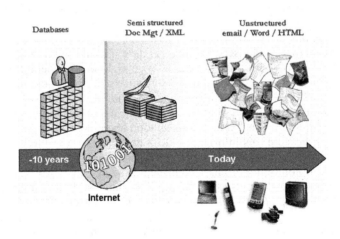

Fig. 1. Evolution of information texture requires automated processes

Following is an analytical description of the platform's desired functionality.

- Language independency: the software should be completely language independent. Usually most software relies on any intimate knowledge of English grammatical structure or that of any particular language.

- Automated Content Aggregation and Management: the software should aggregate content from any data source. It should have the ability to read all widespread file formats and should be able to access all kinds of repositories. Furthermore, there should be no duplication of files into some new repository.
- Concept matching and automated hyperlinking: The software should accept a piece of content as an input and return references to conceptually related documents ranked by relevance or contextual distance.

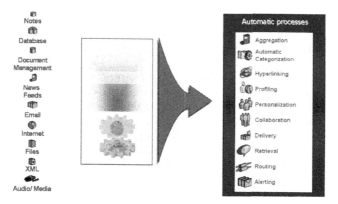

Fig. 2. Required automated processes

- Agent creation and retraining: The platform should accept a piece of content (a training phrase, document or set of documents) and return an encoded representation of the concepts, including each concept's specific underlying patterns of terms and associated probabilistic ratings.
- Agent matching and alerting: The software should accept an agent and return similar agents ranked by conceptual similarity. This is used to discover users with similar interests, or find experts in a field.
- Categorization: The software should accept a piece of content and return automatically categories ranked by conceptual similarity.
- Summarization: The software should accept a piece of content and return automatically a summary of the information containing the most salient concepts of the content.
- Retrieval: The software should support a Boolean term or natural language query and return a list of documents containing the terms ordered by contextual relevance to the query.

A software platform would be a very effective solution when processing of unstructured information is needed, as it reduces costs and processes any kind of data automatically.

3 Case Study

The case study that is presented here is from OTE. OTE is the operator that formerly was the only player in the Greek telecom market, as it was the organization with which the Greek government provided services to telecom users. Three years ago OTE transformed to the major but not only telecom player, as regulatory changes derived new alternative providers. This case study is useful because it reveals issues that must be coped with when a governmental organization shifts from a process based model to a customer or individual based model. The software used in this case was built by Autonomy.

Following is a description of how OTE coped with the two major issues presented in this paper: individual and issue management with the use of Autonomy's software.

3.1 Issue Management

First of all what was strongly needed by this Enterprise was a mechanism that would monitor the enterprise's business environment. This can be thought of as issue management, a technique that is widely used in the security field. Until the utilization of KM practices, this process was carried out by a group of people that constantly searched content that showed up in various sources such as internet sites, news feeds that the enterprise subscribed to and internal documents. As it can easily be understood, the results of the manual operation where not adequate, specially in a changing market where new and thus unknown competitors show up every day and change their commercial habits very frequently. First of all these workers could not cope with the vast amounts of information that overloaded them. This simply means that they could not read thoroughly every bit of information that showed up every moment. It is easy to understand that the automated content aggregation and management feature provided by Autonomy's software solved the problem of information overload. This is because this process was automated and thus executed thoroughly by computers.

The solution that was built on Autonomy's technology was the utilization of the concept matching feature in order to assign documents to specific categories. The approach was to describe the category and let the software match documents to each category description. In this way the enterprise now manages categories which are its main interest and not a vast set of documents. Another feature that expanded the enterprise's categorization capability was agent retraining. This feature allows the retraining of a category. This is done by using the concepts used in a document in order to describe a category.

Beyond category creation a major issue that must be solved is that of alerting. Every time a concept appears that is relevant to a users profile or an expertise description, the platform can alert the specific user. This implies that the enterprise can now respond to an issue, even if it has not been formally identified and assigned to individuals until the moment it appears. The alerting is accomplished with the software's agent alerting feature. This implies that as soon as an issue appears and not when someone finds out that it has occurred, categorizes the document and then inform a person that might not be able to react, because of the improper categorization that has been performed.

The areas in which this telecom provider utilized these issue management techniques were legal issues, competition awareness and benchmarked market leader observation. It is obvious though that these matters are encountered in every issue management initiative.

3.2 Individual Management

The second KM application requested by the telecom operator was to build an ICT infrastructure that would enable the transition towards a customer based environment. The need to shift towards individual telecom users from the service centric view implied that regardless of services that are provided, the customer must be managed as a discrete individual that exhibits specific habits regarding the use of telecom and other adjunct services.

As said above, a major objective for e-government that has not been coped with until today is to accomplish the shift from the management of services to the management of civilians. The need for this shift though is not the same as it is for an enterprise that manages customers. But at the bottom line customers are individuals, so useful lessons can be taught from customer based transitions that are accomplished in the private sector. The public sector is built on a service based logic. This means that for each service provided, there is some kind of organizational structure in place. This structure exists only because the specific service is needed. This implies that every structure is ignorant about the other structures in place that provide different services. The utilization of ICT in the public sector until today has induced major wins in the governmental structure. The services described above have become faster, the localization distribution is not any more a drawback and paperwork is much less. The truth is that public services are improved and cheaper, because of the utilization of ITC. There is though one major drawback that keeps e-government away from the goal of treating citizens rather than services; this is that the use of ITC reproduced the organizational structure that was in place already. This means that all the ICT systems that are in place today do not exchange information. Information about citizens is stored in systems that are built to manage services.

The case of OTE again shows the strength that derives from the aggregation of multiple data sources when such transitions are needed. There where vast amounts of data regarding customers available on many different systems. These systems where managed by many different organizational units, ranging from the IT Division to the CEO's secretariat. This implies that it was very difficult to establish a organizational unit that could exploit this information. Of course, most of this information was unstructured. The result of this fact was that there was no way to see if a customer was profitable or not, because data was built in a way that allowed the monitoring of services and not individuals.

4 Conclusions

Appearance of citizen-centered technologies that make it possible for organizations to understand and respond to the needs of those they serve are influencing the information technology decisions made. The solution presented above supports:

- The growth of standards to allow different applications to exchange data, as it evolutes any kind of digital format, including voice and video. Virually any standard, existing or to be developed, is supported.
- The integration of documents and other unstructured information within applications. Local federal agencies are able to receive incoming information from

the public that can be aggregated with the existing content, for example held on an environmental issue. Therefore enabling the authority to respond publicly in the appropriate manner. This can include external news feeds and newsgroups and can be particularly relevant with such public events as the US Presidential Elections.

- The arrival of network-based services that change the costs of using IT.

Issues to be solved

Although this approach seems appealing, there are various issues that must be resolved in order to maximize the benefits that arise from the presented solution. One of these issues is the utilization of unstructured information that resides on non electronic means of storage. Governmental organizations exist way before the use of ICT. This issue is partially solved, as the exploitation of ICT has lead to the digitalisation of most such data. The problem mostly occurs with data that follows an unstructured nature and is very rich in the term of concepts. The solution to this issue can not be different to the one that has been followed until today; data entry and/or scanning, OCR and manual error detection and correction.

Finally, there are some key points that show how the use of KM software that automates manual processes could push the transition to true e-government from where it is today. These points can be identified in the light of KM applications that have been deployed in large private sector organizations that utilize ICT infrastructure that is similar to that being used in the governmental structure. These main points are:

Issue Management

The development of government policy depends on the analysis of multiple information sources. Civil servants need accurate, timely information (in the form of Government reports, White Papers, etc.), which they then marshal in order to give rise to effective decision-making.

Globalisation

Many government operations will be spread throughout the world. In a military department's case, maintaining contact and ensuring that field personnel have access to information regardless of their position is vital. The importance of sharing information on a worldwide basis also highlights the importance of a scalable solution, Autonomy helps facilitate these operations.

References

1. Clarke T., Rollo C.: Corporate initiatives in knowledge management. Education & Training, volume 43, number 4/5, 2001, p206–214. MCB University Press
2. Clarke S.: Knowledge Suite. Butler Viewpoint, February 1999
3. Harty J., Balla J., Andrews L.: White Paper on Functional Assessment of Autonomy products, Doculabs, December 1999.

Using Knowledge Management to Improve Transparency in E-voting

Alexandros Xenakis and Ann Macintosh

International Teledemocracy Centre, Napier University
10 Colinton Road, Edinburgh, EH10 5DT, UK
Telephone: +44 (0) 131 455 2545   Fax: +44 (0) 131 455 2282
www.teledemocracy.org
{a.xenakis, a.macintosh}@napier.ac.uk

Abstract. In this paper we argue that knowledge management is required to improve transparency in e-government processes and to support their social acceptance. We present the main information flows and knowledge management issues identified in the case of the UK Local Authority elections 2nd May 2002 electronic voting pilots. We provide a comprehensive view of the major areas of information flows either provided to or produced by the main agents (namely voters, administration staff, local authorities and commercial suppliers) involved in the projects. In doing so we highlight the issues of security, data protection, and transparency of information flows and their relation to the social acceptance of electronically services elections.

1 Introduction

This paper was produced as part of a doctoral research program exploring the use of business process re-engineering (BPR) methodologies to provide management, modeling and analysis methods for electronic voting.

In August 2002 the UK government issued a consultation paper on a policy for electronic democracy [HM Government, 2002]. This consultation document usefully argues that e-democracy can be divided into two distinct areas – one addressing e-engagement and the other addressing e-voting. In the case of latter the paper argues that e-voting should be viewed as a technological problem. In the case of the former, the document sets out the possibilities for greater opportunity for consultation and dialogue between government and citizens. One of the actions taken to promote new methods of voting was to conduct 30 voting pilot schemes in the 2nd May 2002 Local Authority Elections. The pilots were funded by the DTLR (Department of Transport Local Government Regions) and approved by the Electoral Commission [Modernizing elections, Electoral Commission 2002]. Out of 30 pilot schemes, 16 were concerned with e-voting applications. All 16 local authorities used electronic counting schemes – 7 of which combined with traditional paper ballots only, 6 provided e-voting in the form of touch-screen voting kiosks, 5 provided internet voting, 3 provided phone (touch tone) voting and 2 SMS text message voting [Pratchett 2002]. This paper identifies the main knowledge and information flows within e-voting as undertaken in the above mentioned pilot projects as well as the new

M.A. Wimmer (Ed.): KMGov 2003, LNAI 2645, pp. 274–284, 2003.

knowledge which was produced during the process. In doing so we indicate how knowledge management could be used to address major issues in e-voting such as security, data protection, transparency and social acceptance. Elections are a government initiated process providing citizens with a service. The product of this process is the electoral result. According to Coleman [Coleman et The Independent Commission of alternative voting methods, 2002] :

" *The public can only be expected to have confidence in the electoral system if it is based upon transparently fair and robust procedures and working methods* "

One of the major issues in the case of e-voting is therefore to gain public confidence in the process as well as its results. In simple terms, citizens and administrative staff must trust any new electoral process introduced. Appropriate knowledge management could provide all interested agents with a better understanding of the new e-voting processes.

This paper is based on the evaluation reports produced following the 2002 pilot projects. The UK 2002 e-voting pilots were the first to be followed by a systematic evaluation and description of the gained experience, where as most existing e-voting reports focus mainly on providing guidelines for future projects [CalTech MIT Voting Technology Project, 2001], [OASIS Election and Voter Services Technical Committee].

We are aware of the vast literature on knowledge management and the equally varied definitions of the term. We use the following as our definition of the concept of knowledge management:

"the identification and analysis of available and required knowledge assets and knowledge asset related processes, and the subsequent planning and control of actions to develop both the assets and the processes so as to fulfill organizational objectives." [Macintosh, 1999]. These knowledge assets can reside in people's heads, in paper documents in filing cabinets, in electronic format, etc. In this paper we focus specially on those assets that have been explicit through knowledge embedded in documents. Dieng-Kuntz and Matta (2002) argue that one of the main objectives of knowledge management is to "improve relationships with the external world (such as customers, or privileged partners" we extend this to include citizens. This 'improvement in relationships' is why we are motivated to consider KM for e-voting.

2 Knowledge Provided to and from the Voters

Prospective voters had to be educated in the use of the newly offered voting channels such as touch screen kiosks, and all three forms of remote voting (internet voting, SMS text, touch tone telephony). The dissemination of passwords, personal identification numbers and voter registration numbers should be regarded as necessary information flow between the administration and citizens, as well as the promotion campaigns which preceded the pilots so as to raise awareness of the pilots actually being conducted and increase turnout

There were indeed some cases in which one could identify some information management efforts. In Chorley [The Electoral Commission Chorley Borough Council p.s.e.[1], 2002] a dedicated website was set up (http://www.chorleyelections.co.uk) .

It provided advice on how to vote, a full list of nominations, interactivity during the count – with results updated as they were announced. The website was linked to the Council's main site and although this pilot was in the area of electronic counting, which meant that citizens voted through the traditional or postal channels, the content of the website also explained the reasons for which the Council was undertaking the pilot scheme. In this case voter education was provided for, although voters did not actually themselves have to use any kind of new voting technology.

However this was not the case in pilots using only touch screen kiosk voting. In Stratford on Avon [Electoral Commission, Stratford on Avon p.s.e.2002], there were no voter education efforts, although the same kiosks had been used in 2000 in the first pilot of its kind in the UK. Nevertheless the 2000 e-voting pilot was on a much smaller scale, therefore in the 2002 elections, voters who had never seen a piece of equipment were called upon to use it. This generated concerns among voters about not knowing who they had actually voted for. In Bolton [Electoral Commission, Bolton Metropolitan Borough p.s.e. ,2002], where the same kiosks were used, road-show demonstrations were organized, and administration staff were issued with a prompt sheet which was used to guide voters through the process. In Chester [Electoral Commission, Chester City p.s.e., 2002] two demonstrations were held and an election website was set up giving details on the pilot and providing results the day after the elections. In contrast, in Newham [Electoral Commission, London Borough of Newham p.s.e.,2002], the Council's website provided links to list of candidates, details of demonstration days, advanced voting locations and more importantly an on-line demonstration of the touch screen unit.

In Swindon [Electoral Commission, Swindon Borough p.s.e,2002], although the scheme included a multiplicity of new voting channels – including kiosk, internet voting and telephone voting – no voter education was provided in a smart form, a lack covered by the use of a help-line and a helpdesk. In St. Albans [Electoral Commission, St. Albans City and District p.s.e.,2002] a comprehensive educational programme was undertaken including a frequently asked questions page on the voting website, and the production and dissemination of a CD-ROM with video and demonstration of the use of new voting methods. In Crewe [Electoral Commission, Crewe and Nantwich p.s.e.,2002] although the pilot was contracted to the same vendors as St.Albans' – BT and Oracle – no similar effort was undertaken. In Liverpool and Sheffield [Electoral Commission, Liverpool City p.s.e. 2002] [Electoral Commission, Sheffield City p.s.e. 2002], a common approach was used – probably because of the use of the same contractors BT-Election.com -. The voting website provided a frequently asked questions page and in both cases a special website was created, targeting young voters providing demonstration of the use of new voting channels using graphics to do so. The Liverpool young voter site (http://www.voteeasyliverpool.co.uk reviewed Nov. 2002) is still active six months after the scheme providing the same context and demonstrations to those potentially interested, therefore contributing to further education of prospective voters.

---

[1] pilot scheme evaluation

Out of the above comparison of practices followed, one can identify the diversity of different approaches. The aim of future research should focus on the effectiveness of each approach and the introduction of best practice guidelines .There is an apparent need for accumulating and managing all the knowledge that a prospective voter may need to :

• Use all new voting channels – technologies – effectively
• Understand the new processes well enough to trust their result

One major input in such an effort is voter feedback. In the case of the recent pilots in question, voters' views on the new methods of voting were gathered by traditional opinion survey methodologies such as exit polls, interviews, mailed questionnaires,

voter comments recorded by help-line operators, a telephone survey conducted by NOP [NOP ,2002] on behalf of the Electoral Commission. Only in the cases of Swindon and Crewe were the voters given the opportunity to fill in an on-line questionnaire.

3 Knowledge Provided to and from Administration Staff

By the term administration staff we mean the Returning Officers, polling clerks, counting staff paid by the local authorities and in general all local authority personnel involved in any stage of conducting the pilots. In all cases where any kind of machinery was used, which administrative staff had to operate (like counting equipment of paper ballots) or instruct voters on how to use (like touch screen kiosks) some training was provided by the technology providers. In Westminster [Electoral Commission, Westminster City p.s.e., 2002] a counting center handbook was produced and in Chester a manual was provided to assist polling staff in the use and processes of operating the touch screen kiosk.

In all evaluation reports surveyed there is no mention of any kind of knowledge gathering from the administrative staff other than anecdotal data. In this case there is an obvious lack of a system to record any experience gained by the staff who operated the voting technology. This in turn prolongs the dependence of local authorities on technology providers and deprives any future staff training exercises of learning based on colleague experience.

4 Knowledge Provided to and from Local Authorities

Regarding the dissemination of results as a procedural information flow towards all interested parties (citizens, candidates, media, political parties) at the end of every electoral process, the main knowledge that local authorities had to offer was their accumulated experience in traditional elections. Nevertheless this was neither structured nor documented knowledge and it was mainly up to experienced staff members to provide their expertise to the project management of the pilots. While this formula provided acceptable results again this was limited to formal and informal consultation rather than organized knowledge management.

However a greater issue arises when looking into the knowledge that was actually provided from the technology providers to the local authorities. In all cases except

Broxbourne [Electoral Commission, Broxbourne Borough p.s.e. 2002] the technology used was provided by an external commercial technology vendor. Although the technology providers engaged their own staff in working along with the administration staff during the whole conduct of the pilots, that does not necessarily mean that the local authorities had a full understanding of how the technology performed the tasks in question whether that be counting, casting the vote or transmitting the data from remote voting to secure data bases. It was therefore due to trust from the local authorities towards the technology providers that it was possible to conduct these pilot projects as was indicated in the Electoral Commissions' general report on the pilots [Modernising Elections 2002]. This issue will be further discussed in the transparency section later on .

5 Security and Data Protection

Security and data protection are closely related to the specific kind of technology used in each e-voting pilot. The following table aims to facilitate the reader's understanding.

Table 1. Technology used in each of the UK e-voting pilots (source DTLR)

	Touch-screen kiosk	Internet	Touch Tone Telephony	SMS Text	e-count
Bolton	*				*
Broxbourne					*
Chester	*				*
Chorley					*
Crewe		*			*
Epping Forrest					*
Hackney					*
Liverpool		*	*	*	*
Newham	*				*
Rugby					*
St Albans	*	*	*		*
S. Tyneside					*
Sheffield	*	*		*	*
Stratford	*				*
Swindon		*	*		*
Westminster					*

In the cases of Westminster and Rugby where the same supplier was contracted [Electoral Commission Westminster p.s.e. 2002, Electoral Commission Rugby p.s.e. 2002] each stage of the vote counting process could be accessed only by authorized staff after scanning a bar coded identity card. Data was stored in an SQL server database regulated by two administrators each holding a 12 character password. The database itself was password protected and a report was run before the start of the count to ensure that there were no pre-loaded votes. However no precaution was taken against access through a default ID created at the time of the installation of the operating system. In Broxbourne [Electoral Commission, Broxebourne p.s.e. 2002] the ballot papers contained a bar code against each candidate's name which was later scanned and logged into a database. Access to the counted votes was allowed to two officials who theoretically could alter the votes with their actions being nevertheless logged. However this process was never conducted and all operators of the system used the same user ID not allowing tractability of their actions.

In Epping Forrest [Electoral Commission Epping Forrest p.s.e. 2002], South Tyneside [Electoral Commission S. Tyneside p.s.e. 2002] and Chorley [Electoral Commission Chorley p.s.e. 2002] where the same counting machinery and result collating software were used, although the software allowed different levels of access to each user this feature was not used. In Stratford [Electoral Commission, Stratford on Avon p.s.e. 2002] and Bolton [Electoral Commission, Bolton p.s.e. 2002] where the same touch-screen voting kiosk was used the data was automatically recorded on a module and later kept for six months to provide an audit trail ; the data on each module were protected and once stored then could not be altered. As the module should be physically detached from the kiosk and transferred to the counting centers physical security was also needed. In the case of Stratford a virtual private network was used to transfer the final results to the Council's intranet. The kiosk used in Chester [Electoral Commission, Chester p.s.e. 2002] and Newham [Electoral Commission, Newham p.s.e. 2002] had a triple data recording system. Each vote was recorded in the machine's flash memory, and to data cartridge and at the end of the vote a print out audit was produced. The merged table – containing the results of all cartridges - was locked to prevent any alterations of the produced results. In the case of Newham three administrators had access rights and another three had "super-user" access rights but the system required two of them being present simultaneously for any changes to be made.

In Swindon [Electoral Commission, Swindon p.s.e. 2002] all voters were provided with 10 digit PINs (personal identification numbers) but a date of birth was also required to allow remote voting. Once the vote was cast it was encrypted and stored in a secure server. The vote was transferred through a secure sockets layer (SSL) system to avoid tampering with the vote until stored to the server (similar to standard e-commerce practice). Data files were date stamped however no encryption was provided over telephone voting and there was no check whatsoever that the technical supplier had recorded the votes correctly.

In St.Albans [Electoral Commission, St.Albans p.s.e. 2002] and Crewe [Electoral Commission, Crewe and Nantwich p.s.e. 2002] voters were issued separately with a 4 digit PIN and a 16 digit VIN (voter identification number) for remote voting. The votes as well as voter information were encrypted and passwords to the UNIX servers were issued to the supplier's staff although different people had access to their relevant part of the software. Firewall and intrusion software was in place and server penetration testing was applied.

A different approach was used in Liverpool {Electoral Commission, Liverpool p.s.e. 2002] and Sheffield [Electoral Commission, Sheffield p.s.e. 2002]. All voters were issued with 6 digit VRNs (voter reference numbers), 8 digit Pins and 10 digit passwords all delivered in the same instance – possibly reducing the security effectiveness of the PIN. Other than that the same security measures were taken as above (standard e-commerce technology), BT being a partner in all four supplier combinations although we cannot be sure about data base security as it was handled by a different supplier (election .com) for which no specifications were given in all the evaluation reports reviewed.

6 Transparency and Social Acceptance

The Representation of the People Act requires that votes cast in UK elections should be traceable, but only in the event of legal challenges to the outcome, for example where there are allegations of malpractice[www.uk-legislation.hmso.gov.uk/acts].

Bearing in mind the above is essential for understanding the context in which the 2002 UK e-voting pilots were devised. We should also make the distinction between the transparency of operation of a process and the transparency of the knowledge that this process produces. In this case the process would be casting the vote or counting the votes cast and the knowledge produced out of this is twofold :

- How was the result produced (the result itself being a data flow)
- Who voted for whom (referring to the possible mishandling of data relating each voter to the candidate of his/her choice for purposes other than judicial)

A further issue to address is the dependence of social acceptance on transparency regarding the first, and understanding of safeguards to protect the second.

In the case of Westminster there were voter concerns about asking them not to fold their ballots – in order to facilitate the electronic counting – as this would undermine the secrecy of their choice. People complained about being too far from the actual place where the counting took place and it was suggested that the bar code on the ballot paper could link it to the voter. Nevertheless this was not the case since the system used had no details of which voter the ballot paper was issued to. Therefore only the local authority had access to that data and only after combining it with voter registration records. Being unable to observe individual ballots was also the case in Hackney. In the cases of S. Tyneside, Epping Forrest and Chorley, trust in the system of counting was developed through demonstration and testing of the machinery and adjudication took place later on for contested ballots. In the cases of Stratford on Avon and Bolton votes were recorded on modules therefore no physical evidence of the votes cast existed. In Bolton trust was gained through demonstration and past use of the kiosk in other elections in the Netherlands and Germany. However in this case too there was no possible connection between the voter and his/her vote as authentication of the voter's identity was done in the traditional way by polling clerks. The touch-screen kiosk used in Chester and Newham did not relate voters to their choice as authentication was done separately but produced a paper audit which increased the possibility of verification.

It is much more interesting though to address the same questions in the cases of remote voting. In Swindon [Electoral Commission, Swindon p.s.e. 2002] the commercial vendor never got to know which PIN related to each voter as the PINs once created were sent to the local authority to attribute to each voter on the register. Vice versa the local authority had no log of the votes cast nor an understanding of how the records were created but only trusted the commercial vendor of fulfilling his part of the deal. In this case voter anonymity was preserved but knowledge of how the result was produced was not transparent. In the cases of St.Albans [Electoral Commission, St.Albans p.s.e. 2002] and Crewe [Electoral Commission, Crewe and Nantwich p.s.e. 2002] neither the process of producing the result was transparent nor voter anonymity was preserved as the database administrators had access to the full data of voters as well as their voting choices, the administrators themselves being employees of the commercial suppliers and not local authority staff. Maybe it is worth mentioning that the commercial suppliers were funded with £1m by the DTLR

(Department of Transport, Local government and the Regions.) although the commercial rights to the application remained with the suppliers.

A pattern similar to the one followed in Swindon was followed in Liverpool and Sheffield [Electoral Commission, Liverpool p.s.e. 2002] [Electoral Commission, Sheffield p.s.e. 2002] . The commercial vendor provided the local authorities with VRNs and in turn these were matched by the local authority to the register. Neither the commercial partner knew the details of the voter related to each VRN, nor did the local authorities know each voter's PIN and password. However the two sets of data were put together on one occasion in order to print the voter polling cards thus creating a record which could relate voters to their choice. The process of producing the result was not transparent nor understandable to all interested parties as the software source code was not open to scrutiny. Testing prior to the official use was conducted to cover for this lack of transparency and improve local authority and candidate trust in the system.

The NOP report clearly indicates that the major obstacle that e-voting has to overcome to gain social acceptance is the voter reservations on the issue of security and fraud [Public opinion in the pilots, 2002]. According to the assessment of the ICAVM[2] [Electoral Reform Society 2002] :

' Scrutiny of the voting and the counting processes is not possible with remote on-line voting to nearly the extent that is possible under the current system. Many of the processes are just not visible in the same way'

It is therefore necessary to promote public awareness of the safeguards in place [Electoral Commission, Modernizing elections, 2002] .

In Swindon a special reference is made in the Commission's report regarding the Deputy Returning Officer and the acceptance that the project gained due to his good leadership. That can also be related to the results of the Council's on-line survey giving high user confidence in the system.

7 Discussion

Out of all the above it is quite evident that local authorities and, in prospective scalable pilots, even larger government organizations, are dependent on the expert knowledge of external commercial technology suppliers. There are however certain issues to be addressed ; the source code of systems is one of them. According to the ICAVM :

'What is clear is that the source code of the system must be made available on an official basis to those who have the qualifications to ascertain just how secure the program really is '

Co-operating on an equal basis with the technology suppliers is one thing while being totally dependent on them – as were most of the local authorities in the examined pilots – is quite another. The legal responsibility for conducting the election remains with the local authority and therefore those in office assume legal accountability as well .

The issue of managing new forms of knowledge is also a matter of great importance.

---

[2] Independent Commission on Alternative Voting Methods

In the case of e-voting, an electronic vote audit trail positioned in the hands of commercial vendors, relating voters to their choice, cannot simply be regarded as a set of data. Knowing who voted for whom is valuable knowledge for political parties, candidates, political analysts, political marketing experts, certain parts of the media (how famous people cast their vote), political activists and any agent with a genuine interest in the outcome of elections. It is therefore rather unethical to trust personal data produced through state administrated processes to commercial suppliers and in general any kind of organization working for financial profit.

The same could be said not only about voter trails but any kind of government produced personal data such as medical records from state hospitals or tax records.

The need is quite obvious ; to regulate the co-operation between technology suppliers and government organisations in the delivery of e-government processes. Furthermore user anonymity must be retained and the new knowledge produced should either be protected from unlawful use or used by accredited organisations to support government functions. The case of distributing disconnected knowledge to different agents seems to be a working solution. The idea of a third trusted party, an independent organization providing its expert knowledge as suggested by the ICAVM or a third party mirroring of the process seems to lead in the right direction.

8 Conclusions

From this analysis of the May 2002 UK Local Authority e-voting pilots, it is possible to identify the following areas of gained experience :

- In the case of electronic voting, regarded as a new e-government service [Electoral Commission, Modernising Elections 2002] prospective users of the newly introduced technology, in this case voters, need to be properly educated in its use. In doing so, knowledge management can provide a comprehensive educational platform so as to convey user familiarity features in ways which will have the maximum effect to the largest number of people. Such efforts should be incorporated in a continuous citizen education planning. It is therefore impossible to do so in the pilot phase of e-voting as strategic decisions have to be made upon which technologies will be followed prior to planning a long term citizen-voter education program.
- The knowledge acquired through the opinion surveys, which was based on after voting experiences of voters who used the new voting channels, can provide invaluable experience in the design and implementation of new e-voting pilots. Up to now, no such effort to organize and structure the voter surveys has been identified.
- The knowledge acquired by the local authority administration staff during these pilots and the experience gained can also provide a comprehensive understanding of what local authorities can expect in future pilots, and educate staff to be used in future electronically enabled elections. Up to now, no such effort to organize and structure the administration staff's knowledge has been identified.
- Local authorities need access to the set of knowledge that commercial suppliers will not provide, in order to be able to audit the process efficiently. If commercial

suppliers do not conform to the ICAVM[3] guidelines about source code being open to scrutiny, using commercial confidentiality reasons, then a knowledge management system under the audit of a third specialized agent would be a first solution.

- Although security and data protection are related to the technology used, the ways of conveying their existence and effectiveness to all interested agents is crucial to the progress of electronic voting.
- Transparency of all procedures, is essential in the implementation of e-government applications especially when the traditional process to be substituted involves a high level of transparency and the ability of the public to scrutinize.
- The greatest risk in the social acceptance of e-voting is the voters' understanding about the security provided and the possibility of fraud and malpractice within the new voting applications. Misunderstanding and total lack of knowledge about the safeguards provided in a process, provide a further area for organized conveying of knowledge not only to voters but also to non-voters (users- non users).
- There is an ethical issue in the matter of trusting non-government agents (commercial partners) with sets of data produced during an e-government process, which could provide knowledge on user preferences (who did one vote for) to non intended third parties. The practice of mirroring processes owned by commercial partners and dividing related data to distributed agents can minimize that risk.

This paper has presented some major issues of knowledge management implications in the field of e-voting. We should however note that as elections are a government motivated process, core e-government applications can benefit from the understanding of all accumulated knowledge gained in the field of e-voting. Further pilots and more over their subsequent evaluation can provide an invaluable resource to this end.

Acknowledgements. We are grateful for the support of ITC staff in critiquing this paper. Particular thanks go to John Fraser and Angus Whyte.

References

1. Dieng-Kuntz, R., and Matta, N. Knowledge Management and Organizational Memories; published by Kluwer Academic Press; 2002
2. HM Government. (2002) In the Service of Democracy – a consultation paper on a policy for electronic democracy. Published by the Office of the e-Envoy, Cabinet Office, London.
3. Macintosh, A., I. Filby and J. Kingston, Knowledge Management Techniques: Teaching & Dissemination Concepts. International Journal of Human Computer Studies (Special Issue on Organizational Memories & Knowledge Management), vol. 51, no. 3, Academic Press, September 1999.
4. The Electoral Commission, pilot scheme evaluation Bolton Metropolitan Borough 2 May 2002, 2002
5. The Electoral Commission, pilot scheme evaluation Broxbourne Borough Council 2 May 2002, 2002

---

[3] Independent Commission on Alternative Voting Methods

6. The Electoral Commission, pilot scheme evaluation Chester City Council 2 May 2002, 2002
7. The Electoral Commission, pilot scheme evaluation Chorley Borough Council 2 May 2002, 2002
8. The Electoral Commission, pilot scheme evaluation Crewe and Nantwich Borough Council 2 May 2002, 2002
9. The Electoral Commission, pilot scheme evaluation Epping Forrest District Council 2 May 2002, 2002
10. The Electoral Commission, pilot scheme evaluation Hackney Council 2 May 2002, 2002
11. The Electoral Commission, pilot scheme evaluation Liverpool City Council 2 May 2002, 2002
12. The Electoral Commission, pilot scheme evaluation London Borough of Newham 2 May 2002, 2002
13. The Electoral Commission, pilot scheme evaluation Rugby Borough Council 2 May 2002, 2002
14. The Electoral Commission, pilot scheme evaluation St Albans City and District Council 2 May 2002, 2002
15. The Electoral Commission, pilot scheme evaluation South Tyneside Metropolitan Borough Council 2 May 2002, 2002
16. The Electoral Commission, pilot scheme evaluation Sheffield City Council 2 May 2002, 2002
17. The Electoral Commission, pilot scheme evaluation Stratford on Avon District Council 2 May 2002, 2002
18. The Electoral Commission, pilot scheme evaluation Swindon Borough Council 2 May 2002, 2002
19. The Electoral Commission, pilot scheme evaluation Westminster City Council 2 May 2002, 2002
20. The Electoral Commission, Modernising Elections : A Strategic Evaluation Of the 2002 Electoral Pilot Schemes, 2002
21. Pratchett, L. " The implementation of electronic voting in the UK " LGA Publications, the Local Government Association, 2002
22. NOP World " Public Opinion In The Pilots 2002, A report summarizing the aggregate findings from surveys carried out by NOP Research in May 2002 In 13 electoral pilots scheme areas', 2002
23. Coleman, S. *et* Independent Commission on Alternative Voting Methods *Elections on the 21st Century: from paper ballot to e-voting* Electoral Reform Society, 2002
24. www.voteeasyliverpool.co.uk as reviewed Nov. 2002
25. CalTech MIT Voting Technology Project, Voting: What is, What Could Be , 2001
26. OASIS Election and Voter Services Technical Committee, Election Mark-up Language (EML): e-Voting Process and Data Requirements, 2002
27. www.edemocracy.gov.uk as reviewed Nov.2002
28. www.uk-legislation.hmso.gov.uk/acts as reviewed Nov.2002

KIWI: Building Innovative Knowledge Management Infrastructure within European Public Administration. The Case of Prefecture of Milan

Lara Gadda[1], Emilio Bugli Innocenti[2], and Alberto Savoldelli[1]

[1]Politecnico di Milano, 20133 Milano, Piazza Leonardo da Vinci 32, Italy
Tel. +39 02 23992796; Fax. +39 02 23992720
lara.gadda@polimi.it
[2]Netxcalibur, 50123 Firenze, via Alamanni 25, Italy
Tel. +39 055 285859; Fax. +39 055 285760
ebi@acm.org

Abstract. The paper is composed by two parts. The first one is to show the main findings of the "as is" process analysis and "to be" process definition in the Prefecture of Milan, one of the users of KIWI project. This allows to present the improvement interventions in order to highlight the main user requirements for KIWI platform. It lets public employees access anywhere and anytime to relevant knowledge, transformed from implicit to explicit, through mobile devices. The second objective is to describe the development stage of KIWI platform that should be used to improve the efficiency and the effectiveness of public organisations. In particular, the project aims at developing innovative, user-relevant, wireless technologies which make the relationship between PA and citizens easier.

1 Introduction

In the last few years, industrialised Countries faced up the necessity of reforming Public Administration (PA), a crucial problem since that context is quickly evolving. The change in progress is moving along two directions: on one hand, the users require a Public Sector's "product" risen in value and, on the other hand, there's the need to provide better services using the same resources [1].

Public Sector reform started with the adoption of a new set of rules which led to the *decentralisation* and the *modernisation* [2], but the mere political rules' transformation is not enough and it is necessary to develop a specific method in order to enhance organisations' performance, efficacy and efficiency [3]. The *technological innovation* and *web oriented technology* are the necessary starting point for improving Public Administration performance. They need to be constantly accompanied by complementary changes in administrative and organisational fields. There is the necessity to use a "*change management*" which should combine with information technology, change of organisation and human resources management [4].

The dynamic environment, where Public Administration operates, requires the need to access information regardless of distance and language, paving the way to make mobile public services affordably and securely available by anyone, anytime and anyplace.

In this context KIWI project, a shared-cost RTD within Information Society Technologies (IST) programme, aims at developing innovative knowledge

M.A. Wimmer (Ed.): KMGov 2003, LNAI 2645, pp. 285–296, 2003.

management (KM) infrastructures able to transform *public administrations* at any level inside Europe into knowledge driven and dynamically adaptive learning organisations and empower public employees to be fully knowledge workers.

The choice of focusing attention on KM arises from the fact that the *Knowledge is more and more becoming the most valuable asset within an administration and KM is the key to the administration reaching its potential.* Each government aims at making information easily accessible to everyone, including citizens, suppliers and partners, and converting that information into knowledge. Knowledge management can provide benefits to an administration's employee. Sharing and reusing intellectual capital increases effectiveness, productivity, and quality in many ways. The KM infrastructures are a *support to remote workforce*: it's essential to help public employees to access important information when they need to make decisions avoiding mistakes and learn from other employees' experience. Indeed, they provide efficient and time-saving solutions: leveraging the knowledge gained from experience enables a better workload distribution within organisations adding value to citizens' services.

The innovation of KIWI project consists of transforming relevant PA services in anywhere and anytime ones, leveraging the PA intellectual capital in their relevant processes, embedding knowledge management in the PA relevant processes and using mobile technology as enabler for managing knowledge in the PA relevant processes. In order to achieve its objectives, the project starts analysing the *user requirements* of the three Public Administrations involved in it: *Prefecture of Milan in Italy, Gironde Department in France and Turku Local Authorities in Finland.* This article focuses its attention on the case of the Prefecture of Milan.

2   The Case of the PREFECTURE of MILAN

The Prefecture of Milan is one of the 103 Italian Prefectures based in Italy depending by the Ministry of the Interior. The Prefectures are the natural liaisons between the central headquarter of the Ministry based in Rome and the local branches of the Interior Administration.

The Prefecture is a local body of the state Administration in charge of general affairs and government representative at provincial level. The chief of the Prefecture is the Prefect who is in charge of the role of mediator with the local Authorities in order to be able to solve citizens' problems. Therefore, the Prefect:

- represents the government at provincial level;
- carries on all functions of a local state administration not conferred on other Offices;
- supervises to the remaining administrative functions carried on by the State, in order to co-ordinate them those carried on by the Local Bodies, directly or through the presidency of the permanent Conference of the officers of the state Offices;
- keeps an eye on the administrative Authorities which operate in the province and replaces them, in case of urgent necessity, adopting the appropriate measures.

With regard to KIWI project, it's important to underline that the Ministry of the Interior and subsequently each Prefecture is especially interested in *making its employees professionals knowledge workers and gaining more efficiency.* Already equipped with laptops and mobile phones, *the public employees are a highly mobile workforce with high information and communication needs.*

Indeed, employees need to communicate each other country-wide, need to exchange data, documents and opinions with other Government administrations at local (municipalities, health care centres, chamber of commerce, police, etc.), regional and national level (pension system bodies, etc). The main benefits from a well-structures knowledge management process will be:

- faster and better informed decision making;
- improved customer service;
- returns on investment as productivity increases;
- innovation further stimulated by capitalising on knowledge and expertise;
- reductions in customer and staff frustration savings in time and effort;
- reductions in costs.

Today, the added value of a Public Administration doesn't consist in the realisation of a series of standard products, administrative acts, but rather in the *orientation towards the citizen-user* and, therefore, in the creation and integration of services which answer to real needs (multifunctional desks, call centres, etc.), in the capability of feeling and interpreting the signals and needs of the environment and in developing on real time innovative solutions by an interactive way. The allocation of the services implies a direct relationship with the citizens-users who are interested to the satisfaction of specific areas of needs.

An undifferentiated manpower, dedicated to routine activities, is not useful; the new Public Administration needs a lower and qualified number of people who are able to provide competence, initiative, know-how and co-operation and innovation ability, referred either to the use of technologies and to the process management or to care of interpersonal relationships. *The human resource is the critical one.* The capability to innovate and increase the quality and reduce costs and answer times depends not only on material, financial and technological investments, but also on the immaterial ones: on the people, on their training, on the relationship system and on the organisation culture.

3   Presentation of the "As-Is" Analysis

The Prefecture of Milan could be divided in five sectors: *Cabinet Office, sector I, sector II, sector III, the decriminalisation.* Each sector is characterised by several activities. KIWI project focuses its attention on the crucial ones as identified in table 1. The choice of the core activities has been done on the basis of the following elements:

- *volume of work*: this means the activity is relevant for the sector;
- *presence of less standardised format*: this means the realisation of a Knowledge Management System can help the employees in their work;
- *interaction with Bodies which are external to the PAs involved in the project*: this means there is the possibility to interact through the mobile devices.

It is possible to identify six classes of knowledge that result indispensable for PREFECTURE activities. The matrix, reported in table 2, shows the correspondences between knowledge and activities. This is just an indicative representation, because generally the activities are not completely separate and also various knowledge present some overlapping areas.

Table 1. The core activities in PREFECTURE of Milan

		Protection civil	Rent of barracks	Vigilance Institutions	Explosives	Driving licence sanction	Drug administration	Juridical status acknowledge	Recurrence to violations	Legal department	Immigration procedure
	Cabinet Office	✓									
SECTOR OF PREFECTURE	Sector I		✓	✓	✓						
	Sector II					✓	✓	✓			
	Decriminalisation								✓	✓	
	New activity										✓

The *operative rules* are, for their own objectives, explicit and easily transferable. This knowledge is structured, almost fix, and can be easily communicate to employees. These rules are fix in the sense that they are rarely changed, because once a procedure is accepted it normally passes quite long time before to modify it.

The distinction between operative rules and Best Practices is very weak, in general it can be said that *Best Practices* become directly from the experience on particular problems, so they are generally less structured and verified, and they need some common background and/or context explanation to be properly understood. Moreover, this knowledge is continuously developing, depending on the actual needs and activities of various sectors.

The *basic information* and the *in-depth knowledge* of laws and rules required are other two examples of explicit, mainly fix, and easily transferable knowledge. Currently, various sectors have already arrange manuals and reference documents to collect this information and support the training and the daily activity of each activity.

The *historical data* are a whole of data and information that are used for various activities. In general, these are explicit and well structured information, so they are easily storable and transferable, even if these data are continuously developing and increasing.

The *experience* is the most difficult to manage because of its complexity. In fact, it is a whole of information that help the employees (usually at high level) to take the best decision on line with the context. In general, these are tacit and not well structured information, so they are hardly storable and transferable, also because these data are continuously developing and increasing.

Finally, *legal competencies* are often maintained at an informal level, even when it could be explicated, because it requires a certain effort to formalise and explicate it. Moreover, it's a developing knowledge, continuously increased and enriched by new experiences, new studies, or new situation. This requires an additional effort for maintaining information and knowledge constantly updated, otherwise it would lose its usefulness. At the same time, these competencies are quite difficult to communicate and transfer, because they need a specific and professional background to be understood.

Table 2. The Knowledge-Activities matrix in PREFECTURE of Milan

		Protection civil	Rent of barracks	Vigilance Institutions	Explosives	Driving licence sanction	Drug administration	Juridical status acknowledge	Recurrence to violations	Legal department	Immigration procedure
		ACTIVITIES									
KIND OF KNOWLEDGE	Operat rules & Best Practices	✓	✓	✓	✓	✓	✓	✓	✓	✓	✓
	Basic inform	✓				✓					✓
	In-depth knowledge		✓	✓	✓	✓	✓	✓	✓	✓	✓
	Historical data	✓			✓	✓		✓	✓	✓	
	Experience	✓	✓	✓		✓	✓	✓			✓
	Legal competencies									✓	✓

A first aspect to be underlined is the frequent use of informal methods to diffuse and share knowledge. Inside each sector, people have regular reunions and meetings, plus the possibility to co-operate for particular activities and to ask experts for any doubt. All these activities are positive and necessary, especially for creating a common vision and behaviour inside the sector, for strengthening relations and for motivation purposes, but they are not the most efficient solutions to diffuse explicit knowledge.

Training courses are not obligatory. In this case each sector is autonomous, but it's generally difficult to organise these courses because of the public expenditures and permits. Consequently sectors can't organise a course for any new employee. The most common solution is to collect relevant information in papery manuals and documents that are given to the new employees, then the core part of the training is "on the job" and new employees learn from the most experienced ones. Concerning manuals and documents, it's important to note that generally each sector has its own material that is not shared with other sectors. The consequence of this behaviour is the lack of uniformity among sectors and the duplication of many activities, since each sector dedicates time to prepare its own documents.

The table 3 resumes the outcomes of the "as-is" analysis of Knowledge Management process using the approach of the SWOT (Strengths, Weaknesses, Opportunities, and Threats) analysis. This allows to highlight the strength and weakness points of the organisation concerning Knowledge Management, but also to underline the opportunities that could be exploited and the threats that should be faced in introducing KIWI platform and new managerial approaches.

Table 3. Knowledge Management SWOT analysis in PREFECTURE of Milan

Strength points and Opportunities	Weakness points and Threats
☞ PREFECTURE is quite used to collect and store data and information	☞ Explicable knowledge is often maintained in implicit form
☞ The most part of relevant data/knowledge can be easily explicated and formalised	☞ Knowledge is not shared among the organisation
☞ PREFECTURE generates useful and value-added knowledge	☞ Internal communication is quite poor and the sectors are not used to co-operate
☞ The PREFECTURE offices collaborate with many external bodies. Therefore, there is the opportunity to share the knowledge and information through mobile devices	☞ Training activities are mainly informal with loss of effectiveness
	☞ IT tools are little diffuse inside PREFECTURE and currently used tools are little suitable for supporting knowledge diffusion
	☞ A lot of knowledge/documents are in papery format

4   Presentation of the "To-Be" Process

The objectives of the improvement intervention on *Knowledge Management* in PREFECTURE could be resumed in five major points:

- to increase the efficiency of the knowledge management process, eliminating duplicate and inefficient activities;
- to increase the usefulness and the effectiveness of existent knowledge, improving its diffusion and usage;
- to favour the communication and the sharing of knowledge among different public bodies, facilitating the co-operation;
- to increase the uniformity among sectors, introducing common methods of work to ensure high quality services;
- to facilitate the organisation of training courses and improve their effectiveness.

Various instruments and interventions are necessary to reach these objectives, also because each typology of knowledge requires proper solutions. In general, it's possible to identify four major kind of interventions:

- a *standardisation intervention*, aimed at increasing the formalisation of information facilitating the processes of explication, collection, storing and diffusion of knowledge;
- the *definition of rules and procedures* common to all sectors, in order to increase the uniformity of action, obtain a common quality level, and facilitate co-operation and co-ordination among bodies;

- the introduction of *proper electronic databases* for collecting, storing, and sharing information in an effective and efficient way. These "repositories of knowledge" should be useful also for training the new employees;
- the introduction of the use of the *new mobile devices and methods of work* aimed at increasing and supporting information sharing and co-operation among bodies.

More specifically, the standardisation intervention is the first step for the introduction of proper electronic databases. At this moment, some sectors have already developed their own database that generally are simple Excel or Access databases made by employees. The possibilities of these systems are quite limited and, most of all, they are not shared among other sectors and public bodies. What KIWI plans to do is the introduction of proper Knowledge Warehousing system that allows to store various kind of knowledge, to make queries, researches and statistical analysis on stored data, and to share them inside the whole Public Administration.

Analysing the specific reality of PREFECTURE, the standardisation process appears to be necessary mainly for *operative rules*, together with the definition of common and shared rules for all bodies involves in a specific activity to increase the uniformity of action and quality, *basic information*, *in-depth knowledge* and *historical data*. The output will be a *series of databases* and *common procedures* that could be used for the daily activities, for the training courses, for making specific researches and analyses, and for substituting current reference manuals that are different for each sector.

On the whole, this intervention will increase the uniformity among sectors and public bodies facilitating co-ordination and co-operation, but will also improve the overall efficiency through the elimination of duplicated activities and a more effective access to information. In addition, the proposed system shall permit the realisation of statistical analysis and researches, especially, but not only, for the historical data. This will add further value to the data stored in the database, increasing the advantage of their use.

Concerning *experience* and *Best Practices*, it has been already told that this is a more complex and partially not explicable knowledge. In this case the improvement intervention aims at developing adequate databases to collect this know-how and proper methods of work for increasing their diffusion inside the whole Public Administration.

The databases for this kind of knowledge haven't to be too rigid, even if a minimum of structure is necessary for effectively retrieving stored information. The better solution will be probably the definition of *electronic databases* where to insert various kind of documents, that will be mainly texts, but also images. Afterward, a full text research system is necessary, for effectively retrieving information among stored documents independently from their structure. This solution facilitates the use of the database, because it doesn't bind the possibilities of data insertion and, at the same time, ensures a good effectiveness for the research phase.

Nevertheless, a database can store only those knowledge and information that can be explicate and described in a written document, however correlated by images or photos. For those know-how that can't be completely explicated because is too related to specific competencies or to the context, the better solution is to provide a list of "internal experts" and proper mobile tools for supporting direct communication, as internal e-mail, electronic forums, or systems for video-conferencing. This systems allow people to directly discuss various cases and situations, sharing those part of knowledge that can't be put in a database. Obviously, this system is useful and valuable not inside the single sector, where people can directly meet and co-operate, but most of all among various public bodies, to increase knowledge diffusion and sharing inside the whole organisation, with the final result to increase its overall knowledge and the quality of services.

4.1 The Improvement Plan

Once the possible interventions for improving the Knowledge Management process inside PREFECTURE has been defined, it's necessary to translate these ideas and suggestions in operative plans that shall be then implemented.

Due to the specificity to the public sector, it could be preferable to limit the breadth of the interventions in order to easily manage it and increase the probability of a success. At the same time, it's important to produce real and tangible results for the considered organisation, and this is not possible with a too small field of intervention. In the case of PREFECTURE the better solution seems to be to concentrate the attention on one of the main activities, *the immigration procedure*.

This solution allows to analyse different kind of knowledge and includes all the typologies of intervention described above (actually, the knowledge of the historical data is not indicated, but only because the activity is a new one for the Prefecture. In the future also the knowledge of the historical data will be essential). On the same time, concentrating the effort on a specific activity, the analysis and intervention phases are simpler and the final results will be more tangible and verifiable. The table 4 reports the reasons for choosing this field of intervention and the expected results for it:

Table 4. Reasons and objectives of the fields of intervention

	Reason of the chose	Objectives of the intervention
Immigration procedure	☞ It represent s an innovative process since it is a new activity also for the Prefecture; ☞ It involves different kind of people characterised by different knowledge. Each of them is in charge of a part of the whole procedure; ☞ It offers the opportunity to use the mobile technologies	✓ To increase the efficient and the effectiveness of the service; ✓ To obtain uniform and high standards of quality; ✓ To ensure an high level of users satisfaction

4.2 User Requirements for KIWI Platform

It is now possible to define the User Requirements of PREFECTURE of Milan for the KIWI platform as indicated in table 5:

Table 5. User Requirements of Prefecture of Milan for KIWI Plat

Relevant characteristics	Intervention Objectives	User Requirements
Great information and knowledge: procedure by procedure, the experience grows up and it" essential to allow its transfer to all employees	• Help remote workforce to access important information when they need to make decisions avoiding mistakes and learn from other employees' experience	• Support to remote workforce
Wrong workload distribution within organisation; no addition of value to client (citizens, businesses) service	• Increase the efficiency, reducing duplicated activities, sharing best practices, automating some repetitive or easy activities, introducing IT tools	• Efficient and time-saving solutions
Difficult communications and information exchange among Public Bodies	• Increase the sharing of data and information inside and among the Public Bodies; • Facilitate the internal communication	• Support asynchronous and long distance communications; • Provide a safe, common environment where to share documents
Tendency to maintain the knowledge implicit	• Facilitate the formalisation, the storing, and the diffusion of the know-how	• Introduce of proper databases and document management systems; • Manage both structured and non-structured data; • Use of a full text research system for retrieving information
Difficulty in organising the training courses for the new employees	• Use the stored know-how and the communication facilities for improving the training courses	• Definition and use of standard training modules with proper support documentation
Difficulties in measuring organisational performances and citizens satisfaction	• Introduce instruments and methodologies for measuring the performance of the organisation and citizens/supporter satisfaction	• Powerful databases of people; • Statistical and analysis capabilities
Low familiarity with IT tools	• Increase the usability and easiness of the proposed solution	• Friendly and simple interface; • Efficient assistance service

5 KIWI System Architecture

The KIWI platform will be structured around the following items:

- A web-based *Intranet Knowledge Warehousing* Toolset that will allow to build a wirelessly accessible knowledge warehouse. The knowledge warehousing will amass *internal* and *external knowledge*;
- A *Mobile Collaborative Environment* to support a realistic collaboration and knowledge sharing and transferring also among geographically distributed workforces, within and between public administrations. It will represent the convergence of technologies such as multimedia document/image management, videoconferencing, and mobile 3G technologies helping public administrations transcend all sorts of boundaries by *making available the right information to the right employee at the right place and at the right time*.

5.1 The Components

The KIWI platform is based on a *Intranet Knowledge Warehousing* Toolset. These tools will allow to build a wirelessly accessible knowledge warehouse (knowledge resources will includes manuals, letters, responses from citizens/companies, news, technological, organisational, legal and other relevant information from administrations, as well as knowledge derived from work processes) applications that support inter-organisational learning process.

At the hearth of the system lies the information hierarchy which acts as the conceptual/semantic glue linking our Knowledge Warehouse. Surrounding this core, the XHTML, the new XML-based W3C/WAP standard for wireline and wireless information and Java agents technologies will stand.

The final layer of this processing layer will contain the needed tools to support Knowledge Warehousing activities, and namely, the *Browsing*, *Query* (support ad-hoc queries, reporting and analysing information, which will rely on existing OnLine Analytical Processing systems) the *Smart Profiling*, and the *Suggesting Engine*.

The KIWI Knowledge Warehouse will be set to deliver the right information to the right employee at the right place and at the right time.

The Browsing Tool will allow for locating and accessing information throughout the Knowledge Warehouse. Client applications consulting catalogues will access both information and meta-information so as to achieve a full multimedia (including video, audio, image, text, web pages, CAD & GIS, etc.) Knowledge Warehousing functionality.

The KIWI Smart Profiling Engine will drive any specific content from employee records and interests. KIWI will combine rule-based (ie, using pre-specified rules to take action), collaborative filtering (ie, by automatically comparing attributes of one set of employee data with other employees, suggesting ideas for personalisation).

The KIWI *Suggesting Engine* will analyse each employee's feedback and generates their profile, which it refines further and further. It will use its learning to recommend information items appropriate to each employee's record, tastes and preferences.

The second Tool which composes the KIWI platform is the *KIWI Mobile Collaborative Environment*. The Groupware can help Public Administrations transcend all sorts of boundaries. Geography, time and organisational structure fade in importance in the groupware-enabled process.

At the same time, mobile technologies are increasingly penetrating businesses, offering anytime/anyplace access to enterprise information. The novelty of the KIWI approach lies in the convergence of these two technologies.

The challenge of Mobile Groupware Tool development within KIWI is twofold:

- firstly, to allow for web-based, mobile groupware by supporting both *synchronous* (ie, real-time interaction such videoconferencing, chatting, electronic whiteboard, etc.) and *asynchronous* (ie, email, group discussions, etc.) communication, including live video/audio/text communications. The foreseen work will be centred around the metaphor of a mobile sharable desktop, storing artefacts that are related to projects, such as documents and reports and organising communication between group and team members through the organisation of email, messaging and calendar management. Additionally, automated wireless workflows on-the-fly set up will be also crucial not only to automate repetitive tasks but also to tracking and incorporating employee comments and feedback within the process;
- secondly, to take full advantage of the Knowledge Warehousing tools, by integrating mobile groupware facilities within the KIWI Toolset. *This will lead to set up of a full Mobile Collaborative Environment.*

The project will look at the recent advancements in the mobile groupware standardisation such as the GroupDX initiative, proposing an industrial grade XML Document Type Definitions (DTDs) and Object Schemata for Internet groupware applications. This new standard, called Groupware Mark-up Language (GML), is being established in order to facilitate data exchange among the various groupware applications, and facilitate data synchronisation among groupware applications and their individual counterparts.

6 Conclusions

The KM will result into a decisive improvement in inserting an information database. This allows the public employees to access easier to the needed data, independently from the place where they are.

Concerning the exploitation of project outcomes for the industrial component of the Consortium, this will mainly result in the commercialisation of the prototypes produced within the project. Indeed, all prototypes will be used as basic elements to develop and produce marketable results: as in-house developments by each partner and in collaboration with project partners. A quick process of research transfer in production will assure to the Consortium partners an essential competitive advantage for a further consolidation of the respective positions on the market. Moreover, the specific techniques implemented in the project will be used by most of the Partners to enhance the techniques already in use, contributing to consolidate a competitive advantage.

Once the innovative technologies are implemented, the idea is to realise a mobile groupware which let in-house functions be used at distance. It involves an organisation and a management changes between headquarter and branches.

Within this structure, the willingness of the Public Authorities involved in the project to provide a common exploitation of the project results, constitutes the cornerstone of the KIWI Exploitation Strategy.

References

[1] AIPA, "La reingegnerizzazione dei processi nella pubblica amministrazione", (1999)
[2] Klages, H., Loffler, E., "Administrative modernisation in Germany – a big qualitative jump in small steps", International Review of Administrative Sciences, pp. 373–384, (1995)
[3] Hammer, M., Champy, J., "Reengineering The Corporation: A Manifesto for Business Revolution", HarperCollins, New York, (1993)
[4] Osborne, D., Gaebler, T., "Reinventing Government. How the entrepreneurial spirit is transforming the public sector", New York, Plume, (1993)

Business Process Modelling and Help Systems as Part of KM in E-government

Alexandra Dörfler

Chief Information Office, Austria
alexandra.doerfler@cio.gv.at

Abstract. According to the e-Europe Action plan all traditional government services, where citizens are in contact with different public institutions have to be online by the year 2005. E-government services differ from the traditional services offered by administrations in many ways. Therefore these new processes have to be modelled, preferably using special software. Business Process Modelling is a part of Knowledge Management because understanding the processes is the basis of an organisation's knowledge. Using online services will cause a need for special "help-mechanisms" for both citizens and administrations in "one-stop-shops": Help Systems will support the users of online-services during their use. Presenting some case studies this paper will show the first steps in Business Process Modelling and adapting Help Systems for e-government scenarios in Austria.

1 Introduction

The implementation of e-government via online transactions in case of the traditional ways of interaction between administration and citizen calls for an extensive reorganisation of all government processes.[1]

"Opening" of these procedures is a main characteristic: procedures that have been handled internally so far will be handled by an external customer on the portal level.

Both the citizen and the civil servant need structured and accurate knowledge about the underlying processes, the procedures and competences for the implementation and application of these new processes.

The question is not "which division is responsible for the process" but "which processes are executed by whom within the process-chain". The mostly functional orientation of the internal organisation of administrative units must be considered. Government procedures must be examined concerning the possibility of non intervention by the person in charge. This reduces the expenditure and accelerates the procedures´ running time. (e.g. *electronic criminal record*: usually no intervention of the person in charge concerning online application, online payment and online notification)

---

[1] Government processes are processes where the interests of customers/citizens are accomplished. The main features are customer-orientation, usefulness concerning the duration of the procedure, *amount of administration contacts* etc.

M.A. Wimmer (Ed.): KMGov 2003, LNAI 2645, pp. 297–303, 2003.

In case of any ambiguity in executing online transactions the conception and planning of help-mechanisms for both citizens and the administration is already a big challenge. These mechanisms shall support the users while utilising e-government procedures and when they have problems with the operation of the application system. As these procedures are often used outside office hours, mechanisms that are time- and location independent are required.

Business process modelling of e-government procedures is the basis for an understanding of the mostly complex target-processes and the design of Help – mechanisms.

This paper will deal with some aspects of knowledge management in e-government. The first steps in Business Process Modelling and the design of help-systems in Austria will therefore be illustrated.

2 General Aspects of Business Process Modelling and Help Systems

2.1 Business Process Modelling (BPM)

2.1.1 Changes in the Future

E-Government will change the administration processes. In the future the citizen will – instead of the official in charge – execute the procedure. Therefore the procedures have to be oriented according to the citizens' view. Furthermore these procedures have to be designed process-oriented, the administrations´ functional orientation has to be considered not too much respectively adjusted to the new processes.

Besides online applications also processable attachments (XML) are available and will allow a much higher level of automatisation. Automated exchange of data with other government procedures is another module to reduce the administrations´ intervention.

Online electronic payment of administrative fees occurring in a procedure is user-friendly and a factor for the reduction of the running time.

Electronic notifications (XML) with electronic signatures are another milestone in the e-government lifecycle. These notifications can be processed automatically in other government procedures. The question of electronic delivery has not been solved yet but is also a main part of the new e-government strategies.

2.1.2 BMP in the Context of Knowledge Management

The design and revision of business processes is the subject of BPM. In the course of a process knowledge is currently generated. At the same time the process accesses on knowledge.

Knowledge about the process, the different functions and their coherences is called process knowledge. This knowledge can be used for optimising, customer orientation and acceleration of the process. Knowledge needed for a certain step of the process is called functional knowledge.

The integrated management of knowledge and processes can be defined as administration and control of organisational processes. Besides there are a certain abilities, skills and knowledge generated.

2.1.3 Why BPM?

In many parts of the administration the actual processes are documented inadequately. The complex processes cannot be redesigned by one person alone. Different divisions of an organisation like operating department, IT department and often consultants have to work together. The use of software tools facilitates communication for the members of the "process-management-team".

Transparent procedures allow the concerned persons to understand the processes and coherences. Every concerned person identifies his or her task along the process chain (citizen, system, administration).

Documenting and analysing the organisations´ processes is the basis for efficient organisational knowledge. Graphical illustration brings objectivity and clarity.

Reduction of costs can only be achieved when knowing the potential of economisation which is located by analysing and possibly simulating the target process model in comparison with the actual process model.

2.1.4 Software Tools

For the modelling of simple processes a graphic tool like MS Visio is sufficient. The majority of processes deal with complex processes where a business process management tool is necessary. BMP software supports the analysis, the modelling of the processes, documentation and simulation of business processes, organisational structures and information systems with integrated aspects activity-based costing etc.

The amount of BPM software offered is high. They differ extremely in functional range and complexity. Some of these tools are already in use in the Austrian administration (e.g. ARIS, Adonis). The focus should be put on user friendliness, to enable also non specific users who do normally not have a good knowledge of these tools to work with them.

Main characteristics of a BPM software tool are the following modules; modelling and optimisation of processes, where optimising comprises the possibility of simulation and analysis of workload. Standard interfaces (import/export) to workflow management software on the one hand and to office products for documentation and acquisition of data on the other hand as well as support in making the documentation are desirable. Finally far-reaching flexibility in configuration is important to adjust the software to the specific needs of public administration.

2.2 Help Systems

Some years ago Help Systems were printed handbooks where the users could look for the desired information. Later they were the first online handbooks.

"Help" in e-government procedures can be manifold; it reaches from expert-systems, to call centres, web-phone, virtual agents (these are programmes that present different topics, lead trough a guided-tour or answer to questions of users), forums, chats, newsgroups (moderated or not), FAQs and collaborative desktops (which is the collaborative working on a specific case/procedure, collaborative browsing or filling in of government forms).

Modern Help systems offer besides different search mechanisms in the system context-sensitive help (Information to the input field). The answers delivered help the users to avoid timely search activities, but they do not always answer the question raised originally.

Many requests come from the applications that are not designed user-friendly. IT-designers do not often realize the difficulties for non-experienced users that arise from insufficiencies of the system.

Modern Help-mechanisms allow the free formulating of questions in original spoken language. These systems are self-learning[2], once a question is answered (e.g. by the call center) it is integrated in the system as answer for future questions concerning the same topic. By collecting these questions and requests FAQs are generated, administered and updated automatically. These systems are able to cover a high amount of help-requests after a short introduction period, because usually a limited number of different requests have occurred in a certain period of time. The level of automatisation determines the size of the call center. When users do not get a satisfying answer via these mechanisms the request should be routed to the call center where in a first step a written dialogue with a call center agent via chat-mechanisms should take place. Future answers are generated and can be processes automatically by the system.

Help-text-blocks that are normally provided in e-government sites are often not applicable and do not support the citizen. Therefore the drop-out rates are high, because once a citizen was not able to do her or his government procedures online she or he will choose again the traditional way of interaction with the administration. Users with these experiences will avoid e-government procedures for a very long time.

3   Case Studies /Pilot Projects

3.1   E-scholarship (BPM)

This project was initiated by Microsoft and Siemens. The company offered the Austrian administration to support the implementation of new e-government procedures.

The reasons for choosing *"e-scholarship"* were the high level of e-skills of students, a high amount of penetration of the student card and that a large number of public access points will be installed in the university institutes in the future. The goal was to have a signed electronic application for a scholarship for a student until fall 2003. Also the act ruling scholarships was one of the first who allowed applying for scholarship by electronic means using secure electronic signatures. To deliver first results for this date the e-application was based on the traditional (paper-) application

---

[2] Definition: a special capability of a device or machine such that it can improve its capability in decision-making as programmed with instructions and based on information received, new instructions received, results of calculations or environmental change.

which means that the order of entry masks in the e-application was adjusted to the "single steps" in the traditional application.

In the course of the implementation of *"e-scholarship"* the project and working group "BPM of e-scholarship" started. This was argued with the changing of processes in the "scholarship authority" because of e- scholarship. The analysis of the business processes was done by documenting the facts and by examining the entry masks that already existed. Interviews with the persons in charge showed that some of them had different views about the scholarship-procedure. By visualising the procedure with a software tool and by common description of the fact the team agreed on a common view. Most of the time was spent on discussion.

3.1.1 Results

Phase 1
- The order of entry masks for the initial application was changed.
- Facts and basic data were queried and acquired only once.
- Data exchange with other authorities has to be considered and established.
- Due to the fact that the application is very complex, the aspects of overview and storage have to be considered.
- Once data has been saved and displayed later, the problem of identification arrises.
- Data from other procedures have to be requested and provided online.
- The question of signing of notifications is still unsolved.

Phase 2
- The procedure was modelled as an online dialogue from application to notification.
- Data of the Population Register, the social security insurance, income data of the financial authorities and data (study success, etc.) of the university were integrated.
- First thoughts were spent on automatic processing of the procedure without any intervention of the administration.
- The possibility of requesting the status of the procedure for the student is planned.

Phase 3
- Data saved once can only be displayed with secure identification; therefore the use of the citizen card is unavoidable.
- This applies also to the requesting the status of the procedure.
- The initial application was structured in several blocks which consist of several pages. Additional mechanisms are necessary for navigating trough the application. A survey-mask is necessary.
- The data must be signed electronically at the end.

3.2 Finanz-Online (Help System)

As already mentioned before Help-text-blocks that are normally provided in e-government sites are often not applicable and do not support the citizen. Therefore the drop-out rates are high, users with these experiences will avoid the e-government procedures for a very long time.

"Finanz-online" (http://www.bmf.gv.at/egov/fonline/_start.htm) is the method of electronic data transfer within the Austrian financial administration based on Internet technology. Citizens can to do their tax adjustments since the beginning of 2003.

It was planned to install a proactive help-system based on a knowledge database for *"Finanz-online"*. A help-system like this is independent of the application system and is linked at specific positions. All standard help-texts can either remain in the application system or be integrated in the independent help-system.

The questions and answers occurring when working with the application are developed with a determined number of users during the pilot-phase and are then released for operation. The application can supply a customer-friendly help-system: all requests can be answered.

Another aspect of knowledge-based Help-mechanisms is the possibility of free formulating of questions which means that the user does not have to navigate trough a help-system and look for the corresponding answers but that he can formulate with his own words and terms his question. He must not be aware of "administrative language". The user gets a list of 1-n corresponding answers (percentage of probability) and selects one answer. Additionally he clicks if the answer was suitable for him. With this information the system can self-learning build up knowledge; FAQs are generated automatically.

The reason why this project has not yet started is the high licence fee for software and the consulting fees for the implementation of the Help-Mechanisms.

4 Conclusion

E-Government means an enormous change for the administration and for the authorities on all levels.

By the end of 2002 the administration was not yet fully aware of the importance of Business Process Modelling and of the designing of help-systems for planned e-government services.

BPM must be started as soon as possible. The later a BPM-project starts, the more resistance comes from persons and organisations involved. BPM of e-government procedures is the basis for the understanding of these very complex processes and a basic requirement for the design of help-systems.

Awareness must be raised among the Administration showing the advantages of BPM software tools. The Austrian Chief Information Office is promoting the use of BPM-software and will assist interested administrative units in working with these tools. Future projects are BPM for "paperless foreign trade administration" and for "Criminal record".

To meet the goals of the e-Europe Action plan government services have to be online by the year 2005. Complex e-government procedures must be designed using BPM software to reduce the procedures` running time, to reduce the administrations` expense and to run automatically.

Complex procedures must also be supported with the use of help-systems, based on knowledge about these processes. The two pilot-projects presented were the first in this new area. Many others will follow to make e-government successful.

References

1. Federal Ministry of Public Service and Sports, Autria, 17.9.2002, „ Bilanz der Verwaltungs-reform"
2. Bullinger, Hans-Jörg, Fraunhofer IAO, Knowledge meets Process, Stuttgart 2001
3. Meir, Joel „Prozessmanagement als Grundlage für integriertes eGovernment", Bulletin des Kompetenzzentrums eGovernment der Berner Fachhochschule, «eGov Präsenz» Ausgabe 02/2001
4. Schaffroth, Marc, „Welches Informationsmanagement braucht eGovernment?, Bulletin des Kompetenzzentrums eGovernment der Berner Fachhochschule, «eGov Präsenz» Ausgabe 02/2001
5. Seifried, Patrick, Eppler J., Martin, Evaluation führender Knowledge Management Suites; NetAcademy Press, 2000
6. Traunmüller, Lenk, „Electronic Government" First International Conference, EGOV 2002, Aix-en Provence, Sept. 2002
7. Wimmer, Maria, Wissensmanagement in eGovernment, Bulletin des Kompetenzzentrums eGovernment der Berner Fachhochschule, «eGov Präsenz» Ausgabe 01/2001
8. Wimmer Maria, 2002, Tagungsband zum ersten egov Day des Forums egov.at.

A Knowledge Management System for E-government Projects and Actors

Roberta Morici, Eugenio Nunziata, and Gloria Sciarra

Irso-Butera e Partners, Via Maria Cristina, 2, 00196, Rome, Italy
{morici, nunziata, sciarra}@irso-bep.it

Abstract. The paper presents a knowledge management system designed for the Italian Department of Technology and Innovation (Dipartimento per l'Innovazione e le Tecnologie, www.mininnovazione.it)[1]. The Department need is to promote the realization of e-government projects on a local basis, supporting all actors involved in the design and implementation of e-government projects in Italy. In the pursue of this objective, the Department needs at the same time to maintain consistence among e-government projects, without restricting the freedom of Local Authorities, who are autonomous in carrying out their projects. In this scenario, a knowledge management system has been designed to support work and knowledge sharing for all actors involved, who will have a chance to re-use experiences, to be guided in the projects implementation, and to join a community of people involved in e-government projects. Since the system is oriented to support different groups of users, for each of them a specific online environment has been designed. Members of departmental e-government projects, innovators within Local Authorities, Internet users, all have the chance to share resources on e-government: the higher involvement, the more resources are available. At the core of the system, there are private rooms designed as working environments for those strictly involved in an e-government project. Together with the design of the km system, the project faced the issues of the organisational framework for maintaining the content and of community building among users.

1 Problem Setting

At the beginning of 2002 the Italian Government, through the Department of Innovation and Technology[2], launched a call for proposals for e-government projects addressed to Regional and Local Authorities. The call for proposal was aimed at funding projects based on cooperation among different levels of local Authorities. After the assignment of funds, Local Authorities are now in the position of carrying

---

[1] The project has been carried out by a team lead by Giulio De Petra (Department of Technology and Innovation) and composed by Stefano Kluzer, Piero Luisi, Luca De Pietro (Formez) and Eugenio Nunziata, Roberta Morici, Gloria Sciarra (Butera e Partners).

[2] The Department of Innovation and Technology– www.mininnovazione.it - provides support to the Ministry for Innovation and Technologies. The Ministry acts in the areas of technological innovation, the development of the information society and related innovations for government, citizens and businesses.

M.A. Wimmer (Ed.): KMGov 2003, LNAI 2645, pp. 304–309, 2003.

out the approved projects. For the purpose of providing them with appropriate support, specific organisational units have been introduced by the Department, called *Regional Competence Centres* (RCC). Their mission is to help Local Authorities in the implementation phase and to guarantee integration between different projects carried out in different areas of the Country. The RCC are mixed teams formed by both people from each regional area and people from the central government.

Although Local Authorities are autonomous in carrying out their projects, the Central government needs to maintain consistence among them without restricting their freedom. In this scenario the knowledge management system is created in order to support actors in keeping in contact, sharing resources, approaches, solutions and problems occurring in the implementation of e-government projects.

The benefit for Local Authorities is to have a chance to re-use experiences, to be guided in the implementation, to join a community of people involved in e-government projects, to discuss and share problems and solutions. Specific goals of the KM system are:

- Create a network of all actors involved in e-government and information society projects, and support community building among them: Central and Local Governments, providers, professionals, researchers, etc;
- Provide a reserved workspace for RCC involved in supporting Local Authorities;
- Give visibility to resources on e-government and the information society in Italy in terms of documentation, events, discussions, hot issues, updates;
- Give visibility to the variety of projects and approaches on e-government implemented in different areas of the country.

2 The Design Approach

The design of the km system has followed an approach focused on two dimensions:

Fig. 1. The picture shows the concept of the KM system.

Content management issues have been addressed focusing on the creation of a knowledge map. The knowledge map represents a framework of keywords to classify, organise, access and retrieve all resources around the domain of e-government and the information society.

The map has been designed ad hoc for this system since no similar map was existing so far within the Department and the Ministry.

The map is a flexible tool, always evolving in order to follow the evolutions of the topic (e.g. introduction of new concepts or applications of e-government). It consists of four main domains which can be combined in order to classify each available resource in the system:

- *"Type of Project"* – the topics of e-government and information society projects
- *"What to do"* – Steps for the planning and implementing e-government and information society projects
- *"How to do"*- Tools, both technological and organisational, to carry out e-government and information society projects
- "Where to do" – the level (Government vs. Local) where projects of e-government and information society can be carried out.

Each macro-area is articulated at a more detailed level, as the following picture shows.

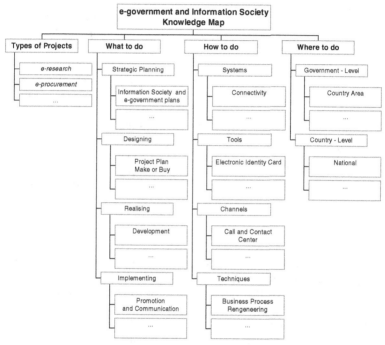

Fig. 2. The picture shows the main elements of the knowledge map.

Community building issues have been addressed focusing on the definition of actors and their roles in the KM system. The solution is designed for a network of actors operating both at local and at central level that need to cooperate and to share.

Different groups of users have been identified with different needs and roles; for each group some "user scenarios" have been designed in order to identify different types of resources and different functionalities.

In order to promote and encourage community development, the system is oriented to problem solving starting from specific knowledge needed in specific e-government projects and during specific project's phases.

The groups are:

- ***Regional Competence Centres and Central Staff:*** these are mainly representatives of the Innovation Department acting both at the local and the central level, whose role is to assist Local governments during the implementation phase. Their main activities are:

- Codification and Upload of documents
- Organise events
- Answer Local Governments and users requests
- Facilitate discussion spaces and animate the community
- Coordinate with the other Regional Competence Units
- System Management

- *Local Authorities,* made of representatives of Local Governments involved in the implementation of e-government projects. Their role is *to carry out* e-government projects. Their main activities are:

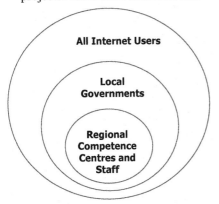

- Implement e-government projects
- Orientation and access to specific documentation
- Communicate and exchange opinions and resources with a community of other actors implementing e-government projects
- Contribute to the system (input of documents and resources)
- Participate to a regional workspace with dedicated resources

Fig. 3. The picture shows the main users of the system.

- *All Internet users:* these are all local and central Administration, external actors (Universities, providers, etc...) and people interested in the subject. Their need is *to be informed* about e-government and to carry out the following activities:

- Access and browse public content
- Input events and documents
- Contribute to the discussion within the community
- Request to join a workspace
- Be informed about new topics and about "what is going on" in e-government.

3 The km Solution

The solution consists of three different environments, one for each group of users: the more a user is involved in e-government projects, the more resources are available. The three environments reflect different levels of access: a public level, a registered level, a private level (working space). A specific interface has been designed for each environment, even if consistency of design has been respected.

The Regional Competence Centres and Central Staff have mainly access to the Back-office environment. The group has the widest access to the system resources, and can input and modify all the resources (the Regional Centres can only work on local level, the Central Unit can work on everything). The group works on content and site management and on community building.

The Local Authorities uses an online environment with local resources accessible with password; the environment presents both content and community functionalities. The Working Areas have the following functionalities: Be aware of who is online; Document management; Event notification; Shared agenda; Address book; Chat; Forum.

Internet users have access to the Internet site (with registration) where they can: Browse resources (according to knowledge map criteria); Search (mixing different knowledge map criteria); Personalise the navigation according to interests; Read the most voted; Send to a friend; Vote; Comment and discuss; Add documents (central staff filter).

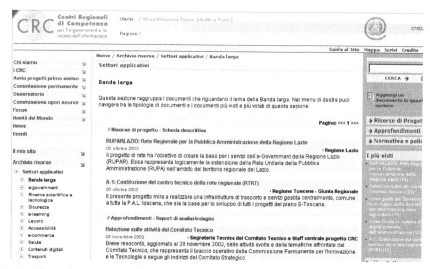

Fig. 4. The picture represents a screenshot of the KM system, accessible online at www.crcitalia.it

4 The Design of Organisational Specs

In order to guarantee maintenance of the system, an organisational framework has been designed. The central staff is responsible for feeding the system with contents, retrieving existing materials on e-government (laws, articles, papers, projects, etc) and to classify them according to all dimensions of the knowledge map. The central staff is in charge of quality control of documents submitted both from local staff and from other users of the system, and of the updating of knowledge map according to new topics emerging in the e-government domain of knowledge.

The local staff – Regional Competence Centres – is responsible for feeding the system with contents coming from projects' implementation (plans, strategic documents, design of services, etc.) and for the updating the section regarding their activity within the territory they belong to.

The registered users to the website could submit documents (which are afterwards checked by central staff before the publishing).

The network and the community will be built with the support of training, experimentation and continuous involvement.

A program of training and involvement is being deployed especially with the Regional Competence Centres.

Various meetings have been carried out in order to explain all the system features and to observe the system in use; findings from these meetings will be used for further training sessions and for fine tuning the system.

Some communication actions will be carried out in order to give visibility of the system to the generic public.

Some further specific organisational actions will be adopted. Some of them are:

- Identifying specific roles of *experts* responsible for site sections to check contents;
- Monitoring knowledge map evolution;
- Supervising the homogeneous use of classifications;
- Identifying specific policy and actions to develop the "community" section, besides the "content" one;
- Spreading capabilities of activating and promoting community;
- Identifying moderation and coordination modalities within workspace.

References

1. Albolino S., Mesenzani M., Multimedia Interaction for Learning and Knowing: inspirational knowledge management to create value for individuals in organisations, TAKMA (2002).
2. Albolino S., Morici R., Schael T., Sciarra G., "A KM solution for the empowerment of Local Authorities", international Workshop "Knowledge Management in e-government - KMGov2002" (2002).
3. Amy Jo Kim, Community Building on the Web: Secret Strategies for Successful Online Communities, by, Paperback, (2000).
4. Butera, F., L'organizzazione a rete attivata da cooperazione, conoscenza, comunicazione, comunità: la R&S. Studi Organizzativi. 2(6):99–130 (1999).
5. De Michelis, G. Cooperation and Knowledge Creation, in Knowledge Emergence: Social, Technical and Evolutionary Dimensions of Knowledge Creation. In Nonaka I. and Nishiguchi T. (eds.): Cooperation and Knowledge Creation, Oxford University Press Inc (2001).
6. Kluzer S., Pizzicannella R., De Marco A., E-Government Project in Italy "A network of Regional Competence Centres (RCC) to support collaboration among Italian Public Administrations in the development of e-government" OECD Seminar 23–24 September (2002).
8. Wenger E., *Communities of practice, learning meaning and identity*, Cambridge University Press, New York, (1998).

E-government Attempts in ESCWA Member Countries

Hasan Charif and Maya Ramadan

United Nations Economic and Social Commission for Western Asia (UNESCWA),
Sustainable Development and Productivity Division, P.O.Box 8576, Beirut, Lebanon
hcharif@escwa.org.lb, ramadan@un.org

Abstract. Many ESCWA member countries have felt the need to initiate e-government applications thus making use of the latest information and communication technologies. However, none of these countries has yet achieved a well developed and fully functional e-government system, in spite of the plans put and sporadic actions taken for this endeavor. On the other hand, countries that resisted for some time the incorporation of ICT in governmental organizations and in citizen's everyday life, have felt the urgency of having national plans taking such innovations into consideration, otherwise they will be left behind in the stream of development.

1 Introduction

E-government allows for more transparency, greater convenience, smoother flow of information, better coordination between different agencies, rapidly delivered services for citizens and businesses, less corruption, revenue growth, cost reduction, and service provision for 24 hours over 7 days per week. If all of this is gained, what hampers e-government from moving-off? Barriers to e-government can be summarized in the following factors: resistance to change, lack of public awareness, public skepticism, poor telecommunications infrastructures and services, lack in human capital readiness, poor information security, hardware and software availability, and public access to Internet for common people, etc...

McConnell International report on e-readiness stated six ESCWA countries as having the potential to impact the new global economy. These countries are Egypt, Jordan, Kuwait, Lebanon, Saudi Arabia and United Arab Emirates. However none of these countries seem to satisfy the conditions needed for full transactions for e-government and e-business [1]. Though e-government provides a wide range of information for decision makers to benefit from, it does in many ways threaten the control and power entitled to political leaders [2].

This is a comparative study describing the situation of ESCWA member countries with regard to e-government applications with consideration of the cultural and political contexts of these countries. Comparative studies concerning e-government applications hold special importance for many reasons: they allow countries sharing similar culture and geographical location to find common grounds and identify common obstacles, thus opening the door for joint planning and coordination for future action. Furthermore, knowing that e-government system is a new concept, internationally as well as locally, and that there is no standard blueprint to launch it,

M.A. Wimmer (Ed.): KMGov 2003, LNAI 2645, pp. 310–318, 2003.
© IFIP 2003

gathering the different experiences in this field allows one country to benefit from another's experience (let it be success or failure) particularly established best practices. Finally, such comparative studies tend to be carried out by non-profit and non-politically oriented organizations, thus giving them an objective and transparent dimension [3], [4], [5].

2 Countries Experience

2.1 Bahrain

The Bahraini society seems ready to make use of IT in daily life, this is reflected through the growing number of Internet and mobile users; the number of mobile phones is almost ten times more than the fixed phone lines. The National Bank of Bahrain has introduced a new service allowing customers to make online transactions [6]. On the other hand the Bahraini government has set for itself a goal to become the telecommunications hub of the gulf [7]. Thirty ministries and departments have been connected to each other, which facilitates administrative procedures, like purchasing, auditing, budgeting and human resources management. This project was directed by the Ministry of Finance and National Economy, and is expected to positively affect the productivity in the concerned ministries [8]. Furthermore, the government had put under trial an e-voting system, called the (2D) Bar Coding Technology. This system holds personal information on every voter and allows citizens to voice out their opinions effectively and efficiently [9]. As for the commerce, the Bahraini government is still drafting a telecommunication act to promote open market and an e-commerce environment [6]. This year Paramount has been given the major role in dealing with information security in Bahrain [10]. Caution ought to be considered when sending politically suspicious emails or launching a Web site that might hold a threat to the ruling family, jail will be the measure taken to punish the suspect [11], [12]. Bahrain is working on developing laws for e-commerce that will keep its reputation as the financial capital of the Middle East [13].

2.2 Egypt

Internet access is affordable for the average Egyptian citizen. The government has an e-government plan that will start by building a media city and smart villages. These villages will provide software development and ICT training. Furthermore, once the plan is implemented it will provide a network linking ministries [14]. An Egyptian company is building an Internet infrastructure promising to procure a very fast connection [15], [16]. The Egyptian government committed itself to reduce software piracy and enforce copyright laws [17]. An official Web site provides wide range of information in a one-stop-shop manner [18]. The government is keen on guaranteeing the climate for IT to flourish; legislations fostering e-signature are underway, international agreements promoting trust in the progress towards an IT society are signed [19]. Nilesoft is committed to develop e-commerce sector in Egypt. This company considers that both the financial sector and the number of Internet users are encouraging to seriously tackle such a project [20].

2.3 Iraq

Until few months ago Internet connection was not available to the Iraqi community. Previously Internet was allowed merely in the ministries, and sending emails was not possible even in the ministries. Nowadays Internet cafes are widespread and it is even possible to have Internet at home. However, there is one Internet provider in Iraq (Urulink) and it is handled by the government. Hotmail, Yahoo or other similar email services are not possible, Urulink will deny access to such services. Home Internet is considered expensive for the average Iraqi costing about 25 USD each three months so usually citizens opt for Internet cafes [21]. It is worth mentioning that until the present moment mobile phones are not allowed in Iraq. Back in 1999, computer spare parts were not allowed to enter Iraq due to UN sanctions after the Gulf War [22], [23].

2.4 Jordan

In 1999, King Abdullah II announced his commitment to strengthen IT sector in Jordan. The REACH initiative (Regulatory framework, Estate, Advancement, Capital, Human resources) was launched. REACH is based on public-private partnership aiming to deliver e-services to citizens, businesses and government [24]. Jordan IT Community Centre was launched on December 2000 in order to spread computer and Internet literacy among inhabitants of remote areas. Computers have even been installed in Bedouin and rural areas to facilitate information access and improve the economic condition of women, students and others from different sectors. Computer skills are already taught in public schools as early as elementary levels [25], [26], [27]. Home Internet connection is also accessible to any citizen [28]. However the digital gap between the poor and the rich is still big in Jordan due to the high cost of connectivity. The government is planning to connect universities and schools (by 2003) and to liberalize the telecommunications sector (by 2005) [29]. Few months ago, the Ministry of Information and Communications Technology held a meeting for civil servants from over a hundred government institutions to discuss their roles and responsibilities in the development of e-government in Jordan [30].

2.5 Kuwait

Internet is widely used in Kuwait and the connection is fast. Every citizen in Kuwait beyond the age of nine has an ID card with a pin number; this card is used for a multitude of purposes like searching for a job and many others. Soon enough this ID will be used for financial transactions. This has already solved the problem of long queues in government departments, hospitals and others. Furthermore, unlike other gulf countries, telecommunications sector in Kuwait is liberalized which encourages both businesses and consumers [31], [32]. The National Bank of Kuwait is providing secure online services allowing the use of credit card for purchase and other transactions [33].

2.6 Lebanon

Lebanon is one of the first countries in the region to have Internet access open to the public. Internet connection penetrated the community as early as 1994, reaching universities and schools as well as average citizens' homes [34]. On the other hand rural areas are not privileged as urban areas with telephone system. The communication and Internet access costs in Lebanon are one of the highest in the region. This situation may change with the privatization of the telecommunications sector. Currently, the Lebanese government is interested in developing e-government. Lebanon has a modern infrastructure throughout the country. Thousand of computers have been deployed, civil servants have been trained on ICT products, and ICT awareness campaigns are run by the government. A one-stop-shop Web page is now available facilitating access to information for citizens [35]. The old law for intellectual property rights has been lately updated to suit the new technologies and the parliament approved it in 1999, which opened the door for many international ICT companies to launch new branches in Lebanon. However, actual market shows that this law is not being respected, for example 80% of software in Lebanon are pirated. The most well developed e-commerce is found in the banking sector [36], [37]. The complete e-strategy for Lebanon is under preparation by the Office of the Minister of State for Administrative Reform (OMSAR) in collaboration with many academics, policy makers, private businesses, citizens and others. This strategy will be ready by the end of year 2002 [38].

2.7 Oman

Internet is currently available for the Omani community [39]. The Omani government is trying to promote IT in the society. For example, the government is trying to increase Omani graduates in software and IT related disciplines, and the latest technologies have been installed in Sultan Qaboos University to make this plan possible [16], [40]. The Ministry of Civil Services is working to build a network connecting 45 ministries with the Ministry of Finance and the Ministry of Civil Services; this project will allow human resources management to update information regarding 86,000 government employees [41]. On last October the government signed a contract to launch the smart card containing personal information for both citizens and residents of the Sultanate; this card is supposed to allow the accomplishment of many public services like getting a driving license, voting, money withdrawal and many others [42]. The Central Bank of Oman is planning to develop the infrastructure necessary for electronic banking products and services [43]. Intellectual property rights is a serious matter in Oman; three large companies in Oman have been invaded because of their possession of illegal software and they have been given a week to legalize these software [44]. TradaNet is a new company launched in year 2000 and is now leading e-commerce in Oman [45].

2.8 Palestine

A report issued by Human Rights Watch in 1999 mentioned that the Palestinian Authority didn't try to control Internet content accessible to the public. Palestinians can have access to information covering a wide range of political and human rights information. This online freedom is making up for the shortage in publications and media due to the war situation [46].

2.9 Qatar

Internet services in Qatar is provided by one agent, Qatar Public Telecommunications Corporation (Q-Tel); no other Internet supplier is allowed to enter the market without an official governmental approval [47]. In September 2000 the government announced its will to have e-government; the e-government plan will be implemented by 2004 hoping to provide electronically 74% of the government activities offered by 22 ministries for both residents and citizens [48], [49]. It is worth mentioning that Qatar was the first Arab Country to announce its will to have e-government [16]. Qatar e-Commerce Committee was introduced to deliver within two years and a half the strategy for e-commerce with individuals and businesses [50].

2.10 Saudi Arabia

Saudi Arabia gained access to the Internet in 1994, however it wasn't before 1999 that the general public was able to make use of this service; furthermore, the connection is still not fast and the Internet service providers are asking the Saudi government to improve the infrastructure [16], [51], [52]. It is known that the government censors some Web sites [53]. The Saudi government is developing a national e-government plan and the related legislations [54]. Acknowledging the scarce human power in the IT field, e-government plan will give special attention to human capital and IT education [52], [55]. A government committee has been assigned to formulate a law to protect information security. The first steps that have been undertaken were training government employees [56]. Though the number of Internet users is showing an average growth of 8%, and the IT sales in the Kingdom make more than 40% of the region's, it was proven that the general public doesn't yet trust the concept of e-government [52], [57], [58]. This trust problem could be due to two main factors: infrastructure and security [59]. The Ministry of Interior is taking actual steps to launch Smart Card containing information including fingerprints and enabling its holder to have access to a range of public services [60]. Furthermore, there is a plan to establish an IT hub and science park in Jeddah [16].

2.11 Syrian Arab Republic

Syria has the most expensive Internet connection rate in the Middle East, allowed only through a local service provider. In 1997 Internet started in Syria, however the public didn't have access to it [16], [61], [62]. Until now the government constantly checks incoming and outgoing emails [63]. The Syrian Telecommunications Establishment blocks certain Web site. However the Syrian government has noticed the drawbacks of having poor Internet services. This not only affects residents of Syria, but it makes foreigners reluctant to visit the country especially if they rely on daily emails to run their work. Thus the government is seriously considering the improvement of its IT infrastructure while encouraging e-business and e-literate society [64].

2.12 United Arab Emirates

The eminent achievement in e-government is Dubai Internet City. Dubai has started a plan to provide 100 percent of its GDP from non-oil sources by 2010. Dubai Internet city, built on 163 hectares surface area, will shift the economy towards IT, multimedia and telecommunications businesses. It is already acknowledged internationally and hosting important IT meetings. International standards of the City have attracted big IT companies like Microsoft, Oracle, IBM, Hewlett-Packard, MasterCard International, Arabia Online, Compaq, and many others. Sheikh Mohammed bin Rashid al Maktoum, Crown Prince of Dubai, inaugurated Dubai Internet City on October 2001 (as scheduled 18 months earlier) and asked civil servants to provide all public services online otherwise lose their jobs. By 2003 every schoolchild will be provided a computer and Internet access [65], [66], [67]. Zayed University is offering a new MBA programme in e-commerce for professionals working in both the private and the public sector [68]. Dubai police is providing eleven services on the Internet and eight services on the WAP (wireless application protocol) [69]. Payment of traffic fines, renewal of driving license and many other services are now possible through WAP [70]. As for e-security, it is more or less protected by the government; for example, fines must be paid by Internet criminals but jail was never a possible verdict [56]. UAE scored the second on 'e-government index' in the Middle East region, after Israel [71].

2.13 Yemen

Yemen started a 10 years project in e-government aiming to guarantee more efficient services to citizens. There is one Internet provider for Yemen (Teleyemen) and connection is possible to the public; however some Web sites are blocked. Some services are already provided online, like payment of postal services. It is worth mentioning that Yemen scored the least in 'e-government index' in the region [71], [72], [73], [74].

References

1. Ready? Net. Go! Partnership Leading the Global Economy. McConnell International (2001)
2. Dahan, M.: Internet Usage in the Middle East: Some Political and Social Implications. Department of Political Science. The Hebrew University of Jerusalem (www.mevic.org/papers/inet-mena.html)
3. Van Bastelaer, B.: e Europe and User Aspects of ICT. Cost Working Paper No.1 (2001) (http://www.info.fundp.ac.be/~cita/publications/e_Europe.pdf)
4. Rubino-Hallman, S.: E-Government in Latin America and the Caribbean. Reinventing Governance in the Information Age. CLAD (2002) (http://www.clad.org.ve/fulltext/0043107.pdf)
5. Risk e-Business: Seizing the Opportunity of Global e-Readiness. McConnell International (2000) http://www.mcconnellinternational.com/ereadiness/ereadiness.pdf

6. Communication in Bahrain. Trade Partners UK
    (http://www.tradepartners.gov.uk/telecom/bahrain/profile/overview.shtml)
7. Assignment B, Information Infrastructure, Telecommunications and International
    Perspectives. Nova Southern University (2000)
8. Bahrain Claims Regional e-Government Lead. M3 New Media Consulting
    (http://www.m3newmedia.com/bahclaimrege.html)
9. Bahrain Become Middle East's First e-Voters. Symbol News (2001)
    (http://www.symbol.com/news/pressreleases/pr_releases_inter_bahrain.html)
10. Affan, M.: Paramount Brings Full Security Solutions Portfolio to Gitex 2002. ITP (2002)
    (http://www.itp.net/news/103390742974222.htm)
11. Bahrain Blocks Opposition Websites. New Monday (2002)
    (http://www.newmonday.co.uk/News/1130509)
12. The Internet in the Mideast and North Africa: Free Expression and Censorship. Human
    Rights Watch (1999) (http://www.hrw.org/advocacy/internet/mena/summary.htm)
13. Corder, R.: Bahrain Drives Toward e-Commerce Laws. ITP (2002)
    (http://www.itp.net/news/101963076345767.htm)
14. Regulatory Development, Mediterranean Area, Synthesis of Master Reports (2001)
    (http://www.eu-esis.org/esis2reg/synthMED7.htm)
15. Seizing e-Government Opportunities: Assessment, Prioritization and Action. McConnell
    International, The World Bank Group (2001)
    (http://unpan1.un.org/intradoc/groups/public/documents/apcity/unpan003917.pdf)
16. E-Initiatives in the GCC Region, Vol. 2, No.11. Middle East Intelligence Bulletin
    (http://www.meib.org/articles/0012_me2.htm)
17. Egypt Launches e-Government Initiative with Microsoft. The Egyptian State Information
    Service (2001) (http://www.sis.gov.eg/online/html4/o040421.htm)
18. http://www.alhokoma.gov.eg/
19. The Government Now Delivers. Ministry of Communications and Information
    Technology (http://www.mcit.gov.eg/)
20. Intershop and Nilesoft Address Egyptian e-Commerce. ITP
    (http://www.itp.net/news/100600796822224.htm)
21 Internet Arrives in Iraq. Aberdeen News (2002)
    (http://www.aberdeennews.com/mld/aberdeennews/news/world/4165387.htm)
22. The Internet in the Mideast and North Africa: Free Expression and Censorships- Iraq.
    Human Rights Watch (1999)
    (http://www.hrw.org/advocacy/internet/mena/iraq.htm)
23. Reply to Human Rights Watch Letter Received From Officials of Iraq. Human Rights
    Watch (1998) (http://www.hrw.org/advocacy/internet/mena)
24. The REACH Initiative (http://www.reach.jo/about.shtml)
25. Volunteer Brings Computers to the Bedouin. Computer World (2000)
    (http://www.computerworld.com/careertopics/careers/training/story/0,10801,524
    80,00.html)
26. Jordan IT Community Centers. JITCC Web site
    (http://www.jitcc.gov.jo/mission.htm)
27. IS Promotional Activities. Summary Report. ESIS Extension (2001)
28. Reply to Human Rights Watch Letter Received From Officials of Jordan. Human Rights
    Watch (1998) (http://www.hrw.org/advocacy/internet/mena)
29. A Road Map for Developing IT Services in Jordan. Jordan Ministry of Information and
    Communications Technology (2002) (http://www.mopc.gov.jo/news2.asp?id=330)
30. Civil Servants to Discuss e-Government Portal. The Jordan Times (2002)
    (http://www.jordantimes.com)

31. Should We Carry a Personal Identity Card?
(http://government.blogspot.com/2002_07_07_government_archive.html)

32. GCC Insights: Kuwait Ahead of the Rest in Telecom Liberalization. Gulf News (2002)
(http://www.gulf-news.com/Articles/news.asp?ArticleID=58890)

33. Corder, R.: Our Gulf and NBK Agree on e-Ccommerce. ITP (2001)
(http://www.itp.net/news/98077342820809.htm)

34. Regulatory Developments. Lebanon Master Report. EU-ESIS (2001)

35. http://www.informs.gov.lb/

36. IS Promotional Activities. Summary Report. EU-ESIS (1999-2000)

37. The Lebanese e-Government Experience. OMSAR (2002)

38. E-Strategy for Lebanon. UNDP
(http://www.undp.org.lb/programme/governance/ict4dev/eStrategy.html)

39. OmanTel – Oman Telecommunications Company (http://www.omantel.net.om)

40. HP Switch Technology Brings Multimedia Applications to Omani Students. HP
(http://www.hp.be/egov/en/references/om_quaboos.asp)

41. Times of Oman (http://www.tariq.net/english/news13.htm)

42. Multi-Purpose Card to Usher in e-Government. Times of Oman (2002)
(http://www.timesofoman.com/newsdetails.asp?newsid=17383)

43. CBO Proposes Electronic Fund Transfer System Omani Information Center (2002)
(http://www.omaninfo.com/cgi-
bin/webnews/ShowArticle.asp?article_id=682232083)

44. Omani Anti-Piracy Raids. Arab Trust (2002)
(http://www.arabtrust.com/midnews/more.html#Oman%20anti-piracy%20raids)

45. Portal on Oman's Non-Oil Exports Launched
(http://www.khaleejtimes.co.ae/ktarchive/270902/middleeast.htm)

46. The Internet in the Mideast and North Africa: Free Expression and Censorship. Human
Rights Watch (1999) http://www.hrw.org/advocacy/internet/mena/summary.htm)

47. Reply to Human Rights Watch Letter Received from Officials of Qatar. Human Rights
Watch (1998) (http://www.hrw.org/advocacy/internet/mena)

48. Qatar Launches e-Government Plan. World Information Technology and Services
Alliance Newsletter (2000) (http://www.witsa.org/news/00aug.htm)

49. Qatar's e-Government Project Making Progress. E-Government Project to be
Implemented in 2004. Development Gateway (2002)
(http://www.developmentgateway.org/node/130619/news/item?item_id=295644)

50. Wilson, G.: Qatar Builds e-Government Portal. ITP
(http://www.itp.net/features/97556902273780.htm)

51. Is the World e-Ready? Maybe Not. US-Egypt Presidents' Council (2000)
(http://www.us-egypt.org/istheworld.html)

52. Al-Sudairy, M. A. T.: Electronic Government (eGov): Implementation Strategies. King
Abdul Aziz University (2002)
(http://www.egov.org.sa/new/ecom/ecom_02speakers.asp)

53. The Internet in the Mideast and North Africa: Free Expression and Censorship. Human
Rights Watch (1999) http://www.hrw.org/advocacy/internet/mena/summary.htm)

54. Kingdom's Interest in e-Government is Growing Rapidly. Saudi e-Commerce (2002)
(http://www.egov.org.sa/new/ecom/ecom_index.asp)

55. 1000 Schools to be Equipped by Kingdom's Internet Initiative. Requirements Valued at
Over 480 Million USD. Saudi e-Commerce (2002)
(http://www.egov.org.sa/new/ecom/ecom_index.asp)

56. Corder, R.: GCC Governments Race to Create Cyber-laws. ITP (2001)
(http://www.itp.net/news/98973640889530.htm)

57. Participate at the Heart of the Largest and Fastest Growing Market in the Middle East. e-Commerce Saudi Arabia (2002) (http://www.recexpo.com/html/ecomm.html)
58. Internet Users ... Official Interest ... Drive Sector's Growth in Full Speed. e-Commerce Saudi Arabia (http://www.recexpo.com/html/ecomm.html)
59. Browne, C.: Saudi e-Commerce Conference Lauded by Major Saudi Industry Experts. ITP (2001) (http://www.itp.net/news/98578363361827.htm)
60. Contracts Signed for Smart Card Technology. Arab News (2002) (http://www.arabnews.com/Articles.asp?ID=18543)
61. The Internet in the Middle East and North Africa: Free Expression and Censorship. Syria. Human Rights Watch (1999) (http://www.meib.org/articles/0012_me2.htm)
62. The Internet in the Mideast and North Africa: Free Expression and Censorship. Human Rights Watch (1999) (http://www.hrw.org/advocacy/internet/mena/summary.htm)
63. Blakeley, C. J., Matsura, J. H.: E-Government. Is e-Democracy Inevitable?
64. Syria, A New IT Strategy. Special Exclusive Report. (http://government.blogspot.com/2002_11_10_government_archive.html)
65. E-Government Launch on Schedule (2001) (http://www.sheikhmohammed.co.ae/news)
66. Dubai Grows as Region's e-Hub (2001) (http://www.sheikhmohammed.co.ae/news)
67. Dubai: New Chip on the Block (2000) (http://www.atimes.com/reports/B128Ai01.html)
68. Zayed University to Offer MBA in e-Business (2000) (http://www.sheikhmohammed.co.ae/news)
69. Dubai Police Launch e-Government System (2001) (http://www.sheikhmohammed.co.ae/news)
70. Renewal of Driving License on the Net (2000) (http://www.sheikhmohammed.co.ae/news)
71. Reply to Human Rights Watch Letter Received from Officials of Yemen. Human Rights Watch (1998) (http://www.hrw.org/advocacy/internet/mena)
72. Yemen Kicks off US$ 60 Million e-Government Initiative. ITP (2002) (http://www.itp.net/news/103405825848780.htm)
73. Electronic Payment Online. Yemen Times (2002) (http://www.yementimes.com/02/iss39/lastpage.htm)
74. Benchmarking e-Government: a Global Perspective. Assessing the Progress of the UN Member States. United Nations Division for Public Economics and Public Administration, American Society for Public Administration (2002)

Author Index